MATTHEW COLLIN

Also by Matthew Collin

Altered State
This is Serbia Calling
The Time of the Rebels
Pop Grenade
Rave On

DREAM MACHINES

Electronic Music in Britain from Doctor Who to Acid House

MATTHEW COLLIN

OMNIBUS PRESS
London / New York / Paris / Sydney / Copenhagen / Berlin / Madrid / Tokyo

Copyright © 2024 Omnibus Press
(A division of the Wise Music Group
14–15 Berners Street, London, W1T 3LJ)

Cover designed by RK Graphics

Hardback ISBN 978-1-9131-7255-8

Matthew Collin hereby asserts his right to be identified as the author of this work in accordance with Sections 77 to 78 of the Copyright, Designs and Patents Act 1988.

All rights reserved. No part of this book may be reproduced in any form or by any electronic or mechanical means, including information storage or retrieval systems, without permission in writing from the publisher, except by a reviewer who may quote brief passages.

Every effort has been made to trace the copyright holders of the photographs in this book but one or two were unreachable. We would be grateful if the photographers concerned would contact us.

A catalogue record for this book is available from the British Library.

Printed in Poland
Typeset by Evolution Design & Digital Ltd (Kent)

www.omnibuspress.com

CONTENTS

Introduction   vii

1. Journey into Space – Musique Concrète and Radiophonic Sound   1
   - Daphne Oram, Tristram Cary: Sonic Explorers   1
   - The Opening of the BBC Radiophonic Workshop   4
   - The Music in Janet Beat's Head   18
   - F. C. Judd and the Reel-to-Reel Club Scene   21
   - Uncommon Characters: Desmond Leslie, Delia Derbyshire   28

2. An Electric Storm – Space-Age Pop and Psychedelia   35
   - The Radiophonic Workshop's Greatest Hit   35
   - Joe Meek Cranks It Up   38
   - The Beatles Take a Trip   41
   - Pink Floyd, 'London's Farthest-Out Group'   51
   - John Baker's Radiophonic Swing   55
   - Peter Zinovieff, EMS, The Rolling Stones and White Noise   59
   - Ernest Berk, Basil Kirchin, Ron Geesin: Musical Misfits   68

3. Other Side of the Sky – Space Rock, Prog and Ambient   73
   - Hawkwind: Psychedelic Warlords   73
   - Prog Rock: Rick Wakeman, Curved Air, Arthur Brown, Pink Floyd   80
   - Live From Planet Gong   88
   - Stonehenge, Ozric Tentacles and the Strange Tale of Zorch   94
   - Roxy Music, Brian Eno and David Bowie   98
   - The Afterlife of Delia Derbyshire   108

4. This Is Entertainment – Industrial Music and Post-Punk Futurism   113
   - Cabaret Voltaire, Electronic Dadaists   113
   - Throbbing Gristle and the Art of Brutal Noise   119
   - Thomas Leer, Robert Rental and Daniel Miller   127
   - The Human League, Clock DVA and Vice Versa   131
   - John Foxx and Ultravox   136
   - The Coming of Gary Numan   139
   - Thomas Dolby and Landscape Get Scientific   143
   - Blitz and Some Bizarre, New Romantics and Futurists   145

5. Just Can't Get Enough – Synth-Pop and Art-Rock   153
   - Soft Cell and the New Electronic Pop   153
   - The Human League and Heaven 17   160
   - Depeche Mode, Perpetual Futurists   164

	Joy Division, New Order and the Electronic Side of Factory	168
	Trevor, Malcolm, Frankie and the Fairlight	176
	Bronski Beat, Imagination: Countering Conformity	184
	Pet Shop Boys' Love Letters to Pop	188
	Japan, Simple Minds and Other Art-Rock Adventurers	190
	Peter Gabriel, Kate Bush and ORCH5	196
	The Last Days of the Radiophonic Workshop	201
6.	Coughing Up Fire – Dub Reggae and Sound Systems	205
	The Roots and Culture of Sound Systems	205
	Dennis Bovell, Jah Shaka and Saxon Sound International	211
	Mad Professor Goes Boom	219
	Adrian Sherwood, On-U Sound, Mark Stewart and Tackhead	222
	Digital Dub and UK Steppers	228
7.	Tearin' Down the Avenue – Electro and Hip-Hop	235
	B-Boys, Buffalo Gals and the Rise of Electro	235
	Electronic Dancers: TW Funk Masters, Freeez	241
	Hybrid Beats: Cabaret Voltaire, Big Audio Dynamite	244
	UK Hip-Hop Finds Its Voice	246
	Mastermind, Soul II Soul, The Wild Bunch, Smith & Mighty	253
8.	Unnatural History – Experimentalists, Industrialists and Noise-Musicians	263
	Chris and Cosey, Psychic TV and Coil	263
	Whitehouse and Power Electronics	271
	The Incredibly Strange World of Nurse With Wound	273
	DIY Noisemakers and the Cassette Underground	278
	Muslimgauze, Bourbonese Qualk, Nocturnal Emissions	282
	Portion Control, 400 Blows, Nitzer Ebb and 'Funky Alternatives'	288
9.	Pump Up the Volume – Samplemania, Hi-NRG and Dance-Pop	293
	M/A/R/R/S and Bomb the Bass	293
	S'Express, The Beatmasters and Plunderphonic Pop	298
	Coldcut, The JAMs – and Brian Eno (Again)	303
	Hi-NRG: Gay Disco Strikes Back	310
	Stock Aitken Waterman Seek Pop Perfection	317
10.	Emotions Electric – House, Techno, Acid	323
	The Foundations of UK House	323
	Acid House and Rave Culture	327
	A Guy Called Gerald and 808 State	334
	The KLF, The Orb and 'Ambient House'	341
	Bleep Techno and Breakbeat Hardcore	346

Acknowledgements	357
Notes	359
Index	377

INTRODUCTION

'To me, electronics were like magic.'

Neil Fraser, the artist-engineer known as the Mad Professor, likes to tell a story about a childhood incident that set him off on a lifelong journey of sonic exploration – a story that captures some of the sense of wonder at the heart of electronic music.

As a boy, he was fascinated by the sounds coming from his mother's radio, believing they were being conveyed by some form of wizardry. 'But the answers my mother would give me when I asked her about this magic were not enough. I wanted to know how the man was singing in the radio, but my mother said there was no man in the radio,' he remembers.

'So I opened it up with a screwdriver and I looked and saw the wires and transistors there. But that still wasn't enough, so I had to build my own electronic equipment to find out more about it. And that's how I started out, looking for this magic.'

The quest for the extraordinary, the thrill of exploring new possibilities, is a thread that runs through the history of electronic music in Britain and through this book. Its narrative begins in the 1940s with experiments using oscillators and tape recorders, and follows the trajectory of the music's development via small circles of enthusiasts in the classical avant-garde and bohemian alternative scenes into pop culture, tracking developments through the studios, concert halls, clubs, dancehalls, festivals and raves that served as testbeds for new forms.

Dream Machines takes an inclusive approach to what may be considered 'electronic music'. As well as the musique concrète pioneers, synth-pop stars and noise sculptors, it examines innovations within genres like psychedelia, space rock, industrial music, dub, electro and hi-NRG, as well as the crucial roles played by DJs, sound systems, sampling and remix culture.

World War II had a powerful impact on the development of electronic music in Britain, as it did on so many other aspects of national life. Out of tumult and violence came new beginnings, grounded in the desire for a better future. Demobbed servicemen returned with new skills and ideas for peacetime; women who began careers in creative and technical industries while men were away fighting offered fresh perspectives. Military surplus equipment that could be adapted to make unusual noises became available cheaply. Composers experimented with new technology and radio producers sought out new sounds to enliven drama or comedy broadcasts, while the rise of television would open up uncharted territory for creative activity. The years that followed the war also saw an influx of new arrivals from Britain's Caribbean colonies, whose influence would transform the musical culture of the country.

Contrary to its dominance of synth-pop in the 1980s, Britain was not one of the great powers in the early years of electronic music. Most of the pre-war electronic instruments had been invented in the United States, Russia, France or Germany, and the two major avant-garde movements of the late 1940s and early 1950s, musique concrète and elektronische musik, were French and German in origin.

But electronic instrumentation was not unknown in mid-20th century Britain, and the song that might contentiously be described as the country's first electronic pop anthem dates back to 1939, the year the war began. Better known in its later, orchestrated version, it was a ballad of hope in dispiriting times, plaintively phrased by a 22-year-old woman and simply arranged around the chords of an early Hammond Novachord synthesizer: Vera Lynn's 'We'll Meet Again'.

There were also electronic novelty acts in the pre-war period – popular variety entertainer Joseph Forrest Whiteley, who called himself Musaire, was known for humorous music-hall performances with his Theremin, an instrument whose phantasmal tones would become familiar on the soundtracks to films like Alfred Hitchcock's *Spellbound*. Its inventor, Leon Theremin, gave a concert billed as *Music from the Ether* at London's Royal Albert Hall in 1927, while German-born Martin Taubman gained renown in Britain in the 1930s for recitals with his Theremin-style Electronde.

There were British inventions too. Back in 1899, electrical engineer William Duddell built an instrument called the 'Singing Arc' – by manipulating the voltage of a carbon-arc streetlamp, he produced tones that could be controlled from a keyboard. In what is believed to be one of the first performances of electronic music, Duddell used the Singing Arc to play 'God Save the Queen' at the Institution of Electrical Engineers in London. Another British electronic instrument was the Luminophone, which generated sounds using a photoelectric technique and was created in the 1920s by Harry Grindell Matthews, an eccentric inventor who became famous for claiming to have developed a 'death ray'.

But the Singing Arc and the Luminophone were never really more than curiosities. It was the commercial availability of the tape recorder after World War II that made a genuine impact, turning sound into what Brian Eno later described as 'a substance which is malleable and mutable and cuttable and reversible',[1] enabling it to be reordered, manipulated and repurposed.

This new technology offered access to sonic worlds in which the minuscule could become colossal and the ephemeral infinite. It also made the means of avant-garde musical production accessible to the wider public, and a subculture of amateur tape-recorder enthusiasts experimenting in rudimentary home studios emerged in the 1950s, the predecessors of the post-punk electronic musicians and bedroom techno producers of later decades.

Electronic music's post-war development in Britain was deeply intertwined with developments in broadcast media. The BBC was central to this, setting up its Radiophonic Workshop to supply sound effects and signature tunes for dramas, current affairs, schools broadcasts and entertainment shows like *Doctor Who*, bringing electronic sounds into the nation's living rooms. In an era when linear broadcasting is no longer dominant, it's sometimes hard to recall how powerful a grip terrestrial television once exerted on the public consciousness, and how deeply the Radiophonic Workshop's creations could affect the imaginations of the nation's children. Decades later, some of them remain convinced that these esoteric sounds set them on the path to becoming electronic musicians themselves. (Other quaint anachronisms to be found within these pages: the importance to the national cultural discourse of the weekly pop charts and the prime-time TV show *Top of the Pops*; the huge influence once exerted by the printed music press).

Technological advances and the introduction of new instruments – from the reel-to-reel tape recorders of the 1950s to the Fairlight sampler-synthesizers of the 1980s – enabled the continuous creation of new genres and styles. In his history of music production, Richard James Burgess explains that new technologies come inbuilt with the 'potential for previously unsuspected applications',[2] which are then exploited in novel ways by recording artists.

But innovators haven't always needed the latest gear. From Hawkwind's oscillators and Jah Shaka's dub sirens to techno's reanimation of semi-obsolete Roland drum machines, some of the most exciting electronic music has been made with cheap, secondhand or homemade equipment, sometimes rigged to perform functions not envisaged by the manufacturers. The history of electronic music in Britain, this land of hobbyists and tinkerers, is also a tale of do-it-yourself creativity.

As electronic music has always been interlinked with visions of the future, its story contains no shortage of progressive thinkers, as well as more than a few starry-eyed dreamers, militant iconoclasts, brilliant loners and other unconventional characters. So often in its history, this has been a music made by outsiders and nonconformists.

But as well as acknowledging important individuals, this book also explores the social and cultural environments, the subcultures, scenes and communities that collectively nurtured innovations through mutual cooperation and creative competition. As Daphne Oram, one of the key figures in early British electronic music, wisely cautioned: 'New developments are rarely, if ever, the complete and singular achievement of one mind.'[3]

Nor are they the singular achievement of one country: the development of British electronic music was informed by ideas from America and Europe, and in return exerted its own influence on subsequent developments across the Atlantic and on the European mainland. This was particularly evident in electronic dance music, which thrived on complex, cross-continental interactions between musicians and technologies from the United States, Britain, Germany, Jamaica, Japan and elsewhere.

All cultures are shaped by their time and place, as are histories of cultures, which inevitably reflect the preoccupations, orthodoxies and prejudices of the periods in which they are written. It's only relatively recently that major figures like Oram and Delia Derbyshire have gained retrospective prominence, after years of male-dominated histories of electronic music in which there was a 'black hole of no info'[4] about the involvement of women, as composer Annea Lockwood described it. But there are other important characters who still deserve more substantial recognition too.

From war veterans using electronic engineering skills gained in the forces to build their own equipment to Jamaican immigrants bringing sound system culture to their new homeland, the story of electronic music shadows British social history since 1945. Post-war austerity and the subsequent consumer boom, the cultural freedom-seeking of the 1960s, the rise of movements for equality and civil liberties, the political turbulence of the 1970s and 1980s: all of these developments found some expression through the electronic music of their time.

Electronic music has also reflected people's hopes, fears and fantasies about technology, with its dreamlike visions of idyllic futures and nightmares of dystopias created by scientific overreach or catastrophic malfunction, awe at the speed of progress and fear of machine power harnessed for oppression.

It's no coincidence that space travel and all things cosmic have been recurring themes within electronic music, expressing the desire to traverse the frontiers of reality and float freely into some celestial utopia untainted by earthbound evils and follies – 'to escape from this world into a whole new universe where you can be whatever you want to be,' as techno musician A Guy Called Gerald said in one of the interviews for this book.

So much electronic music embodies this yearning for transcendence – the desire 'to reach "out there"',[5] in the words of John Lennon, another musician who plays a role in this story. This also indicates why the long association between psychedelic drugs and electronic music is no chance phenomenon: both hold out the promise to take human consciousness beyond its limits.

This book's narrative concludes at the end of the 1980s, when electronic music had established itself as the most vital creative force within pop culture and few recordings were being made that did not use at least some of its techniques. Although the technology and the music continued to evolve in the years that followed with the dizzying array of styles that emerged from post-acid house electronic dance culture, this is the story of its formative decades, when it still had the power to surprise and to shock, as well as to lift the spirits into the realms beyond.

It's a journey through some remarkable times and places, so in the words of *Star Trek* creator Gene Roddenberry, prominently sampled on one of the most exuberant electronic dance records of the 1980s, *enjoy this trip...*

British electronic composer Daphne Oram in her home studio, February 1962.
©National Media Museum/Getty Images.

1

JOURNEY INTO SPACE

Musique Concrète and Radiophonic Sound

Daphne Oram, Tristram Cary: Sonic Explorers
'It will be interesting to see what guiding principles emerge from this completely uncharted world.'
Letter to Daphne Oram about electronic music from Yehudi Menuhin[1]

OUT AT SEA ON A ROYAL NAVY SHIP as the world waged war around him, Tristram Cary dreamed of a new era in music.

Cary had joined the British armed forces in 1943, at the age of 17, like so many other teenagers who volunteered to fight Nazi Germany. He was trained in electronic engineering and became a radar specialist – skills that would have a profound effect on his life's work.

The teenage Cary was a radio enthusiast and had heard about a new invention called the tape recorder. Whilst on active service on the aircraft carrier **HMS** *Triumph*, he started to imagine how he could use it. 'None of us had seen a tape recorder... so you had to imagine what it was like,' he recalled later. 'But I thought, well if this *is* true, there's a new way of editing sound and a new way of dealing with sound and you can bring all sorts of sounds into music that were not possible to bring in before. So this was the amazing idea of musique concrète, you know, and also that with oscillators and electronically-generated sound you could have no restrictions like twelve notes to the octave, for example – you could have any pitch you liked…'[2]

Cary realised he could create novel musical pieces by cutting and splicing magnetic tape, reordering and combining sounds to construct new sequences that could not have previously existed. 'It occurred to me,' he reflected, 'that here was a chance to have a new sort of music altogether. The editing capacity meant that you could cut sounds together that were not normally together. Also, if you were writing a piece for orchestral music you could say, "Well, we won't have drums here we'll have a recording of thunder instead." Those were the first ideas that I had.'[3]

Born in 1925, Cary came from a family of artistically-minded intellectuals. As a child, he had been a talented pianist but was also fascinated by electrical devices and built his own radios. He went to public school and had begun studying music at Oxford University when World War II broke out, disrupting previous certainties for Cary and so many others.

On July 8, 1945, Prime Minister Winston Churchill announced the unconditional surrender of all German forces in Europe. 'It is the victory of the cause of freedom in every land,' Churchill declared. 'In all our long history we have never seen a greater day than this.'[4]

It came at a high price. Britain struggled economically after the war and its population endured a long period of austerity; food rationing continued for another nine years; bombsites and rubble-strewn plots blighted the great cities where German air raids had destroyed hundreds of thousands of homes. Social conservatism was still all-pervasive, with its values of class hierarchy, deference and strict conformity in gender roles; divorce came with a terrible stigma; homosexuality was a criminal offence; a sense of British imperial superiority remained almost ubiquitous and racism was taken for granted.

But the war had stoked desires for change and a more equitable future. The Labour Party defeated Churchill's Conservatives in a landslide election victory in 1945, promising to tackle the 'five giant evils' of want, disease, ignorance, squalor and idleness. Labour's government established the basis of Britain's modern welfare state, setting up the National Health Service to provide free universal healthcare and the National Insurance scheme to provide unemployment and sickness benefits as well as retirement pensions. Despite the economic gloom of the immediate post-war years, there was genuine optimism as Britain started to rebuild and people used make-do-and-mend ingenuity and new skills learned during wartime for peaceful goals.

One of them was Tristram Cary, who would become one of Britain's first independent electronic music-makers. When he got out of the Royal Navy, he wanted to buy a tape recorder. But at this point they were much too expensive, so he spent his £50 demobilisation pay instead on an acetate disc-cutting lathe and other basic equipment and started out as a 'lone experimenter', as he put it.

Living at his parents' house in Oxford, he made trips to London to search through shops selling surplus electrical equipment from the armed services. On Lisle Street near Leicester Square and around Tottenham Court Road were shops selling military surplus radio and electronics, with components heaped into boxes that sometimes spilled out onto the pavement, attracting ham-radio enthusiasts and technically-minded tinkerers. 'There was the junk of three armies, the American, the German and the British Army was in the London junk shops and you could go around, pick up gear cheap, sometimes absolutely brand new still in the original case. Probably designed for another purpose, but if you knew what you were doing, you could make it do something different,'[5] Cary observed.

He moved to London, where he built up an assemblage of sundry pieces of electronic equipment in his flat, including oscillators built with parts cannibalised from secondhand military equipment and a wired-up keyboard from a gutted harmonium. Technology intended for other functions was repurposed for creative objectives – a theme that recurs throughout the history of electronic music in Britain.

A sketch from 1947 shows Cary gazing nonchalantly at his elaborate contraption with its jumble of wires and keys and bulbs and valves – a 'ramshackle apparatus which only I would dare to use,' as he described it.[6] He initially made money to support himself by charging people to record them on acetate discs: three shillings and sixpence for two minutes of speech or four shillings and sixpence for the same amount of music. He also started to write to BBC producers, seeking commissions.

At that point, the kind of music he was making was completely new in Britain. 'I didn't feel with electronic music that I had any rules to break,' he reflected. 'If I did something and I liked it, I would claim it was music. Certain friends, of course, would say, "Well you've got some interesting noises there but it's not music, is it?"'[7]

When he started out, he didn't even know about the musique concrète experiments that had been ongoing in Europe for several years, until a friend came back from a visit to France and told him: 'You know they're doing stuff in Paris rather similar to what you're doing.'[8]

But Cary wasn't the only person in Britain who had been dreaming of a new music amid the violence of World War II. 'It was in 1944, at the age of 18 that I first became interested in the possibilities of electronic music,' composer Daphne Oram would recall. Reading Kurt London's book *Film Music*, Oram said she became fascinated by his descriptions of 'sounds, which one can produce from nothing with the help of science' and 'methods of recording which achieve the most astonishing effects by technical means.'[9]

Born the same year as Cary, in the Wiltshire market town of Devizes, Oram had studied music as a child and had also developed an early interest in electronics, experimenting by building basic radio equipment. As a schoolgirl, she said she was 'intrigued by strange sounds' and created what she described as a John Cage-like '"prepared piano" with tissue paper, paper clips etc, to shock mother and her prim guests.'[10] She joined the BBC in 1943 and was subsequently trained as a studio engineer.

The corporation would play a crucial role in the development of electronic music in Britain, offering an initial outlet through experimental drama broadcasts on the post-war, high-culture Third Programme, the precursor to Radio 3, and then, as television took over as the main popular medium, through programme soundtracks and theme tunes.

The BBC would also allow several talented and determined women to develop careers within this new genre as it evolved. During the war, the absence of men who had gone to fight opened up spaces in formerly male-dominated environments that women like Oram filled with vigour. The corporation recruited 900 women during the war to replace male staff who had been called up, creating previously unknown opportunities for female technicians and engineers.

Within three years, Daphne Oram had become a BBC studio manager, but she was resolved to achieve more. She wanted to make music with machines.

The Opening of the BBC Radiophonic Workshop

'You take a sound. Any sound. Record it and then change its nature by a multiplicity of operations. Record it at different speeds. Play it backwards. You add it to itself over and over again. You adjust filters, echoes, acoustic qualities. You combine segments of magnetic tape. By these means and many others you can create sounds which no one has ever heard before.'

Donald McWhinnie, introduction to Private Dreams and Public Nightmares, *a 'radiophonic poem' by Frederick Bradnum with sound effects by Daphne Oram, BBC Third Programme, 7 October 1957*

Magnetic tape recording was developed in Germany in the 1930s and reel-to-reel machines started to become commercially available, initially at large cost, after World War II. Forward-thinking composers saw the possibilities immediately. When Tristram Cary finally managed to acquire his own tape recorder in 1952, he felt liberated. Any noise could now be used in composition: 'You immediately crossed the frontier between "legitimately musical" sounds such as trumpets and triangles, and "non-musical" sounds, because anything that could be heard and recorded was valid material.'[11]

Perhaps the earliest piece of musique concrète was 'The Expression of Zaar', a piece assembled from noises and music from the streets of Cairo, made by Egyptian composer Halim el-Dabh using a magnetic wire recorder that captured sound signals on steel wire. In 1948, French composer Pierre Schaeffer, who gave musique concrète its name, presented his earliest noise-music collages, 'Cinq Études de Bruits', which were built from sounds cut onto discs and then arranged using turntables.

Schaeffer got access to tape recorders when he and fellow composer Pierre Henry set up an electro-acoustic research unit called the Groupe de Recherches Musicales at Radiodiffusion Télévision Française, the French public broadcaster, in Paris in 1951. National broadcasters across Europe also started to establish studios for electronic music: the Studio für Elektronische Musik des Westdeutschen Rundfunks, where Karlheinz Stockhausen became assistant director and created his early works, was founded the same year in Cologne.

The Paris and Cologne studios were followed by the Studio di Fonologia Musicale di Radio Milano in Milan, used by composers like Luciano Berio and Bruno Maderna, and the Studio Eksperymentalne Polskiego Radia in Warsaw, where Andrzej Dobrowolski and Krzysztof Penderecki created early pieces. In the United States, there was the Columbia-Princeton Electronic Music Centre in New York, founded by Vladimir Ussachevsky, Otto Luening and Milton Babbitt, and later the San Francisco Tape Music Centre, where Morton Subotnick, Ramon Sender and Pauline Oliveros experimented with new sounds. But until the late 1950s, there was nothing similar in Britain.

Initially there was a divide between the creators of this new music in France and Germany. In Paris, composers like Schaeffer and Henry called their works musique concrète and built them out of recorded sounds, while Stockhausen and his German colleagues only used purely electronic sound sources and described what they did as elektronische musik.

In Britain however, Cary wasn't overly concerned about the differences between the continental European ways of working, which soon intertwined anyway. 'Personally I found these distinctions academic – I don't care, I'll mix and match, I'll use some electronics and some real sounds,' he said. With his beard, glasses and pipe, roll-neck jumpers and corduroy jackets, Cary didn't look like a sonic radical, but he saw himself as someone who was 'operating at the fringes of what people generally thought of as music.'[12]

The lack of rules was a vital part of the excitement he felt about the new form. 'Electronic music seemed to have no limits,' Cary explained. 'We all dreamed about in the early days that it was a music *sans frontières*, it had no boundaries.'[13] Daphne Oram expressed similar enthusiasm about making music with tape recorders: 'Once the composer can write without the limitations of performance his palette is extended enormously,' she wrote. 'Rhythms become anything the composer can visualise without them having to be playable. Timbres have no registration and theoretically any sound, musical or otherwise, is within his grasp.'[14]

As early as 1950, Oram had already completed the score for an orchestral piece, 'Still Point', which was fizzing with new ideas, using live sound manipulated in real time and manipulated recordings played back on discs – an early form of turntablism. But the BBC rejected the work: 'I was told they couldn't understand it, it didn't make any sense at all,' she said.[15] Oram had also asked the corporation's management to provide her with technical equipment to realise her musical ideas, but was brusquely rejected by the BBC's Head of Research: 'He pulled himself up to his full height and said, "Miss Oram, we employ a hundred musicians to make all the songs we want. Thank you".'[16]

In an article she wrote several decades later, Oram looked back on how dismissively creative women were treated in the fifties and sixties. 'On the musical scene, some of the various groups of establishment male musicians found it to their advantage to ignore women, treating them as if they were just not there,' she said. 'If I was allowed to proffer an idea and they thought it of value they did not say so. They commandeered the idea for their own use, for no one would credit that a woman could have thought of it.'[17]

She was not alone; even though more women had been going out to work since the war, their employment status usually remained low and their average pay was around half that of men. 'On the radio, in films, in women's magazines, femininity was almost exclusively identified with the home and the nurturing of children,' historian David Kynaston said in his book about the post-war years.[18]

But Oram was a formidable character and not easily discouraged. Frustrated that the BBC wasn't allowing her to develop her ideas, she seized the initiative and began to exploit the corporation's resources for nocturnal sonic research. For several months, after her working day had finished in Broadcasting House and most people had left the building, she would gather up all the tape recorders she could find and use them to work on her own sound collages until they had to be put back the next morning.

'Having, usually, only one tape recorder available to me in my office, I continued to book Broadcasting House studios from midnight to 04:00 – collecting Ferrographs from many studios to make a "night only" electronic studio where I could compose,' she recalled.[19] She would then go home to sleep for a while before returning to Broadcasting House to start her day job over again. Such autonomous DIY experiments, circumventing rules in the cause of creativity, would become another recurring theme in British electronic music.

Oram had started to lobby the BBC to set up a permanent facility for creating electronic music; drama producer Donald McWhinnie was also urging the corporation to establish an experimental sonic workshop. Without their campaigning, electronic music in Britain might have developed very differently.

BBC engineer Alex Nesbitt, aided by Oram, McWhinnie and others, submitted a report to BBC management in November 1956, explaining how broadcasting organisations in Brussels, Cologne, Hamburg, Milan and Paris already had specialist facilities for creating electronic sound effects, listing what kind of staff would initially be needed – a recording engineer, tape editors and 'devisors of special effects' – and what kind of equipment (six tape machines, plus some audio frequency generators and filters). Their report argued that although the studios in Cologne and Paris have 'developed this medium primarily as an art form' and are 'specifically charged to make new compositions', the BBC unit would be used to create unusual sounds for radio dramas and productions for the features department.[20]

Culturally conservative managers in the BBC Music Department were fiercely opposed, arguing in letters to senior executives that an electronic studio could pose a threat to 'British musical tradition' and the 'rational development of musical aesthetics in this country.' They also claimed that some European composers in their 'expensive laboratories' had produced 'little beyond freakishness'. One memo pleaded that there should be 'no undue haste to exploit sound effects, under a pseudo-musical label, for their novelty, freak or feature value.'[21]

Decades later, it's hard to clearly picture what a crucial role the BBC played in British life in the post-war period, or what a powerful hold its three radio stations and one television channel once had over the public consciousness in the absence of competition. 'During and after the war, the BBC was the fount of all knowledge and entertainment, so you can't underestimate its importance in society at that time,' recalls Dick Mills, who was employed as a technician by the corporation after he finished national service as a radio mechanic with the Royal Air Force. 'Radio was a central point in everyday life, families would sit down and listen together.'

In her history of the BBC, Charlotte Higgins argues that as an institution, the corporation became deeply embedded in the British collective consciousness. 'As well as informing, educating and entertaining, it permeates and reflects our existences, infiltrates our imaginations, forms us in myriad ways,' she wrote. 'If nationhood consists of sets of intangibles, of common reference points and belief systems, the BBC threads us together through shared experience and memory.'[22]

That social binding had become even stronger during the collective trauma of World War II and the years of austerity that followed. Because of this, the corporation's managers took their roles as the nation's cultural gatekeepers very seriously indeed, as the BBC Music Department's memos of concern about alien influences showed.

But outside the Music Department's sphere of influence, BBC producers were starting to create sound effects for experimental drama programmes and radio comedy series like *The Goon Show*. The first BBC radio programme to use electronic effects – oscillator noise fed through a reverb chamber – was *Journey into Space*, a children's sci-fi serial about a spaceship's travels that went on air in 1953. As they would be so often in the years that followed, electronic sounds were cast as cosmic transmissions, conjuring mental images of unknown worlds and extraterrestrial odysseys to uncharted frontiers.

The first original musique concrète score commissioned by the BBC was for a drama called *The Japanese Fishermen*, about a fishing boat contaminated with radiation from a US nuclear weapons test in the Pacific Ocean. It was broadcast in 1955 on the Third Programme and its score was composed by Tristram Cary: an early example of how electronic music would also be frequently used as the soundtrack for menacing scenarios of scientific catastrophe and gross technological malfunction.

At the end of 1956, after seeing the proposal for an experimental studio, BBC managers set up what was initially called the Electrophonic Effects Committee to investigate 'the facilities required to set up a combined technical and operational "workshop" to provide electrophonic effects as supporting sound for certain programmes.'[23]

By this time, as well as Daphne Oram, there were other people at the BBC exploring ideas that grew out of musique concrète. Desmond Briscoe, a balding, avuncular ex-drummer and former big-band leader who was working as a sound engineer in the corporation's radio-drama department, had been intrigued by early recordings of Schaeffer and Stockhausen and by watching a BBC colleague cut up extracts of dialogue from the soundtracks of films to produce radio versions of movies. 'Suddenly sound on tape was for me an entirely different thing with limitless possibilities,'[24] he would recall. Briscoe started to integrate increasingly imaginative sound effects into the BBC's drama productions.

In 1957, producer McWhinnie recruited him to provide sound effects for what would be a critically acclaimed radio adaptation of Samuel Beckett's play *All That Fall*. Briscoe used tape-recorder manipulation techniques to create disorientating flutter-echo effects, which he said were 'particularly good for suggesting that slightly "fantasy feeling" of things happening in a larger-than-life way', as well as speeding up, layering and filtering human voices to paint a dreamlike sound picture.[25] (Briscoe had a long-term interest in imaginative effects. A couple of decades later, he would contribute electronic textures eerily combined with whale sounds for Nicolas Roeg's 1976 film *The Man Who Fell to Earth*).

Oram, Briscoe and others then created what *The Daily Telegraph* accurately described as a 'strange and discomfiting' soundtrack for a 'radio poem' called *Private Dreams and Public Nightmares*.[26] The broadcast on the BBC's Third Programme was preceded by an announcement by McWhinnie, explaining to the audience that what they were about to hear was something rather out of the ordinary. He described it as 'radiophonic sound'.

9

'What is radiophonic sound? It is new sound – suggestive of emotion, sensation, mood, rather than the literal moaning of a wind or the opening of a door,' McWhinnie declared. 'Created by technical means from basic sounds which may vary from the rustle of paper to a note from an electronic oscillator, radiophonic sound provides the writer and producer with an entirely new field in which to convey his intentions with the utmost subtlety of expression.'[27]

The concept was so novel that, before the broadcast, the BBC felt it had to warn its studio engineers who were working on the programme: 'Don't attempt to alter anything that sounds strange – it's deliberately meant to sound that way.'[28] Although one critic was repulsed by the soundtrack's 'shrieks and reverberations', others were excited by the possibilities of using radiophonic sound to enhance drama programmes. *The Times* hailed its 'power to support, indeed to transfigure, the most commonplace writing.'[29]

Not long afterwards, the BBC commissioned Oram to create sound effects for the televised comedy play *Amphitryon 38*, the first musique concrète soundtrack to be broadcast by BBC television. In tribute, one local newspaper headline offered the accolade: 'Devizes girl constructs new type of music for the BBC.'[30]

The interest generated by programmes like *Private Dreams and Public Nightmares* and the growing demands from BBC producers for futuristic effects for drama broadcasts finally led the corporation to inaugurate a dedicated studio to supply what it called 'special sounds'. The BBC Radiophonic Workshop officially opened on April 1, 1958, down a long, low-ceilinged corridor in Rooms 13 and 14 of the BBC's studio complex at the former Maida Vale Roller Skating Palace and Club in west London.

'A "workshop" for producing synthetic sounds, partly by electronic oscillators and partly by trickery with conventional sounds recorded on tape, has been set up by the BBC,' *The Times* reported.[31] Oram and Briscoe were employed to run it, with Dick Mills joining later as their engineer. Its initial budget was £2,000 and much of its equipment was either cast-offs sourced from other departments or from the BBC's Redundant Plant, a facility for obsolete and discarded gear.

The Radiophonic Workshop was not intended to be the kind of studio that Oram had envisaged, like those in Cologne, Paris or Milan where Stockhausen, Henry and Berio laboured intensively over complex avant-garde works. What the BBC's management had in mind was a relatively cheap little unit to serve the corporation's radio and television output, rather than nurturing the development of music for its own sake, with a minimal investment in equipment.

An article hailing the opening of the Workshop in *BBC Sound Broadcasting News* explained that 'radiophonic sound' was a purely practical innovation: 'Its functions are quite different from those of what is usually termed *musique concrète*, and although some of the techniques are similar radiophonic sound is not an art in itself – it is used to provide an additional "dimension" for radio and television productions,'[32] the bulletin declared.

'In France and Germany, they were building studios with all the latest equipment because they wanted to make art music. But the BBC just wanted a sound effects department for creating special sounds for cutting-edge drama,' explains the Radiophonic Workshop's archivist, Mark Ayres. 'So they rather grudgingly gave Daphne and Desmond two rooms and anything they wanted from the redundant equipment stores department, so anything that didn't quite work they could have, and that informed a lot of that early music and sound that they produced.'

As if to illustrate this, one of the Radiophonic Workshop's first commissions was to create a series of intestinal gurglings to accompany an absurd *Goon Show* skit about the gastric disorders of Peter Sellers' comedy character Major Denis Bloodnok. Briscoe and Mills even appeared as a novelty double-act billed as 'Weird and Wonderful', in a music hall-style revue intended to promote the Workshop at a BBC event at Earl's Court in 1962. The sound of Briscoe hitting a row of bottles was tape-manipulated into a rhythm, which was then augmented by a jazz trio who sprang out of the wings to take up the groove. It's hard to imagine a 'serious' composer like Stockhausen performing such a comic turn.

The establishment of the Radiophonic Workshop represented a major achievement for Oram, who had struggled for years with conservatives inside the corporation in her campaign for the BBC to embrace new sound techniques. It would also ensure her place in history as one of the founding figures in British electronic music.

After her death in 2003, composer Hugh Davies recalled in an obituary how her 'independent outlook' played a vital role in bringing the Workshop into existence 'despite resistance and indifference'.[33] Brian Hodgson, who began his long and illustrious career at the Workshop in 1962, framed her achievement even more directly: 'Without Daphne, it would not have started, because the BBC did not want an electronic music studio.'[34]

But although the BBC was not seeking to emulate developments in mainland Europe, it did nurture innovation. The Radiophonic Workshop was established within a culture of radio that had been experimenting with formats, styles and techniques for several decades. Whatever the limitations and stylistic parameters imposed on it from above, the Workshop would take this even further. It would make both musique concrète and electronic music. It would make sonic art.

On the door of the Workshop, Oram pinned up a quote from philosopher Francis Bacon's 17th century utopian novel *New Atlantis*, which seemed to predict the electronic music of the 20th century. For Oram, it represented a kind of statement of intent: 'We have also sound-houses, where we practice and demonstrate all sounds and their generation. We have harmonies which you have not, of quarter-sounds and lesser slides of sounds… We have also diverse strange and artificial echoes, reflecting the voice many times.'[35]

Oram and Briscoe were tasked with producing sound effects for drama and entertainment, signature tunes for radio and TV shows and broadcasts for schools, and 'interval music', which was played between programmes. A lot of the Workshop's early output was musique concrète-style creations made from recorded sounds, manipulated using tape machines and modified with echo or reverberation. Tapes were meticulously cut and re-spliced by hand to form new sequences.

'If you're using natural sounds, you could use anything. You can use a door banging, you can use glass breaking, you can use the wind that's blowing down the road… and you record it and play it backwards, forwards, echo, double it up, speed it up, slow it down,'[36] said Maddalena Fagandini, who joined the Workshop in 1959.

Workshop archivist Ayres has described the unit's early techniques as 'analogue sampling', a method involving huge amounts of patience and dedication. 'Each note was individually recorded onto magnetic tape, the playback speed altered so as to produce the correct pitch, copied to a new piece of tape, cut to length and spliced in order,' he wrote in the sleevenotes to the *BBC Radiophonic Music* compilation album. 'With multitrack tape not available until 1965 (and even then, rarely), multiple layers were created by repeatedly copying the tapes or by manually synchronising a number of separate machines.'[37]

Bulky tape recorders the size of launderette washing machines dominated the studio, alongside a bank of twelve oscillators linked to a primitive, purpose-built control unit, while hundreds of loops of tape hung from hooks on the walls; echo effects were created in a basement room and the mixing desk had been salvaged from the Albert Hall. 'There were no synthesisers, no computers, no samplers; just a few oscillators, crude filters, aged tape recorders, razor blades, miles of recording tape, an ancient microphone and a collection of noise-producing old junk – the piano frame rescued from a junk heap and liberated from its case, metal lamp shades, a burst copper hot water cylinder, empty bottles of all shapes and sizes, mad ideas and lots of laughs,' Hodgson later recalled.[38]

An article in the BBC's *Radio Times* magazine in December 1960 described the Workshop as 'one of the newest and strangest departments' at the corporation, set up to supply 'scenery in sound' for radio and television. 'Fantasy of any sort is our ideal medium,' Desmond Briscoe told the reporter, who seemed fascinated by Fagandini's 'weird "orchestral" score' for a science-fiction radio play, made up of whimsical descriptions rather than musical notations and by sound effects created for a *Goon Show* sketch – 'genuine explosions, whoops from electronic oscillators, water splashes, synthetic burps, and cork-like pops.'[39]

According to a BBC Engineering Division monograph, the Workshop provided special effects for a whole variety of programmes in its initial years, from wacky noises for *The Goon Show* and Fagandini's chilling effects for Jean Cocteau's play *Orpheus* to soundtracks for the *Music and Movement* schools series, including Jenyth Worsley's quirky theme 'The Magic Carpet', as well as documentaries about steam trains and science-fiction dramas.[40] It was all rather eccentrically British – strange electro-acoustic sequences that might have been thought of as 'serious' music in continental Europe were being broadcast to the general public as part of children's television programmes, comedy shows and educational documentaries, rather than to high-culture aficionados at concert halls.

At this point, electronic music was often seen as an amusing novelty or oddball diversion, rarely as 'real music'; some even regarded it as a cultural monstrosity. 'How can one dignify with the word "music" a series of sounds manufactured on a tape recorder?' a writer for *The Times* demanded in 1957.[41] A newspaper review of a piece by Oram at the Edinburgh Festival in 1961 described her 'conglomeration of tape recording equipment and electronic devices' on stage as looking like a 'George Orwell fantasy'.[42]

'There are those who claim that these electronically conceived compositions are the natural development of modern music forms. While there may be a certain amount of art-form in the experimental effects, the claim can hardly be entertained seriously. This was musical madness,' the review chuntered. It allowed that Oram was 'obviously a very gifted woman', but concluded by approvingly quoting a disgruntled audience member who left the show early: 'This eerie stuff's alright for cranks and beatniks.'[43]

But there were also wonderstruck articles like a *Daily Mirror* report about Oram in 1962, which was published under the admiring headline, 'She makes music for the age of machines.' The reporter expressed amazement at Oram's 'weird, out-of-this-world' compositions and urged his readers not to be too quick to mock because 'Beethoven and Stravinsky sounded pretty odd to a lot of people at first.'[44]

Dick Mills acknowledges that the sounds being made at the Workshop were, initially at least, unintelligible to many people: 'It all sounded very alien to them and there were complaining letters in the *Radio Times*, saying that what we did sounded like skeletons doing naughty things on corrugated iron roofs: "Who needs nightmares when we've got the Radiophonic Workshop?" They would say we were making sounds and music that nobody liked for radio plays that nobody could understand.' Indeed, letters to the *Radio Times* complained of BBC incidental music that sounded like a 'lunatic asylum' or a 'nightmare in a railway train'.[45]

'People didn't really understand it, they thought it was outlandish and disgusting that the BBC should spend money on this experimental unit,' says Brian Hodgson. But he also recalls how perceptions started to change after the serial *Quatermass and the Pit*, one of the Workshop's first big commissions for television, attracted popular acclaim when it was broadcast from late 1958 onwards.

Quatermass and the Pit, created by SF-horror teleplay maestro Nigel Kneale, was 'the first television programme to hit a wide audience with strange and weird electronic sound',[46] according to Desmond Briscoe. These included 'great electronic churnings and throbbings' created by tape recorders feeding back to each other and 'great splats of sounds' made by connecting and disconnecting amplifiers, Briscoe recalled. As many as eleven million people tuned in for the final episode, giving the Workshop's splats and churnings a nationwide impact.

Television ownership had risen dramatically during the 1950s. Queen Elizabeth II's coronation in 1953 was a breakthrough moment for the medium, cementing BBC TV's central role in British public life. After rationing was lifted, austerity had given way to a consumer boom as spending escalated on domestic goods that had been luxuries – washing machines, vacuum cleaners, refrigerators and televisions. It's been estimated that in 1950, there were only around 350,000 television sets in Britain, but by the end of the decade, some three quarters of the country's households had one. Television became the new focus of British domestic entertainment, giving the Radiophonic Workshop a huge audience, but also placing limitations on the kind of pieces its staff could create.

The Workshop's output was qualitatively different from German elektronische musik or French musique concrète because of its functional nature. Musicologist Louis Niebur has described it as 'British populist modernism'[47] – sounds tailored for a specific purpose, encompassing familiarities of rhythm and melodic sequencing as well as some of the dissonance and abstraction of continental European art music.

'The people on the continent who were doing peculiar things with musique concrète, they weren't doing it for a specific purpose and to a deadline, they were doing it as exploration and research to satisfy themselves, not a programme-maker who had given them a list of requirements,' explains Mills. 'But within those requirements we were given, we were free to experiment as far as we wanted, in whatever direction we thought the programme ought to take.'

But the BBC's conception of the Radiophonic Workshop as a practical facility to create 'special sounds' rather than original electro-acoustic music was a bitter disappointment to Daphne Oram. She had hoped it could become an experimental institution, exploring the frontiers of a new audio art form. A visit to the Philips Pavilion at Expo 58 – the 1958 Brussels World's Fair – reinforced both her ambition and her frustration.

Commissioned by electronics company Philips and designed by Le Corbusier, the pavilion's remarkable structure housed an immersive multimedia environment, within which Edgard Varèse's specially-commissioned 'Poème Eléctronique' was played through several hundred speakers, accompanied by film projections and a lightshow, prefiguring how electronic music would be presented on stage in the techno era. The Philips Pavilion made a huge impression on those who came to see it, including

Stockhausen, Berio, Schaeffer, American composer John Cage and Britain's Tristram Cary.

Not long after her trip to Brussels for Expo 58, Oram resigned from the BBC, exasperated by what she saw as the corporation's institutional conservatism. She left behind the Workshop she'd helped create, less than a year after it started operating. 'On Nov 1st 1958 I handed in my resignation as, by that time, I could see that the Workshop was going to handle very little music – only extended sound effects... I wished to continue to compose,'[48] she later explained to the managing director of BBC Radio, in a letter preserved in her archive at Goldsmiths, University of London.

Yet again, Oram had the courage to follow her own path. Part of the impetus for going it alone dated back to the war years; on a BBC training course in 1944, she had encountered the cathode ray oscilloscope, which displays the waveforms of electrical circuits, and inquired whether it would be possible to create a machine that converts waveforms into sound. She then started developing the ideas for what would become her 'Oramics' system, an electro-mechanical composition machine that scanned dots, lines and squiggles hand-painted onto strips of 35mm film and glass slides, converting them into sounds. In Oram's archive, there are yellowing papers with pencil diagrams of the concept for the Oramics machine, dating back as far as 1951. It seemed to be a descendant of the pre-World War II explorations of optical sound synthesis by Soviet avant-garde composer Arseny Avraamov, or the experiments in generating sound by making marks on cinematic stock by animator Norman McLaren and filmmaker Jack Ellitt in the 1930s. (McLaren described the noise he created by scratching, drawing and painting on film as 'a small orchestra of clicking, thudding, buzzing and drumlike timbres'[49]).

Leaving the Radiophonic Workshop behind, Oram cashed in her BBC pension and used the money to set up her own independent studio in a converted oast house in Kent called Tower Folly, where she worked on developing her prototype Oramics unit. '[The Oramics machine] does away with all the limitations imposed by the range of conventional instruments,' she told a visiting reporter in 1960. 'You can achieve completely new tone colours and rhythmic patterns.' She even seemed to predict the digital audio workstations of the late 20th century, informing the journalist: 'There is no reason why there should not eventually be cheap, make-your-own-electronic music sets in thousands of homes instead of the conventional piano.'[50]

A British Movietone News report from 1962 showed Oram 'engaged in scientific research into electronic music' in her Tower Folly studio, surrounded by banks of equipment, using a sound generator to create swooping tones, looping tapes to build rhythms and then adding reverb to compose the haunting 'Bird of Parallax'.[51] Long before she was 'rediscovered' by 21st century electronic music enthusiasts, Oram was recognised as an innovator – by her peers at least. 'A Remarkable Woman Pioneer' declared the headline of a report by specialist magazine *Tape Recording* in 1960.

'Miss Daphne Oram is today probably Britain's busiest and most successful producer of electronic music and musique concrète and an increasing number of amateur enthusiasts are now benefiting from her professional knowledge and skill,' the article declared. It quoted Alan Sutcliffe, a student who recounted his experiences of a weekend electronic composition course at Oram's studio, where 'countless loops of tape festoon the walls.'[52]

In the early sixties, Oram acted as a mentor for keen young men like Sutcliffe, who went on to become an electronic composer and part-time director of British synthesizer company EMS, co-found the Computer Arts Society and create computer-animation sequences for the 1979 film *Alien*. She was also a creative catalyst for Hugh Davies, who visited Tower Folly as an 18-year-old student before going to work as Stockhausen's assistant in Cologne and becoming a renowned composer.

Whilst developing the Oramics machine, Oram earned money by working on pieces of music for film, television and theatre, as well as advertisements for companies like Lego and Nestlé. One of these commercial commissions was a whimsical 7-inch single entitled 'Electronic Sound Patterns', released by HMV Records in 1962 as a soundtrack for 'Listen, Move and Dance' classes in primary schools. Because it has thudding, bass xylophone-style echoed riffs and a lolloping groove, it has since been jokingly described as the world's first electronic dance record, although its sleeve notes more modestly claim it is only 'intended for children to enjoy and may lead them into movement of dance-like character.'

Oram also continued to create her own, more serious compositions. Her work was featured alongside pieces by Tristram Cary, Delia Derbyshire, Ernest Berk and Peter Zinovieff at what was billed as the 'First London Concert of Electronic Music by British Composers', at the Queen Elizabeth Hall in January 1968. The event was a sell-out and a reviewer for *The Daily Telegraph* was impressed by the large crowd, writing that 'it would seem that there are many people who would never dream of attending a conventional avant-garde concert yet are interested in the possibilities of electronic music.'[53]

Oram's best works had a delightfully otherworldly character: the exquisitely delicate tones and subterranean rumblings of 'Four Aspects', the cosmic exoticism and marionette-jig melodies of 'Bird of Parallax', the séance-like vibrations of 'Pulse Persephone' and the supernatural overtones of 'Contrasts Essconic'. But the musical possibilities she envisaged for her own optoelectronic instrument, the Oramics unit, were never realised in the end. She tried to develop a prototype Mini Oramics for production, but it was never completed. When her machine was put on display at the Science Museum in London in 2011, eight years after her death, it looked like a strange relic of a lost potential future.

The Music in Janet Beat's Head

'I was drawn to people who were outsiders, because they experimented.'
Janet Beat

Daphne Oram and Maddalena Fagandini were not the only women composers of musique concrète in Britain at the end of the 1950s. Born in 1937 in the West Midlands town of Streetly, Janet Beat was another early adopter of the new techniques who rejected social orthodoxies to dedicate herself to a career in electronic music.

Like Oram, she had started experimenting with her family's piano when she was young. 'I would climb on the armchair which was next to the piano, open the top of the piano and drop knives and forks and spoons inside, and then they would jingle-jangle when you played piano,' she says, describing sound-modification strategies that John Cage used when composing his prepared piano pieces – 'although as a small child I didn't know anything about John Cage, of course.'

She also broke the family's wind-up gramophone by trying to play records backwards and slowing them down while they were spinning, much to the dismay of her parents: 'I heard my mother once saying to my father: "I don't think that child is quite right in the head. We'll have to put her in a [children's care] home to knock the music out of her".'

Beat realised early that women who wanted to be composers faced serious obstacles. She had started writing music as a young girl and wanted to enter

Janet Beat in her home studio. Photo courtesy of Janet Beat.

a piece she had written for a BBC *Children's Hour* competition, but her mother wouldn't allow her to post it and threw the envelope in the fire. 'The attitudes to women were so different then. Your job was to get married off. We were supposed to be baby machines and look after the household for a man,' she says. 'So my parents didn't want me to have a career in music: "Women don't write music. What would the neighbours say?"'

In the late 1950s, she heard musique concrète on the radio for the first time: a piece by Pierre Henry. 'I was fascinated, so when I was 21, I used my twenty-first birthday money to buy my first tape recorder, a Brenell Mark 5, and I started experimenting with that.' She created her first recorded piece from the tape-manipulated sounds of a pair of antique cymbals in 1958. But her early reels were destroyed by her father while she was away at university studying music. 'He used them to tie up his raspberry canes and other fruits and flowers in the kitchen garden. He just referred to them as "Janet's junk".'

Her university lecturers were also disparaging. 'They were very hostile to musique concrète and they made fun of composers like Stockhausen, so I didn't dare let them know I was fascinated by all this new music or I'd have been thrown off the course.'

Beat persevered, and eventually went on to set up an electronic studio at the Royal Scottish Academy of Music and Drama – though spiteful misogynists tried to sabotage some early concerts staged there by tampering with the equipment. 'It was the time when women weren't supposed to write music, or only just to write a wee hymn tune. You were allowed to do that. But you certainly had to have nothing to do with technology,' she recalls.

Nevertheless, she managed to gain recognition as a composer and lecturer, and would attract renewed acclaim at the age of 83, when her first ever album was released by archivist label Trunk Records in 2021. It featured a selection of her delicately alluring electronic recordings like the exquisite 'Dancing on Moonbeams' and the disorientating keyboard chimes of 'Piangam'. 'I've become a sort of historic monument,' she says. 'The second woman electronic music composer in the UK, Daphne Oram being the first of course. I'm getting the sort of attention that you usually get just after you die – and I must admit, I'm enjoying having it while I'm still alive.'

Like Janet Beat, the avant-garde electronic composers of the time had to be strongly self-reliant, often working alone and finding their own paths by trial and error. The BBC Radiophonic Workshop largely maintained a closed-door policy to outsiders, with the notable exception of the Catalan political exile Roberto Gerhard, who assembled his electronic soundtracks there for BBC radio plays like *Asylum Diary* and *The Anger of Achilles*, as well as the tape-manipulated sounds incorporated into his orchestral work *Collages*.

British universities, like the BBC, were slow to set up electronic music departments compared to their European counterparts. This meant that the culture developed differently from continental Europe, with a blurring of the lines between 'serious' music, pop music, film soundtracks, functional music for dramatic or educational purposes, and commercially-commissioned music for advertisements.

Composers in Britain had fewer accessible resources and had to rely less on state institutions and more on their own personal initiative. People like Oram and Cary, who might in other countries have been granted the resources to concentrate on composing art music, had to hustle for a living, chasing commissions from television, film and advertising or making marketable electronic pieces they could sell to library music companies for commercial use. Meanwhile, outside the cultural establishment, autodidacts and hobbyists had begun to set up their own amateur studios, making their own contributions to the development of Britain's distinctive DIY electronic music culture.

F. C. Judd and the Reel-to-Reel Club Scene

'Many of the methods applied to electronic music and *musique concrète* can be adapted by the amateur in the making of interesting electronic sounds.'
F. C. Judd, Practical Electronics, October 1965

For around a decade from the late 1950s onwards, an amateur tape-recording scene flourished in Britain, with specialist clubs and societies proliferating across the country as enthusiasts experimented with a new sonic technology that was starting to become more affordable amid the post-austerity consumer boom.

F. C. Judd at home with his Chromasonics electronic music visualisation machine. Photo courtesy of Public Information.

Most of these tape-machine hobbyists were not using their equipment to create music, however. In his fascinating book *Tape Leaders*, which documents this long-overlooked era of British domestic creativity, author and musician Ian Helliwell explains that their interests were usually more conventional, 'with much activity based around actuality recordings, hospital radio broadcasts, recordings for the blind and tapespondence' – communication via tapes sent through the post.[54] But some tape-recorder club members did experiment with musique concrète, and their meetings occasionally hosted speakers who staged demonstrations of the new form.

One of these expert orators was F. C. Judd, perhaps the most industrious proselytiser of amateur electronic experimentation in 1950s and 1960s Britain. Born in 1914, Fred Judd was a remarkably prolific composer, inventor, author and specialist magazine editor who travelled around the country giving lectures and demonstrations. He became one of the most important figures in the early development of British electronic music, although his indefatigable efforts have long been underappreciated.

Judd had worked with radar equipment and electronics while serving with the RAF Coastal Command during World War II. In the mid-fifties, before the BBC established the Radiophonic Workshop, he started building his own studio for electronic music at his house in the east London suburb of Woodford, where he also created his own prototype voltage-controlled, keyboard-operated synthesizer in 1963, around the same time as the better-known American inventors Robert Moog and Don Buchla developed theirs. From his home, he helped to run the independent label Castle Records, which released sound effects recordings and a series of his own electronic compositions. His three EPs were later compiled as an album of library music entitled *Electronic Age*.

In 1961, Judd published the do-it-yourself guide *Electronic Music and Musique Concrète*, a manual for the aspiring electronic musician illustrated by photographs of serious-looking gents in suits in front of banks of dials and reels. 'The composer of electronic music has little need to offer a justification of his work. He can regard this as an experiment in an unexplored field and can supply musical motive by pointing to the fascination of creating new sounds,'[55] he wrote.

The book included circuit diagrams for hobbyists to construct their own equipment, which many did. 'Mixers, oscillators, ring modulators and even complete tape recorders were built by enthusiasts, and the more seriously committed constructed their own recording dens at home; in spare rooms, garages, sheds, under the stairs or even in the lounge,'[56] Helliwell observed in his book.

British Recording Club magazine *Amateur Tape Recording*, one of several publications that catered to the craze, published pictures of some of these 'dens', profiling a Mr B. Whibley of Gravesend, Kent, who had assembled a fully-equipped studio in his lounge to record musique concrète. 'Mrs Whibley put up with three months of construction chaos while her husband built this console in the window bay,' the magazine noted.[57]

From the late fifties onwards, *Tape Recording* and *Amateur Tape Recording* provided DIY tips on how to make field recordings, homemade film soundtracks or unusual sound effects. *Amateur Tape Recording*, which Judd edited, offered a series entitled 'How to make modern music with a tape recorder', along with dozens of adverts for various types of tape machine and readers' letters offering recordings for the magazine's library. 'My tapes of Workingmen's Clubs will now definitely be ready by the first week in June, as I have arranged to record in Rotherham on Saturday, Sunday, 23rd and 24th May,' promised one such letter-writer in the August 1959 edition.[58]

The magazine's liveliest section was 'Tape Club News', to which hobbyists' clubs from towns and cities around the country sent despatches detailing their activities in the most banal detail – recordings of birdsong, theatre plays, old songs. 'All members of the Wakefield and District Club had a really enjoyable time at the last meeting when Messrs. Wood and Appleton gave a first-class demonstration of "sounds mysterious",' reported one correspondent in March 1960. 'These were produced by using some pre-recorded sounds of everyday life, and by distorting, cutting, looping, dubbing, re-dubbing, and splicing these in various permutations. Much laughter was heard at some of the unusual noises produced.'[59]

Some of the clubs staged exhibitions or public demonstrations in municipal meeting rooms and parish halls or debated their endeavours at members' houses. Enthusiasts could compete in the annual British Amateur Tape Recording Contest, and some of the winners' pieces were aired by the BBC. By the end of 1960, the size of the scene in Britain and Ireland was indicated by *Amateur Tape Recording*'s listing of around ninety clubs and societies from Aberdare to York. The British Recording Club, which published the magazine, even opened its own Centre of Sound complex in London's Soho to promote sonic technology. Judd reportedly gave a lecture and concert there in July 1961 featuring works by himself and Daphne Oram, one of the first electronic music events ever staged in the UK.

There was a distinct vibe of suburban hobbyism around this early sixties cult. 'I think a lot of them would have been just very ordinary people, not particularly well-versed in avant-garde music or advanced classical music, but they saw that there was something really quite fascinating because that was the first time really that the public had any chance to play around with sounds themselves,' says Helliwell.

'From the early fifties onwards, tape recorders really started to become affordable and there were so many different competing manufacturers, so many different models to choose from. A staggering amount in fact, so I suppose it was inevitable, really, that that although people may not have been that enamoured by contemporary music, they wanted to play around and were thinking, "This musique concrète, what's all that about?"'

The sounds produced by club members have sometimes been dubbed 'outsider electronics' – recordings by obscure figures who had no connection to the BBC Radiophonic Workshop, the classical avant-garde or the commercial pop world, who assembled amateur musique concrète pieces using their own equipment in spare rooms, sheds or garages. In his book, Helliwell relishes the stories of marginal characters like Ralph O. Broome, a member of the Doncaster and District Tape Recording Club in South Yorkshire, who was one of the few to get his work released on disc: a track called 'Nuclear Madness', created using tape recorders, an oscillator and a tremolo unit. It was issued on a promotional 7-inch as one of a selection of tracks from 1960's International Tape Recording competition, according to Helliwell. He also documents the tiny oeuvre of Trevor F. Holmes, a '21-year-old toolmaker of Redditch, Worcester', whose only known work is a 1965 composition called 'No Title', the recording of which probably no longer exists.[60]

Decades later, some of the surviving recordings were released on compilation albums by archivist labels like Trunk and Public Information. Most of the amateur tinkerers faded from history, however, although a few managed to pursue careers in electronic music. Years before Malcolm Clarke became a composer at the BBC Radiophonic Workshop and produced his brilliant piece for narrator, vocoder and synthesizer, *August 2026: There Will Come Soft Rains*, adapted from Ray Bradbury's SF story, he was recording homemade, tape-manipulated music as a teenage member of the Leicester Tape Recording and Hi-fi Club.

The obscure influence of the tape-recording societies continued long into the 1980s, when readers of hobbyist electronics magazines played a significant role in the industrial and post-punk scenes, right up to the techno era. Helliwell's book documents the story of a 13-year-old who conducted 'amateur experiments by creatively soldering an old intercom to make electronic sounds'[61] back in 1968. The boy, Ian Loveday, would go on to become respected London club DJ Ian B, one of Britain's first wave of acid house producers in the late eighties, recording a series of electronic dance tracks under the aliases Eon, Minimal Man and Rio Rhythm Band before his death at the age of 54.

One of the great themes explored by both amateurs and serious composers in the late 1950s and early 1960s was the near-universal obsession of the period: space travel. The relationship between electronic sounds and cosmic exploration in the popular imagination, which continued into the 21st century, dates back to radio programmes like *Journey into Space* and was cemented in 1956 when *Forbidden Planet* became the first major Hollywood sci-fi movie to have an entirely electronic soundtrack, composed by Bebe and Louis Barron.

The reverb-drenched oscillator noise and electronic bleeps used for *Journey into Space* were followed into the nation's living rooms in 1957 by the real-life bleeping of the Soviet satellite Sputnik, which could be picked up on short-wave radio receivers as it circled the globe, generating awe in the minds of many who heard it. Meanwhile comic strips featuring tales of space-age derring-do – flyboy hero Dan Dare of the International Space Fleet in the *Eagle* comic and Captain Condor in the *Lion* – sold hundreds of thousands of copies. 'As a kid, I was very excited about space travel, but of course everybody was at that time,' recalls the Radiophonic Workshop's Brian Hodgson, who was a dedicated schoolboy listener to *Journey into Space*. 'Even more so after the Russians put Gagarin into space.'

The first manned space flight by Yuri Gagarin's Vostok 1 in April 1961 set off a surge of enthusiasm that spilled over onto the streets of Britain when the Soviet cosmonaut visited three months after his historic voyage. Thousands gathered to greet him in London, clapping, cheering and waving to the Russian hero of the skies. 'I am deeply moved by the overwhelming welcome which I have received here in Britain,'[62] Gagarin said.

He then travelled on to Manchester, where he was driven through town in an open-top Rolls-Royce with the number plate YG 1, standing and saluting the crowds by the roadside. 'There were thousands of people here, and the girls were running to Yuri Gagarin's motorcade, wanting to hold his hand, screaming in excitement – as if he was some major pop star,' Ray Smith, a teenager at the time, told the BBC.[63] Some tried to push past the police cordon to get the cosmonaut's autograph, or to touch his talismanic green uniform.

The public's excitement about space travel inevitably had an impact on radio and television producers as they sought to create fresh material that would intrigue and entertain. Popular fascination with science fiction themes was compounded by scientific advances, as well as by technological disasters like the deadly accident at the Windscale nuclear power plant in 1957. As the Cold War became a potentially life-exterminating US-Soviet stand-off and Britain announced it had successfully tested atomic weapons, catalysing the foundation of the Campaign for Nuclear Disarmament, anxieties about global annihilation also had a huge impact on public consciousness.

The science fiction of the time channelled such fears about dystopian or apocalyptic futures, with TV programmes like the *Quatermass* serials and novels by authors like John Wyndham exploring concerns about technological progress leading mankind towards catastrophe. The popularity of space travel and science fiction gave a significant boost to electronic music: as more SF programming was commissioned by British broadcasters, more strange sounds were needed to express feelings of awe and terror, increasing the demand for soundtracks from the Radiophonic Workshop and independent musique concrète producers.

The commercial network Independent Television (later to become ITV) first broadcast the British children's sci-fi series *Space Patrol* in April 1963, with a soundtrack composed by F. C. Judd. Opening with crashes, booms, bleeps and the atonal call-sign of a spinning spaceship, Judd's score for the animated marionette serial was distinctly abstract, but it had a strong impact on younger viewers with fewer preconceptions about what music should sound like.

The *Space Patrol* soundtrack was created at Judd's home studio, which resembled a miniature version of the Radiophonic Workshop relocated to suburbia: stacks of metal-housed generators and modulators, snaking coils of cables and homely, floral-patterned curtains. Judd himself seemed an unlikely avant-gardist, with an appearance that was anything but bohemian. In a photograph taken at the time, he posed with his electronic devices in shirt and tie, as if preparing to give an after-dinner speech. The image was somewhat deceptive; although some of his quirkily melodic sound-sketches with jaunty tape-loop rhythms had a hint of the variety club, he also made off-kilter proto-electro-pop tunes and disorientating dronescapes that foreshadowed the dark ambient genre.

In his book *Electronic Music and Musique Concrète*, Judd's tone was practical rather than intellectual, like an electrical-appliance salesman. But he briefly allowed himself to fantasise about where electronic music might go in the years to come, arguing that it would increasingly depart from musical traditions, 'for there is little point in producing a purely synthetic version of an orchestra playing a well-known composition,' he asserted. 'The next step must therefore be an entirely new conception of "music" with new sounds and acoustic effects.'[64] This unlikely suburban prophet had unwittingly predicted techno.

Judd was a tireless inventor who was also active on the ham-radio scene, another hobbyist subculture, and designed two short-wave aerial antennae that proved popular among his fellow amateurs. He went on to develop what he called Chromasonics, a system to generate abstract patterns on a TV screen triggered by sound inputs, but it never went into commercial production. The apparatus was lost after his death in 1992, as were many of his recordings. Interest in his music waned too, though it saw a revival on the intellectual fringes of techno in the 21st century and a tribute album by contemporary electronic musicians interpreting his work was released in 2013. 'There is something really fascinating about F. C. Judd as an artist,' said one of the contributors, American composer Holly Herndon. 'I won't pretend there is not some romance to how committed he was.'[65]

Judd was one of several independent tape composers who achieved some kind of success in Britain in the late fifties and early sixties; others included Stuart Wynn Jones, who created homemade soundtracks for his animated experimental films, and Terence Dwyer, an art-college lecturer who later wrote two educational books on the subject, *Composing with Tape Recorders* and *Making Electronic Music*.

Closer to the mainstream was Barry Gray, who set up a home studio to make music for advertisements and TV shows like Gerry and Sylvia Anderson's 'Supermarionation' series *Stingray*, *Thunderbirds*, *Captain Scarlet and the Mysterons* and *Joe 90*. Their soundtracks incorporated ethereal noises he called 'musifex', created using the Ondes Martenot, an early electronic instrument with a mysterious, quivering sound similar to the Theremin. Like the Radiophonic Workshop's output, Gray's work would be credited by later generations of electronic musicians as a formative childhood influence.

Uncommon Characters: Desmond Leslie, Delia Derbyshire

'We spend quite a lot of time trying to invent new sounds – sounds that don't exist already, sounds that can't be produced by musical instruments.'
Delia Derbyshire interviewed on BBC One's Tomorrow's World, *December 1965*

In its early years, electronic music was an unusual art form that attracted free-thinkers and adventurous spirits, as well as some distinctly unusual characters. One of the most unusual of them all was Desmond Leslie: a plummy-voiced, aristocratic figure who was a distant cousin to Winston Churchill, owned a castle in Ireland, flew Spitfires as a fighter pilot for the RAF during World War II and worked on propaganda films aimed at undermining the Nazis. He was married to the German-born cabaret singer and film star Agnes Bernelle, who had fled Hitler's regime with her parents in the 1930s.

Leslie was enthralled by the esoteric and the idea of extraterrestrial life, and co-wrote a cult book about alien contact, *Flying Saucers Have Landed*, with George Adamski, an American mystic huckster. 'George Adamski was a very charming con man and had claimed to have been up in a UFO, and my father wasn't sure whether he had or not, but he was fascinated by anything to do with space and by anything futuristic,' says Leslie's son Mark. SF author Arthur C. Clarke called the book 'a farrago of nonsense', but it became a US bestseller and Bernelle told Leslie it had made him 'a household name with the lunatic fringe'.[66]

Leslie's career as a film composer began in the late 1940s, when he ran out of money for the soundtrack for his own project *Stranger at My Door* and had to improvise. Bernelle said he used reels of music he bought from libraries and then mixed them up, 'playing some of these tracks backwards or re-recording them on top of one another until he had achieved the desired effect.'[67] He continued to experiment with reel-to-reel machines and turned the spare room in his London house into a studio, amassing a huge collection of tapes of sound effects including 'people marching, birds singing, bombs exploding, lathes turning, storms raging, cars starting,'[68] *The Times* reported in 1962.

Adjacent to his home studio was young Mark Leslie's room. 'I was a small child in the next bedroom, and the neighbours would complain about all these weird noises going through the building. And my father would go, "It's the plumbing, it's the plumbing." He set up his own studio really for making commercial sound effects, general sort of noises that went to sound libraries and were used by people like the BBC. There were also a lot of television advertisements, people asking for "bloop bloop bloop" noises for adverts for bottles of port. But as he was of an artistic bent, he could envisage this as an art form.'

Leslie's music was part F. C. Judd novelty amateurism, part Stockhausen-like austerity and part indefinable weirdness, with titles like 'Music of the Voids of Outerspace' that reflected his extraterrestrial obsessions. Although most of the recordings made at his London studio were sold for use as soundtracks for films and plays, or as library music, some were compiled on the album *Music of the Future* – pressed as a single acetate copy in 1960 and only made publicly available in 2005, four years after his death.

In the sleeve notes, Leslie explained that he was not aiming for natural sounds but something marvellously artificial: 'One of the advantages of electronic music is that it is pure sound. As it relates to no recognisable source it exists in its own dimension and is capable of exerting fully its conscious and subliminal impact without the usual string of conditional references in the mind of the listener,' he wrote.[69]

Perhaps his most high-profile work was the *Living Shakespeare* series of albums, a 1962 commission from His Master's Voice to write electronic music for recordings of twelve of the Bard's plays. But the year afterwards, Leslie gave up producing music completely when he returned to Ireland to oversee the family estate, Castle Leslie.

'I think it was a great loss to musique concrète. He was so far out ahead in terms of what he was doing, nobody really had latched on. And just when he was taking off and getting reviews and being interviewed on television, he inherited the castle and got stuck into trying to farm it and then develop it as a tourist venue,' Mark Leslie explains. 'He moved the whole recording studio and all the kit and created a sort of musique concrète studio in the basement of the castle, but he just never really got back to doing it.'

Leslie, who was described by a local newspaper after his death as a 'pioneer of the unusual', was one of the unconventional characters whose inquisitive nature and yearning for artistic adventure drew them to musique concrète in the post-war period. Another was a young woman who went on to achieve exalted status in the history of British electronic music: Delia Derbyshire.

Born in 1937, Derbyshire was the gifted daughter of a car-factory worker. 'I came from – what they'd like to call themselves – an upper working class Catholic background in Coventry,' she told interviewer John Cavanagh. The city was heavily bombed during World War II and it made a significant impression on the young Derbyshire's aesthetic sense. 'I was there in the Blitz and it's come to me, relatively recently, that my love for abstract sounds [came from] the air-raid sirens: that's a sound you hear and you don't know the source of as a young child... then the sound of the "all clear" – that was electronic music.'[70]

Derbyshire went to Cambridge University and gained a degree in music and mathematics, which as she said herself was 'quite something for a working-class girl in the fifties.'[71] 'I was always into the theory of sound even in the sixth form. The physics teacher refused to teach us acoustics but I studied it myself and did very well,' she recalled. 'It was always a mixture of the mathematical side and music. Also, radio had been my love since childhood because I came from just a humble background with relatively few books and radio was my education.'[72]

She initially tried to get a job at Decca Records but was told they did not employ women in their studios. She then joined the BBC as a trainee studio manager, and was transferred to the Radiophonic Workshop in 1962. Unusually for the period, the Workshop employed a significant amount of women who played key roles in some of its most important achievements. Maddalena Fagandini recalled that when Derbyshire arrived, her more scientific approach brought the Workshop new capabilities: 'She knew maths and was very organised from that point of view. She began to use the oscillators in a more structured sense, because she could. She knew the harmonic structure of certain sounds, she could put them together.'[73]

Like Daphne Oram, Derbyshire came to the Workshop with the ambition of creating her own electronic music, but soon learned it would not be easy. 'I was told in no uncertain terms that the BBC does not employ composers, and so it was only by gradually infiltrating the system that I managed to do music,' she said.[74] As Oram had found, the BBC saw the Workshop's staff as providers of soundtrack effects, not music.

But Derbyshire was another strong-willed character who sought to push the boundaries. She made common cause with some of the Workshop's other musically-oriented staff: John Baker, a pianist with a talent for creating kooky tunes with household implements, and Brian Hodgson, a special-effects creator with a background in theatre who became interested in electronics while working as a radio mechanic during national service with the RAF.

All of them could make music from the most unlikely sources; Derbyshire once said her favourite instrument was 'a tatty green BBC lampshade' with 'a beautiful ringing sound to it'.[75] She used it on 'Blue Veils and Golden Sands', her extraordinary music for David Attenborough's 1967 *The World About Us* programme about the nomadic Tuareg people of the Sahara, which painted expressionist sonic images of camel trains passing through the desert, the striking beauty of the Tuareg men with their blue cloaks swirling in the wind and the shimmer of the heat haze against the horizon.

As well as the sonorous lampshade, Derbyshire also used a rhythmic cut-up of her own voice for the camels' hooves. 'I hit the lampshade, recorded that, faded it up into the ringing part without the percussive start,' she explained. 'I analysed the sound into all of its partials and frequencies, and took the twelve strongest, and reconstructed the sound on the Workshop's famous twelve oscillators to give a whooshing sound. So the camels rode off into the sunset with my voice in their hooves and a green lampshade on their backs.'[76]

Such creative inventiveness was not unusual at the Workshop in its early years. Senior engineer David Young described it as 'a very Heath Robinson set-up';[77] he would repair damaged secondhand equipment and build custom gear to order, some of it assembled from cast-off military tech. During World War II, Young had been shot down over Germany in a Lancaster bomber and spent the rest of the conflict in a prisoner-of-war camp. 'He managed to get hold of valves and build radio sets in the camp, so they could listen in to the broadcasts from overseas from the BBC,' says Paddy Kingsland, who joined the Workshop later. 'He was generally brilliant at improvising and was just in tune with equipment and machinery, and he was also an original thinker. He loved picking up old junk components and making something out of them.'

Hodgson says that the Workshop's creativity thrived on 'loads of imagination and cheek'. The most original of all its composers was Derbyshire, he insists: 'Delia was just bloody brilliant. She had about a million times more talent than I ever did. She was a mathematician and her mind was just incredible, she was into analysis and resynthesis. We all loved and respected her.'

Dick Mills recalls how Derbyshire 'immersed herself' in her sound projects, sometimes frustrating her colleagues who wanted her to finish commissions more quickly and efficiently. 'She was such a talented, creative person, but it wasn't particularly easy to work with her,' he acknowledges.

Derbyshire would go on to forge links with the 1960s pop world, but she was also connected to the classical avant-garde. In 1962, she assisted Luciano Berio with sessions on electronic music at the Dartington International

Summer School and also worked with Peter Maxwell Davies and Roberto Gerhard. Later in the decade, one of her pieces featured alongside works by Berio, Tristram Cary and Pierre Henry on the programme of the first concert of electronic music in the northwest of England, at Liverpool University's Mountford Hall in April 1968.

She once said she wanted to make electronic music beautiful, to challenge its common perception as the soundtrack for tragedy and horror. When the BBC's popular science show, *Tomorrow's World*, filmed her at the Workshop in 1965, she elegantly demonstrated how to cut tapes into loops and run them together in synchronicity to construct an attractive piece of polyrhythmic musique concrète.

The report showed her building a pulsing electro-acoustic track from natural sounds using multiple tape recorders to create the bassline and percussion, then layering what sounded like a one-note Euro-techno pulse-riff over the top as she tapped her shiny slingback court shoes to the beat. 'We can build up any sound we can possibly imagine, almost,'[78] she asserted.

Intentionally or not, the composers who made music for TV and radio in the early sixties using tape machines, oscillators and other primitive sound-generators changed the public perception of what music could be. The sounds they made were disseminated to mass audiences rather than being played to limited numbers of high-culture aficionados at concert halls, opening up minds to new possibilities. The Radiophonic Workshop's output was practical rather than theory-based, intersecting with pop culture and film, and had a crucial influence on the way that electronic music developed in 1960s Britain, away from the European avant-garde strongholds of Paris, Cologne and Milan.

In 1963, the Workshop would also create one of the most beloved pieces of music for television in the BBC's history, a piece that would play an immeasurable role in popularising electronic music in Britain: the theme tune for a new science-fiction series called *Doctor Who*.

Brian Hodgson producing sound effects for Doctor Who at the BBC Radiophonic Workshop. ©Hulton-Deutsch Collection/Getty Images.

2
AN ELECTRIC STORM
Space-Age Pop and Psychedelia

The Radiophonic Workshop's Greatest Hit
'When I started work on the sound effects for *Doctor Who*, I had to ask myself a question: how does a time machine move? Does it go upwards or downwards, or maybe sideways? I thought about it and decided it goes forwards, and also backwards. But there was another question: what sort of sound would it make?'
Brian Hodgson

'THERE'S A CHILDREN'S SCIENCE FICTION SERIAL that's going to run for six weeks. Can you do a signature tune?'[1]

This was the question television producer Verity Lambert asked when she telephoned the BBC Radiophonic Workshop's director, Desmond Briscoe, in 1963. 'I want a new sound… way out and catchy,'[2] Lambert told Briscoe, according to a report in the *Daily Mirror*.

The series went on air on 23 November 1963, and the signature tune delivered all that Lambert wanted. 'Nothing quite like this as a title tune has been heard before on TV,' the *Mirror* declared. 'It is a noise with rhythm and melody which continually pulsates in a weird, fluid and uncanny way.'[3]

The story featured a mysterious but benevolent time-traveller known only as the Doctor, and its intended six-week run would extend for decades, on and off, into the next millennium. Its opening theme would also become one of the most influential pieces of electronic music ever made in Britain.

Australian composer Ron Grainer was chosen to write the tune and Delia Derbyshire, a recent recruit to the Radiophonic Workshop, was tasked with realising the piece sonically. However, Grainer only provided a 'very slight' score for the theme, with 'just the bare bones' of the piece on a single sheet of paper, no harmonies and 'the occasional chord symbol',[4] according to Peter Howell, a Workshop composer who found the composer's rudimentary manuscript in a filing cabinet many years later.

Grainer also provided some rather vague directions, Derbyshire recalled: 'He used delightful expressions for the sort of noises he wanted: "wind bubbles and clouds".'[5] She said that Grainer intended the score to complement the hypnotic visuals of the programme's opening title sequence, created using a video feedback technique known as the 'howlround effect'.

Derbyshire and engineer Dick Mills set to work, using oscillators to produce soaring, swooping, melodic tones. 'Each one of the swoops you hear is a carefully-timed handswoop on the oscillators,'[6] she explained. Filtered white noise was used for rhythmic hissing effects and a tape-manipulated twanging sound to create a propulsive bassline. 'We recorded the twang of a steel string and speeded up and slowed down the recording to different pitches to make the notes for the bassline, then cut them together with tape edits to get the rhythm,' Mills remembers.

The result was a thrillingly elemental piece of music that seemed to whirl the listener away into cosmic realms, spinning outwards through space like the Doctor's TARDIS time machine. Six decades later, Mills was still marvelling at their achievement: 'It's a rattling good tune, but it's ethereal – nobody had a clue as to what instruments were playing, because there weren't any, but it was not obviously machine-made either, it had these the magic of these new, new sounds that were not exactly tangible so it had this spacey, mysterious feel.' Musician David Vorhaus, who later worked with Derbyshire, describes it as 'the first ever piece of electronic pop art'.

Derbyshire's Radiophonic Workshop colleague Brian Hodgson recalled what happened next: 'When Grainer heard the result, his response was "Did I really write that?" Most of it, Delia replied. She deserved at least half the royalties, insisted the composer. She did not get them. At that time the BBC preferred to keep members of the Workshop anonymous and uncredited.'[7]

Hodgson also helped build the sonic architecture of the *Doctor Who* series: he created the noise of the TARDIS taking off by scraping one of the strings of an old piano with a key and tape-manipulating the sound, and used a ring modulator to create the merciless monotone voices of the Doctor's perennially vexed adversaries, the Daleks.

In another sign of the adventurous spirit of the times, avant-garde composer Tristram Cary, whose work could sometimes be challengingly angular and abrasive, was engaged to compose the music for the first *Doctor Who* episodes featuring the Daleks, at the end of 1963. His sinister, metallic drones provided a suitably menacing backdrop to a confrontation between the Doctor and his extraterrestrial foes. Cary, however, once dismissed his work for *Doctor Who* as 'a load of rubbish'[8] – like many composers using electronics at the time, he subsidised his more adventurous projects by taking what he sometimes saw as inferior commercial commissions. He went on to make music for several other *Doctor Who* episodes and write soundtracks for around fifty feature films and documentaries, working for Disney, Ealing Studios and Hammer Films.

By 1963, when *Doctor Who* was launched, there were television sets in over 80 per cent of British homes. As a prime-time series, it brought avant-garde sonics into the living room, where the impact on young viewers' minds was enhanced by the programme's suspenseful storylines. Throughout the 1960s, the Workshop extended its influence over a generation of young people, some of whom would become important figures in electronic music in the decades to come. As well as *Doctor Who*, it created theme tunes and sound effects for programmes like *Bleep and Booster* – a cartoon series about an alien and his earthling boy sidekick, broadcast from 1964 as part of the popular *Blue Peter* children's show – and for educational broadcasts on BBC School Radio.

'School Radio was the Workshop's biggest customer because it went out five days a week,' says Mills. 'So while the kids were being taught at school, they would assimilate our background sounds and tunes at the same time, and the real hidden value of all this was that it educated a whole generation of youngsters into a new art form.'

It was not considered particularly odd that the state broadcaster was immersing schoolchildren in experimental weirdness. 'It was part of the soundscape you grew up with,' says composer James Gardner, who played with electronic band Apollo 440 in the early 1990s. 'You only had three TV stations then, so chances are at some point in the day you were going to hear something that the Radiophonic Workshop had done. So it's not surprising that by the time people of my generation got into our twenties and thirties, that influence came out again in the music that we were making.' Indeed, this may well be one of the reasons why British musicians would dominate synth-pop in the 1980s.

Joe Meek Cranks It Up

'Yes! This is a strange record; I meant it to be.'
Joe Meek, sleeve notes for I Hear a New World

The *Doctor Who* theme was not the first British recording to bring esoteric sounds to a mainstream audience. In 1962, the year before the series launched, Joe Meek's production of The Tornados' enchantingly naive space-age instrumental 'Telstar' reached number one in the UK charts. The song, a tribute to the Telstar communications satellite launched earlier that year, soars and spins skywards, an irrepressibly optimistic celebration of human technological advances in an era of surging prosperity.

Meek himself was as complex as 'Telstar' was simple – a tormented, unpredictable, idiosyncratically creative character whose mood swings were exaggerated by the amphetamines and barbiturates he regularly consumed. In his Meeksville studio in a flat above a leather goods shop on north London's Holloway Road, he developed his unorthodox production techniques, pushing what limited equipment he had as far as it would go to make recordings with sonic characteristics that were impossible in live performance – not just reproducing sounds, but artificially enhancing them, transforming them into something new. Before King Tubby, Lee Perry or Brian Eno, non-musician Meek was using the studio as an instrument.

Wired on pills, Meek liked to crank it up, using distortion and overcompression, cascades of echo and a spring reverb unit he built himself to add power and drama, speeding up tracks to give them an adrenalised urgency. 'Certainly I try to inject punch and drive into my productions,' he said. 'There's not a record made yet that wouldn't benefit from speeding up a little bit.'[9]

Meek was making what he intended to be commercial recordings, but his idea of pop music was highly individual. Some of his innovative sound engineering techniques were seen at the time as eccentric, or even downright deranged. 'He compressed practically every sound; routinely pushed his input and tape levels into the red; drenched nearly everything in reverb, echo, and delay; recorded bass big enough to cause needles to jump the record grooves; sometimes added homemade sound effects; and frequently sped up masters,'[10] Barry Cleveland wrote in his book about Meek's production methods.

Meek used suitably cosmic sound effects to open and close 'Telstar', while for its careening melody he multi-tracked the tones of an electronic keyboard instrument, the Selmer Clavioline (although some claim it may have been a Jennings Univox). Coming the year after Del Shannon's number one hit 'Runaway', which used a Clavioline variant called a Musitron, 'Telstar' showed that electronic sounds could be the stuff of pop, not just of TV sci-fi and experimental radio drama.

Meek had long been an outsider. Growing up in the small West Country market town of Newent, he began by building his own electrical equipment in a shed in the garden, where he would also put on theatrical shows. The neighbourhood children bullied him and called him a 'cissy'. 'We always said he ought to have been a girl,'[11] said his brother Eric. After leaving school at 14 and being put to work as a farm labourer, he earned extra money by playing records at the local dancehall and as soundtracks for amateur dramatic societies.

Meek did his national service with the RAF as a radar mechanic, then worked as a TV and radio-repair technician, while running his own mobile DJ unit. He also experimented by editing tapes of comedy sketches and noise effects, layering the sounds using a second tape recorder. 'He was always interested in weird sounds and had us doing all sorts to get them,' said Eric Meek. 'He used to get up at three o'clock in the morning and put microphones out on the walls so that he could record the early morning birds singing; he'd have me spinning round the corners, ripping on the brakes and smashing glass to sound like a car crash... The local people quite possibly thought that he was a nutter.'[12]

After moving to London, Meek worked for recording studios before setting himself up as one of the Britain's first independent pop producers. He was fascinated by the esoteric – psychic phenomena, UFOs and alien beings – and in 1959 recorded a charmingly guileless, pre-psychedelic concept album about life on another planet called *I Hear a New World*. It was assembled from hand-crafted special effects created via household objects, the Clavioline and recordings of a skiffle combo called The Blue Men, sometimes with over-the-top, helium-pitch vocals, all of it tape-processed to sound cartoonishly extraterrestrial. Some of the tracks were issued as an EP but the full album would not see release until decades after his death.

The heavy reverb and severe compression on Meek's productions fuelled controversy in the British music press about the use of sound effects in pop, with some critics complaining that the practice was gimmicky and inauthentic. 'Popland: The machines are taking over!' warned a 1964 headline in *Melody Maker*, illustrated by a photograph of 'robot' musicians.

The 'real talents' of contemporary pop were now 'the factory workers on the conveyor belt of pop – recording engineers, sound mixers, recording managers – assembling the record like a new car', the writer presciently declared.[13] One of the pop stars criticised for being 'too electronic' was Meek's protégé John Leyton, best known for his hauntingly echo-drenched hit 'Johnny Remember Me'. Leyton had already stated his defence a couple of years earlier: 'Even Frank Sinatra has echo effects,' he argued. 'Pop records today must be as exciting as possible.'[14] Meek dismissed his critics for being out of touch: 'I make records to entertain the public, not square connoisseurs who just don't know.'[15]

What Meek certainly did not want the public to know was that he was homosexual, fearing that it would damage his career. Sex between men was illegal until 1967 and was seen by many as morally repugnant. Prosecutions for 'gross indecency' were commonplace, as the police mercilessly targeted homosexuals seeking furtive intimacy. The press delighted in exposing them and ruining their lives, forcing men like Meek to live under constant psychological pressure. Homophobic abuse and discrimination, which he reputedly experienced while working at recording studios, were commonplace.

Calls for legal reform had been growing, however; there were also moves towards greater visibility, particularly in the arts. The 1961 British film *Victim* sympathetically depicted actor Dirk Bogarde as a repressed gay man targeted by blackmailers, while playwright Joe Orton's black comedy with queer overtones, *Entertaining Mr Sloane*, was a West End success in 1964 and popular BBC radio serial *Round the Horne* featured two flagrant queens trading suggestive quips in the covert gay slang known as Polari. Meek's own 1966 production for a Tornados B-side, 'Do You Come Here Often?', included what was meant to sound like a catty conversation between two camp characters in a nightclub, one of the first overtly homosexual records ever released by a major record label in Britain.

Despite Meek's fear of exposure, he often cruised public toilets and parks for sex, and in 1963, he was arrested and fined £15 after pleading guilty to 'persistently importuning for an immoral purpose'. The case appeared in the newspapers, causing several would-be extortionists to pressurise him for cash in return for not revealing other indiscretions. As he maintained his intake of pills, Meek became increasingly fearful of the police and blackmailers, while his outbursts of rage became more extreme.

By 1967, his pop success had waned and royalty payments for the multimillion-selling international hit 'Telstar' were frozen because he was being sued by French composer Jean Ledrut, who accused Meek of plagiarising music he wrote for the film *Austerlitz*, although the claim was eventually dismissed.

Wracked by drug-fuelled anguish and paranoia, Meek shot his landlady and then turned the gun on himself. He left behind nearly 2,000 tapes of unreleased recordings and a legacy of sonic experimentation that would make him a cult figure for decades to come.

The Beatles Take a Trip

'With any kind of thing, my aim seems to be to distort it... to change it from what it is to see what it could be... It's all trying to create magic, it's all trying to make things happen so that you don't know why they've happened.'
Paul McCartney, speaking in 1967[16]

George Martin couldn't have been more unlike the tempestuous Meek, but this urbane, middle-class Royal Navy veteran would become even more important to the development of electronic pop music. In the early sixties, Martin was a record-company executive and producer of recordings for British comedians like *Goon Show* funnymen Peter Sellers and Spike Milligan. He also knew about musique concrète and had begun experimenting with then-unusual studio techniques like alternative tape speeds, reverse echo and backwards recording.

Hoping to score a novelty hit, Martin adapted a piece of percussive, tape-manipulated TV interval music produced by BBC Radiophonic Workshop composer Maddalena Fagandini into a quirky lounge-beat single called 'Time Beat' under the pseudonym Ray Cathode. Promotional photographs for the 1962 release showed Martin posing with 'Ray the robot' – a rack

The Beatles at a press call to promote the song 'All You Need Is Love' at Abbey Road Studios in London, 24 June 1967. ©Ivan Keeman/Getty Images.

of studio equipment with dials for eyes, a fake moustache and a sombrero. 'BBC Radiophonics' was credited as the song's composer; Fagandini went unmentioned.

'Time Beat' wasn't a big seller, but this would hardly matter to Martin. In the summer of 1962, he began work as producer for a promising young quartet from Liverpool called The Beatles, after they were turned down by Joe Meek, who dismissed them as 'just another bunch of noise.'[17]

Meek's unconventional studio techniques had offered new directions for popular music; with The Beatles, Martin would go much further. From the mid-sixties onwards, The Beatles' recordings opened up pop music to tape loops and musique concrète, sonic manipulation and synthesizers, just as composers like Pierre Schaeffer and Karlheinz Stockhausen had brought sounds that weren't considered music into the classical world in the previous decade. As the best-loved band in the world, whose every musical idea was intensively analysed in the media and often emulated by other musicians, The Beatles became a prism through which sounds from the avant-garde were refracted into pop and became part of its musical vocabulary.

'As the Beatles began kicking over the traces of popular musical conventions, it gave me the freedom to do more of what I enjoyed: experimenting, building sound pictures, creating a whole atmosphere for a song,' Martin would retrospectively reflect.[18] The producer revealed to them the possibilities of the recording studio as a compositional tool, but The Beatles themselves, in tune with the times, were also exploring new ideas on their own initiative.

By 1965, as London's bohemian scene thrived, Paul McCartney had begun to seriously investigate the avant-garde, listening to experimental jazz players like Sun Ra and Pharoah Sanders and classical composers like Cage, Berio and Stockhausen, who he described as making 'the farthest-out music yet'.[19] Martin played him *Music from Mathematics*, an album of electronic recordings made at Bell Laboratories in the US of an IBM 7090 computer with a digital-to-sound transducer creating rudimentary melodies like 'A Bicycle Made for Two', while the Beatle also set about exploring contemporary art and new developments in cinema. 'People are saying things and painting things and writing things and composing things that are great, and I must *know* what people are doing,' he enthused.[20]

This was a time of great optimism about technological progress, as well as concomitant fears about its potential consequences. In a famous speech in 1963, soon-to-be prime minister Harold Wilson declared that a prosperous and egalitarian society could be forged in the 'white heat' of the 'scientific revolution', although he cautioned there would need to be 'far-reaching changes in economic and social attitudes which permeate our whole system.'[21]

The urban landscape was also changing rapidly: slums were being demolished and new housing estates and shopping centres built; towerblocks reached ever higher; ring roads encircled cities and motorways cut across the country, as concrete sprawled outwards amid a mood of hopeful modernism. The future was fun: children played with toy spaceships, plastic astronauts, home-science kits and chemistry sets, while their parents bought shiny new cars and household appliances.

But at the same time, as the Cold War saw technology exploited for military purposes, there was a sense of existential unease about a possible nuclear confrontation between the United States and the Soviet Union. Many people genuinely feared a war that might 'terminate the entire species', Jeff Nuttall wrote in *Bomb Culture*.[22]

As Nuttall's book recorded, all these enthusiasms and anxieties filtered into the popular culture of the time. But there were other new influences too;

it wasn't just avant-garde music and art that helped to change bands like The Beatles' perception of what they were doing and what they could do. The impact of drugs like marijuana and LSD on the way music was heard and made from the mid-sixties onwards was substantial; the musicologist Michael Hicks has suggested that acid in particular helped to erode the dominance of standardised musical structures and timescales. 'Psychedelic drugs transformed fixed shapes into shifting shapes,' he wrote.[23]

The Beatles are believed to have started smoking marijuana in 1964 and taking acid in late 1965 and early 1966, at a point when LSD was still legal in Britain, and when the four young men were seeking new directions. George Harrison described acid as 'a key that opened the door and showed a lot of things on the other side.'[24] McCartney, meanwhile, said he believed that the drug fuelled their musical and spiritual inquisitiveness: 'With acid you get like a Woody Allen film – asking all these questions: what is the meaning, why am I doing it?'[25]

It was McCartney who immersed himself most deeply in the splendours and eccentricities of London's mid-sixties bohemian scene. One of his guides was Barry Miles, a journalist, scene 'face' and dedicated advocate for the capital's emerging counterculture – the underground, as it became known. Miles co-founded the Indica alternative bookshop, co-edited counterculture newspaper *International Times* (*IT*) and was connected with Beat Generation writers like William S. Burroughs and Allen Ginsberg as well as The Beatles and The Rolling Stones. According to underground musician and writer Mick Farren, Miles 'moved in some high hip circles, in which the first acid was making the rounds' and operated as 'a crucial link between the rock elite and the intelligentsia of Swinging London.'[26]

Miles recalls how he and McCartney would sometimes meet up at the house of the Beatle's actress girlfriend, Jane Asher, to get high on hash brownies and talk about Burroughs, Buddhism, drugs, the possibilities of electronic sound and the testing of musical boundaries in jazz. 'Favourite stoned listening included electronic music by Luciano Berio,' Miles remembers. Also on the turntable were the IBM computer album, minimalist music by Terry Riley and 'lots of the latest squeals and shrieks' by free-jazz players like Albert Ayler and Ornette Coleman.

McCartney said he found their meetings inspirational. 'We discussed all these crazy ideas together. We put down these lines of research together. I'd come home from an exciting crazed sort of think meeting with Miles, a stoned think tank, which was great fun and I'd love it and I'd be very enthusiastic about all these ideas and I used to tell John [Lennon] about this stuff. I'd spew 'em all out the next day. John would say, "Wow, wow, wow! Well, why don't you do that? Why don't you do that?" I remember saying to him I had an idea for an album title, *Paul McCartney Goes Too Far*.'[27]

'Paul was open to everything, as he put it, he liked to go around with his antenna out,' says Miles. 'He would see [music-hall revivalist] Tessie O'Shea at the Talk of the Town [mainstream nightclub] one night and an American underground film the next.'

In early 1966, the two friends went to hear a lecture on electronic music by Berio and attended radical noise-improv band AMM's sound workshop at the Royal College of Art. The Beatle contributed to the exuberant din by running a penny along a radiator and then using the coin to 'carefully tap his pint glass beer mug', Miles recalls. In the 1960s, free jazz and freeform improv, with their carefree disregard for structure, were factors in the opening up of pop music to dissonance and noise. 'You don't have to like something to be influenced by it,' McCartney pointed out to Miles after the AMM session.

McCartney also came into contact with William Burroughs, the literary exponent of artist Brion Gysin's 'cut-up' technique, and discussed the creative possibilities of tape recorders with him. Burroughs' lover, electronics technician Ian Sommerville, installed two Brenell reel-to-reel machines for McCartney so he could experiment. 'I used to make loops mainly with guitar or voices, or bongos, and then I'd record them off on to this other Brenell so that I had a series of loops,' the Beatle recalled. 'It would start with a thing that sounded like bees buzzing for a few seconds, then that would slow down and then an echo would kick in and then some high violins would come in, but they were speeded-up guitar playing a little thing, then behind them there would be a very slow ponderous drone... they were going to be little symphonies, all made with tape loops done by varispeeding the tape.'[28] The symphonies didn't happen, but other important things did.

McCartney wasn't the only Beatle who was checking out new developments in music. In an interview with Miles in *IT*, Harrison described Indian sitar virtuoso Ravi Shankar as his 'musical guru', but said he also rated the Western avant-gardists. 'Stockhausen and all the others, they're just trying to take you a bit further out or in, further in, to yourself,'[29] he explained in the turned-on vernacular of the time.

But it was John Lennon's encounter with LSD that would provide the context to express the various Beatles' fascinations with the avant-garde and Eastern mysticism. Lennon had used Timothy Leary, Ralph Metzner and Richard Alpert's interpretation of *The Tibetan Book of the Dead* in their trip manual, *The Psychedelic Experience*, as a guide for his own encounter with LSD. 'Tomorrow Never Knows', the closing track on 1966's *Revolver*, was the Beatle's attempt to translate the feelings he experienced into music. 'Whenever in doubt, turn off your mind, relax, float downstream,'[30] urged Leary and his fellow acid evangelists' psychedelic-era version of the Tibetan Buddhist text. Lennon said that after he dropped the acid, he followed the trip manual's instructions as closely as he could: 'I did it just like he said in the book, and then I wrote 'Tomorrow Never Knows' which was almost the first acid song.'[31]

At the time, 'Tomorrow Never Knows' must have been a total headrush, as The Beatles burst free from the orthodoxies of pop into another space altogether. Delivered in the voice of a mystic seer over tambura drones, Mellotron tones, backwards guitar, the mesmerising churn of tom-toms and loops swirling and twirling like Spirograph circles, its trance-like style and Indian raga vibrations set a template for tripped-out psychedelic pop.

As The Beatles were the most famous pop group in the world, it was effectively a global advertisement for the psychedelic experience. Critic Kenneth Tynan wrote in an effusive letter to McCartney later in 1966 that it was 'the best musical evocation of LSD I have ever heard'.[32] Echoes of its influence continued to ripple outwards for decades afterwards, through space rock, ambient techno and beyond.

During the recording, Lennon is said to have told producer George Martin: 'Make me sound like the Dalai Lama chanting from a mountaintop.'[33] To achieve what he wanted, his voice was fed through a sound-modifying Leslie rotary speaker system to give it a unique texture, while fuzzed-out guitar was played backwards and a series of overlapping loops spooled through several tape machines simultaneously.

McCartney had been making loops for the song at home; engineer Geoff Emerick remembered in his autobiography how the Beatle brought them in to the studio in a plastic bag. 'Paul had assembled an extraordinary collection of bizarre sounds, which included his playing distorted guitar and bass, as well as wineglasses ringing and other indecipherable noises. We played them every conceivable way: proper speed, sped up, slowed down, backwards, forwards,'[34] Emerick said.

According to musicologist Ian MacDonald, the loops that were eventually used for 'Tomorrow Never Knows' were a treated recording of McCartney laughing, a manipulated sitar phrase, a chord played by an orchestra, and flute and string sounds generated by a Mellotron. 'We had no sense of the momentousness of what we were doing [with 'Tomorrow Never Knows'] – it all just seemed like a bit of fun in a good cause at the time – but what we had created that afternoon was actually the forerunner of today's beat- and loop-driven music,' reflected Emerick.[35] As this was The Beatles, every other pop group in the world was listening and so its impact would be immense.

The Beatles were not only feeding on avant-garde techniques; experimental music wasn't even their primary influence. They adored the Black American R&B and soul of Stax and Motown; their minds were blown by The Beach Boys' *Pet Sounds* and by Indian classical music. They picked up on all these various currents and then, rather than trying to strictly emulate them, repurposed them for their own ends. There were no precedents for the world's most famous band launching all the way out into the unknown. It had never happened before, and could never really happen in quite the same way again.

As the sixties progressed, The Beatles' recordings became increasingly adventurous, like the times themselves. 'Using the overdub facilities of multitrack recording, they evolved a new way of making records in which preplanned polyphony was replaced by an unpredictable layering of simultaneous sound-information, transformed by signal-distortion and further modified during the processes of mixing and editing,'[36] Ian MacDonald wrote.

This was music which could not, at the time, have been created or reproduced by live musicians. It existed on tape and in the heads of its creators. Lennon seemed to grasp why this was such a monumental shift when he explained why The Beatles were giving up touring after releasing *Revolver*: 'What we're saying is, if we don't have to tour, then we can record music that we won't ever have to play live, and that means we can create something that's never been heard before: a new kind of record with new kinds of sounds.'[37]

That record, released in 1967, was *Sgt. Pepper's Lonely Hearts Club Band*, on which Martin and The Beatles further explored the possibilities of the studio as an instrument, using multitracking techniques, sound effects, esoteric instrumentation and tape-splicing to create imaginary sonic worlds. 'The Beatles were constantly coming to me and saying "What can you give us?

What instruments do you know about that we could use? What recording ideas can you give us?"' Martin recalled. 'Their inquisitiveness pushed us into new territory.'[38]

The prequel to *Sgt. Pepper* was the high and hazy 'Strawberry Fields Forever', which used a Mellotron to entrancing effect. The Mellotron, an electro-mechanical keyboard instrument first marketed in the UK in 1963 by three brothers from Birmingham, was a kind of precursor to the digital sampler, playing back sounds of strings, brass, wind instruments, guitar and piano that came prerecorded onto pieces of magnetic tape.

Martin was disdainful of its design. 'The Mellotron was a Heath Robinson contraption if ever there was one; you could virtually see the bits of string and rubber holding it together,' he grumbled. 'It was as if a Neanderthal piano had impregnated a primitive electronic keyboard.'[39] This did not prevent the hybrid beast from going on to create some of the most memorable textures in what became known as progressive rock in the years that followed.

On *Sgt. Pepper*, the Beatles were 'trying to create magic', as McCartney told Miles; they distilled what they learned from their musical and psychedelic experiments into an audacious set of compositions full of charm and ambition.[40] A couple of decades later, Martin described the album as 'a musical fragmentation grenade, exploding with a force that is still being felt… Nothing even remotely like *Pepper* had been heard before. It came at a time when people were thirsty for something new, but still its newness caught them by surprise.'[41] Fittingly, considering their influence on some of the ideas that shaped the record, Stockhausen and Burroughs were among the collage of characters portrayed on its pop-art cover.

Sgt. Pepper showed that four working-class lads from the north-west of England could not only succeed on their own terms but also become globally-renowned musical innovators. Reviewing the *Magical Mystery Tour* EP later in 1967, the *New Musical Express* declared they were 'stretching pop music to its limits'.[42] But as they grew their hair longer, wore ever more flamboyant clothes, embraced avant-garde art, explored pacifist politics and Eastern mysticism, and admitted to smoking marijuana and taking LSD, they moved further away from the mainstream of British society, which remained predominantly conformist, opposed to sexual freedom and women's rights, racially prejudiced, homophobic and largely unaffected by the radicalism of the underground, despite all the hype about the 'swinging sixties' and the 'permissive society'.

The Beatles' unconventional lifestyles even caused some conservative figures to express fears that they posed a genuine threat to social morality. Despite this, the four Liverpudlians' commercial success granted them the power to venture even further artistically.

As Lennon's relationship with Japanese conceptual artist Yoko Ono deepened his interest in the avant-garde, he was inspired to create what could be the most widely heard piece of noise-music ever, simply because it appeared on a Beatles record that sold millions of copies around the world: his sound collage 'Revolution 9' on 1968's *The Beatles* (popularly known as 'The White Album').

Lennon compared the track to an action painting: 'There were about ten [tape] machines with people holding pencils on the loops – some only inches long and some a yard long. I fed them all in and mixed them live,' he said. Ono, who had been involved in the Fluxus experimental performance-art movement in New York and knew all about Dadaist playfulness and John Cage's ideas about chance and indeterminacy, was a key player in the recording. 'Yoko was there for the whole thing, and she made decisions about which loops to use,' Lennon acknowledged.[43]

This was the point at which The Beatles' fascination with experimental music peaked. Stockhausen recalled that around the time of 'The White Album', 'Lennon often used to phone me. He was particularly fond of my *Hymnen* and *Song of the Youths* [*Gesang der Jünglinge*] and got many things from them.'[44]

'Revolution 9', however, was no equal to the German's cerebral soundscapes and attracted critical scorn. A *Melody Maker* review described it as 'a huge, shifting cacophony of sound... noisy, boring and meaningless.'[45] The *New Musical Express* was even harsher, calling it 'a piece of idiot immaturity' attempting to posture as mysterious or intelligent: '"Highlights" include cackles and screams,' the reviewer noted.[46] McCartney also said dismissively that 'Revolution 9' was similar to some of the tape experiments he had been doing 'for fun' but were not 'suitable for release'.[47]

The same month that 'The White Album' came out, Lennon and Ono released their experimental set *Unfinished Music No. 1: Two Virgins*, which almost made 'Revolution 9' sound like 'Love Me Do'. Made up of loops, clatterings, spoken interjections and screeches, the album became best-known for the controversy sparked by the full-frontal naked cover photograph of its creators.

49

Miles believes Lennon's infatuation with the avant-garde was intense but temporary: 'He was certainly keen on using new sounds in rock'n'roll, as in 'I Am the Walrus', but a lot of that was collaborative – done in Abbey Road with the other Beatles and George Martin all making suggestions,' he says. 'And of course there's his famous line: "Avant-garde is French for bullshit."'

The year after *Two Virgins*, George Harrison released an underwhelming album of doodles called *Electronic Sound*. 'It was George learning how to use a Moog synthesizer,' Miles says scornfully. 'I was not very impressed by it, and, as far as I remember, nor were the critics.' The record gained attention because it was made by a Beatle and due to controversy created by Moog sales representative Bernie Krause claiming one of its tracks was actually a recording of him demonstrating the new instrument to Harrison.

The Moog played a much more aesthetically satisfying role during the sessions for the *Abbey Road* album – one of the first uses of a synthesizer on record by a major pop group. The Beatles displayed their artistic percipience by using the synth to subtly enhance some of the songs, rather than as a novelty instrument belching out astro-bloops – though Harrison later dismissed the electronic noises on 'Here Comes the Sun' as 'very kind of infant sounds'.[48]

With his Brenell loops, McCartney had been making experimental noise before either Lennon or Harrison. A couple of years earlier, he had sought out Delia Derbyshire of the BBC Radiophonic Workshop to ask her about the possibility of providing electronic sounds for his ballad 'Yesterday'. 'We'd already recorded it with a string quartet, but I wanted to give the arrangement electronic backing,' he explained.[49]

The idea went no further, but in 1967 McCartney instigated the most avant-garde (and most obscure) Beatles recording ever: 'Carnival of Light': a fourteen-minute sound collage specially created for the Million Volt Light and Sound Rave, an experimental multimedia show at London's Roundhouse that also featured music from Delia Derbyshire, Brian Hodgson and Peter Zinovieff's Unit Delta Plus project.

'Carnival of Light' was recorded at Abbey Road under McCartney's direction. 'I said all I want you to do is just wander around all the stuff, bang it, shout, play it, it doesn't need to make any sense,' he told the other Beatles. 'Hit a drum then wander on to the piano, hit a few notes, just wander around. So that's what we did and then put a bit of an echo on it.'[50]

The audio collage was played at the Roundhouse event, as Miles remembers – 'but even though it was announced, very few people realised what it was and continued talking and carrying on raving.' It was never released and few have heard it. One of those who has is Miles, who describes it as having 'no melodies, rhythms or lyrics, just more or less random sound à la AMM': lots of feedback, distortion and reverb-laden shouting, slowed-down drums and organ, plus whistling, coughs and fragments of chatter, concluding with the echoing voice of McCartney asking: 'Can we hear it back now?'

Looking back over fifty years later, Miles doesn't give 'Carnival of Light' a glowing retrospective review: '"A curio of the period" is a good description,' he says. 'Basically the other three Beatles were not very interested and were clearly reluctantly going along with Paul's new interest in "random" sound. It's not much different than the tapes we used to make at Paul's and at [Indica bookshop co-owner] John Dunbar's flat sitting around banging on pots and pans with a Studer or Revox on full echo.'

Asked what she recalled about The Beatles' piece at the Million Volt Light and Sound Rave, Delia Derbyshire quipped: 'Well, they'd played around with, er… sounds.'[51] McCartney later said he wanted to release it on one of The Beatles' *Anthology* compilations in the 1990s, 'because it would show we were working with really avant-garde stuff,'[52] but the other surviving band members refused.

Pink Floyd, 'London's Farthest-Out Group'

'The Pink Floyd reproduces the sound equivalent of LSD visions, acclaimed by promoters and fans as "psychedelic". It has taken part in curious way-out events, simulating drug ecstasies, known as "freak-outs", in which girls writhe and shriek, and young men roll naked in paint or jelly.'
Daily Express, 2 March 1967

The sixties in London were a period of cultural fluidity, when musique concrète composers made music for TV shows and sci-fi films and hung out with pop stars, when pop crossed over with the classical avant-garde and the wilder fringes of jazz and its boundaries started to dissolve as it explored the possibilities offered by new technology.

It was also a time of distinctly high idealism. 'We thought we were going to change the world,'[53] Richard Neville, publisher of counterculture magazine *Oz*, later declared. Although the hippie movement was overwhelmingly white and male-dominated, and initially had much less impact outside the capital,

Pink Floyd in London, January 1967. ©Michael Ochs Archives/Stringer.

it nurtured ideas that would continue to develop in a multitude of ways for years to come.

Electronic music became part of a free-thinking continuum that encompassed Eastern spiritualism, psychedelic drugs, pop art, free theatre, free improvisation, Fluxus-style 'happenings', arts labs, art schools, alternative newspapers and comicbooks, the new wave of British science fiction championed by writer Michael Moorcock at *New Worlds* magazine, anti-Vietnam war demonstrations, be-ins, sit-ins and love-ins. Underground newspaper *IT* displayed interest in electronic music from its first issue in 1966. Alongside articles about the war and an advert for Yoko Ono's art show at the Indica Gallery (where she met John Lennon), it reported on American electronic composer Morton Feldman visiting Britain, quoting him as saying that 'ideas are more important than music at the present time.'[54]

Drugs were also increasingly important that year. 'LSD changed everything: it stretched time as well as encouraging the blurring of sight and sound in the environment – the definition of synaesthesia in that period – and, by the end of 1966, the twin ideas of psychedelia as a Happening and a drug culture were taking hold in the UK,'[55] Jon Savage argues in his book *1966: The Year the Decade Exploded*. Perhaps not coincidentally, this was also the year when pop music vaulted daringly forwards from the three-minute single format to *somewhere else*...

In March, a new band initially called The Pink Floyd Sound played at a mixed-media party called Spontaneous Underground at London's Marquee Club. One of its organisers, photographer and scene catalyst John 'Hoppy' Hopkins, described it as 'an absolutely new kind of rave', with abstract film projections, absurdist comedic performances and improvised music. 'Floyd's music was new but it wasn't completely foreign to what was happening elsewhere,' Hopkins said. 'We were all listening to avant-garde jazz, and my girlfriend at the time had brought back tapes of The Velvet Underground from New York. John Cage had also given a concert at the Saville Theatre [in London's West End] in 1964 or 1965, and that had made a dent on people's musical consciousness. Floyd were different, but they fitted right into all that.'[56]

Various members of Pink Floyd had already had experiences with LSD by the time they became the latest sensation on London's acid-influenced underground scene. 'There were a lot of people experimenting with it as a way of finding a greater consciousness,' guitarist David Gilmour said. 'The intention was to have a quasi-religious-cum-scientific experience, and I rather concurred with that. I'm an atheist, and I didn't start suddenly believing in God, but the claims were that it accessed parts of your brain that were not normally accessible, and the first couple of times I took it, I found it to be a very *deep* experience.'[57]

The band's stage show became increasingly psychedelic as they pioneered an immersive sound-light experience that simulated an acid trip. An advert for an early gig at the London Free School, a community centre for political and cultural activists in Notting Hill, paraphrased Timothy Leary: 'The Pink Floyd. Turn on, tune in, drop out.'

Pink Floyd and The Soft Machine became the house bands at London's first all-night psychedelic club, UFO, which opened in December 1966. These were two remarkable groups of musicians: one exploring the new frontiers of white psychedelic rock in a very English way, the other utilising elements of avant-garde jazz and Black American music. As well as the bands and hallucinatory projections by lightshow artist Mark Boyle, UFO hosted bizarre theatrical performances and poetic recitations, and screened old Charlie Chaplin and W. C. Fields movies along with experimental films by Andy Warhol or Kenneth Anger. 'It was all like a trippy adventure playground really,' said Paul McCartney.[58]

The club's liberating atmosphere provided a suitably receptive audience for Pink Floyd's more unusual, freeform material. Songs like 'Interstellar Overdrive', 'Astronomy Dominé' and 'Set the Controls for the Heart of the Sun' identified the psychedelic experience with a yearning for the cosmic and the accelerating rush of an LSD trip with a rocket lift-off, as Syd Barrett used his Binson Echorec delay unit and experimental techniques adapted from AMM's Keith Rowe to explore the frontiers of guitar noise. 'The Pink Floyd was the first free-form acid consciousness music,'[59] argued journalist and underground scene face Jenny Fabian.

But this apparent connection between their music and drugs led to them being targeted alongside other bands in an early tabloid exposé about rock musicians and 'the cult of LSD' published by the *News of the World* in February 1967. 'The Pink Floyd group specialise in "psychedelic music", which is designed to illustrate LSD experiences,'[60] the newspaper asserted. The tabloid's sensationalist campaign led to police raids that netted several musicians, including Mick Jagger and Keith Richards of the Rolling Stones. In a subsequent parliamentary debate in July that year, Home Office minister Alice Bacon claimed that pop stars like Paul McCartney were 'trying to influence the minds of young people and trying to encourage them to take drugs', as well as 'questioning traditional values and social judgments of all kinds'.[61]

Pink Floyd might not have been actively encouraging young people to take drugs, but they were keen to conjure up some derangement of the senses.

Bassist Roger Waters began experimenting with musique concrète techniques for a multimedia performance at London's Queen Elizabeth Hall in May 1967. 'I was working in this dank, dingy basement off the Harrow Road, with an old Ferrograph. I remember sitting there recording edge tones off cymbals for the performance – later that became the beginning of 'A Saucerful of Secrets','[62] he said.

The title track on *A Saucerful of Secrets*, the band's second album, opened with his Delia Derbyshire-like cymbal drones into an ambitious, experimental suite that channelled ideas from composers like György Ligeti and John Cage, utilising gothic organ, heavily echoed guitar, a hypnotic drum loop, dissonant piano strikes and treated noise.

But unlike German contemporaries Tangerine Dream and Kraftwerk, Pink Floyd never wanted to become a fully electronic band. Instead, like other British musicians in the late sixties who were experimenting with unconventional sounds – from effects like phasing and echo to non-rock instruments like sitars and harpsichords – they were simply seeking new ways to blow people's minds.

Artistic adventurousness was seen a counterpart to progressive social and political ideas, with rock musicians embracing experimental techniques as 'a cipher of liberation from convention and the market', the musicologist Robert Adlington has suggested: 'Indeed, there was a widespread conviction that aesthetic experiment and social progressiveness made natural bedfellows.'[63] For the sixties underground, weird was good and radical was very chic indeed.

John Baker's Radiophonic Swing
'It was fantastic, what [John Baker] did. He could cut tape in syncopation and produce the most astonishing rhythms and cross-rhythms, and then he would bring in a drummer and an oboe player and he would play the piano himself and produce these sort of jazz/electronic fusion pieces.'
BBC Radiophonic Workshop archivist Mark Ayres[64]

Pink Floyd visited the BBC Radiophonic Workshop in October 1967, during the period in which *A Saucerful of Secrets* was recorded. A photograph from the time shows the shaggy-haired psychedelic rockers resplendent in the denim, corduroy and flowery prints of the era. Delia Derbyshire was impressed with them: 'I realised they'd done serious listening to whatever electronic music was available on record. They mentioned 1966 composition *Praxis For 12* by [Greek composer] Jani Christou,' she said. Despite this apparent affinity, however, Roger Waters would later describe avant-garde music as 'absolute nonsense'.[65]

By this time, Derbyshire had made a variety of artistically important and emotionally powerful works, like her collaboration with playwright Barry Bermange on *Inventions for Radio*, an experimental series that started broadcasting in 1964. In the first programme, 'The Dreams', disconnected voices describe dreams about running, falling, colours and the sea, set to ethereal, drifting ambient tones intended to illuminate the dreamers' interior lives. The second programme in the series, 'Amor Dei', collaged people's voices as they tried to describe their perceptions and experiences of God. Bermange told Derbyshire he wanted a sound like a 'gothic altar piece';[66] she responded by manipulating a recording of a boy soprano and an angelic choir.

Derbyshire said that during her time at the BBC, she tended to produce music for scenarios 'either in the far distant future, the far distant past, or in the mind.'[67] Some of her most intriguing pieces were included on the 1968 album *BBC Radiophonic Music*, released to mark the Workshop's tenth anniversary, including 'The Delian Mode', a drifting sound-sculpture of drones, tones and decelerated chiming noises that predated the dark ambient genre by a couple of decades. Also on the album was the tense, urgent 'Pot au Feu', whose insistent signal-riffing sounds like it had been teleported back from the hardcore rave era, and 'Ziwzih Ziwzih OO-OO-OO', a tune that seems to prefigure art-rockers The Residents, composed for a BBC dramatisation of an Isaac Asimov story about robots who reject their human masters and begin to worship an energy converter.

Around the same time, Derbyshire also created a peculiar electro-pop number called 'Moogies Bloogies', with lascivious lyrics by hit-making actor-singer Anthony Newley, one of the most popular British stage and screen stars of the sixties. 'I'd written this beautiful little innocent tune, all sensitive love and innocence, and [Newley] made it into a dirty old raincoat song,'[68] she said.

This was just one of Derbyshire's unusual collaborations. She also composed soundtracks for a short film that showed Yoko Ono wrapping one of the ornamental lions in London's Trafalgar Square in white cloth and for Peter Hall's 1968 comedy film about a psilocybin enthusiast, *Work is a Four-Letter Word*. 'I did the electronic part of the music – the bloopy bits when they'd taken the magic mushrooms,'[69] she said. Then in 1971, she provided suitably disorientating sounds for the BBC short film *Crash!*, in which author J. G. Ballard explored ideas that would inform his subsequent techno-fetishistic novel. Ballard and British electronic music would become close companions in the years that followed.

The *BBC Radiophonic Music* tenth anniversary album also featured tracks by two very different but equally unique Workshop composers. The first was David Cain, who brought a Middle Ages-inspired retro style to the music he composed for radio productions of *The War of the Worlds* and *The Hobbit*, like a technologically-enhanced version of musical medievalist David Munrow.

'Desmond Briscoe famously described David Cain as our only living medieval composer,' says Workshop archivist Mark Ayres. 'David loved the fact that very basic, raw, rough sound of untreated electronic sound sounded like shawms and other classic medieval instruments.' Cain also made the dark and eerie techno-primitive music for BBC School Radio's *The Seasons*, a series of poems intended to soundtrack children's drama classes, although its verses and sounds often seemed a little too disturbing for its youthful audience.

The Workshop album further showcased the quirky stylings of John Baker, one of the most important composers of what's become known as the Radiophonic Workshop's 'first golden era' in the 1960s. Jazz pianist Baker's recordings were far from the dystopian clichés that dominated some of the electronic music of the time. He was the man for a cheery jingle made up of wacky noises – twanging rulers, boinging springs, popping corks and bottles blown like flutes. He played as mischievously with taped sounds as Art of Noise would play with sampled sounds in the 1980s, and his creations were increasingly in demand as signature tunes and musical idents as the BBC started to launch local radio stations around the country in 1967.

Baker was creating a kind of radiophonic jazz – musique concrète with a jaunty gait. 'John was our most talented razor-blade-and-chinagraph-pencil music editor. With tape editing, if you cut music according to mathematical lengths and times and seconds and microseconds, there's a chance that it is going to turn out to be quite predictable and robotic, but John could edit with a built-in swing,' Dick Mills explains. 'He'd make one note a bit longer or a bit shorter and the whole thing would suddenly spring to life as though somebody was actually playing it rather than it coming out of a machine.'

It is Baker's plinky-plonk aesthetic that many people whose childhood years spanned the late sixties and early seventies associate with the Radiophonic Workshop, like the perky sign-off from children's TV news show *John Craven's*

Newsround. While some Workshop composers spooked youngsters with their eerie soundtracks, Baker was having fun, playing games with sound. 'It was just amusing to express the commercialisation of Christmas by using the Christmas carol 'O Come All Ye Faithful' and playing it on a cash register,' he once said.[70]

Like other British electronic composers at the time, Baker supplemented his earnings by working freelance on advertising jingles and recordings for commercial music libraries that were licensed for use in films and TV productions. Among his non-BBC compositions was the incidental music for director Ridley Scott's 1965 black-and-white student debut, *Boy and Bicycle*. Photographs from the 1960s show Baker as a cheery but diffident chap in a chunky woollen jumper. After his death, his obituary in *The Times* described him as a 'shy, sensitive and courteous man' who was 'blessed with a heightened sense of the ridiculous' but troubled by stress and ill health. It concluded: 'He was unmarried.'[71]

The background to these allusions was eventually illuminated by a poignant tribute written by his brother, Richard Anthony Baker, a BBC radio presenter. John Baker was gay and came of age in the dark period when male homosexual sex was illegal, his brother explained. Although he did have boyfriends and, as a pianist, was 'happy to accompany sing-songs at Southend's only gay pub', his brother lamented that he suffered from being 'born into a world for which he was too tender'.[72]

The Sexual Offences Act 1967 decriminalised sex between men under the age of 21 in England and Wales (although Scots had to wait until 1980 and gay men in Northern Ireland until 1982); it was one of several pieces of progressive legislation introduced by the Labour government that constitute a genuine legacy of sixties social liberalisation: alongside laws relaxing restrictions on divorce and abortion, the state provision of contraception and the abolition of capital punishment.

Baker's Radiophonic Workshop colleague Paddy Kingsland recalls that the BBC in the late sixties and seventies was a relatively liberal environment, where people knew and accepted that Baker was gay: 'The thing is that the BBC was a kind of an artistic place, really. People were quite happy with being in the company of gay people.' Baker's brother also said that the composer met many of his boyfriends at the BBC.

Nevertheless, Kingsland believes Baker suffered psychologically from his experiences in the years when male homosexuality was still a criminal offence.

'He had been through a time when it wasn't legal and it was very soon after it had become legal, so it was very hard for him to really be open about it.' Baker was a drinker, and the harder he worked, the more he drank. 'His intake of alcohol and the intense pace of his work fuelled bouts of severe depression and in August 1970 he suffered his first breakdown,' his brother wrote.[73]

Kingsland also remembers how, after the Radiophonic Workshop got its first synthesizers, Baker struggled to cope with the change. 'He didn't really want to learn the synthesizer things, he had his own very good way of doing music. But that tape-cutting was being slightly superseded and I think he found it more and more difficult.'

'In 1974, the BBC sacked him and he never recovered from the shock,' his brother wrote. 'From the day he left Maida Vale, he never wrote another note of music nor played in public again.' Baker lived off his royalties and 'spent the next few years in an alcoholic stupor' until he died of liver cancer in 1997.[74] Thirteen years after his death, his legacy of innovation was belatedly honoured by Trunk Records' release of a two-volume archive compilation, *The John Baker Tapes*.

Peter Zinovieff, EMS, The Rolling Stones and White Noise

'At the beginning, nobody else actually understood how my computer worked. It was a mystery to everybody.'
Peter Zinovieff, computer music pioneer and founder of EMS

For almost a decade, the Radiophonic Workshop remained the only state-funded electronic music studio in Britain, highlighting a lack of institutional support in stark contrast to the government funding for the new art form in France and Germany. But as the 1960s progressed, basic studios slowly started to be established at several universities around the country, including York, Manchester and Goldsmiths in London. In 1967, Tristram Cary set up the Royal College of Music Electronic Studio. Ever in search of an income, he composed the soundtrack for the Hammer Films adaptation of SF-horror tale *Quatermass and the Pit* the same year.

Cary was also involved in what has been described as the first solo performance by a computer in London, at the Queen Elizabeth Hall in 1968: Peter Zinovieff's 'Partita for Unattended Computer'. Dressed up like a music-hall impresario in dinner jacket and bowtie, Cary introduced the proceedings with a theatrical flourish from a lodge above the packed hall, promising the audience nothing had been prerecorded and that 'the performance you are about to hear is unique and unrepeatable.'

Zinovieff and Delia Derbyshire, who also had a piece on the bill, then checked and loaded the composer's DEC PDP-8/S computer. As they left the stage, a ping-ponging percussive sound began to reverberate erratically around the hall, with the computer as the lone focus of attention – a stack of boxes and wires blinking and blooping inscrutably at the audience. In the concert programme, Zinovieff predicted: 'One of these days, a computer could produce a sound as emotionally satisfying as a full symphony orchestra.'[75]

Zinovieff had first set up his own home studio back in 1962. The son of aristocrats who had fled the Russian revolution, he had studied geology at Oxford and briefly worked as a mathematician at the British Air Ministry before deciding to explore experimental music. Just as Tristram Cary had done several years earlier, he bought his first electronic equipment on London's Lisle Street, where stores that had specialised in military surplus items were still selling electrical paraphernalia in the 1960s.

'In those days Lisle Street, a poky little side-street around the back of the Odeon Leicester Square was just a mass of electronics shops, most of them had started by selling ex-Air Ministry stuff post-war,' reminisced one contributor to an online forum for electronics hobbyists. 'Nearly every shop in the street had piles of boxes spread across the pavement full of all sorts of magical items, acorn valves, precision servo pots, crystals (the Bakelite ones where you could take them apart), circuit boards, you name it!'[76]

Zinovieff was delighted with what he found. 'I got all these great bulky things – oscilloscopes, sine wave oscillators, waveform generators, filters and so on.' But he needed someone to teach him how to actually make music, so he approached a former BBC Radiophonic Workshop luminary for tuition.

'I went to have lessons and Daphne Oram taught me about tape-splicing and speeding up tapes and slowing them down,' Zinovieff recalled in an interview for this book, not long before his death in 2021. 'It made me resolve not to do tape-splicing – it was very time-consuming, and anyway it seemed idiotic because the whole thing of electronics was advancing, so it was pretty obvious to try and do it electronically rather than mechanically.'

After installing the equipment he had amassed in an outhouse at the bottom of his garden by the River Thames next to Putney Bridge, he decided to try to compose music using a computer as a 'mega-sequencer' to control his gear, and bought a DEC (Digital Equipment Corporation) PDP-8/S, one of the first such machines in private ownership. He financed the £4,000 purchase, a huge amount in 1967, by persuading his wealthy wife to sell a tiara she owned.

What is believed to be the first recording of primitive computer-generated music had been made back in 1951 at the University of Manchester, where mathematician and cryptanalyst Alan Turing had enabled a gargantuan Ferranti computer to generate musical notes. Turing, renowned for his World War II codebreaking achievements as well as his role in developing computer science, managed to effectively transform the Ferranti into a musical instrument. It was recorded by the BBC hooting out a rudimentary medley, including the British national anthem, 'Baa Baa Black Sheep' and Glenn Miller's 'In the Mood', in a tone that sounded like a vintage car horn.

Technology had moved on significantly by the time Zinovieff bought his computer, but using it was still laborious. 'Programming wasn't like nowadays, it was extremely cumbersome, there was no screen and everything had to be done on this very slow keyboard, and you had to produce a punch tape, which had to be fed in, you had to use machine language and it was extremely slow and there were errors, and there was no hard drive so nothing was stored – when you turned on the computer, it had nothing in its memory at all,' he said.

Zinovieff was aided by his talented engineer-collaborator David Cockerell, but as this was the only home studio for computer music in the country, it was a lonely mission: 'Nobody else had a computer in their house. So there was nobody to ask, you know, "How do you do this?" So it was much harder to find out about things,' recalled Zinovieff. 'I mean, there were people with tape studios like Tristram Cary or the Radiophonic Workshop, but there was nobody using a computer.'

In 1966, Zinovieff, Delia Derbyshire and her BBC colleague Brian Hodgson established a short-lived production team called Unit Delta Plus to develop electronic music projects at Zinovieff's home studio. They gave an initial concert in September that year of works they had written, accompanied by lightshow projections, at the Watermill Theatre in the village of Bagnor near Newbury, Berkshire – an obscure location for one of the first electronic music events in Britain – and also contributed music to the Million Volt Light and Sound Rave alongside The Beatles' 'Carnival of Light'.

But differences of opinion caused the trio to split up not long afterwards. 'It never worked out because [Derbyshire and Hodgson] never had the patience to cope with this amazing studio I had, they were used to very quick work at the Radiophonic Workshop and they were interested more in making commercial music for advertising jingles and selling it, and that wasn't what I was interested in,' Zinovieff claimed. 'I was interested in the equivalent of classical music, working with serious composers in a new way.'

Hodgson had mixed feelings about working with Zinovieff, whose haughty self-confidence could be perceived as patrician arrogance. 'Zinovieff was very clever and didn't suffer fools gladly. He behaved like a Russian aristocrat, and he was utterly infuriating but wonderful to work with,' he says.

A BBC One *Tomorrow's World* programme that profiled Zinovieff in 1968 ventured inside his semi-subterranean, bunker-like studio, packed wall-to-ceiling with electronic equipment: dials, lights, switches, buttons, spools, cables and sockets, and his PDP-8/S computer with an assistant typing out code on paper, which was then transferred onto punched tape and fed into the computer that oversaw the musical output. The outcome, when played, was a series of woozy, wobbly tones that sounded a bit like the space creatures from the BBC children's series *The Clangers* stumbling home after a long night on the town.

It's been argued that Zinovieff was more important as an animateur than a composer, and his technological entrepreneurialism undoubtedly had a huge and lasting effect. After he and David Cockerell built a rudimentary synthesizer for Australian composer Don Banks for $50, he realised there might be a market for such gizmos that could subsidise his computer experiments. So in 1969, Zinovieff and Cockerell teamed up with Tristram Cary to start a company called Electronic Music Studios (London), which would market the first commercially-produced British synthesizers, as well as operating as a private studio for his own work. 'When I started EMS, the point was to design and sell synthesizers in order to fund the studio because it was so expensive,' he explained.

At his studio, Zinovieff worked with software designer Peter Grogono to create MUSYS, an early programming software for composing electronic music using a computer. He also collaborated on pieces with contemporary classical luminaries like Hans Werner Henze and Harrison Birtwistle, whose sonorously percussive 'Chronometer' was based on computer-manipulated recordings of watches and clocks, including Big Ben.

'There was no real English equivalent of [French sonic research institute] IRCAM or Columbia Princeton [Electronic Music Centre] or Bell Labs at that time,' says composer James Gardner, an expert on EMS and Zinovieff's work. 'Zinovieff's studio was in his house and it was underfunded. But he made it possible for composers of art music to do computer music work before they could do it anywhere else in England.'

Like other synthesizer manufacturers operating at the time – Moog, Buchla and Electronic Music Laboratories, all in the United States – EMS was a small-scale operation with few employees. Its first product in 1969 was the VCS3, a compact analogue synth with an idiosyncratic pin-matrix patchboard and joystick control that could generate and modify sound. EMS kept the costs low during the prototype development stage by using parts from budget electronics stores. 'Nearly all the components were bought on Lisle Street,' Cockerell said. 'Being an impoverished amateur, I was always conscious of making things cheap.'[77]

The profile of American engineer Robert Moog's synthesizer had been raised the previous year by the popular novelty album *Switched-On Bach*, Wendy Carlos' recordings of the baroque composer arranged for the modular unit. But the price of the VCS3, at £330, was much cheaper than any synthesizer made by Moog, whose least expensive model would have cost around £1,800 at the time. (Decades later, after they became cult items, vintage VCS3s would sell for thousands on the synth nostalgia market).

As avant-garde composers, Zinovieff and Cary initially seem to have envisaged that the VCS3 would be used by people like them. 'The new instrument for the new music,' proclaimed the slogan on the cover of the brochure, which pictured the synth next to a pair of professorial glasses and some kind of music textbook. Educational establishments were their other target. 'We thought we could design a package that would appeal not only to composers but also to schools and people like that. A very good teaching instrument for acoustics and so forth,' said Cary.[78] But instead, many of the early adopters came from rock music which, in the wake of *Sgt. Pepper*, had been sonically diverging from pop as its leading protagonists sought new ways to proclaim their originality.

One early EMS client was Ringo Starr, who Zinovieff attempted to instruct in the techniques of VCS3 manipulation. 'I would go to his house in Hampstead. He wasn't particularly good. But then neither was I,' the EMS founder said of the Beatle.[79] Soon EMS would realise that wealthy rockers, rather than lesser-paid classical avant-gardists, represented their most lucrative market. A later ad depicted a pop art-style cartoon woman asking:

'Have you heard about the VCS3? Curved Air have, so have Pink Floyd, the Moody Blues and King Crimson.'

Nevertheless, Zinovieff remained immaculately snooty about his rock clients, whose music held little interest for him. 'I didn't really like it very much. I was into experimental music,' he declared imperiously, insisting he was much more excited when Stockhausen visited his studio than when Paul McCartney turned up.

Zinovieff also had little interest in the counterculture, disdainfully rejecting the idea that avant-garde musical exploration had any connection to the quest for new perceptions through psychedelic drugs and freeform artistic happenings. 'I don't see what all that's got to do with electronic music,' he grouched. 'This was experimental music, it was nothing to do with drug-taking or hippies. People have always experimented.'

When it was first produced, the VCS3 did not have a keyboard. Catering to their own preferences, Zinovieff and Cary never envisaged its users would want to use the equal-tempered scale. They were mistaken, and Cary was disappointed when EMS started selling a keyboard accessory. 'I was quite shocked when keyboards came in because the whole thing about electronic music for me was you were getting away from keyboards, one thing you wanted to avoid in electronic music was twelve notes to the octave,' he said.[80]

It was a view shared by American synthesizer inventor Don Buchla, who described keyboards as 'dictatorial' because they imposed a specific frame of thinking about music. 'When you've got a black and white keyboard there it's hard to play anything but keyboard music,' he argued.[81] The debate about whether electronic devices should emulate existing instruments was not new. As far back as 1940, John Cage had complained that the Solovox and the Novachord, both electric keyboard instruments, were examples of a 'desire to imitate the past rather than construct the future'. Cage argued that the electronic instruments of the future should instead 'make available for musical purposes any and all sounds that can be heard.'[82]

Although rock stars were intrigued by synthesizers, most would initially only use them for novelty value. The Rolling Stones, who had experimented with sound effects and a Mellotron on their psychedelic period piece *Their Satanic Majesties Request* in 1967, were among the first owners of a Moog in Britain. Not long before his death, guitarist Brian Jones came to see the Radiophonic Workshop's Brian Hodgson and Delia Derbyshire to ask for advice. 'He said, "Oh, we've just bought a Moog synthesizer",' Hodgson recalls. 'So we said,

"Well, what are you doing with it?" And he said, "Well, nobody is really quite sure so it's just lying around the studio while we get our heads around it." So we said, "Terrific, can we come and see it?" And he said, "Yeah, I'll arrange it, come up and have a play." But unfortunately, he died within weeks of that visit and it never actually happened.'

As Barry Miles points out, The Rolling Stones gave up on psychedelic exploration soon afterwards: 'The Stones only really had that one psychedelic album, *Satanic Majesties*, in response to *Sgt. Pepper*, and certainly tracks like '10,000 Light Years from Home' were LSD-inspired. But once Brian Jones was gone they reverted to their R&B-based sound.'

A Moog was also used to create unsettling incidental music for some of Mick Jagger's scenes in Donald Cammell and Nicolas Roeg's 1970 cinematic psychodrama, *Performance*. Played on the film soundtrack by American synthesizer expert and Moog promoter Bernie Krause, its ominous throb and whine gave a supernatural edge to tracks like 'Poor White Hound Dog'. The Stones' singer used a Moog himself to create the soundtrack for Kenneth Anger's experimental short film from 1969, *Invocation of My Demon Brother*. Jagger's electronic effort was no masterpiece, however, sounding like someone trying to execute a three-point turn on a remote-control car.

A little better was an audacious experiment by British psychedelic blues-rock band Spooky Tooth, who made an entire album in 1969 with French musique concrète innovator Pierre Henry. On its release, underground newspaper *IT* hailed *Ceremony: An Electronic Mass* as 'a major experimental breakthrough'.[83] But most other critics agreed the mismatched collaboration didn't gel and the album would remain a historical curiosity rather than a creative or commercial triumph.

Probably the most significant British electronic pop album of the late sixties was made by a group that included the woman who had already made the most important piece of early electronic music for TV – Delia Derbyshire. In 1967, Derbyshire and Brian Hodgson gave a lecture in London that attracted a curious American student called David Vorhaus. 'It was a very experimental time in those days and I didn't even know I was going to be a musician – I'd studied physics and I was aiming to be a physicist, music was just meant to be a hobby. So this was a life-changing moment,' recalls Vorhaus.

Derbyshire and Hodgson asked him to join them in setting up a studio, Kaleidophon, which produced soundtracks for theatre plays, advertising jingles and recordings they sold to the Standard Music Library. Some of their delightfully trippy vignettes, including compositions with suitably sixties titles like 'Far Out' and 'Delia's Psychadelian Waltz', were released as an album called *Electronic Music* in 1969, with Derbyshire using the pseudonym Li de la Russe and Hodgson credited as Nikki St. George. Some of the album's contents were later used on the soundtrack to the 1970s science-fiction series about adolescents with paranormal abilities, *The Tomorrow People*.

Island Records founder Chris Blackwell then offered Derbyshire, Hodgson and Vorhaus £3,000 to make an album, so in 1969 they began recording under the name White Noise. *An Electric Storm* was the one album they made together (although Vorhaus would use the White Noise name for later releases), and it was as striking as its lightning-flash sleeve – a tour de force of musique concrète pop, aural drama, discombobulating sound effects and intricate loop-and-splice work. Some of the music was subversively eroticised, some of it steeped in gothic camp, some of it suggestive of ideas that would be explored by industrial bands like Throbbing Gristle a decade later.

'Nobody was doing this except us and because nothing like it had been done before, you had to kind of dream up what you wanted to do and how you were going to do it and try it,' says Vorhaus. 'At the time, there was this huge space between pop music, which was completely unelectronic, and avant-garde classical music, which was very experimental stuff and much weirder than it is today. There were these two extremes and so much space in between, and I would say White Noise fitted in the middle of it – it was much too weird to be pop music but it was definitely psychedelic, even though I hadn't even taken LSD until I finished that record.'

The closing track, a demented phased-drum freakout called 'Black Mass', was so unnerving that it was used in the Hammer horror film *Dracula AD 1972*, soundtracking a scene in which the count is brought back to life in a bloody invocation ritual by thrill-seeking hippies. Although *An Electric Storm* was released after electronic rock albums by US bands Silver Apples and The United States of America, it was a landmark for British futurist pop.

At this point in sixties Britain, electronic music was attracting 'serious' composers and pop stars as well as hobbyists and eccentrics, but also creative artists from other disciplines; this was a time of experimental cross-fertilisation. Historian Dominic Sandbrook has described how artists, designers, filmmakers and musicians 'borrowed from one another's work, so that, say, the paintings of Bridget Riley or the music of The Beatles had unexpected reverberations in completely different fields.'[84] Experimental composer Ron Geesin puts it more directly: 'Everyone was pinching things off everyone else back then – or perhaps we should say that there was an "exchange of creative energy" across all the media.'

Annea Lockwood, who later became the creator of environmentally-inspired ambient assemblages of field recordings from the natural world, has recalled how, in the culturally liberated environment of sixties London, she was involved in all manner of uncommon musical experiments. She performed with a band called Naked Software using a map of Mount Everest as a score, placed microphones in a piano and set it on fire in an attempt to record the sounds it made while burning, and created an installation of noise-making glassworks at hippie club Middle Earth. 'I was working in a world in the late sixties in which, in all the art forms, really, we took for granted that we could work with any material in any way we could imagine,' Lockwood said.[85]

Composer Deirdre Piper, who helped set up a small studio for producing electronic and tape music at the University of Manchester in the late sixties, has spoken of a similar feeling of freedom. Piper recalled how she felt 'the sense of being part of something radical and of historic potential... We were a small community sharing visions of a new music for a new age.'[86]

Various British musicians were inspired by the ideas of indeterminacy and chance explored by John Cage, whose audio-visual piece 'Variations V' for tape recorders, short-wave radios and video projections was performed in London with choreography by Merce Cunningham, whose dancers manipulated sound via their movements on stage. Lockwood spoke for many when she described Cage as 'a very liberating influence' at the time.[87]

In May 1968, experimental concert promoters organisation Music Now programmed the first in a series called Sounds of Discovery in London, promising 'experiments in indeterminacy, live electronics, [and] improvisation', beginning with a performance led by British composer Cornelius Cardew of 'In C' by Terry Riley.[88] 'In C' forged a crucial link between psychedelia and classical minimalism – it was trance-like, druggy and free-flowing; a soundtrack for inner journeys and communal happenings. Like other works by Riley, it was a powerful creative stimulant for British musicians who went on to make psychedelic electronic music in the years that followed.

Ernest Berk, Basil Kirchin, Ron Geesin: Musical Misfits

'I was always against any kind of clique or gang or movement.'
Ron Geesin

Writing in *IT* in 1968, Barry Miles described London's alternative scene as 'a "test-bed" for new sounds and talent.'[89] The sixties underground also offered space for alternatively-minded and sometimes rather peculiar characters to thrive. Among them was Ernest Berk, one of several hard-to-classify figures who was involved in electronic music composition but also worked in other artistic disciplines – in his case, contemporary dance.

Berk was born in Cologne but fled Nazi Germany before World War II with his Jewish wife Lotte, who became a renowned dancer and exercise teacher. He started making musique concrète in London in the 1950s – works that he described as 'music-paintings, reflections of a wild and uncontrolled world.'[90] A pacifist, Buddhist and committed naturist, Berk rejected social norms in search of a higher form of artistic expression through movement, attracting an entourage of dancers who were seeking to explore the possibilities of the moment.

'He was fascinated by the new and the now and breaking the rules, and a lot of that played into what interested us in the hippie era from 1966 onwards,' says Christopher Thomson who was a member of Berk's Dance Theatre Commune. 'It was about free expression, an expressive response to the moment, not bothering about technique or conventional structures.'

Thomson remembers how Berk set up his self-assembled electronic equipment in a corner of his little dance studio near London's Baker Street – 'always wearing dance clothes or maybe motorbike leathers, if he was wearing anything at all' – and would sit cutting tape with razor blades for abstract pieces used to soundtrack his experimental dance works. 'His work was expressive. He was expressive. He was someone who was always moving and alert and alive,' says Thomson.

Berk would hold freeform, trance-inducing dance sessions soundtracked by recordings of African drumming or rhythmic tape loops to liberate the creative energies of his company. Sometimes they took off their clothes and danced naked. 'It didn't seem unusual, it didn't seem weird or anything like that. It was a way of just getting in touch with your physical body and your muscles and feeling how you moved,' says another former member of the Dance Theatre Commune, Julia Dunn. 'A lot of the dances were about freedom, escaping, breaking out – I think it was part of that whole era. I didn't realise at the time how liberating it was.'

Like Daphne Oram, Tristram Cary, John Baker and others, Berk sold some of his electronic pieces for commercial use as library music for television and films, but mostly created tracks to accompany his own choreography. He also collaborated on occasion with other electronic music mavericks, like Desmond Leslie and an even more curious character called Basil Kirchin.

Kirchin had lived a highly unusual life: at the age of 13, during World War II, he had been a big-band drummer on the London jazz scene; he then travelled to India in the 1950s to live in a temple and investigate Hindu mysticism. He subsequently worked as the musical director of a theatre in Sydney before returning returned to London, where he spent the 1960s writing film scores and producing library music.

Using a tape recorder, Kirchin manipulated field recordings of birdsong, animal noises and children's voices, assembling abstract lattices of natural sounds and slowed-down drones. He combined these elements with free-jazz playing by saxophonist Evan Parker and guitarist Derek Bailey to create the first of his two *Worlds Within Worlds* albums in the early 1970s, both of which were decidedly uneasy listening experiences.

'Basil realised long before the rest of us did that sound could become a malleable material,' said Brian Eno, who wrote the second album's sleeve notes.[91] Eno would credit Kirchin as an inspiration for the album he made later with David Byrne, combining found sounds and electronic manipulation: *My Life in the Bush of Ghosts*.

Both *Worlds Within Worlds* albums sold poorly and Kirchin disappeared from view until he was tracked down decades later, impoverished but full of ideas, in a council house in Hull by Jonny Trunk, owner of Trunk Records. Trunk subsequently rereleased a lot of Kirchin's music to significant acclaim. Despite being in his mid-seventies and suffering from cancer, Kirchin was enthused by the unexpected accolades and completed a final album before he died in 2005. Trunk's description of his sound was a fitting obituary: 'His music will consume you, entertain you, thrill you, and scare the living daylights out of you.'[92]

While Kirchin had an impact on Eno's work, another uncategorisable experimentalist from the wilder fringes of the sixties avant-garde exerted influence on Pink Floyd's musical methods. Ron Geesin, a former trad-jazz pianist, gained a cult reputation for his jocular sound-collage recordings that drew comparison to Ivor Cutler and Spike Milligan, as well as his soundtracks for avant-garde films by Stephen Dwoskin and John Schlesinger's 1971 movie *Sunday Bloody Sunday*.

The wild-bearded Geesin was a steadfastly independent character who had turned down Desmond Briscoe's offer of a job at the BBC Radiophonic Workshop. 'It didn't take long to consider. I said, "No, I'll go my own way, thank you." I didn't want to get institutionalised,' Geesin explains. Instead, he set up his own studio in his basement flat in Notting Hill, where he pursued his craft 'surrounded by a collection of recording machines, spools, miles of tape, and a number of bespoke and proprietary musical devices', according to Pink Floyd's Nick Mason.[93]

In 1970, Geesin worked alongside Roger Waters on the soundtrack to Roy Battersby's controversial documentary film about human biology, *The Body*, and created orchestral settings for Pink Floyd's *Atom Heart Mother*. Mason said that Geesin's 'idiosyncratic techniques and modus operandi' helped steer the band away from conservative thinking about musical arrangements; he also credited Geesin with influencing the tape-delay effects and wacky noises on 'Several Species of Small Furry Animals Gathered Together in a Cave and Grooving with a Pict' from the *Ummagumma* album, and on the abstract cosmic section of 'Echoes', the opening track on *Meddle*. 'Ron passed on a variety of tricks with Revox tape recorders hooked up in tandem that went well beyond the bounds of standard use as recommended in the manufacturer's manual,' Mason said approvingly.[94]

Geesin became known for his confrontational stage performances, during which he says he tried to 'create a lot of energy by picking a fight with the audience'. But he also recorded delightful electronic vignettes, like his pieces for library music label KPM that were released as the album *Electrosound* in 1972. He just wanted to be as uncategorisable as possible, he explains: 'To me it didn't matter if I was manipulating a voice or a musical noise. Backwards banjos, shouting, strange voices, all pitch-shifted, I would use whatever I'd got. I've always called it painting with sound.' As a guest lecturer at colleges in the 1970s, Geesin would make a significant impression on two inquisitive students who went on to become electronic musicians, Daniel Miller, who recorded as The Normal and founded Mute Records, and Dave Ball of Soft Cell.

Many of the fringe composers of the 1960s, like Geesin, Berk and Desmond Leslie, were listed in the *International Electronic Music Catalog*, a book by composer Hugh Davies that ambitiously sought to document every piece of music made using electronic techniques anywhere in the world up to April 1967. His gargantuan list included rock bands like The Beatles as well as composers like Stockhausen and Berio.

Davies himself was another fascinating figure, involved in a myriad of experimental projects, whose contribution to British electronic music's development is sometimes not fully credited. He made his first piece of musique concrète, 'Essay for Magnetic Tape', with a friend at Daphne Oram's Tower Folly studio in 1962, while still a teenager, then set up his own makeshift studio whilst studying at Oxford. He was apprenticed to Stockhausen as his assistant in Cologne for a couple of years in the early sixties and became part of the German composer's live electronics ensemble for a while.

A photo from the period shows Davies at home, sitting cross-legged on a carpet surrounded by a jumble of electronic gizmos, cables, tape loops and other technological bric-a-brac. For the live shows he staged, he constructed his own amplified instruments, continuing the DIY tradition of early electronic music. The first electro-acoustic device that he made, which he called the 'shozyg', was built out of fretsaw blades, a spring, a ball castor and two contact microphones, mounted inside the hard cover of an encyclopaedia; it made a scratchily metallic noise like a hamster trying to escape from a toolbox. Davies built various other instruments from bits and pieces of junk over the years that followed, including several versions of the shozyg – one of which he'd later play on 1980s prog-pop band Talk Talk's *Spirit of Eden* album.

He claimed to have been the first electronic musician to play live in Britain: 'When I first began working in live electronic music in England in the summer of 1967 I was the only musician in the country to do so,' he asserted.[95] The following year, he also started the first British live electronic duo with composer Richard Orton.

At the start of the 1960s, a lot of this might have been unimaginable. But by the end of the decade, the once obscure concepts of musique concrète and elektronische musik had entered the popular consciousness through soundtracks to radio and TV programmes, London's avant-garde art scene and the bohemian underground, and through inquisitive musicians like Paul McCartney and John Lennon, who embraced experimental sound as one of the artistic totems of progressive culture. Championed by the most famous band in the world, electronic music had gone pop.

Stacia Blake of Hawkwind, 1972. ©Gijsbert Hanekroot/Getty Images.

3
OTHER SIDE OF THE SKY
Space Rock, Prog and Ambient

Hawkwind: Psychedelic Warlords
'Hawkwind were very keen to attempt things that nobody else had done before, experimenting with sounds on the edges of what was acceptable at the time. It sounded mad and it sounded weird.'
Dave Anderson, bass player for Hawkwind from 1970-71

THE ISLE OF WIGHT, AUGUST 1970. Out beyond the corrugated metal fences, away from the swarming crowds and stellar attractions of the most multitudinous festival of the hippie era in Britain, the impecunious refuseniks of the underground were freaking freely. In a raggedy whirl of churning riffs, tranced-out rhythms and rushes of oscillator noise, a band of scruffy hippies called Hawkwind had attracted what alternative newspaper *IT* described as 'a motley collection of drug-crazed idiot dancers, anarchists and Hells Angels' to an enormous inflatable tent called Canvas City.[1] This was a free jamboree promoted by the White Panthers anarchist group as a politically-motivated alternative to the Isle of Wight Festival. Staged right next to the official festival site, it confirmed Hawkwind's reputation not only as standard-bearers of the counterculture in Britain, but also as musical adventurers bringing otherworldly noise to post-sixties rock'n'roll.

For the Hawkwind crew, it was a wondrous, chaotic, disturbing weekend. While Jimi Hendrix, The Doors and The Who headlined the main stage and hippie activists besieged and battered down the metal fences to make the main festival free for all, Hawkwind played on and on for hour after hour; outside in the sunshine by day and inside the bulbous bubble of Canvas City after dark.

'One night we went into the tent late evening and just played through the night,' says Thomas Crimble, the band's bassist at the time. 'There was very much a trance element to it, we had the echo chambers rigged up so you could get an echo going on a beat, you'd get a repeat pulse going and you'd fit a riff into that and build it up and then you'd just take off. We came out of the tent at about eight o'clock the next morning having not stopped at all.

'We were experimenting on stage and what came out was new to everybody then. We were creating new sounds, especially with DikMik [Michael Davies] doing the electronics – he had an audio generator he'd bought from an army surplus store that he was putting through a bunch of guitar pedals and an echo chamber. We were making music that hadn't been heard before.'

Isle of Wight Festival organiser Ray Foulk was infuriated by the rival free event, calling it 'a honey pot for freaks and nutters who seemed to be mainly acid trippers, down-and-outs or agitators', and dismissing Hawkwind as purveyors of 'anarchistic and drug-fuelled agitprop stunts'.[2] But rock journalists were fascinated. 'When it comes to mind-blowing, Hawkwind are really into it,' declared a headline in the music paper *Sounds* not long afterwards. The reporter expressed naive amazement at DikMik's use of apparatus which he described as emitting 'strange electronic force waves'; he observed how the band had noticed these drones and squeals were 'having a profound effect on audiences, not to mention themselves' and had started to worry that they were playing with mysterious forces that could distort their perception forever. 'The sounds send out a force field and things really came to a head at the Isle of Wight,' bandleader and guitarist Dave Brock told the music paper. 'We were playing a heavy riff for about four hours with strobe lighting going on and off, and it freaked me out so badly I just had to get away.'[3]

What had actually happened was that someone had dosed the band's fruit juice with LSD, causing Brock to wander off to wrestle with his hallucinations, while on stage guitarist Huw Lloyd-Langton felt he was losing his mind as he played on, praying desperately to God for salvation. 'All around me, there were people freak dancing and turning into devils,' he would remember.[4] Meanwhile, saxophonist Nik Turner painted his face silver and roamed the festival site, attracting press photographers and intriguing Hendrix, who dedicated a song from the stage to 'the cat right there with the silver face'.[5]

As the *Sounds* article highlighted, Hawkwind's use of electronics to enhance their hypnotic jams was a distinct novelty at the time. 'I suppose Pink Floyd had done some of this, but not to that degree of taking off and going places where nobody really knew where it was heading,' says Crimble. 'It was very exciting if it didn't completely screw up. And the audience picked up on that and then the room and everyone in it was all in this great sonic experiment.'

IT had entered 1970 with an obituary for the 1960s, its liberties and its counterculture. 'Underground music is dead. As The Rolling Stones observed, "the hype of the Love Generation triumphed over its own reality",' declared a dejected commentary. The writer, *IT* columnist Arthur Pitt, despaired that the musicians involved in the counterculture were fakers, not really trying to build an 'alternative society' at all: 'We've all been kidding ourselves, including the so-called British underground press, that there is something inherently, socially different about progressive music and the people who make it,' he wrote.[6] But the same month, in the same magazine, another comment piece expressed a completely contrary point of view: that the sixties' cultural movements would thrive in this new decade. Its author, musician Edgar Broughton, placed his faith in 'the spread of free concerts throughout the country along with the many commercial festivals… powerful well organised togetherness under the trees and in the sunshine', which he argued could become a 'rallying point for the spread of community action'.[7]

The band who would come to embody this spirit of community action was that gang of hirsute rogues with guitars, oscillators and a seemingly endless supply of drugs, Hawkwind. They were the instigators of what became known as space rock – a mixture of German *kosmische* psychedelia, hard-jamming pre-punk rock and Floydian atmospherics with a load of wild electronic noise squalling away over the top. Seen at the time as a kind of British counterpart to Amon Düül II, or even Can, they toured relentlessly, spreading their sonic strangeness and utopian-dystopian cosmology across provincial Britain while upholding the ideals of the sixties underground by playing countless benefit concerts and free festivals.

Hawkwind founder Dave Brock was a long-haired street busker who was into Hendrix and the electric blues, but also listened to The Velvet Underground,

Can and US electronic duo Silver Apples. Brock had been to the UFO club, where he saw Pink Floyd and Soft Machine taking rock apart and propelling it into another state of consciousness. Whilst working temporarily in a studio producing soundtracks for cartoons and TV commercials, Brock came into contact with musique concrète techniques. 'We used to make huge tape loops on Revoxes and around door handles. It was interesting work and I was able to experiment with a lot of weird sounds,' he recalled.

At home, he would make his own loops and combine them with his guitar playing fed through an echo unit to multiply and layer the sound, inspired by American guitar innovator Les Paul, who had conducted tape-recorder experiments in the early fifties. 'We'd get Sonny Terry's harmonica going backwards on a big loop, then play guitar over it and really get the echo going.' All this fed into the free-ranging music that Hawkwind developed, Brock explained, 'because that was the age where you could be as avant-garde as you liked.'[8]

What made Hawkwind different from other rock groups of the period was the role of Michael 'DikMik' Davies, who was initially the band's roadie but was invited to join after acquiring an electronic signal generator, which he set up on a baize-topped card table and fed through a Watkins Copicat echo unit, a fuzzbox and a wah-wah pedal. 'I've got practically no musical knowledge but I figure if you let it become your whole trip, where your involvement is total, you can do anything you like and do it well,' he was quoted as saying on the sleeve of Hawkwind's debut album.[9]

The noises that DikMik created – flashes of cosmic madness that arced across the band's grungy, hypnotic riffing – variously thrilled, confused and repelled audiences. 'The essence of Hawkwind is that combination; the weird psychedelic stuff with the echo units and all the electronics,' Brock said.[10]

Hawkwind were devoted imbibers of LSD, although DikMik and bassist Lemmy Kilminster preferred amphetamine sulphate; the two drugs representing the Yin and Yang of their cosmic-savage sound. 'We used to record a lot of our earlier albums under the influence of LSD because we used to reckon that all the sound frequencies that we used to get were key little things when people were tripping that they'd feel the same as we did,' claimed Brock.[11]

They liked the idea of a gig as a kind of psychedelic trip and, like Pink Floyd, turned it into an immersive experience – in Hawkwind's case with hypnotic projections by visuals crew Liquid Len and the Lensmen, a hard-flashing strobe and a wildly swaying, body-painted 'interpretive dancer', Stacia Blake. Like being on acid, it could be blissful or frightening, phantasmagorically wonderful or disturbingly dark.

Sax player Nik Turner, assuming the role of psychedelic Pied Piper, would also distribute free acid and copies of alternative magazine *Frendz* to the audience. 'I think it really compounded the band's popularity, because people still come up to me and say, "Wow, that gig you did in 1971 changed my life!" And I say, "You sure it wasn't the LSD?"' Turner told Hawkwind biographer Joe Banks. 'It had a resounding effect. We were doing gigs in the provinces, in the middle of nowhere, giving away all this LSD, and I think it really did change people's lives.'[12]

The Hawkwind experience was further enriched by the outlandish verse and maniacal stage performances of poet-singer Robert Calvert, who suffered from bipolar disorder and occasionally had to be hospitalised for psychiatric treatment. 'I'm not really a vocalist, I'm a sound poet,' insisted Calvert, whose lyrics channelled his personal psychological torments as they sampled imagery from SF writers like Michael Moorcock, J. G. Ballard and Roger Zelazny, or tales of wartime bravery from British comics like *The Wizard* or *The Rover*, projecting the band as intergalactic superheroes, psychedelic warriors battling to save their home planet from oblivion.[13]

There was also a direct literary-poetic input from New Wave science fiction author Moorcock; the grand wizard of British SF provided lyrics and declamatory readings for the band and also used them as characters in some of his writings. Moorcock said he liked them because of their 'barmy, visionary innocence'.[14] (Lemmy had his own picaresque explanation of why he liked playing with Hawkwind: 'It was like *Star Trek* with long hair and drugs.')[15]

An advertisement in *IT* for Hawkwind's first album, depicting the band playing in front of a kind of Stonehenge made of speaker stacks as the Earth rose behind them, identified their sound as 'space rock'. The term had already been used to describe Pink Floyd, who had provided some of the music for the BBC's coverage of the Apollo 11 moon landing in 1969. But Hawkwind's sound was altogether *filthier* than the ethereally melodic Floyd. 'The thing about Hawkwind was, they were more raw, they were more rough'n'ready, and you could dance to them,'[16] said Simon Dunkley, Hawkwind's tour DJ, who sometimes dressed as a wizard. Lemmy, in typically emphatic style, rejected any Floyd comparison outright: '[Hawkwind] were a black fucking nightmare. A post-apocalypse horror soundtrack. We wanted to make people's heads and sphincters explode.'[17]

When Del Dettmar, a second roadie turned electronics player, joined the band in 1971, they added an EMS VCS3 and their sound spun even further out. It was a long way from Peter Zinovieff's high-culture vision of the British-made synthesizer's functions. 'I don't think there was any other band, at least not in England, that was doing anything quite like this – playing long stretches of freeform, experimental electronic music with spoken poetry being read to it, in the way that earlier poets read their work to jazz,'[18] said Calvert.

IT's first feature on Hawkwind in 1970 had shaped their image, describing them as a 'community band' who were 'strongly rooted in the freak sub-culture of Ladbroke Grove and Notting Hill.'[19] They played free gigs under the Westway flyover and innumerable benefits for Underground causes – the Campaign for Nuclear Disarmament, drugs charity Release, imprisoned LSD advocate Timothy Leary and the Legalise Cannabis campaign – while their lyrics addressed fears about man-made environmental destruction.

'We were an ideals band. We were living those ideals and totally fucking believing them and trying to put them about as much as possible,' insisted drummer Terry Ollis, who like dancer Stacia Blake sometimes took his clothes off on stage.[20] Turner concurred: 'My whole motivation and stimulation within the context of the band was spreading peace and love,' he said. 'It wasn't just a musical thing. It was a whole concept, it was about raising people's consciousness.'[21]

But for the counterculture, the early seventies was a time when peace and love turned to turmoil and dread amid an establishment backlash and high-profile prosecutions of key figures from underground newspapers *IT* and *Oz*, as well as comicbook *Nasty Tales*, for obscenity and morality-related 'crimes'.

It was also a period that saw the trial of nine Black activists for 'inciting a riot' at a demonstration against police raids on the Mangrove restaurant in Notting Hill, the arrests of Gay Liberation Front protesters and the increasing radicalisation of some activists who started to believe that only violence could achieve their goals. In 1972, Hawkwind played a benefit concert for the Stoke Newington Eight – members of leftist group the Angry Brigade, who were being tried for a series of bomb attacks. (Calvert's satirical song inspired by the Angry Brigade, 'Urban Guerrilla', was subsequently banned by the BBC when the Irish Republican Army launched a bombing campaign in England).

Despite all this, long after the optimism about the sixties dawning of the Age of Aquarius had begun to fade, Hawkwind continued to hold aloft the standard for the alternative society, committed to being permanently tuned-in, turned-on and dropped-out. Music paper *Melody Maker* described them in 1972 as the 'people's band', beloved in provincial towns where loon pants, joss sticks, tie-dyed shirts and shaggy Afghan coats were still in vogue in the early seventies as the longhair culture of what historians call the 'long sixties' continued to spread outside London even after the decade itself had ended. 'There's a Hawkwind cult now that's almost as vital to their gigs as the music. Every gig is a stage for local fantasies. Bottled up extrovert tendencies explode into fancy dress and painted faces,' a *Melody Maker* reporter enthused.[22]

Stacia Blake said she knew why they were so popular: 'The kind of music Hawkwind played appealed to a certain kind of person… basically all freaks and misfits, like the rest of us.'[23] The band even scored an unlikely chart hit in 1972 with 'Silver Machine', a propulsive acid-rock anthem that took flight on the synthetic whoosh of a VCS3.

As Hawkwind took their urban sci-fi revue across Britain, bringing druggy weirdness with them, they made a substantial impact on the consciousness of teenagers who subsequently became musicians. 'When I saw them live, I got a full sonic psychedelic onslaught that was kind of punk before punk, very raw, and it was great the way that they were using synths not with a keyboard, just as noises, and how you never knew where one song started and another one began,' remembers Stephen Morris, who would later become the drummer with Joy Division and New Order.

They also continued to experiment with their own distinctive formula. Tracks like the euphoric 'Opa-Loka' on 1975's *Warrior on the Edge of Time* album, with double drummers clattering hard and a VCS3 careening across the sonic landscape, took them close to the German motorik rock of bands like Neu!.

'They were much more influential than they've been given credit for,' says Nigel Ayres of post-punk electro-acoustic duo Nocturnal Emissions. 'This was radical electronic music at that point – they had this connection with the counterculture, they were playing at free festivals, they put this multimedia show together. But also there was the idea of the band being not as important as the communal experience.'

This vibe of collective abandon has led to suggestions that Hawkwind were not only a kind of precursor to post-punk electronic music, but also to the

British rave scene; a view endorsed by Harvey Bainbridge, who played bass and keyboards for Hawkwind, and for Dave Brock's satellite bands Sonic Assassins and Hawklords, from the late seventies onwards.

'The rhythm is the key to this,' argues Bainbridge. 'Because the whole idea of rave music is the eternal rhythm, isn't it? And when you listen to some of Hawkwind's stuff, it's just that almost ceaseless rhythm. It's repetitive, hypnotic – it's got that trance thing going on. It makes you want to move.'

Prog Rock: Rick Wakeman, Curved Air, Arthur Brown, Pink Floyd

'It was felt after *Sgt. Pepper* anybody could do anything in music. It seemed the wilder the idea musically, the better.'
Bill Bruford, drummer for King Crimson and Yes[24]

At the start of the 1970s, although electronic music wasn't as obscure and alien-sounding as it had been a decade earlier, most of the synthesizers on the market were still prohibitively expensive and only accessible to the relatively affluent few. They were however starting to become familiar to the public by 1971 through early albums by progressive rock bands like Yes, King Crimson and Emerson, Lake & Palmer (ELP).

By 1972 and 1973, Moogs, ARPs and VCS3s were being used on songs as diverse as Hawkwind's 'Silver Machine', Elton John's 'Rocket Man', Black Sabbath's cold and doomy 'Who are You?' and Chicory Tip's irrepressibly catchy 'Son of My Father', written by German producer Giorgio Moroder and his British collaborator Pete Bellotte – the first synth-led UK number one hit. But despite their growing presence in rock and pop, synths were still sometimes seen as a musical novelty, a perception endorsed by albums like *Moog Party Time* and *Great Hits of the 70s Moog Style*, which featured Moogifications of such classics as 'The Wombling Song' and 'Chirpy Chirpy Cheep Cheep'.

In the US, synthesizers became associated with adventurous Black keyboard prodigies like Stevie Wonder, Herbie Hancock and Billy Preston. Wonder's early seventies records also had a British connection: London-born Malcolm Cecil, who, like several other early electronic experimenters, had trained as a radar engineer while doing his national service with the Royal Air Force. Cecil and his American collaborator Robert Margouleff built their own hybrid synthesizer called TONTO (The Original Neo-Timbral Orchestra) using Moog, ARP and EMS modules combined with other electronic units. It was a gargantuan construction, standing 6 ft tall and stretching out over 20 ft in its semicircular cabinets.

The two men started an electronic duo called Tonto's Expanding Head Band, whose first album, 1971's *Zero Time*, was a landmark in cosmic electronics; a reviewer for Manchester-based underground newspaper *Mole Express* even claimed it was 'possibly the only *true* psychedelic music to emerge so far.'[25] *Zero Time* also impressed Stevie Wonder, who recruited the duo to help him produce a series of albums that offered new directions for soul music, including *Music of My Mind*, *Talking Book* and the magisterial *Innervisions*.

Wonder was fascinated by the possibilities offered by TONTO. 'He was the first person who would really take it to the extreme,' said Cecil, who recalled how the singer told him he wanted to use electronic techniques to create his own idiosyncratic arrangements because, under Motown's production regime, they 'came out nothing like the music I had in my mind.'[26]

In Britain, the advent of the synthesizer allowed non-musicians like Peter Sinfield of King Crimson or Brian Eno of Roxy Music to invent new creative roles, using the EMS VCS3 to electronically process sounds made by other band members. But synthesizers became most closely identified with progressive rock, more specifically with so-called 'keyboard wizards' like Keith Emerson and Rick Wakeman – flamboyant extroverts, sometimes clad in capes, prancing around in front of banks of electronics as they twiddled out as many notes as they could fit into each bar.

British pop had started to ransack jazz and folk music in the late sixties, as bands sought to develop beyond the 7-inch single and *Sgt. Pepper's Lonely Hearts Club Band* convinced them they too could play out a concept over two sides of a vinyl album. Prog rockers took these ambitions much further, delighting in incorporating motifs from the European classical canon. 'Most rock music was based upon the blues and soul music, and to some extent country and western, gospel. Whereas a lot of progressive music takes its influence from more European roots,' explained Greg Lake of ELP.[27] Prog's top players seemed keen to show off their music's supposed aesthetic superiority to R&B-derived pop, revelling in grandiose displays of musical virtuosity and tricky time signatures. 'We just refused to play anything that sounded anything like a Tin Pan Alley pop song. So if it sounded at all popular, it was out,' said King Crimson's lyricist and occasional VCS3 player, Peter Sinfield. 'It had to be complicated.'[28]

Albums that plundered ancient legends, pastoral fantasias, sword-and-sorcery tropes, science fiction and epic fantasy novels by J. R. R. Tolkein and Mervyn Peake for what Sinfield described as 'an audience of really educated university students' made some prog-rock records targets for mockery, as well as the subsequent contempt of the punks.[29] And yet prog was a genre that valued experimentation, risk-taking and the rejection of banality. Its musicians were quick to adopt new technology – Keith Emerson bought a Moog after he heard Wendy Carlos' classical synth opus *Switched-On Bach*, Carl Palmer was one of the first users of electronic drums, guitarist Robert Fripp of King Crimson pursued a series of innovative projects with Brian Eno, while many other prog bands like Camel and Gentle Giant incorporated Minimoogs, ARPs or VCS3s into their sound. And for a few years in the seventies, prog was immensely popular and sold in massive quantities: bands like Yes, Genesis and ELP all had multiple Top 5 albums.

Most improbable in hindsight was the commercial success of Rick Wakeman's series of faux-classical 'symphonic rock' suites with electronic embellishments – *The Six Wives of Henry VIII*, *Journey to the Centre of the Earth* and *The Myths and Legends of King Arthur and the Knights of the Round Table* – which all became major hits between 1973 and 1975, despite being scorned by critics at the time as exemplars of excess. Wakeman even staged *The Myths and Legends of King Arthur* as an extravaganza on ice at Wembley Arena with an orchestra, a choir and skaters in period costumes acting out the concept.

Born in 1949, Wakeman's first contact with electronic music had come through the BBC Radiophonic Workshop's output for TV and radio. He studied piano at the Royal College of Music and was interested in the experimental work that Stockhausen, Schaeffer and Berio were doing at their studios in Cologne, Paris and Milan, although it didn't motivate him to explore the avant-garde himself. 'I'm very much a melody man and that always comes first with me,' he explains. His first encounter with a Moog synth, also via *Switched-On Bach*, was much more inspirational – Wakeman describes it as 'the equivalent for me of seeing a brand-new colour for the first time.' After dropping out of college, he became a session keyboard player for musicians including David Bowie – he played Mellotron on 'Space Oddity' – before joining Yes and developing a parallel solo career as the pre-eminently ostentatious icon of prog.

Wakeman was happy enough to chuckle self-deprecatingly at some of prog rock's excesses, although he argues now that its keyboard players were highly creative as they had to program their own electronic sounds rather than relying on presets. This meant his sounds came from his own imagination rather than that of an unknown programmer. 'I was able to be a self-contained orchestra, colouring parts of the music that no other instrument could achieve,' he says. He saw prog's ethos as stretching the limits of what was possible at that point in time. 'Simply breaking the rules… but in order to do that, you really must know the rules in the first place.'

Asked whether, in hindsight, he accepts the punks' accusation that prog was self-indulgent, he responds simply: 'Of course it was indulgent – all music is.'

Few women featured in progressive rock bands; among the exceptions were Dagmar Krause, who sang with the distinctly left-field Henry Cow for a while, and Sonja Kristina, lead singer of Curved Air. Despite being objectified as a sex symbol by the music press, Kristina insisted later that rock's male dominance didn't deter her from following her own path. 'I was very much in charge of what I wanted to do, always. There was nobody who dictated to me,' she declared. 'I contributed to the writing… There was no difference in status between all of us [in the band].'[30]

Curved Air were named after Terry Riley's 'A Rainbow in Curved Air'; their keyboard player, Francis Monkman, had taken part in the first performance of Riley's 'In C' in Britain in 1968. For Monkman, like many other musicians in the late sixties, encountering Riley was a transcendent experience: 'I was listening one day to the record of 'A Rainbow in Curved Air' at the college library with the sun streaming in through the windows and thinking that we no longer need Beethoven, which was nonsense of course, but perhaps shows what a revolutionary effect Terry Riley's particular invention of minimalism through repetition had on those fortunate enough to hear it at the time,' he recalled in an interview before his death in 2023.

As with Wakeman, the Radiophonic Workshop had played a key role in Monkman's musical development. 'The *Doctor Who* theme was a revelation; techniques of musique concrète applied in a mainstream and particularly melodic context represented a new crossover,' he said. 'Additionally the background music to the series was of course supplied by "serious" electronic composers such as Tristram Cary, which opened many ears to a whole new range of sonic possibilities.'

Monkman used a VCS3 to process some of the instruments and vocals with Curved Air, whose complex interpretation of rock incorporated avant-garde electronic sounds as well as influences from classical music. The band worked on some tracks for their third album, *Phantasmagoria*, at the EMS studio, using Peter Zinovieff's computer equipment to manipulate Kristina's voice on 'Whose Shoulder are You Looking over Anyway?' and the huge Synthi 100 for Monkman's 'Ultra Vivaldi' track. Monkman was an admirer of Zinovieff, seeing the VCS3 as a kind of portable studio unit capable of 'creating soundscapes from electronic sound sources'. But he was less interested in synths as keyboard instruments. 'I was quite disappointed with the advent of the Minimoog when it became clear that "a keyboard and a few oscillators" was going to be the direction in which synthesizers were headed,' he said.

Kristina recalled how Monkman's dedication to experimentalism and love for the 'shamanistic energies' of 'real out-there cosmic rock jamming' ultimately caused a creative rift with Curved Air violinist Darryl Way, who favoured a more organised and melodic approach. 'Neither really liked the other's direction and sensibilities that much,' she said. 'Darryl did try, but Francis is very idealistic and has his vision of how he wants things to be and he's not one to compromise at all.'[31]

Monkman left the band after *Phantasmagoria* was released. He would later play in the art-rock supergroup 801 with Eno and Phil Manzanera of Roxy Music, and compose the grimily evocative, semi-electronic soundtrack for the 1980 British gangster film *The Long Good Friday*, as well as adding synth to a 1978 Afro-funk album by Nigerian band The Apples, *Mind Twister*. Like Wakeman, he believed the prog years were a period when unusual and sometimes difficult music could gain a large audience and bands had more freedom to experiment: 'I would say "travelling without a map" sums it up very well.'

Indeed, there were some distinctly peculiar records released during the prog era, although few were as odd as Tony McPhee's 'The Hunt', a song from the Groundhogs vocalist's 1973 solo album – a completely deranged nineteen-minute electro-prog track with McPhee declaiming anti-bloodsports, anti-aristocracy lyrics over two ARP synths and a drum machine pumping out an abrasive industrial rhythm.

Equally bizarre were some of the records made by Kingdom Come, a psychedelic prog band led by Arthur Brown, the UFO club veteran known for performing his hit 'Fire' in a flaming helmet. On the hippie-futurist album *Journey* in 1973, Brown's band used a VCS3 and an ARP, a Mellotron and a Theramin; the spindly guitar on the opening track anticipated Cabaret Voltaire's Richard H. Kirk, while the beats were provided by a rudimentary Bentley Rhythm Ace drum machine.

'There was a great love of free expression in that band, and the way that it came together was through the spirit of being open to whatever might come,' Brown recalls. 'We'd had a series of drummers but it didn't really work out, and so we just thought, "Let's do something different." So the idea of the drum machine came in, and I said, "Right, I'll play it, I'll control the rhythm and we'll do without a drummer".'

Primitive, non-programmable drum machines with basic presets had been on the market for a couple of decades by this time, and Brown's Kingdom Come were hardly the only band using one: Sly and the Family Stone, Kraftwerk and Cluster were all recording tracks without drummers, while Bee Gee Robin Gibb's melodramatic ballad 'Saved by the Bell' was one of the first British hits to use a rhythm box, a Bentley Rhythm Ace again, in 1969. (The Bee Gees later even marketed their own novelty drum machine-synth mini-unit, the Mattel-built Bee Gees Rhythm Machine, which Kraftwerk would actually use on 1981's 'Pocket Calculator', alongside a Stylophone). Drum machines were becoming increasingly popular despite an attempt in 1967 by the Musicians' Union to get its members to boycott them, arguing that they were a 'danger to the profession', and that up-and-coming percussionists were under threat from 'the competition of the robot'.[32]

Brown, who later went on to contribute his theatrical vocals to several records by German *kosmische* synth maestro Klaus Schulze, thought the beatbox could work as a distinctive feature and helped him capture 'that feeling of something from the future' on the *Journey* album. 'It was at once totally limiting and totally freeing,' he says. 'Once you accepted the limitations of the machine, it was great – a new way of expressing your feelings and finding new patterns.' But he found the Bentley Rhythm Ace could sometimes be as unpredictable as a human drummer. 'One night we were playing in the Marquee Club, it was a very hot night and everybody was sweating and so it started to drip from the ceiling. It dripped into the drum machine and its patterns started to jump, it went off on its own and we had to follow it, improvising for the whole set with me making up lyrics. The audience loved it.'

Some of Brown's fellow denizens of UFO had also been exploring electronic techniques: The Soft Machine did an experimental collaborative session with Delia Derbyshire, Brian Hodgson and Paddy Kingsland at the BBC Radiophonic Workshop in 1970, using a VCS3 to create a gloriously tripped-out version of their instrumental track 'Eamonn Andrews'.

Another was The Who's Pete Townshend, who got his own VCS3 in 1970 as he sought new directions after the success of the rock opera *Tommy*, worrying that the band was becoming 'a cartoon of itself'.[33] Composer Tim Souster, who later in the decade created music for *The Hitchhikers Guide to the Galaxy* on BBC Radio 4, introduced Townshend to musicians like Stockhausen as he tried to recapture the experimental mindset of his days as an art student, making electronic demos for a dystopian SF song cycle called *Lifehouse*. 'I envisaged the practical integration of synthesizers into the regular rock-band format. I imagined The Who playing along with rhythmic synthesizer sounds, or pre-prepared backing tracks on tape,' Townshend wrote in his autobiography.[34]

The project was abandoned and the songs channelled into the *Who's Next* album instead, but Townshend's experiment with feeding a Lowrey organ through his VCS3 did create the swirling rhythmic sequence that The Who locked into and followed through 'Won't Get Fooled Again', making the track something more than a fist-in-the-air rocker. He also said the synthetic ostinato introduction to 'Baba O'Riley' emerged from 'experiments I'd been doing with tapes and synthesizers', inspired by the minimalist composer Terry Riley and made using a repeating marimba sequence on the Lowrey.[35]

Townshend saw himself as an innovator; his website would later describe him as a 'pioneer of electronic music' and recount how he had used electronics for a lot of his preparatory work on The Who's *Quadrophenia* album and for the soundtrack for Ken Russell's film of *Tommy*, creating pseudo-horns and strings but also stylised 'natural' effects. 'The synthesizer was used for all kinds of things; the planes flying at the beginning, the explosions, even [actor] Oliver Reed singing,' Townshend explained.[36] His raw demos for tracks like 'Wizardry' sounded like psychedelic electronica and only had faint hints of The Who's thunderous rock dynamic. The guitarist was so enamoured with his electronic devices that he even appeared, looking singularly bug-eyed, in advertisements for ARP synths that proclaimed: 'Who wrote the first ARP opera? None other than Pete Townshend.'

The album that overshadowed most others in the mid-seventies, in commercial terms at least, was also deeply textured with synthetically-generated sounds: UFO alumni Pink Floyd's *The Dark Side of the Moon*. The band had first used a synthesizer on the title track of 1972's *Obscured by Clouds*, with its sweeping VCS3 drones and slow-rolling pre-'Autobahn' motorik groove, but *The Dark Side of the Moon* was a step beyond their previous work with its deft merging of experimental techniques and rock music. Musique concrète methods were used to create the brief opening track, 'Speak to Me', with its voices speaking of madness reminiscent of Delia Derbyshire's *Inventions for Radio*, while engineer Alan Parsons' collage of recordings of clocks ticking and chiming embellished 'Time' and a loop of coins jingling, paper ripping and cash registers clanging formed the rhythmic undertow for 'Money'.

The soaring Minimoogs on 'Any Colour You Like' and the frenetic whirling of the EMS Synthi AKS on 'On the Run', in which Philip Glass heard echoes of his electric minimalist style, added a sheen of modernity without being modish gimmicks. *The Dark Side of the Moon* was first and foremost an album of rock songs, but the electronics gave it an anomic, otherworldly feeling that propelled the music beyond the earth's atmosphere and out into that lunar blackness.

After *The Dark Side of the Moon*, Pink Floyd did some work on a proposed musique concrète album tentatively called *Household Objects*, which was to have been made up of found sounds. 'We investigated the domestic sound world in a variety of ways: percussion was created by sawing wood, slamming down hammers of different sizes or thudding axes into tree trunks,' said Nick Mason. 'For the bass notes we clamped and plucked rubber bands, and then slowed the resulting sounds to lower tape speeds. Like some adult playgroup we set about breaking light bulbs and stroking wine glasses, and indulged in various forms of water play including stirring bowls of water before pouring them into buckets. We unrolled lengths of adhesive tape, sprayed aerosols, plucked egg slicers and tapped wine bottle tops.'[37] Although they abandoned the *Household Objects* project, a looped recording of wine glasses, embellished with synthesizers and organ, did form the basis for the introduction to their next record, *Wish You Were Here*.

By this time, in 1975, synthesizers were being widely used in rock music – from the space-gazing, post-Beatles orchestral pop of ELO, augmented by Richard Tandy's synth stylings, to 10cc's 'I'm Not in Love', with its tape-looped voices and Moog. Electronics were already in vogue in dance music too: in Munich, Hertfordshire-born producer Pete Bellotte and his partner Giorgio Moroder produced a libidinous marathon of a Euro-disco track called 'Love to Love to You Baby' for singer Donna Summer.

Bellotte later recalled that they only used a drum machine on the record because the drummer couldn't keep time. 'I'd gone to a lot of clubs where these peculiar Italian bands played a schmaltzy kind of music and they used to have this little drum machine where, if you just pressed a button, it would

87

play a samba, or if you pressed another button it would play a waltz. It was very basic and it had a horrible sound, but of course it played in time, so we sent out for one and we laid that down as a track,' he said.[38]

Over in the US, Casablanca Records boss Neil Bogart fell in lust with the record. 'Bogart was having an orgy at his house, there was a lot of coke going on and, to use his own language, they were all "fucking to this track" and the crowd there had him replay the song over and over again,' said Bellotte.[39] Bogart told them to make the song as long as they could; their sixteen-minute-plus remixed version, with Summer simulating over twenty orgasms, became a scandalous sensation of a hit. But even as Moroder and Bellotte began to make records that would shape the electronic music of the 1980s, there was a lot of creative energy left in the graduates of the 1960s underground.

Live from Planet Gong

'In terms of psychedelic bands, Gong were definitely the real deal.'
Steve Hillage

Daevid Allen left Melbourne at the start of the sixties to escape conservative Australia and live out his Beat Generation fantasies. He moved to Paris and

Gong in the early 1970s. ©Michael Ochs Archives/Getty Images.

spent time at the Beat Hotel, where William Burroughs and Brion Gysin were conducting experiments with tape recorders and cut-ups, and took a job distributing newspapers around the city to earn some money. In the French capital he befriended young American avant-garde composer Terry Riley, who also hung out at the Beat Hotel and introduced jazz-head Allen to the potential of tape loops. 'I educated him about musical ideas and he showed me things about the free bohemian life you could lead in Paris,' Riley recalled.[40]

Riley was already moving towards the trance-pulse compositional style he would use for his landmark motorik-minimalist piece 'In C', and the Australian beatnik was fascinated by his ideas about repeating motifs and shifting patterns. 'Terry was my loop guru,' Allen said. 'He played me his piece 'Mescaline Mix' and opened a Pandora's box of possibility for me. Suddenly with two ordinary tape recorders so much was now possible that I wanted to explore.'[41]

Allen began to use his new knowledge to create backing tracks for performances like the 'Machine Poets' event at London's Institute of Contemporary Arts in March 1963, which included 'permutated poems' by Gysin along with Burroughs and Antony Balch's short film, *Towers Open Fire*. 'I composed voice loops containing parts of my poems and sound collages as backing tapes against which I performed live poems,' Allen said.[42] From 1964 onwards, he also recorded a series of collage pieces like 'The Switch Doctor', an intriguing mix of looped and layered voices, tape-manipulated found sounds and spoken-word whimsy.

Allen became a founder member of The Soft Machine, the psychedelic jazz-rockers who named themselves after a Burroughs novel and became underground stars at UFO. But when the band returned from playing in France in 1967, Allen was denied entry to the UK. Returning to Paris, he and his partner, poet and self-styled 'space whisperer' Gilli Smyth, formed a new band, the cosmic prog-jazz ensemble Gong. The band would continue to perform for decades, in a mystifying multitude of incarnations, even after Allen and Smyth's deaths in 2015 and 2016.

Like Hawkwind, Gong developed and chronicled their own acid-warped cosmology – a fantasy universe inhabited by characters like Zero the Hero (essentially Allen himself), Yoni the Witch (Smyth) and the Pot Head Pixies from the Planet Gong. In the second volume of his fantastical and not necessarily wholly reliable memoir of the band, *Gong Dreaming 2*, Allen explained that they specialised in absurdist humour and 'psycho-spiritual space music'.

'We attempted to take our inspiration from Dada, juxtaposing normally incompatible styles, symbols and attitudes in a light-hearted way,' he wrote. 'We felt that as psychedelic shamans we had the potential through our extra terrestrial music to inspire the planet.'[43] He was similarly enlightening about his part in the Gong project: 'I saw my job as tribal scribe, song cyclist, local vocalist, glissando sphere masseur and sound bite truth dentist.'[44]

As Allen's musings might suggest, acid played a significant role in Gong's creative process. 'At appropriate full moon gigs we would ritually imbibe LSD with the focused intention of creating full moon rituals,' he explained. 'These were known as melting feasts where superficial differences could dissolve in an ecstatic trust generated by the shared sensory/spiritual involvement with the music and the costumes and the light projections.'[45]

For 1973's *Flying Teapot*, the first album of their fabulously barmy *Radio Gnome Invisible* trilogy, Gong were joined by two important figures in the development of British electronic music: guitarist Steve Hillage and synthesizer player Tim Blake, an admirer of Delia Derbyshire's BBC work who had moved in the same circles as Hawkwind in London. 'Seeing DikMik going down Tottenham Court Road and picking up loads of [electronic] gear was very inspiring. Hawkwind were using kit totally differently from these classical, "serious" music people,' Blake says. Later in the seventies, he would go on to stage a series of synth-and-laser spectaculars with French light artist Patrice Warrener under the name Crystal Machine, and also become a member of Hawkwind.

Blake recalls that when he first arrived to meet Gong's manager, 'he put a joint in my hand and said: "Smoke *this* and listen to *this*." And he put on [Terry Riley's] *Rainbow in Curved Air*. Now this at the time was pretty mind-shaking music, you know – all those long echoes. And it knocked me out completely and making those long ping-pong stereo echoes became my fascination for a long time afterwards.'

Hillage was one of the most inventive players in prog rock, influenced by the echoing, arpeggiated style of German *kosmische* band Ash Ra Tempel's guitarist Manuel Göttsching and by Riley's hypnotic loops: 'I first heard *Rainbow in Curved Air* played by DJ Jeff Dexter at a concert at the Roundhouse. I was saying, "What's that? That loop, it's fantastic how it's changing as it goes along,"' he remembers. 'It really blew my head off.' Hillage sees Gong as a futuristic band, part of a historical lineage of sonic exploration – a psychedelic continuum – whose credentials as innovators have subsequently been overlooked because of their madcap hippie image.

'I think growing up in the sixties there was a pre-psychedelic electronic ripple effect – things like Joe Meek's 'Telstar', the soundtrack of *Forbidden Planet*, the Radiophonic Workshop and *Doctor Who*, all this stuff was seeping into our consciousness,' he says. 'And then of course you had all this stuff done with studio work like The Beatles with 'Tomorrow Never Knows' and 'Strawberry Fields Forever', and of course 'Good Vibrations', and then what Hendrix was doing with a guitar on songs like 'Third Stone from the Sun'. And when I first went to university, one of my friends had *Switched-On Bach* and we used to listen to that on acid, and then there was Pink Floyd – *A Saucerful of Secrets*, *Ummagumma*…

'I think that all this work with tapes, with echo and with feedback and effects and then the synthesizer, was part of a quest for the psychedelic experience in music; this was the big thing that happened from 1966, 1967 onwards. I mean, once you heard 'Tomorrow Never Knows', you couldn't ever *un*hear it; it changed your whole outlook on music completely.'

In the early seventies, Gong were living communally in a house in a wood near Voisines in France's Bourgogne region, where they could jam together at any time of the day or night, leaf through books about spirituality and the occult, and take acid. 'Let's be frank, [the *Radio Gnome Invisible* trilogy] was probably the result of the psychedelic experience, or of several psychedelic experiences lived collectively,' says Blake, who was sometimes credited on Gong's records by his pseudonym High T. Moonweed.

The trilogy culminated with the recording of *You* in the summer of 1974 in rural Oxfordshire. Allen kept a diary of the sessions and noted that on day eleven, 'a full moon acid drop and ritual jam was essayed.' As the acid took hold, Allen recalled: 'Moonweed's synthi began spiralling soft feedback and the Yoni's spacey whisper began calling from the far distant future'; Hillage's guitar 'pealed with bell tones', and Allen began to rejoice. 'Ecstasy filled my heart,' he exclaimed.[46] The album justified his exultations: from Hillage's relentless, hypnotic 'Om riff' on 'Master Builder' to Blake's sparkling synth pirouettes through 'A Sprinkling of Clouds', *You* was one of the peak moments of psychedelic prog. 'It had elements of trance music – the repetition, the glissandos – and it all was aimed at enhancing and stimulating a psychedelic state of mind,' Hillage confirms.

Hillage's partner, Miquette Giraudy, also joined Gong in time to appear on *You*, initially contributing vocals. Giraudy would go on to play synthesizer with Hillage on his subsequent solo albums and co-write the ambient classic *Rainbow Dome Musick* in 1979; later, in the 1990s, she and the guitarist would found techno duo System 7. She explains that she became interested in electronic music 'because I started taking acid. And this kind of opened my mind about music – first it was my eyes and then it was my ears.'

Giraudy was a former film editor who had acted for director Barbet Schroeder in films like 1972's *La Vallée* (*Obscured by Clouds*), which was soundtracked by Pink Floyd, and had once interviewed Stockhausen for French television. She went to live in Gong's communal house after meeting 'these completely crazy stoned guys' at a studio in Paris: 'I first did some kind of dancing, tambourine, singing, you know, hanging around getting stoned. And then Tim Blake was there with his synth, and that blew my mind. I wanted a synth like Tim Blake.'

With Smyth and Giraudy, Gong were one of the few prog-rock groups to include women in important roles. Even more unusually, they once had a Black British female singer, Diane Stewart, in their stage line-up for a brief period. There were few role models to follow in the seventies, and Giraudy says she wasn't aware of women electronic composers like Éliane Radigue or Suzanne Ciani: 'I didn't know them. I had no idea.' She also says she didn't really consider how atypical her situation was in rock music at the time: 'I was not examining my position as a woman, I was just doing it. I was living it. I was in it. I didn't think about it or intellectualise it. It was just pure heart, you know?'

After the *Radio Gnome Invisible* trilogy, Blake was fired from Gong. Giraudy and Hillage quit soon afterwards, while Allen and Smyth headed off together on their own eccentric trajectory. Although Allen was a hippie fantasist who could be as mercurial and frustrating as he was whimsically entertaining, Hillage says he admired the Australian for his commitment to the freak cause. 'He was holding a torch for pure psychedelia and he gathered around him a disparate band of people all looking for the same thing,' says the guitarist. 'Of course, it was very volatile mix – everyone in the band with strong personalities, and so in a way it was doomed to disintegrate, which it did. But at the same time, the spirit of Gong carried on.'

Gong played at the Glastonbury Fair (a fledgling hippie iteration of the festival) in 1971, alongside David Bowie, Arthur Brown's Kingdom Come and Hawkwind. Nik Turner recalled an event whose organisers were stoked up with idealistic fervour and whose audience was utterly saturated with drugs: 'It was like the entire site had been invaded by an intergalactic carnival of extra-terrestrial beings,'[47] he said.

There was an even more peculiar sight at dawn one day on the festival's pyramid-shaped stage, when avant-garde electro-acoustic ensemble Gentle Fire premiered their 'Group Composition IV': four men gathered around a communal instrument made up of amplified metal grilles and springs that they called the 'gHong'. Photographs from the time show the sun's rays bursting over the silver pyramid and the looming strangeness of the huge gHong. As early-morning revellers sprawled out in the field in front of the performers, the transcendental reverberations of the hybrid contraption's great grilles made it feel like some kind of spiritual ritual was being conducted.

The reason why the ensemble was booked to perform was rather more prosaic, explains Gentle Fire's Richard Bernas: 'How it happened was that someone called from Glastonbury and said, "We've heard that you play electronic stuff." And I said, "Well, we've just come back from Berlin where we played a piece by Stockhausen which was designed to greet aliens from other planets. And they said, "That sounds fun".'

Gentle Fire had formed in 1968 and performed pieces by Cage and Stockhausen alongside their own compositions that used a VCS3 synth, conventional instruments and tape recorders playing odd 'found sounds', as well as ensemble member Hugh Davies' amplified homemade instruments, the shozygs. 'Hugh's shozygs were delightful objects, like a Pandora's box that was amplified and you opened it and touched it and sounds would fly out,' says Bernas.

Gentle Fire was one of several live electro-acoustic or mixed-media ensembles that began operating around the same time in the liberating atmosphere of the late sixties British avant-garde, including Intermodulation, Naked Software, Half Landing and Quiet Pavement Ensemble. 'There was something in the air at that time,' affirms Bernas. 'People from the older generation, like Stockhausen, he had his own performing ensemble which was there to play Stockhausen music. But we knew the Sonic Arts Union from the States, who were connected to [John] Cage, and they were all composers who performed each other's music. And so it seemed sensible that we would form a live electronic music ensemble.'

Andrew Powell of Intermodulation recalls a lot of cross-pollination between classical music, free improvisation and rock. 'This was happening in both directions – several of the avant-garde/underground groups were influenced by electronic music and "loop" techniques as introduced by Terry Riley,' Powell explains. Intermodulation, who were admirers of The Soft Machine as well as Stockhausen, gave their first concert in a geodesic dome outside the Tower of London in 1970, using a sound system installed by The Who's Pete Townshend, who also mixed the show. Intermodulation member Tim Souster, who had worked with Stockhausen, had been helping Townshend with his own electronic music techniques.

At the concert, Intermodulation performed a suite by Souster entitled 'Waste Land Music', interspersed with readings from the T. S. Eliot poem. Powell invited Nick Mason of Pink Floyd to attend: 'He was fascinated by the VCS3s we were using.' Soon the Floyd were using similar synths, notes Powell.

This fertile period in electro-acoustic music enjoyed a peak moment in August 1972 with the International Carnival of Experimental Sound, ICES 72, a sprawling two-week festival of music, performance, visuals, improvisation and electronics at London's Roundhouse that was described by writer Dave Thompson as 'the Woodstock of the avant-garde',[48] bringing together like-minded experimentalists from around the world.

ICES 72 involved hundreds of participants including John Cage, Intermodulation, AMM, Gavin Bryars, Naked Software and Ernest Berk's Dance Theatre Commune, while Penny Rimbaud and Gee Vaucher, later to found anarcho-punk band Crass, performed under the name Exit. 'The festival's ambitions weren't matched by its administrative skills, but it was a very interesting confluence of many, many different tendencies at the time,' recalls Richard Bernas, who performed at the festival with Gentle Fire. 'Very chaotic, but very exciting.'

Stonehenge, Ozric Tentacles and the Strange Tale of Zorch

'The air was thick with acid. At times, when even the announcers on stage were ripped out of their skulls and jabbering like Jabberwocks, the entire joint was connected in one rubber-flow of guitar-lines, energy ley-lines, power lines, telephone lines.'
Rolling Stone review of the 1971 Glastonbury Fair[49]

The first major free festivals of the seventies were Phun City near Worthing, Sussex, in July 1970, organised by anarchist rocker and journalist Mick Farren, followed by the Glastonbury Fair in 1971. The Windsor Free Festival started the following year in the royal park near Windsor Castle, an idea dreamed up by commune-dweller Bill 'Ubi' Dwyer. 'Tripping on acid in Windsor Great Park he had a Blakean vision of a communitarian utopia, which he thought he could bring to life by holding "a giant festival in the grandest park in the kingdom",' according to cultural academic George McKay.[50]

Dwyer's vision of reclaiming land owned by royalty, with its echoes of the 17th-century agrarian-socialist movement known as the Diggers, was inevitably seen as a potential threat to the monarchy, particularly as the annual festival grew in size. Home Secretary Roy Jenkins later wrote in his memoirs that the hippie gathering was 'causing Prince Philip near-apoplexy'.[51]

In 1973, *IT* estimated that 15,000 people came to revel at Windsor. Hawkwind were among dozens of bands to play; there wasn't even a proper stage, so they just let rip in open parkland. 'The festival was permeated throughout with a warm glow as people boogied together, made love, got ripped, prayed and fell over unconscious,' *IT* reported.[52] But the following year, the party was crashed by approximately 600 police officers who launched a savage raid on the Windsor site at around 8 a.m. on August 29, 1974. 'Hundreds of innocent people were hurt as the police randomly and brutally laid into anyone unlucky enough to be in their way. People were dragged from their tents to be treated to a breakfast of boot and abuse,' Penny Rimbaud later recalled.[53] A total of 220 people were arrested; organiser Ubi Dwyer was convicted of 'incitement to commit a public nuisance' and jailed.

A free festival for the summer solstice around the prehistoric monument at Stonehenge also began that year, initiated by a hippie called Phil Russell, alias Wally Hope. 'He wanted to claim back Stonehenge (a place that he regarded as sacred to the people and stolen by the government) and make it a site for free festivals, free music, free space, free minds,' said his friend Rimbaud.[54] By the late seventies there was a full summer itinerary of free festivals around Britain, with hippie travellers moving from one site to the next in convoys of trucks and buses.

'Free festivals were like medieval fayres, with people selling their wares,' said Dave Brock of Hawkwind. 'Everybody would turn up and someone would get a bit of a stage together, get a tarpaulin up, bring a generator. People would be organised but disorganised in a sense. They came together with a camaraderie. Bands would turn up and play.'[55] Hawkwind themselves played unpaid each year, until the brutal police crackdown on travellers at the 'Battle of the Beanfield' in 1985 ended the Stonehenge revels.

For bands like Hawkwind, electronics were always part of a rock-music paradigm, whereas in Germany, Tangerine Dream and Kraftwerk had disconnected from rock'n'roll. The only British band to go full synth in the early seventies was Zorch, a little-known group of psychedelic explorers and free-festival devotees whose name fell into obscurity after they split.

Zorch were formed in 1973 after a teenager called Howard Scarr, who owned one of the EMS Synthi AKS synthesizers that came housed in a portable case, placed an advert in a music paper for 'like-minded synth players to form a sci-fi band'. Scarr, who adopted the alias Gwyo Zepix', got replies from two other youths who also had access to EMS synths. One of them was Basil Brooks, who had discovered electronic instruments through his uncle, classical composer Edward Williams – the owner of a VCS3 he used in film scores and, later, to process orchestral music for his soundtrack to the BBC's landmark natural history series, *Life on Earth*.

Brooks remembers the music press advert somewhat differently. 'Apparently, it said: "Anybody from Planet X wanting to join synthi freak band?" Well, this was in 1973,' he laughs. The trio moved into a cottage in the Surrey countryside owned by Brooks' grandmother, who allowed them to live there rent-free, and, joined by their girlfriends and a guitarist who used an EMS guitar processor called the Synthi Hi-Fli, embarked on a communal life of cosmic music-making, living the hippie dream. 'We would get up at noon or later and start jamming. The music was quite pastoral,' recalls Scarr. 'We used the sequencer of the Synthi AKS for repetitive kind of basslines and floaty, ethereal fast sequences; there was a lot of tape echo as well,' says Brooks.

Wally Hope invited them to play at the first Stonehenge Free Festival in 1974. A remarkable photograph from the time shows Brooks' Synthi set up in front of the venerable stones; ancient and modern standing together. 'In those days, Stonehenge didn't have loads of barbed wire around it. There wasn't any proper stage or anything so we just sort of set up on the grass and played,' Brooks remembers. 'At one point, we had a microphone and were giving it to people and then processing it through the synths with the filters and the echo; obviously, that was quite a novelty in those days. And I don't think it's just New Age hippiness, but for me that location definitely has a certain power there, for sure.' Scarr recalls that one intoxicated onlooker freaked out and attacked an electricity cable, then later wrote a poem denouncing Zorch for their 'demonic role in his bad LSD trip'.

The band also performed at the doomed Windsor Free Festival in 1974, playing from sometime after midnight right into the dawn. They managed to dodge the violent police crackdown and, even more fortuitously, met John Andrews of Acidica Lights, a psychedelic lightshow, and Tony Andrews, an expert in sound system technology. (Tony Andrews would later found the world-renowned companies Turbosound, which supplied rigs for the rave scene, and Funktion One, whose sound systems were used at 21st-century techno clubs like Berghain in Berlin). Both men moved into Zorch's Surrey commune; now the band had their own in-house PA and visual show. 'Our full-range synthesizers through Tony's system were earth-shattering, especially when Basil fired off his bomb sound at the end of the set,' says Scarr.

They also knew an engineer at Peter Zinovieff's EMS studios, who allowed them to use the company's huge and complex Synthi 100 unit to record an album while Zinovieff – who had little time for 'unserious' music – was away on holiday. But despite all their evident fortune, Zorch would never attain popular renown as British electronic pioneers. *Ouroborous*, the album recorded at EMS, was only released as a limited-run cassette. Faced with a lack of gigs and income, Zorch split in 1976; Brooks joined the Steve Hillage Band and Scarr went on to work as a sound designer for synthesizer companies and Hollywood film soundtracks. 'We weren't the most ambitious of musicians,' muses Brooks. 'If a record company maybe had the vision to say, "Yeah, this is interesting," maybe it would have been different. We did what we could.'

As Zorch's story suggests, festivals like Stonehenge provided a forum for the development of the hairier strains of British electronic music – from Hawkwind and Gong to spaced-out bands like Ozric Tentacles, who later gave birth to psychedelic trance outfit Eat Static, and then onwards to outlaw techno collectives like Spiral Tribe, who updated the free-festival format for the nineties rave era.

Ozric Tentacles first came together at Stonehenge in 1983, playing long, proggy jams in front of a campfire, and soon became known for marathon festival sets that sometimes stretched out into six or seven hours of improvisation. 'We'd play all night, occasionally I would wander off and grab a cup of tea while the band did a bit of ambient stuff, then wander back again and carry on for hours,' explains bandleader, guitarist and keyboard player

Ed Wynne. 'There were certain patterns that we were used to jamming on, but in general we were just following the pathways up into the realms.

'Some of it was slightly chemically enhanced, you must understand. That was part of where the inspiration came from to be able to carry on for that long and to keep it interesting because I didn't find psychedelics were a hindrance in those days to my musical capabilities at all. Quite the opposite. If you're a certain kind of person who can actually ride those pathways, you shouldn't be too scared of that, because it can show you a lot and, for me at that time, it formed a whole musical philosophy.'

Ozric Tentacles' recordings, initially released on home-produced cassettes, forged a link between space rock, prog and the coming sounds of psychedelic trance and ethno-ambient electronica: trippy music for festivals, in other words. Out in the fields, under the skies, a looser, freakier style of electronic music seemed to make more sense, as revellers whose mental states had been significantly altered by illicit substances became attuned to stranger noises.

'Once you've got diesel in the generator, plugged it in and heard it start chugging, then you hear the synths start kicking in and you're in the open air and you hear the noises flying across the sky and all those delicious synthy waterfalls pouring out, you just think: "Right! OK! We're on!"' Wynne enthuses.

'It's the most wonderful feeling, electronic music in the open air. It's one of the greatest pleasures of life.'

Roxy Music, Brian Eno and David Bowie

'Pop music isn't primarily about making music in any traditional sense of the word. It's about creating new, imaginary worlds and inviting people to try them out.'
Brian Eno[56]

Erudite theorist and extrovert pop icon, cerebral innovator and glam prankster in make-up – Brian Peter George St John le Baptiste de la Salle Eno, the son of a postal worker, brought up in the post-war years in the little market town of Woodbridge in Suffolk, has exerted a powerful influence on the way that pop music is made, heard and interpreted.

There were two US Army bases near Woodbridge in the fifties, which meant there were cafés with jukeboxes playing Black American R&B, early rock'n'roll and doo-wop tunes for the GIs. The young Brian Eno was captivated by the overwhelming reverberations of Elvis Presley's 'Heartbreak Hotel', by Little Richard's exuberant glossolalia on 'Tutti Frutti', by Chuck Berry, Bo Diddley and doo-wop: 'Magical music... It could have been from another galaxy for all I knew,' he later recalled. 'I was absolutely entranced by it.'[57]

Eno studied at Ipswich School of Art, where he underwent an unconventional teaching programme that involved the study of cybernetics, conceptual processes and psychological game-playing, designed to challenge socialised behaviour and open up the students to contemplating fresh possibilities – a precursor, perhaps, to the Oblique Strategies playing cards he later created to generate ideas at recording sessions. He read John Cage's book *Silence* and was excited by the American composer's idea of incorporating chance events and indeterminacy into music, and by The Velvet Underground's drone-rock and Steve Reich's perception-altering use of repetition on tape-loop pieces like 'It's Gonna Rain'. In 1966, Eno started making music using twin tape recorders; his biographer David Sheppard said his first ever recorded piece was 'the sound of a pen striking the hood of a large anglepoise lamp, multitracked at different speeds to form a shimmering, bell-like cloud of tones, over which a friend read a poem.'[58]

Eno moved on to study at Winchester College of Art, where he staged avant-garde music events and booked composers like Christian Wolff to give lectures. 'When these composers came down, I thought there were so many ideas there that were ripe for plucking. But it worked the other way around as well: for there were so many practical approaches to music that pop musicians knew about, that the avant-gardists didn't,' he remembered. 'A very good example was the fact that pop musicians knew about studios; they knew about recording – they knew that listening to a record was a different experience to a live performance. They realised that the record had to be a distinct, separate and satisfactory experience; it couldn't just be a memento of a performance.'[59]

He deduced that the concerts of experimental music he attended while at college constantly posed the question of what music could be: 'And from it, we concluded that music didn't have to have rhythms, melodies, harmonies, structures, even notes, that it didn't have to involve instruments, musicians and special venues.'[60] It was a lesson that he would apply in the decades that followed as he brought ideas from classical minimalism, Cagean indeterminacy, musique concrète and dub reggae into pop and rock.

A chance meeting on the London Tube in the early seventies, with a musician called Andy Mackay, would prove decisive for his future. 'If I'd walked ten yards further on the platform or missed that train or been in the next carriage I probably would have been an art teacher now,' Eno said later.[61] Saxophonist and oboe player Mackay had also been involved in the sixties avant-garde. He had checked out the scenes at the UFO club and London's Arts Lab alternative culture centre and was involved in Fluxus-style happenings while studying at Reading University; it was at one of them that he first met Eno, who was presenting a tape-delay piece. When they met again on the Tube, Mackay asked Eno to make some recordings of his new group, Roxy Music, and then lent him a VCS3 synthesizer.

Eno started work as Roxy Music's technical assistant; some of the band's rehearsals were held at the communal house where he lived in south London. 'It was fantastic – a maze of wiring, leads, bits of old speakers everywhere, old amps... an Aladdin's Cave of barely held together technology,' said singer Bryan Ferry.[62] Soon Eno was using the VCS3 not only for unusual sound effects, but as a signal processor to manipulate the sound of the band itself, feeding the other players' instruments through the synth to transform the music.

He revelled in the novelty of being a 'synthesizer player', a role which at that point hardly existed in rock music. 'There were no rules for playing synthesizers, so nobody could tell me I couldn't play one,' he would explain. 'Nobody else could play one either. It was an instrument you made up yourself... its role was waiting to be invented.'[63]

Eno the postman's son and Ferry, whose father had looked after pit ponies for his local colliery in County Durham, were both art-school graduates; the singer had studied with Pop Art pioneer Richard Hamilton. In the sixties, state grants enabled many working-class and lower middle-class youths to become the first person in their family's history to study art, and this had a significant impact on pop music. Attracting free thinkers and rebellious spirits, art schools helped to nurture the development of a specifically British pop-culture sensibility. Going to art school connected students not only to the artistic avant-garde, but also to the works of American beatniks and blues players, to European intellectual discourse and the politics of dissent – to new ideas in general, and sometimes to electronic music.

In their book *Art into Pop*, Simon Frith and Howard Horne suggested that art school students who became musicians 'inflected pop music with bohemian dreams and Romantic fantasies'.[64] The ideas that musicians encountered at art school encouraged them to reject the orthodoxies of pop and embrace new formats, styles and technologies, asserting their autonomy by defining

Roxy Music performing at the Royal College Of Art video studio in London in July 1972. ©Brian Cooke/Getty Images.

themselves as 'serious' and 'progressive'; seekers after aesthetic truths. Art schools acted as a conduit for ideas from the avant-garde and the fine arts in general to enter the realm of pop, as art students saw music as a medium within which they could realise the self-expression they had been taught to cherish at college.

Roxy Music was Ferry and Eno's opportunity to turn their art-school ideas into music. 'We wanted to be able to meld our interest in the Fine Arts – particularly Pop Art for Bryan, and contemporary Cage or [Cornelius] Cardew-type music for me – with this amazing vehicle called pop music,' Eno said.[65] The effervescent sleevenotes for the band's self-titled 1972 debut album, *Roxy Music*, describe their sound as 'rock'n'roll juggernauted into demonic electronic supersonic mo-mo-momentum – by a panoplic machine-pile, hifi or scifi who can tell?'[66] Ferry's showily stylised vocals, Eno's VCS3, tapes and echo unit and Mackay's evocative oboe, as well as the theatrical arrangements and oblique lyrics of some of the songs, made it quite unlike most other music being made in Britain: ambitious, provocative, unashamedly arty – but with great tunes.

Roxy's adventurous music and ostentatiously chic image bemused some critics, who described the band as pretentious, over-intellectualised and simply not 'authentic'. Underground newspaper *Oz* described the first album as brilliantly packaged for 'the current frivolous, ambiguous, divinely decadent mood', but took aim at Eno for tracks it said were 'cut at random with ill-considered bursts of synthesized trifles... the ramblings of a self confessed musical illiterate twiddling the knobs.'[67] Indeed, Eno often proudly declared he was non-musician; he sometimes even described himself as an 'anti-musician', although perhaps he was actually a new kind of musician – the electronics controller; the artist-technician.

Like the music, the first Roxy album's cover was determinedly *un*-rock. On the inner sleeve, Eno flaunted flowing locks and a leopardskin-patterned shirt, while Ferry sported an ultra-stylised breaking-wave quiff and a ritzy gold-and-black tiger-striped bomber jacket, like a nightclub crooner on a space station in a Hollywood movie. Mackay looked like some queer fantasy of a renegade teddy boy in satiny black shirt, lavishly pomaded pompadour and gold rings. Their heavily made-up depictions were an implicit challenge to the gender stereotypes of the time, but from a heterosexual perspective; lovers of the synthetic, they were all 'artifice and exaggeration', as Susan Sontag's definition of camp put it.

Eno said they wanted to 'look beautiful, but in ways that men had not thought of looking beautiful before.'[68] He had started experimenting with women's clothes from secondhand shops and jumble sales, and wearing make-up, while at college. His Roxy stage costumes became increasingly outlandish, with peacock feathers and ostrich plumes, leopard-print shirts and gold lamé trousers, fake furs and diamanté chokers. Dedicated fans loved this exaggerated display of outrageousness and would dress to excess for Roxy gigs: the women in pill-box hats, mesh veils, and leopardskin-print dresses, the men in flash suits with floppy fringes.

The political mood of the time was gloomy and pessimistic, so it was perhaps no wonder that people were attracted to the lurid, tinselled distractions of Roxy and their glam-rock contemporaries. The early seventies were dominated by concerns about the IRA's deadly bombing campaign on the British mainland, rising unemployment and widespread strikes, including industrial action by mineworkers that caused power cuts and led Edward Heath's Conservative government to impose a three-day working week to save energy. Amid the turmoil and violence, a state of emergency was declared in Britain five times within a four-year period; it was widely believed that the country was in serious decline, even though the majority of people were more materially comfortable than they ever had been.

But the sexually-ambivalent images projected by the likes of Roxy Music and David Bowie in the early seventies weren't just glamorous diversions; they also liberated fans to venture across the gender divides. Dave Ball, then a teenager in Blackpool, later to form electronic duo Soft Cell, recalled how 'lads wore their mums' and sisters' clothes and make-up' at Bowie and Roxy nights at his local disco.[69] The impact was even more powerful on youngsters who were growing up gay and fearful in a deeply homophobic country, where male homosexuality had only been decriminalised a few years earlier.

By 1972, the gay liberation movement was gaining momentum as *Gay News* magazine was founded and hundreds of people marched through central London at the first official Gay Pride event. This was also the year when Bowie – clad in 'skintight pantsuit, big hair, huge, red plastic boots' – told *Melody Maker*: 'I'm gay and always have been.'[70] Although Bowie was actually bisexual, his comments had huge resonance for those who followed him: 'Bowie gave me the green light to start exploring my own sexuality,' recalled George O'Dowd, later to become Boy George.[71]

Roxy Music's second album, *For Your Pleasure*, was a glittering whirl of retro-futuristic brilliance offering yet more pointers for future art-rock adventurers. But by the time the languidly echoing title track had evaporated into a haze of electronic reverberations, Eno was already moving on. He had started collaborating with King Crimson guitarist Robert Fripp on recordings that would be issued as the album *(No Pussyfooting)*, feeding Fripp's long, fuzzed-out tones through two tape recorders to build layer upon glittering layer of sound. It resembled the 'time lag accumulator' delay-and-feedback system used in the sixties by American composers like Terry Riley and Pauline Oliveros, though the British guitarist called his set-up 'Frippertronics'.

(No Pussyfooting) was a mesmeric suite of drifting cosmic noise, closer to German groups like Cluster or the solo work of Tangerine Dream's Edgar Froese than anything being made in Britain. But Fripp and Eno's live performances, with their loops and liquid guitar set to avant-garde films projected in the darkness, confused and angered some audience members who thought they would be getting some kind of Roxy-meets-King Crimson superduo.

The years that followed saw Eno release a remarkable quartet of solo albums – *Here Come the Warm Jets*, *Taking Tiger Mountain (By Strategy)*, *Another Green World* and *Before and After Science* – the latter two records in particular mapping a series of ideas for possible futures that remained influential way beyond their era. He also made a series of luminous recordings with *kosmische* bands Cluster and Harmonia, later saying how the Germans' approach to electronic music had fascinated him: 'It was a very uncompromising type of music, consciously experimental, and conscious of which particular experiment it was trying to do.'[72]

He argued that the Germans' music was connected to avant-garde classical composers' ideas about electronics and tape manipulation, but that it also showed that 'the interesting electronic music of our time was being done by rock musicians rather than academic composers. Stockhausen was an example of a charismatic theoretician who inspired a lot of people but whose own work is generally unlistenable,' he declared.[73]

Despite his reputation as an experimentalist, Eno was often remarkably dismissive of avant-garde music, once describing it as 'a sort of research music… You're glad someone's done it but you don't necessarily want to listen to it. It's similar to the way I'm very happy people have gone to the North Pole.'[74] He had much warmer words for Jamaican dub producers like King Tubby and Lee 'Scratch' Perry and their imaginative use of echo and space.

In January 1975 there was a turning point in Eno's career, when he had an accident and was ordered to rest; it was then that he encountered the idea for which he is best known: ambient music. 'I was not seriously hurt, but I was confined to bed in a stiff and static position,' he wrote in the sleeve notes for his first ambient album, *Discreet Music*, released later that year. 'My friend Judy Nylon visited me and brought me a record of 18th century harp music. After she had gone, and with some considerable difficulty, I put on the record. Having laid down, I realised that the amplifier was set at an extremely low level, and that one channel of the stereo had failed completely… [it] played on almost inaudibly. This presented what was for me a new way of hearing music – as part of the ambience of the environment just as the colour of the light and the sound of the rain were parts of that ambience.'[75]

He wondered why no music like this was being made – music that 'could be listened to and yet could be ignored', functional music that mingled with the sounds around it. His sleeve notes compared it to French composer Erik Satie's idea of creating 'furniture music' – an unobtrusive sound that would be 'part of the noises of the environment'. Satie had set out his idea back in 1917: 'I think of it as melodious, softening the noises of the knives and forks, not dominating them, not imposing itself.'[76]

Eno's *Discreet Music*, with its gently repeating melodic figures created with a synthesizer and tape loops, was in some ways an heir to Raymond Scott's *Soothing Sounds for Baby* trilogy of proto-ambient albums, intended to lull infants into tranquillity, which the American composer made in the early sixties using electronic instruments he designed himself with names like the Clavivox and the Electronium. But critics dismissed the Eno record as an arty joke, particularly rock writers who already saw him as a pretentious poseur: 'I remember one review that said "this is a music that lacks rhythm, melody, narrative, personality" and I thought "Oh, great! Those are *exactly* all of the things that I want to leave out".'[77]

The sleeve notes for his second ambient album, 1978's *Ambient 1: Music for Airports*, elaborated on his idea of a functional music that is 'as ignorable as it is interesting', while seeking to differentiate it from the syrupy orchestrated sounds produced as aural wallpaper by American company Muzak Inc since the 1950s. 'Ambient music is intended to induce calm and a space to think,' Eno declared – a function further developed by techno-era chill-out DJs like Mixmaster Morris and Alex Paterson of The Orb, who relocated the idea into the context of the rave environment.[78]

Music for Airports was drifting, elegiac, serenely dissociative, intended as a superior alternative to the tedious background music Eno had heard at New York's JFK airport while waiting for a flight. 'I had in my mind this ideal airport where it's late at night; you're sitting there and there are not many people around you: you're just seeing planes take off through the smoked windows,' he explained.[79]

Eno recorded piano improvisations by Robert Wyatt and Rhett Davies, then cut and slowed them down and put them on a series of long tape loops alongside his own minimal synth chords, allowing the melodic elements to interact and reconfigure themselves as the loops rolled and repeated. In 1978, with punk rock still raging, the album's soporific textures infuriated some critics. A *New York Times* reviewer described it as 'avant-garde Muzak… the album nearly sets one asleep with its still, small voice of calm.'[80] A few did get it however; writer Lester Bangs described the record as having 'a crystalline, sun-light-through-windowpane quality that makes it somewhat mesmerising even as you only half-listen to it.'[81] It was eventually even played in several airports, including New York's LaGuardia, and over the years its stature grew, particularly after the emergence of techno, until it came to be seen as a classic.

Ambient music, as Eno originally shaped it, was a musical style as well as a concept – there were delicate, Satie-like piano phrases, washes of warm electronics and indistinct, heavily reverbed sounds gently repeating. He said he wanted to make an immersive sonic environment – 'music to swim in, to float in, to get lost inside.'[82] At around the same time, New Age composers like Stephen Halpern started releasing similarly uneventful yet melodic electronic music designed for meditation, yoga and other spiritual practices, but ambient musicians like Eno felt no common cause with makers of sounds they considered banal. 'When I hear the words New Age, I reach for my gun,' quipped Harold Budd, who collaborated with Eno on *Ambient 2: The Plateaux of Mirror*.[83]

Nevertheless, ambient music itself would eventually become a stylistic staple in the online streaming era of 'peaceful' or 'relaxing' mood lists on Spotify and other platforms that attracted millions of listeners – a cliché of reverberating piano tones, dreamy waves of synthetic sound and wildlife noises; what writer and musician David Toop called 'industry ambient', the Muzak of the 21st century. But this was hardly Eno's doing; his music was not all weightless wisps – *Ambient 4: On Land*, with its crepuscular textures reminiscent of drizzle-swept afternoons and foggy marshlands, hinted at the post-industrial sound of 'dark ambient' with its ominous drones and rumblings.

In 1976 came another crucial moment for Eno, and for British electronic music, when David Bowie called to ask if he would do some production work on a partly-finished album, the first in what would become known as his 'Berlin Trilogy'. Initially the idea was for Eno to add a sheeny lacquer of synthesizer in the style of *Discreet Music* and the ambient tracks on *Another Green World*, both albums that Bowie loved.

The singer had been listening to German electronic and *kosmische* bands, and had already recorded some sessions using synthesizers and drum machines with arranger Paul Buckmaster on a never-finished soundtrack for Nicolas Roeg's film *The Man Who Fell to Earth*, reportedly inspired by Kraftwerk's *Radio-Activity* album and the motorik rhythms of Neu!, 'I was completely seduced by the setting of the aggressive guitar-drone against the almost-but-not-quite robotic/machine drumming of [Klaus] Dinger,' Bowie said.[84]

Before embarking upon *Low*, he had been living in Los Angeles and had become addicted to cocaine, experiencing psychotic episodes, paranoid delusions and messianic fantasies, obsessing over the occult and raving about Hitler and how Britain needed a fascist regime. 'Adolf Hitler was one of the first rock stars,' he declared in one interview.[85] Bowie later admitted he had basically gone mad: 'I was out of my mind totally, completely crazed.'[86]

His move to Berlin in 1976 offered a new start and a chance to develop a new sound that incorporated what he had heard in Kraftwerk, particularly their rejection of American rock stereotypes for 'European' sonic aesthetics – but using human musicians instead. 'Kraftwerk's percussion sound was produced electronically, rigid in tempo, unmoving. Ours was the mangled treatment of a powerfully emotive drummer, Dennis Davis,' he explained. 'Kraftwerk supported that unyielding machine-like beat with all synthetic sound-generating sources. We used an R&B band. Since [1976 album] *Station to Station* the hybridisation of R&B and electronics had been a goal of mine.'[87] The locomotive-simulating sound effects that opened the title track on *Station to Station* hinted at how this idea could be developed.

Bowie had already used synthesizers and a drum machine before Eno was hired to work on *Low*, while he was co-writing and producing Iggy Pop's *The Idiot*, a stark and moody piece of electronically-textured gutter-rock whose sound the singer is claimed to have described as 'James Brown meets Kraftwerk'. Eno came into the *Low* sessions with his own agenda and ended up part-creating tracks like the rainswept, melancholic 'Warszawa'. 'I was pushing for all this strange instrumental stuff and for the sound to be radical in some way, all nervy and electronic,' he said.[88] Another transformative input was hearing Donna Summer's 'I Feel Love' for the first time; Bowie recalled how Eno came running in with a copy of the motorik disco record and declared excitedly: 'I have heard the sound of the future.'[89]

But it was producer Tony Visconti who brought the electronic device that would create *Low*'s remarkable shattered-metal drum sound – an Eventide Harmonizer, an early digital effects processor which could record sounds and play them back simultaneously at a different pitch. Visconti said he initially told Bowie it could create noises that he had never heard before. When Bowie asked how, Visconti responded: 'Well, it fucks with the fabric of time.'[90]

In his autobiography, Visconti recounted how he would send a feed from the snare drum microphone to the Harmonizer, drop the pitch by a semitone then add feedback from the drum to the original sound. 'In simple terms it means a very deep snare sound that keeps cascading downwards in pitch; the initial impact had the "crack" but then the "thud" never seemed to stop, and, not only did it go on at length, but it got deeper and deeper in pitch, kind of like the sound a man makes when he gets punched in the stomach,' he explained.[91] Stephen Morris of Joy Division was just one of the young post-punk drummers who later pestered studio engineers to try to copy it.

The anthemic title track of Bowie's subsequent album, *"Heroes"*, was one of the peak moments of the Berlin Trilogy, incorporating Eno, guest player Robert Fripp and an EMS Synthi to treat Fripp's feedback-embellished guitar sound, which created the levitating electroglide that drifts and surges through the song. It was the result of a sublime piece of serendipity: after Fripp had recorded several guitar takes, Visconti decided to play them back simultaneously, one on top of the other, to see how they interacted. 'It got a quality that none of us anticipated. It was this dreamy, wailing quality, an almost crying sound in the background. And we were just flabbergasted,' Visconti recalled. 'We just looked at each other and we just couldn't believe our luck, how beautiful it sounded.'[92]

'Tomorrow belongs to those who can hear it coming,' declared the press advertisement for *"Heroes"*. Bowie and Eno had certainly perceived that the future would be electronic, even at a time when synthesizers were still regarded as unacceptably 'inauthentic' by some rock bands. (Queen even stated on several album sleeves in the seventies that no synths were used on the record, although by 1980 they were deploying an Oberheim OB-X to fine effect on *The Game*). Just as The Beatles and George Martin had introduced ideas from musique concrète into pop in the sixties, Bowie's Berlin Trilogy helped to bring synthesizers into the aural language of Anglo-American alternative rock, laying out ideas that would soon be followed up by Ultravox, The Human League, Gary Numan, Joy Division, Simple Minds and many others.

'For whatever reason, for whatever confluence of circumstances, Tony, Brian and I created a powerful, anguished, sometimes euphoric language of sounds,' Bowie said many years later. 'Nothing else sounded like those albums. Nothing else came close.'[93]

The Afterlife of Delia Derbyshire
'I did all sorts of things I was told I couldn't do.'
Delia Derbyshire[94]

British television in the 1970s provided an abundance of science-fiction programming for children, some of it dark and frankly disturbing. As well as *Doctor Who*, there was *The Tomorrow People*, *Space: 1999*, *Blake's 7*, *The*

Boy from Space, *Children of the Stones* – many of which featured electronic soundtracks or used library recordings by composers like Delia Derbyshire, Brian Hodgson, Barry Gray and Dudley Simpson. The eerie atmospheres and unsettling otherworldliness of this music for seventies children's dramas and public information films would recur in the 21st century as spectral, blurrily-recalled memories in the work of electronic musicians like Boards of Canada and The Focus Group, a musical aesthetic that would become known as 'hauntology'.

But while the seventies were a creative 'second golden age' for the BBC Radiophonic Workshop, as Louis Niebur wrote in *Special Sound*, his excellent history of the unit, the decade proved difficult for some of the veterans of its first peak period.[95] The introduction of synthesizers signalled the beginning of the end of the tape-splicing era; compositions could now be completed much more quickly and efficiently, and synth keyboards shifted the focus towards more traditional melodic forms and away from avant-garde abstraction.

The Workshop's razorblade virtuosos, Delia Derbyshire and John Baker, struggled to adapt and became increasingly frustrated as programme producers expected work to be delivered more quickly. The space for musique concrète tinkering shrank and the Workshop increasingly became a production house rather than the experimental research unit Derbyshire had loved.

'You did need ages with the tape techniques but when synthesizers arrived, you could whack things out much more quickly and I think Delia felt slightly concerned about that,' says her former Radiophonic Workshop colleague Paddy Kingsland. 'She was highly original and she wanted to do things her way, and I think wasn't always possible to do that. Things were changing – in broadcasting, things change a hell of a lot very quickly. And the way people made shows, it was getting faster and faster. So Delia, I think, found this very daunting.'

Derbyshire decided to leave the Workshop in 1973; she later said she quit because she was unhappy with how BBC managers were handling her work: 'I didn't want to compromise my integrity any further. I was fed up with having my stuff turned down because it was too sophisticated... they were dead scared of anything that was a bit unusual.'[96] She was due to start working with her Workshop friend and former White Noise bandmate Brian Hodgson at his newly-established Electrophon studios in London, where he made synth-prog albums *Where are We Captain?* and *New Atlantis* with collaborator John Lewis under the name Wavemaker, but ultimately decided not to get involved.

In the mid-1970s, Derbyshire left London and moved to a village in Cumbria, where she was employed for a while as a radio operator on a gas pipeline project. But contrary to the perception that she gave up all creative activity and entered a tragic alcoholic-depressive spiral of decline when she quit the BBC, she was involved in various collaborative art projects over the decade.

'The years weren't lost,' says Hodgson. As well as making atmospheric ambient soundtracks for films by artists Madelon Hooykaas and Elsa Stansfield and collaborating on a resonant score for an experimental documentary by Elisabeth Kozmian, Derbyshire worked as an assistant to innovative Chinese abstract artist Li Yuan-chia at his LYC Museum & Art Gallery in a remote location near Hadrian's Wall.

In the late 1990s, she was contacted by Pete Kember, alias Sonic Boom, former singer and guitarist with neo-psychedelic band Spacemen 3, and another musical collaboration began. 'She taught me pretty much everything I know about the physics of sound,' Kember said.[97] They recorded a short track together called 'Synchrondipity Machine (From an Unfinished Dream)' and were planning on doing more. 'Working with people like Sonic Boom on pure electronic music has re-invigorated me,' Derbyshire said at the time. 'Now without the constraints of doing "applied music", my mind can fly free and pick up where I left off.'[98]

But the alliance was brief. In 2001, Derbyshire died of renal failure in hospital in Northampton. She left behind her a hoard of cereal boxes containing a total of 267 reels of tape, which included music produced for the BBC and as a freelancer. Kember said that even just before her death, she was still excited by new ideas: 'In fact, her last project was looking into the musical possibilities in shapeshifting alloys,' he wrote in a letter to *The Wire*.[99]

After her death, Derbyshire was harshly traduced by several newspapers. *The Times* described her as 'the godmother of modern electronic dance music' but also as a 'hopeless alcoholic' who 'lived in relative obscurity and would rail, between drinks, against her lack of critical recognition.'[100] A feature in *The Mail on Sunday* plotted a grubby narrative that took her from being a sexually-alluring, Biba-clad musical genius in the sixties, an 'unsung heroine to generations of British children' for her *Doctor Who* theme, to 'a victim of her own excess and weakness' in her later years, 'her body wrecked by alcoholism, her good looks all but obliterated.'[101]

In the years that followed, however, her historical stature grew steadily as her importance to electronic music in Britain became more widely understood. With documentary films, academic papers, compilations of old recordings, musical tributes by admirers like Cosey Fanni Tutti, the WikiDelia information portal, the Electronic Church of St Delia page on Facebook, a dedicated archive of personal documents and tapes at the University of Manchester, and an annual Delia Derbyshire Day event, she became a totemic figure, exalted for what she achieved within a male-dominated musical-technical culture and a working environment characterised by institutionalised sexism.

'She can be recognised as a figure of empowerment for women musicians, a representative of a period of modernist popular culture, a technological innovator, and a progenitor for British EDM [electronic dance music],' wrote journalist and academic Frances Morgan. 'Her work and what we know of her life allow for all these interpretations.'[102]

Archive photographs of the coolly confident, black-clad Derbyshire splicing tape amidst stacks of oscillators and tape machines in the Workshop studio projected an inspirational power; the music she made and the life she lived would have an enduring impact.

'When I started out making electronic music I felt like a kind of lone warrior, or like Delia said, like the one fish swimming the other way,' says Caro C, an electronic musician and sound engineer who co-founded Delia Derbyshire Day. 'Then I discovered Delia and Daphne Oram and I realised they were making this weird and wonderful music decades before me, and suddenly I felt I was part of this lineage.'

Cabaret Voltaire in 1981. Photo courtesy of Mute Records.

4
THIS IS ENTERTAINMENT
Industrial Music and Post-Punk Futurism

Cabaret Voltaire, Electronic Dadaists
'We were fascinated by the idea of Dada and its irreverence. It wasn't just an art movement, it was about the exhibitionism, it was about the spectacle, it was about the statements, it was about the shock of it all.'
Stephen Mallinder

IN A PHOTOGRAPH TAKEN IN 1975 IN AN ATTIC IN SHEFFIELD, they look like spindly young deviants from an English pulp novel, faces stark white against black shadows thrown by harsh light: Stephen Mallinder lolling Roxyesque in a dark shirt, pale skinny tie and winklepickers; Richard H. Kirk in a shiny PVC jacket, staring curiously into the camera like a glam-rock misfit; Chris Watson loitering watchfully beside them, the technical fixer in jeans and plimsolls.

It was here, in this cramped loft space at Watson's parents' house, from 1973 onwards, that the three members of Cabaret Voltaire would gather in the evenings to record electro-acoustic collages. 'It was a real kind of junk shop aesthetic, because synthesizers cost a fortune in those days,' remembers Mallinder. 'Me and Richard had a junk shop bass and guitar. Chris was a telephone engineer so he had some practical soldering skills and I got him to build me a fuzzbox from *Practical Electronics* magazine. We got a Copicat delay unit, and Chris built a really primitive synth. Richard had a clarinet, I think because he couldn't afford an oboe like Andy Mackay of Roxy Music had.'

Sounds and voices were recorded from the television or outside on the street, cut up and manipulated: 'It was extremely raw, messy. We'd buy secondhand tape recorders we'd find in [classified advertising newspaper] *Exchange and Mart*, I remember having to carry up to the loft an ex-government reel-to-reel tape recorder which weighed an absolute ton. Those tape recorders were used as more of an instrument, and we'd make little loops and bounce them around. So it wasn't so much electronic but more experimental and built around magnetic tape as a tool to manipulate sound.'

Watson had been cutting and splicing tape since he was given a reel-to-reel recorder as a schoolboy and heard a Pierre Schaeffer piece on BBC Radio 3: 'I realised I could play things backwards, and at different speeds, and be transported into the science-fiction worlds that I was watching on television.' He also acquired a copy of Terence Dwyer's musique concrète guide for beginners, *Composing with Tape Recorders*. 'That was my bible, my manual,' he said. 'That and the tape recorder, the razor blade, the editing block and a microphone – they were my instruments.'[1]

Amid the political and economic chaos of the early seventies, some British pop bands – The Rubettes, Mud, Showaddywaddy – harked back to the perceived golden era of the fifties, while glam rockers like Slade and Sweet lived for the moment, revelling in garish theatricality. Others – David Bowie, Roxy Music – set their eyes on the future. One of the factors that initially drew Kirk, Mallinder and Watson together was seeing Roxy play in Sheffield in 1972; Eno with his VCS3 and his idea that non-musicians could create sonic art excited them.

'I think Eno was our common bond in terms of electronics and processing and technology. He was like a lightning rod for a lot of people,' says Mallinder. 'Before Eno, the technology was inside studios, so these weird techniques happened in another world, but Eno brought it on stage, he showed that this was a tool that people could use.' Watson would soon acquire his own EMS Synthi AKS, as well as a basic Farfisa drum machine and an organ whose melodramatic tones he would exaggerate by playing them through effects units.

Cabaret Voltaire were one of a handful of electronic and electro-acoustic bands that emerged from Britain's post-sixties, pre-punk alternative culture, as the ideas of a self-sustaining non-mainstream culture grew out of the hippie underground through an informal network of alternative arts spaces, community centres and radical bookshops that proliferated across the country in the early seventies.

The trio developed DIY methodologies that picked up on ideas aired in the music press by people like Eno, but were also informed by arthouse films, 'transgressive' literature and early 20th-century movements like Surrealism and Dada. They took their name from an art nightclub that operated in 1916 in Zürich, the Cabaret Voltaire, where absurdist performances and politically provocative happenings were staged. This was where the Dada movement took shape, partly in reaction to the brutal insanity of World War I. 'We couldn't believe that people were getting up to this stuff in the early part of the 20th century, when it would have been genuinely outrageous and clearly unique,' explained Watson. 'I loved the humour and I loved the darkness of it as well.'[2]

Sheffield's Cabaret Voltaire set out to cause outrage too; the young trio would take their attic recordings and play them from the back of a van while driving around the city, or blast them out in local pubs, on the street or even in public toilets to get a reaction. The street playback, intended as a sonic rip in the fabric of normality, was one of the strategies propagated by William Burroughs. The American writer had inspired Paul McCartney to experiment with reel-to-reel recorders in the sixties and would now exert a defining influence over the industrial music genre, with his ideas about tape manipulation and the cut-up technique as tools of subversion and resistance to social control mechanisms.

Burroughs' thinking was shaped by his outsider status as a gay drug user in 1950s America, when homosexuality was seen as a disease. His iconisation as a 'literary outlaw' has increasingly been seen as problematic because of the allegedly accidental shooting of his wife, Joan Vollmer, but his books and ideas enthralled bright young non-conformists in the socially conservative 1970s. Like Kirk, Mallinder and Watson, many were introduced to Burroughs through Bowie's references to the cut-up technique in interviews; some also heard about his work via proto-punk art-rock band Doctors of Madness, who sometimes opened their shows with a reading from *The Naked Lunch*.

Kirk said he started using cut-ups after discovering that Dadaist artist Tristan Tzara created poems by putting words into a paper bag and pulling them out at random; Burroughs then showed how the technique could disrupt literary orthodoxy. 'I thought the idea of applying that to music might make it jump forward in the way that Burroughs had done with words,' Kirk said. 'To do it with sounds and noises is what Cabaret Voltaire started to do originally.'[3]

Cabaret Voltaire were aware of the classical avant-garde but were more interested in rhythm and repetition; Kirk and Mallinder had grown up listening to Motown and Stax and used to go out dancing to soul, ska and early reggae as teenagers rather than sitting at home contemplating the works of Cage and Berio. An insistent pulsebeat was central to their sound, although everything around it was treated, processed, manipulated, distorted – Kirk's creeping, insect-like guitar lines; Mallinder's darkly expressionistic vocals; Watson's sinister keyboards and the agitated voices they taped from TV and radio to provide the strangeness, menace and paranoid unease they sought to convey.

Cabaret Voltaire also loved the deep space textures of Jamaican dub and the trebly, scratchy guitars of The Velvet Underground and sixties psych-rock bands like The Seeds. Like other alternatively-minded young musicians of their generation – Stephen Morris of Joy Division, John Lydon of PiL, Pete Shelley of Buzzcocks, Colin Newman of Wire, Youth and Geordie of Killing Joke – they loved Hawkwind, too. Kirk once described the self-proclaimed 'sonic assassins' as 'probably the nearest we got to Krautrock in England... On *Space Ritual*, they'd have these wonderful moments where there'd be no drums, and you'd just hear electronics and somebody delivering a monologue over the top, and that was very similar to the early Cabaret Voltaire recordings.'[4]

Significantly, Cabaret Voltaire came from the first generation to grow up with electronic music around them. Mallinder dates his influences back to early childhood and a radio series called *Sparky's Magic Piano*, starring a piano that talked back to a small boy in an unsettling, Vocoder-like voice. It was generated by a device called the Sonovox, which picked up vocal sounds from the human throat using transducers. 'It was this weird electronic voice that was somehow "not quite right", and it fascinated me,' he says.

Before they got their Synthi AKS, the technically-adept Watson had built a synthesizer from a kit advertised by the Dorset-based Dewtron company in *Practical Electronics*, a DIY monthly that published construction tips for amateurs as well as articles by the indefatigable champion of the electronic tinkerers, F. C. Judd. The tape-recorder hobbyist craze was waning by the end of the sixties, so *Practical Electronics* had started to print circuit diagrams to help its readers build their own synthesizers – although this was a far harder task than splicing tape. In 1973, the magazine began publishing blueprints for the construction of a low-budget kit synth called the PE Sound Synthesizer, for enthusiasts to build at home from scratch, and for the smaller, brightly-coloured, stylus-operated PE Minisonic. It also printed a score for an electronic piece by composer Malcolm Pointon, designed to be played on the Minisonic; Pointon's own rendition sounded like a rough-and-ready demo of a Radiophonic Workshop soundtrack for *Doctor Who*.

The articles in *Practical Electronics* had the earnest tone of the shed-pottering suburban amateur, but the magazine promoted a self-build philosophy that served to inform aspiring electronic musicians. As well as Chris Watson, its readers included Chris Carter and Bernard Sumner, later of Throbbing Gristle and Joy Division, who would use the knowledge they gleaned in the recordings they would make later in the seventies.

Cabaret Voltaire's first live show was an intentionally provocative performance at Sheffield University in 1975, which ended with infuriated members of the audience attacking the band. 'I had a tape of a steam hammer that we'd recorded,' recalled Watson. 'We made a percussion loop out of it, it was pretty hardcore, it was great. [The gig] ended in complete chaos, a proper Cabaret Voltaire, Dadaist happening, people got really pissed off, it got violent.'[5]

It was not the last time their electro-acoustic Dadaism would spark violence; at their first London gig during the punk era, supporting Buzzcocks, they were showered with plastic pint-pots. (Live electronics still seemed offensive to some rock fans in the seventies, particularly fundamentalist punks who identified synths with prog and would accept nothing but fast, guitar-driven rock'n'roll. When New York electronic duo Suicide supported The Clash on tour in the UK in 1978, they were bombarded by beer glasses, flaming toilet-rolls and other projectiles).

In the seventies, Cabaret Voltaire's Sheffield hometown was a proudly working-class, socialist city that had prospered through steelmaking; the awesome pounding of the steelworks' huge drop hammers could still be heard resounding through the night, although the slow and painful decline of South Yorkshire's steel and coal industries had already begun and would accelerate under Conservative Party rule in the eighties. But the abandonment of redundant industrial premises offered other possibilities; Cabaret Voltaire set up their Western Works studio at a former factory space in Sheffield city centre, where they recorded their early albums as well as sessions for many other left-field musicians of the era, including 23 Skidoo and Eric Random, who made his post-punk electronic classic *That's What I Like About Me* at the studio with Mallinder producing.

Western Works continued to be a cultural hub nurturing Sheffield's alternative music-makers right up into the techno era. Sheffield DJ Parrot, who would make a series of important records with Kirk as Sweet Exorcist, says Cabaret Voltaire consistently sought to encourage 'anyone in the town that was trying to do something different' and 'made themselves and the Western Works available to try interesting ideas out'. Kirk described Western Works as 'Andy Warhol's Factory on a fifty pence budget'.[6]

When punk first erupted, Cabaret Voltaire were stirred by its irreverent attitude. In an interview in February 1977, Kirk hailed the Sex Pistols' 'raw energy': 'Any change is good news,' he declared.[7] But ultimately they found punk a musical disappointment: 'It was still guitar, bass and drums, following an established format, and we were more interested in challenging the established format,' says Mallinder. They were not alone: the cultural energies unleashed by punk would inspire musicians and non-musicians alike to reject the rock-band template and experiment with styles, formats, unorthodox techniques and novel sonic strategies as part of the amorphous cultural movement later codified as post-punk.

The records that Cabaret Voltaire released as a trio in the period from 1979 to 1982 – including their thrilling first three albums *Mix-Up*, *The Voice of America* and *Red Mecca* – were urgent, neurotic, often fearsome sonic despatches full of spooked minimalist rhythms, rasping industrial dub and surging torrents of electronically-mutated garage-band riffing, layered with Mallinder's disjointed declamations, Watson's disruptively garish organ tones, the eldritch wail of Kirk's treated clarinet and the needling frequencies of his distorted guitar. They utilised the taped voices of newscasters, preachers and police officers as signifiers of enforced social conformism and institutional repression, but kept their own political opinions intentionally vague, although they played benefit concerts for human rights organisation Amnesty International and Polish trade union Solidarity. The posters for left-wing gatherings on the walls at Western Works, which the trio inherited from the previous occupants, the Young Socialists, also indicated they were definitely not Tories.

'Being northern and working class, we were very aware of inequalities,' says Mallinder, who had studied history and politics 'from a Marxist perspective' at university. 'If we'd have been a punk band I suppose we would have been writing songs about this but we were very abstract and had a much broader take on things so it wasn't about the British government, it was about wider forces of control.' The ideas they expressed tended to be Burroughsian discontents about media manipulation, state surveillance and politico-religious oppression. 'Basically, I'd like to think that what we do makes people think for themselves,' said Kirk.[8]

Cabaret Voltaire developed their sound amid the political chaos and industrial strife of the mid-seventies, in a country wracked by social tensions that erupted into a wave of public-sector strikes towards the end of 1978: the 'winter of discontent' saw hospitals blockaded by pickets, uncollected refuse festering in the streets and the dead going unburied. This showdown between government and trade unions led to the election of a right-wing Conservative government headed by Margaret Thatcher, who came to power in 1979 on an assertively capitalist, law-and-order platform, vowing to reassert control over unruly workers, restrict immigration, cut taxes and reduce state spending – setting the stage for yet more social discord.

It was a political climate that suited the edgy, unsettling noise-music that Cabaret Voltaire were making; music that vibrated with the turbulence of the times. In 1981, when violent unrest erupted in Britain's inner cities, Kirk told a journalist it was good to see people 'kicking out against the shit', while Watson, ever alert for potentially useful sonic material, tried to record police radio transmissions during the riots – 'for future cut-ups', he said.[9]

Throbbing Gristle and the Art of Brutal Noise
'We were out to break all the rules any way we could.'
Cosey Fanni Tutti[10]

When Hawkwind played St George's Hall in Bradford on their *In Search of Space* tour in October 1971, one of the support acts was a little-known performance art collective called COUM Transmissions. Among its members was 21-year-old Neil Megson, who had changed his name by deed poll to Genesis P-Orridge. (Several decades later, P-Orridge would identify themselves as non-binary and reject any male/female paradigm). As P-Orridge hammered away arythmically on a large assemblage of drums, another member of the COUM collective, 20-year-old Christine Newby, later better known by her pseudonym Cosey Fanni Tutti, wandered around in a school uniform, firing a starting pistol. A poor-quality recording of the event exists, full of cacophonic battering, random guitar noises, feedback and yelling. Afterwards, Hawkwind reputedly asked them what drugs they were on.

As members of Throbbing Gristle, P-Orridge and Tutti would go on to become the instigators of a DIY noise-music culture, alongside Cabaret Voltaire, shifting British electronic music into a new stage of development in the late seventies. But their influences came straight out of the sixties underground.

P-Orridge had grown up despising the deep-rooted prejudices and socially-sanctioned hypocrisies of provincial England, and had been intrigued by the possibilities offered in the freeform multimedia happenings and musical experiments of the late sixties. Tutti, who came from a council estate in the Yorkshire port city of Hull, was similarly enchanted by the liberties of the time: going to free festivals, seeing Jimi Hendrix and Pink Floyd play live, smoking dope, watching arthouse films and 'realising that a different kind of life was possible.'

'The alternative culture was the foundation for everything I've done,' she says. 'I've never looked back since those early days of not wanting to be in the mainstream. The sixties freed me up completely.' Psychedelics were an important creative motivator. 'With acid and stuff, you saw the world in a completely different way and you wanted to access that space when you weren't on drugs,' she explains. 'So the way to do that, for me, was through music and through art, finding different ways of being in the world and expressing how you felt, and that there was more than we're actually seeing and hearing. Because we'd done it on acid, we knew there was more behind the ways our brains had been programmed to see the world. The gates had opened.'

The rise of feminism, the gay liberation movement and environmental activism shows how the ideas of the sixties counterculture continued to spread around the country in the early seventies; in cheaply-rented shared houses, squats and community centres, projects were initiated and actions planned, artistic as well as political. The COUM Transmissions collective's initial activities in Hull were shaped by ideas in play on the artistic fringes of the time: street-theatre happenings and absurdist actions in peculiar hippified costumes, influenced by the cross-disciplinary mischievousness of the Fluxus movement.

They were also fascinated by the physical extremism of the Viennese Actionists, and COUM's playful shenanigans would start to explore more contentious themes – sexuality, gender roles, pornography, violence – particularly after P-Orridge and Tutti moved down to London in 1973. They found a rehearsal room in the basement of Space Studios, an artist-run complex at an old garment works in Martello Street in the then-dilapidated London Fields area of Hackney; this was also where Bruce Lacey, father of COUM Transmissions member John Lacey, had a studio with his wife and creative partner Jill Smith.

The irrepressibly eccentric Lacey started making sound sculptures in the early sixties, when he created two 'electric actors', robots constricted out of junk, for a performance at satirical comedian Peter Cook's Establishment Club. Lacey was one of those unclassifiable characters whose meanderings around the fringes of the creative world brought him into contact with electronic music. He bought a synthesizer from a schoolboy who had assembled it from kits advertised in *Practical Electronics* and made a series of improvised recordings, combining the primitive sounds the monophonic unit emitted with his own effects-treated voice, as well as creating offbeat musique concrète recordings with tape recorders. These were used as soundtracks for performances that he, Smith, his robots and sometimes his children would stage around the country.

Tutti recalled Lacey's workshop in Hackney being 'full of sculptures and robots, an Aladdin's cave of disparate parts awaiting assembly alongside experimental electronic machines, synthesizers, effects units and circuit boards'.[11] His son John Lacey, who sometimes used the alias John Gunni Busck, introduced P-Orridge and Tutti to his friend Chris Carter, an electronics enthusiast. P-Orridge and Tutti initially struck Carter as 'a couple of colourful hippies with a lot of mad ideas', when they first invited him to their Hackney studio. 'They were playing with all these half-working, broken-down and borrowed instruments,'[12] he recalled.

As a teenager, Carter had constructed synths and effects pedals from circuit diagrams in *Practical Electronics*. He said he was inspired to begin tape-manipulation experiments by hearing Joe Meek's bizarre concept album, *I Hear A New World*, on a bootleg cassette; he then pestered his parents until they bought him a cheap, battery-operated reel-to-reel.

He was also intrigued by photographs of the US electronic band Silver Apples playing live with banks of tone generators, and decided he wanted some too: 'There was a shop in Tottenham Court Road called Proops and I used to go in there and buy old oscillators and all sorts of weird stuff,' he says. 'I couldn't afford to go out and buy off-the-shelf synthesizer equipment, so I used to buy *Practical Electronics* magazines and just put it all together myself.' Carter started to perform live with John Lacey using homemade electronics and psychedelic lights under the name Waveforms, putting on 'a little multimedia show that we used to drive around the country doing performances at arts labs and festivals.'

Carter first contributed to a COUM Transmissions performance at the Royal College of Art in October 1974, playing abstract modular synth improvisations with John Lacey; decades later, the recording was released under the title *Music for Stocking Top, Swing and Staircase*. The following year, P-Orridge and Tutti decided to start a new art-music project with Carter and another friend, Peter Christopherson, who went by the nickname Sleazy and was a graphic designer at Hipgnosis, the company that created some of the best-known record sleeves of the seventies, including Pink Floyd's *The Dark Side of the Moon*. They called their group Throbbing Gristle, which Tutti said was 'Yorkshire slang for an erection'.[13]

P-Orridge said that they wanted to take Burroughs and Gysin's ideas about tape recorder experiments and cut-ups into pop culture, combining them with COUM's inflammatorily sexualised post-Fluxus performance art and a firm commitment to anti-musicianship. 'With TG, one of the ideas was that it should be people who could not play their instruments so that they weren't trapped into riffs and traditions. Everything could be included... we absolutely liberated the idea of what music could contain.'[14]

P-Orridge had made contact with Burroughs back in 1972, when the American writer was based in London. Burroughs explained to his young admirer how cut-up tapes of what he called 'trouble sounds' could cause unease and unrest: 'Ominous, negative sounds... Gunshots, police sirens, warfare, bombs exploding, buildings being demolished, screams of fear, loud swearing, crying, fire engines.'[15] These ideas would be incorporated into Throbbing Gristle's methodology alongside the distinctly queer aesthetics of Christopherson, who was openly gay and had a well-researched taste for the perverse and bizarre, as well as a mischievous inclination to disrupt the equilibrium: 'He'd always want to bring in the unexpected,' recalled Carter. 'He was the master of the inappropriate.'[16]

Carter had his own specific tastes: German synth bands like Tangerine Dream, prog rockers Yes and Genesis – and ABBA. Tutti believes that without his technical skills, Throbbing Gristle could not have made the music they did. Her customised Woolworth's guitar sounds and sporadic cornet blasts, P-Orridge's bass blurts, screams and groans, would all be fed through home-made 'Gristleizer' units, built by Carter to a design he adapted from a guitar effects-pedal diagram he saw in *Practical Electronics*, to create surges of delirious noise.

Carter also built a mini-synthesizer called the Tescosynth and a peculiar sound-generating machine for Christopherson with cassette machines hooked up to a little keyboard. 'It's a one-octave keyboard; each line is triggering three Sony stereo cassette machines, loaded with cassettes with prerecorded noises on them. He makes tape loops with constant noises on them – shortwave noises, a tape loop of a piano, screaming voices, and other things,' Carter explained at the time. 'He just has all the outputs running through his keyboard, and he can play with the output. He's got a little sequencer built in that can override the keyboard, that can build up a rhythm if he wants to. And he's got a little harmonizer – for pitch changing.'[17]

Like Cabaret Voltaire, Throbbing Gristle believed that punk rock did not go far enough in subverting musical orthodoxies. 'There was that classic quote about punk: "Learn three chords and form a band." But I thought, *Why learn any chords?* P-Orridge later argued. 'As soon as you learn chords, you've surrendered to tradition.'[18]

Released independently on their own Industrial Records label in 1977, their severe and uncompromising debut album *The Second Annual Report* was the founding statement of industrial music. Its immaculately unpleasant 'songs', with titles like 'Slug Bait' and 'Maggot Death', ranged from sludgy, ugly live improvisations full of queasy electronic noise to chaotic and frightening studio recordings, made even more unsettling by P-Orridge's creepily insinuating vocals.

In an early photograph, the quartet looked like members of a mentally unstable motorcycle gang with their long hair and mirror shades; Christopherson's sardonic smirk only added to the sinister impression. P-Orridge gleefully used distressing imagery intended to confront the listener with the most atrocious acts of brutality humanity was capable of perpetrating: torture, sexual abuse, murder, genocide. 'Art has to ultimately deal with issues of human behaviour, and why we behave in ways that are counterproductive, cruel, destructive, aggressive,' they explained. 'That's what I wanted to find out: why?'[21]

Throbbing Gristle used an image from the Auschwitz death camp for the Industrial Records logo, while their song titles included 'Zyklon B. Zombie', a reference to the poison gas the Nazis used to massacre Jews during the Holocaust, and 'Hamburger Lady', about a severe burns victim – one of the most disturbing pieces of electronic music ever released, with Carter's synths almost weeping in pain. On their second album, *D.O.A: The Third And Final Report*, the use of uneasily suggestive extracts from taped conversations added to the pervasive feeling of corruption, depravity and inescapable dread.

P-Orridge argued they were following the lead of The Velvet Underground, who introduced darkly transgressive themes to popular music: 'The Velvets basically gave permission to tell stories that could be much more unpleasant than had been told in pop music before.'[22] But Throbbing Gristle's critics argued that their ambiguous use of extreme imagery and Holocaust references without overt judgement constituted a kind of irresponsibly exploitative titillation in its own right.

Both consciously and unconsciously, Throbbing Gristle reflected the violence and depravity of the 1970s, the time when multiple murderers like the Yorkshire Ripper and the Black Panther terrorised the country; when serial sexual predators like television presenter Jimmy Savile and parliamentarian Cyril Smith abused the innocent with impunity. Throbbing Gristle's music expressed an indeterminate horror about human corruption and wickedness. 'We had strong moral values and consciences,' said Tutti. 'All we saw was hypocrisy and we hated it.'[23] But there was violence inside the band too, as she revealed when she published her autobiography *Art Sex Music* in 2017, detailing how 'charismatic prankster' P-Orridge, her partner during the COUM and Throbbing Gristle period, was a domineering manipulator who assaulted her on a series of occasions.

Tutti brought her own, specifically female artistic experiences to Throbbing Gristle's music. For several years, she had been earning a living by strip shows in bars and shoots for pornographic magazines, integrating her sex-industry work into the art she made with COUM Transmissions and Throbbing Gristle. 'I was no "victim" of exploitation,' she would insist in her autobiography. 'I was exploiting the sex industry for my own purposes, to subvert and use it to create my own art. It was my choice.'[24] Alongside exhibits featuring used tampons, syringes, knives and a double-ended dildo, images from Tutti's porn shoots were used in COUM's *Prostitution* exhibition in October 1976 at the Institute of Contemporary Arts in London, which was also the forum for one of Throbbing Gristle's earliest performances.

Prostitution caused media outrage, with the politically Conservative *Daily Telegraph* fuming that 'every social evil is celebrated' in the display. 'Public money is being wasted here to destroy the morality of society. These people are the wreckers of civilisation,' Conservative MP Nicholas Fairbairn raged in the right-wing *Daily Mail*.[25] The exhibition ran for a week; each day Tutti and Carter went down to the ICA to add the latest scandalised newspaper clippings to the display as the controversy rolled on, artistically exploiting the press's titillating exploitation of COUM's exhibition on the theme of exploitation.

Throbbing Gristle's records could be morbid and grungy, shiny and erotic, cruel and unpleasant, belligerent and stupid. Sometimes they delighted in puerile humour: 7-inch B-side 'Something Came Over Me' was their techno-pop ode to teenage masturbation. They also enjoyed defying preconceptions. The photo on the cover of their third studio album, 1979's *20 Jazz Funk Greats*, was an attempt to satirise their 'evil' image by showing them posing in leisurewear at seaside beauty spot (albeit well-known suicide location) Beachy Head. 'We were all tired of being so quickly pigeon-holed, even by our fans and supporters in the media, as colourless, gratuitous, bleak, industrial, dark, sombre, and humourless,' explained P-Orridge.[26]

Some of *20 Jazz Funk Greats* was as perverse and discomposing as ever, but there were also pieces inspired by the lounge melodies of American exotica maestro Martin Denny, German *kosmische* synth music and even an electronic disco track, the lubriciously Moroderesque 'Hot on the Heels of Love'. Tutti had come to love disco while working as a stripper in London pubs. 'When I started doing stripping, I had to use records that had rhythm and actually sounded familiar to the audience, so I really got into the disco stuff of the time, Giorgio Moroder and Donna Summer,' she recalls.

Live, Throbbing Gristle would confront and be confronted by their audience. 'It was a two-way assault, at times. They'd assault us and then we'd join in the fight – it was great fun actually,' says Tutti. As a lot of their music was improvisational, it would change with the atmosphere in the room; P-Orridge would berate and goad the crowd; Carter would drop in unexpected beat patterns from his box of rhythm tapes, Christopherson would unleash perverse samples and Tutti would tear screams out of her guitar: 'We wanted to push people out of their comfort zone of what to expect with music,' she says. 'It was about breaking it down to literally sound and how people react to it.'

But they were not the first to explore the use of noise as provocation on a British stage. Back in 1914, Italian Futurist artist Luigi Russolo – author of *The Art of Noises*, the manifesto that predicted a new music made of pure sound – staged a series of twelve concerts with the Futurist movement's founder, Filippo Marinetti, at the London Coliseum showcasing their mechanical *intonarumori* noise-generators. *The Times* reported that the music performed was like sounds that could be heard 'in the rigging of a channel-steamer during a bad crossing', and was greeted by 'cries of "no more" from all parts of the auditorium'.[19] Marinetti quipped back that playing the noise-intoners for the London public was like 'showing the first steam engine to a herd of cows'.[20]

In 1981, the year after releasing *Heathen Earth*, a live album of astonishing power and solemnity, Throbbing Gristle split; a rift made inevitable by the break-up of the relationship between Tutti and P-Orridge. They left behind them the term 'industrial music', a genre that took its name from their record label but would outlive them and fellow travellers like Cabaret Voltaire and SPK – bands who shared their love of confrontation and disruption, autonomous production methods, low-tech instrumentation and rejection of musical proficiency. Indeed, it was only after Throbbing Gristle disintegrated that industrial music became fully codified as a combination of (sometimes rhythmic) noise, harsh electronics, aggressive male vocals, taped or sampled voices, grotesque imagery, the influences of Burroughs and occultist Aleister Crowley, and obsessions with sexual transgression and mortality.

Journalist Jon Savage wrote in 1981 that he saw Throbbing Gristle as seekers after a particular set of truths: 'Truths about the limits of human behaviour that we are encouraged to ignore – love, despair, coercion, bestiality, repose, intense sexuality, frustration and incredible violence.'[27] Their use and perceived misuse of sensitive subjects like fascism and sexual violence would continue to be debated and disputed in the decades after their demise, as their influence continued to grow and 'industrial' became an established genre.

For some of the industrial musicians that came afterwards, Throbbing Gristle's work served as a gateway into deeper darkness, emboldening them to go even further in terms of extreme noise and imagery, and to iconise violent abusers and murderers. All the band's former members expressed discomfort about these subsequent interpretations, with P-Orridge scorning industrial bands who used brutality for shock value – 'people who thought if they accessorised with serial killers or talked about rape they were being bold and special.'[28] 'It was like Frankenstein's monster,' Carter laments. 'It just became something completely different, it became this macho thing. Whereas industrial for us was all about DIY. Do it yourself.'

Thomas Leer, Robert Rental and Daniel Miller
'There was a very specific moment in 1978 when everything seemed to come together.'
Daniel Miller

Genesis P-Orridge and Cosey Fanni Tutti were veterans of the 1970s Mail Art movement, which saw artists around the world sending small works to each other by post, establishing an informal network of independent creatives. Personal connections were vitally important to Throbbing Gristle too; their *Industrial News* bulletin served to put their fans in touch with esoteric information sources, as well as with each other. The newsletter's recipients then began exchanging their own tapes and ideas, and some went on to start bands themselves.

Throbbing Gristle's label, Industrial Records, also encouraged their musical contemporaries by releasing their music: Cabaret Voltaire's 1974-76 compilation of tapes recorded in the Watson family's attic; the debut single by SPK (under the name Surgical Penis Klinik); noise-funk group Clock DVA's *White Souls in Black Suits*; William Burroughs' spoken-word album *Nothing Here Now but the Recordings*; and, most peculiar of all, Black American actress Elizabeth Welch's lounge-jazz rendition of the standard 'Stormy Weather', after it was featured in Derek Jarman's 1979 film adaptation of Shakespeare's *The Tempest*.

One of Industrial Records' finest releases was *The Bridge* by Scottish electronic duo Thomas Leer and Robert Rental. Leer (Thomas Wishart) and Rental (Robert Donnachie) were Can, Faust and Captain Beefheart enthusiasts who had grown up in Port Glasgow, a declining shipbuilding town on the River Clyde. Leer lived in a hippie commune for a while and attended the Stonehenge and Windsor free festivals. He then played in a punk band but found the genre constricting – though he did find inspiration in The Desperate Bicycles, who recorded and released their ramshackle debut single in 1977 for a total cost of £153 and urged others to emulate them: 'It was easy, it was cheap, go and do it!'[29]

The idea that anyone could release their own records on their own label definitively shaped the evolution of post-punk electronic music in Britain. In 1978, Leer released 650 copies of his low-tech but utterly charming debut single on his own Oblique Records label. 'Private Plane' and flipside 'International' were recorded in his flat using a preset-only drum machine, a Watkins Copicat echo unit, an effects pedal and a Stylophone 350S, the deluxe version of a miniature analogue electronic keyboard manufactured by Leeds-based company Dubreq (also used on David Bowie's 'Space Oddity'). The 350S was operated using two styluses with a kind of wah-wah pedal controlled by hand movements over a photo sensor. 'You could wave your hand a bit and get a filter effect like a synthesizer,' says Leer. 'People thought it was a synthesizer, that's why they classified me as an electronic artist. But really I was using this weird little pen organ.'

Leer's vocals had an intimate quality that was also a result of the cheapo domestic recording set-up, he explains: 'I was singing late at night and we were just in a little bedsit and my girlfriend was asleep in bed, so I was singing quietly, so as not to wake her up. I've never sung like that since.'

After he finished recording, the equipment was moved to his friend Robert Rental's flat, where Rental recorded two equally idiosyncratic songs: 'ACC' and 'Paralysis', which he also released in an edition of 650 copies on his own Regular Records label. Leer and Rental designed the sleeves themselves; the black-and-white covers were surreptitiously photocopied after hours at the offices of Virgin Records by Rental's partner, while the labels were hand-stamped using a John Bull printing kit. Some of the sleeves were also hand-coloured using felt-tip pen. 'I think both of us saw them as being kind of like ultimate punk records,' says Leer. 'We felt that the whole idea of what punk was about wasn't three-minute rock'n'roll songs – that it should be about something beyond that.'

This idea of punk being more important as a set of creative strategies than a musical formula was already being discussed at the time. A November 1977 edition of music paper *Sounds* proselytised the idea of an adventurous, post-punk 'New Musick', citing bands like Kraftwerk, Devo and Throbbing Gristle, plus dub and disco. In one of the articles, Jon Savage acknowledged that 'somewhere in the energy of punk lies some kind of life-force', but argued that its accelerated garage-band thrash was creatively obsolescent.[30]

Leer and Rental's adaptation of what they saw as punk principles helped to show that there was another way of making electronic music; in a sense they were the original bedroom boffins, prototypes for a format that would become ubiquitous in the techno era. The The founder Matt Johnson said that Leer's 'Private Plane' showed him how music could be made cheaply and autonomously: 'The fact it was just one guy in his bedroom doing the entire thing made a massive, massive impact on me. He was years ahead of his time and actually inspired me to create The The really.'[31]

The only record Leer and Rental made together was the album they released on Industrial, *The Bridge*. One side was oddball electro-punk, the second was drone ambient. Most of the tracks were made using two Wasp synthesizers – viciously noisy British-made synths with a distinctive gaudy yellow-and-black design. The Wasp had a plastic strip keyboard, a plastic casing and a comical insect logo; it looked like a musical toy but was relatively inexpensive at £199, when UK company EDP – Electronic Dream Plant Ltd – first put it on the market in 1978. 'It was a ridiculous thing, it was like a piece of plastic, but boy, did it sound good,' says Leer.

The Wasp immediately became a staple for independent, post-punk synth players – people who, as EDP's press advert pitched it, 'dream of owning a synthesizer' but couldn't afford it; like obscure British experimental band Metabolist, whose anarchic, post-Faust racket was made even more uncommercial by the caustic emanations from their Wasp. EDP went on to produce an even cheaper version called the Gnat, as well as the Spider digital sequencer, further extending the possibilities of making electronic music on a budget.

As well as their Wasps, Rental and Leer were using the 'time lag accumulator' technique of looping and repeating sounds that was developed by Terry Riley and employed by Robert Fripp and Brian Eno on *(No Pussyfooting)* and Eno's ambient landmark *Discreet Music*, which had a diagram on its cover showing how to hook up the necessary equipment. 'There were two tape recorders and one tape going across the two machines. So the sound would just keep on building up and building up on the tape into this mass of sound, and then we just improvised on top as it was coming through,' says Leer. 'That second side of *The Bridge*, all four tracks, as long as it takes to hear them, that's how long it took us to record them.' Sometimes the ambience of Rental's high-rise apartment was picked up on the recording – the noises of electrical appliances and the duo quietly chatting, coughing or lighting cigarettes, as well as snatches of comments from Joan Collins and John Lydon that could be heard from the television as they appeared on pop programme *Juke Box Jury*.

At a Throbbing Gristle concert in London, Rental met Daniel Miller, an electronic music enthusiast who was working as an assistant film editor. The son of Austrian refugees who had fled the Nazi regime, Miller had studied film and TV at art school, where he had experimented with tape recorders and loops; Ron Geesin once came in to lecture and demonstrated the first synth that Miller ever saw, an EMS Synthi.

Miller had recorded two starkly minimalist, J. G. Ballard-influenced electro-punk tracks, 'T.V.O.D.' and 'Warm Leatherette', using a simple, monophonic MiniKorg 700s synth. 'I used it for everything from drums to melodies to sounds on those songs. I managed to figure out a way of getting a kind of a kick drum and a snare drum from that synthesizer,' he says. 'I recorded both of them in a 24-hour period. It was kind of punk rock. I was listening to the first Ramones album a lot at that time as well as Kraftwerk. As I was recording, I very much had the Ramones in my mind – the brevity, the simplicity, no solos, minimal production.' Like Leer and Rental's initial releases, and The Human League with 'Being Boiled', Miller made a virtue out of his equipment's limitations.

Miller decided to set up his own record label from home and released the tracks as a single in 1978. Mute Records would go on to become one of the world's most creatively important record companies, elegantly straddling the divide between 'pop' and 'art' music. It was one of several independent labels – like Rough Trade, Factory, 4AD and Fast Product – established around the same time by people given confidence by punk's DIY ideals to release records themselves. Like fanzines, independent labels were hardly a new phenomenon, but there was an ideological mood in post-punk culture that it was a necessity, almost a political imperative, to be autonomous; apathy was unacceptable and alternative culture, with its ethics of self-empowerment – be a *participant*, not a spectator or passive consumer – could pose a genuine challenge to the establishment.

Like Thomas Leer and Robert Rental, Cabaret Voltaire and Throbbing Gristle, Daniel Miller was part of a new generation of independent non-musicians that coalesced into the post-punk electronic movement over the course of 1978. 'It was a very special moment in history, I think,' he says. 'There were a number of other people who were doing the same things – The Human League, Cabaret Voltaire, Throbbing Gristle were already recording. We were inspired by similar artists from the earlier part of the seventies like Kraftwerk for instance, or Can or Neu!, and by the liberating influence of punk where you could do anything you really wanted to. Plus there was the increasing affordability of electronic equipment, so you didn't even have to learn three chords, just press a couple of keys and twiddle a few knobs.'

Japanese companies like Korg and Casio had brought relatively affordable, basic synths to the market in the mid-seventies; they were smaller and more portable, therefore easier to use at gigs. 'All these factors came together in 1978 along with the DIY label explosion, where there were a lot of people doing their own releases rather than going to a record company,' says Miller. Andy McCluskey of Orchestral Manoeuvres in the Dark has also cited 1978 as the crucial moment when he heard new records by The Normal, Cabaret Voltaire and The Human League and realised his band were not 'the only people in the whole of Britain who were interested in this kind of music.'[32]

Despite this, there was still significant resistance to the idea of synth-driven groups, even among self-styled punk rebels. The year after Suicide were repeatedly attacked while playing with The Clash, Miller and Rental went out on tour as an electronic duo, supporting punk band Stiff Little Fingers. 'We didn't go down well at all. There were a few gigs where we were really spat at, and bottles and burning cigarettes were thrown on stage,' Miller recalls. 'I think a lot of people at the time associated synthesizers with pseudo-classical prog-rock artists like Emerson, Lake & Palmer, and punk was very much a reaction against that – although I was reacting against that too.'

A single-sided album was released from the tour, *Live at West Runton Pavilion 6/3/79*, an assortment of industrial rhythms, one-finger melodies, electro-punk riffs and wild Wasp noise. It would prove to be one of Rental's last releases before he gave up music, leaving a tiny recorded output and a mystique that grew over the years, particularly after his death from lung cancer in 2000. 'Robert's music was deeply soulful in the truest sense – it came from him completely unfiltered by any musical, emotional or commercial constraints,' Miller wrote in an obituary. 'It was maybe this rawness of spirit that made him his own more severe critic, a self-criticism that sadly led to very little of his music being released.'[33]

The Human League, Clock DVA and Vice Versa

'We were punks for a while but the novelty quickly wore off. We just thought that, ultimately, it was just rock'n'roll. Then you had Eno

essentially saying that rock'n'roll is dead and the future is DIY-style, all you need is a synthesizer, a two-track tape recorder and a microphone. So we took him at his word.'
Martyn Ware, The Human League and Heaven 17

As well as promoting creative independence, the DIY philosophy that emerged out of punk helped bands realise they didn't necessarily have to sign to London-based companies, strengthening regional scenes around the country, particularly in the north of England. Manchester's Factory Records was the first label to provide an outlet for Cabaret Voltaire and early electro-pop band Orchestral Manoeuvres in the Dark, a duo from Merseyside with a tape machine they named Winston and placed prominently on stage when playing live. At the time, it seemed the whole idea of what constituted a 'band' – and indeed what constituted 'music' – was open for reinterpretation.

Orchestral Manoeuvres in the Dark made some of their early records using a low-budget Korg synthesizer they bought from a mail-order catalogue. 'Our great inspiration was Kraftwerk, though we didn't have the technology to emulate them. This helped us define our own sound. We were never purist and robotic, and there was a certain romance in our melodies,' co-founder Paul Humphreys later explained.[34] These twinkling tunes contributed a feeling of innocent sincerity to their winsome early run of singles from 'Electricity' to 'Enola Gay', perhaps the perkiest song ever written about a nuclear attack. Andy McCluskey also said that their prominent use of melody was influenced by the Tornados' 'Telstar', which Orchestral Manoeuvres in the Dark covered as a demo in 1979.

In Sheffield, Cabaret Voltaire's guiding example and beneficence was one of the reasons why the city became a key location for independent electronic music in the 1980s. One of the bands that benefited from their assistance was Clock DVA, who recorded their debut album, *White Souls in Black Suits*, at Western Works. Clock DVA made a restless, moody noise, with singer Adi Newton's gruffly portentous voice echoing over stuttering punk-funk drums and bass, and raucous squawks of Ornette Coleman-style free-jazz sax Newton describes as 'fractured fractals of sound'.

Newton once asserted he wanted to make music that was 'intense, paranoid and totally out of control'.[35] On stage, he harried and insulted the audience. 'I was interested in trying to combine the energy of The Stooges and Velvet Underground, that dark kind of energy, using conventional instruments but pushing them in different ways, and fusing all that together with electronics and creating some kind of hybrid between electronics and the rawness of rock'n'roll,' he explains.

He saw himself as an experimental artist rather than a musician. Before forming Clock DVA, he had been 'making sounds using field recordings, tape loops and treated material' with a short-lived Sheffield electronic group called The Future, alongside two local synthesizer enthusiasts, Martyn Ware and Ian Craig Marsh, both of whom were working as computer operators at the time.

The Future made some demo recordings at a peculiar home studio called Studio Electrophonique, run by a former panel beater and RAF veteran in the chintzily-decorated front room of a council house in a Sheffield suburb, with the tape recorder sitting on the coffee table. 'It was like something out of a sitcom,' recalls Ware. 'We sat down in this front room and had a cup of tea and biscuits, and then started recording these abstract soundscapes with Adi mumbling over the top of them, reciting excerpts from J. G. Ballard and lyrics created by this lyric-generation system we'd invented called CARLOS, which meant Cyclic and Random Lyric Organisation System, which would generate these sentences from a list of prepositions, adjectives, nouns, verbs, et cetera – we were very influenced by William Burroughs' cut-up technique, because we'd heard Bowie did that.'

No record companies were interested in their low-budget recordings, though. Newton quit the band to start Clock DVA, leaving Ware and Marsh to indulge their more melodic sensibilities and attempt to write coherent pop songs using electronic equipment. 'And the closer we got to the pop songs that we loved, the happier we were,' says Ware. They decided to recruit a singer who they thought could help them realise their pop dreams: a hospital porter called Phil Oakey, a Bowie and Roxy freak well-known on the local club scene for his extrovert self-styling.

The band also adopted a new name, The Human League, which they took from a science-fiction board game called Star Force. As with many late-seventies British synth bands, science fiction programmes and the soundtracks made by the BBC Radiophonic Workshop were important childhood influences. Some early Human League tracks like '4JG', a Ballard tribute whose title referenced Roxy Music's Bogart homage '2HB', sounded like proto-techno, but they also made demos of The Righteous Brothers' crooner classic 'You've Lost That Loving Feeling' and a (semi) tongue-in-cheek tribute to electronic disco, 'Dance Like a Star'. 'All we ever wanted was to sound like Donna Summer,' Oakey would declare.[36]

Ware explains that they saw no contradiction between liking dance music and admiring Eno, the Radiophonic Workshop and Wendy Carlos' soundtrack for *A Clockwork Orange*. For him, like for many others who started making low-budget electronic music in the punk era, Donna Summer's 'I Feel Love' and Kraftwerk's 'Trans-Europe Express' both signified the future when they were released in 1977. 'We didn't fall for that stuff propagated by the music press about disco being this great, bland evil. Looking back on that now, it was massively racist,' he says.

The Human League played their debut gig in Sheffield in June 1978; the rhythms and basslines were prerecorded on tape and the playback machine was placed centre-stage – a defiant poke at rock 'authenticity'. 'The show started with us deliberately walking on and turning the tape recorder on, and the stuff would start without us playing anything... which was pretty provocative at the time,' said Marsh.[37] They recruited former film student Adrian Wright to add visual excitement with his light show and slide projections, offering a kaleidoscopic spin through contemporary pop-culture references – *Thunderbirds* puppets, The Bay City Rollers, Iggy Pop, John Noakes of *Blue Peter*, *Star Trek* characters, *Starsky & Hutch* and *Wonder Woman*.

The band's first single, 'Being Boiled', released on independent label Fast Product, was a minimalistic statement of intent with a killer robot-funk bassline and an infectious lo-fi slapback beat. 'We got the rhythm going on the Roland System 100 and we were massively into Parliament, Funkadelic and Bernie Worrell and that kind of Black synthesis, so I said, "I can do a bassline on the Korg 700S that sounds a bit funky – only it's going to be dead simple",' recalls Ware. 'And those were the only instruments on the original version.' With Oakey's weirdly operatic, post-Roxy vocal style, it sounded like pop and anti-pop simultaneously.

'Being Boiled' wasn't a hit as they would have liked; nor was its follow-up, 'The Dignity of Labour', an instrumental concept EP based around Soviet cosmonaut Yuri Gagarin. But they did secure a deal with Virgin Records and their first two albums, *Reproduction* and *Travelogue*, saw them develop a kind of twisted English sci-fi pop. 'Our basic idea was if we aim for a normal kind of pop song writing, but we use this ridiculously abstract palette, automatically it's going to be interesting because you're going to miss the target by a mile but where it lands might be somewhere unique,' explains Ware. They wanted

The Human League to become the first synth-pop band to make number-one records – but a Londoner who called himself Gary Numan would get there first.

Another experimental electronic group from Sheffield with pop aspirations who recorded at the Studio Electrophonique council house was Vice Versa, whose members were slightly younger than The Human League and Cabaret Voltaire, and looked up to them as role models. 'They were so perfectly formed in what they were doing,' recalls Vice Versa co-founder Stephen Singleton. 'We kind of felt we were like schoolboys and they were grown-ups.' The EP they recorded, *Music 4*, was a set of pulsing synthetic song-sketches with Kraftwerk-style beats and dramatic melodies. Released on their own independent label, Neutron Records, it came with a manifesto that grandiosely declared Vice Versa were aiming to 'provide a soundtrack to the second industrial revolution'.

Like Daniel Miller and Robert Rental, they discovered that audiences often didn't appreciate punky electronic bands. 'We played lots of gigs where people just *hated* us because the music was so different at that time,' says Singleton. 'We played at pubs in Sheffield and we'd turn up with a drum machine and they would be going, "Where's your bloody drummer?" And we'd reply that we didn't have one and they'd say, "Well, that ain't right!" But we kind of liked being hated because then we could get a kind of confrontation going on with the audience, which we enjoyed.'

Soon they were writing songs with verve and swagger like 'Stilyagi', a power-surging stomp that hailed the young Soviet hipsters known as 'style hunters'. But they looked set to remain the sort of post-punk cult band that would only get played on John Peel's eclectic late-night show on BBC Radio 1 – until they discovered that Martin Fry, who came to interview the band for his fanzine *Modern Drugs* and subsequently joined as a synth player, had a hidden talent. 'Mark White was the original singer and Martin was kind of really shy at first, he just kind of stood at the back looking menacing,' says Singleton. 'Then we discovered that Martin was a great singer. But we didn't think his voice suited the electronic sound so much and we decided then to change direction.'

Like The Human League, they resolved to quit the radical fringes and make music intended to be popular, under a new name: ABC. 'We wanted to do this raw, funky kind of thing, with the kind of guitar that Chic had, a bit like A Certain Ratio but not as gloomy, and so we recruited a drummer and bassist,' says Singleton, who switched from synth to sax. They also resolved that with Fry as the new frontman and a new band identity, they could even try writing love songs — romance being a subject that was either ignored, satirised, analysed according to Marxist dialectics or treated with utter contempt by most post-punk bands.

'We decided to turn it all on its head. And the very first song we wrote as ABC was [hit single] 'Tears Are Not Enough'. So shortly after we did the last Vice Versa concert in 1980, we did the first ABC concert and shocked all our friends. They would usually come along and politely applaud, but now they were going apeshit, screaming and shouting, "Oh my God, this is incredible, it's fucking brilliant!"' By 1981, ABC were pop stars.

John Foxx and Ultravox

'The availability of affordable guitars and amplifiers had enabled the sixties to happen, and these instruments (plus recording studios and imported blues records) had shaped the music. It seemed to me that this was happening again, with synthesizers and drum machines.'
John Foxx

In 1978, that pivotal year in the development of British electronic music, singer John Foxx and his art-school band Ultravox travelled to Cologne to realise the dream of recording their third album, *Systems of Romance*, with German producer Conny Plank. Foxx was thrilled that they were the first British group to make an album with this esteemed veteran of German electronic recordings with Kraftwerk, Neu! and Cluster.

'Conny was really the human crossroads at that time – the place where everything intersected – experimental, classical, electronic, rock, technology, recording, innovative ideas, art, avant-pop, film music, underground and emergent culture – he understood and loved all of it. I think there was no one else alive at that time who could offer all that,' says Foxx.

Foxx's ideas had been shaped by the 1960s underground, like others involved in 1970s electronic music. Born Dennis Leigh, he was the son of a coalminer from Chorley in Lancashire and moved to London to study at the Royal College of Art in the late sixties. Like Brian Eno and Bryan Ferry of Roxy Music, his time at art school was a transformative experience. Foxx recalls listening to imported American blues records and experimental music by Pierre Schaeffer, John Cage and Terry Riley, reading fringe literature and 'early experimental sci-fi', buying clothes from jumble sales and flea markets – 'art students were instinctive style magpies' – plus parties, alcohol and the occasional experimental imbibing of drugs. 'So you had a complete, immersive culture,' he says. 'When that generation left art school and went back into the world, all this permeated the art, graphics, fashion, clothes and music of the sixties, seventies and eighties.'

Foxx got involved in London's psychedelic scene, attending events like The 14-Hour Technicolor Dream at the Alexandra Palace in 1967; he also started doing some experiments with a tape recorder, 'recording atmospheric monologues with breathing and movement sounds, then street sounds... I also used some recorded drones – traffic sounds from a bridge over the M6 and recordings of Hoovers – to sing to. Then I realised you could slow things down or speed them up, play sounds backwards and cut the tapes and Sellotape them together.'

He said he conceptualised the idea that would become Ultravox (or Ultravox!, as they were known from 1976-78) after he attended a talk by design professor Richard Guyatt at the Royal College of Art about 'design for the real world' in 1973. 'I took it as making art real – not something on a wall in a gallery, but an active part of the real world,' Foxx says. Shortly afterwards, he decided that he wanted to 'design a rock band'.

According to Foxx, the band took in references from Burroughs and Ballard, from European films and from German bands Kraftwerk and Neu!, from The Beatles' 'Tomorrow Never Knows' and from Roxy Music noisemaker Eno. 'Roxy Music were the ultimate art school band,' he says. 'They really had it all – glamour, fun, surrealism, futurist nostalgia – and hit records, all on their own terms.'

The eponymous *Ultravox!* debut album was deep in post-Roxy, post-glam, art-rock territory; it was even co-produced by Eno, whose work with bands like Devo and Talking Heads was crucial in shaping some of the ideas identified with the post-punk period. The album used largely conventional instruments, apart from 'My Sex', which Foxx claims was 'the first synth ballad'. He said he originally wanted to use human heartbeats in place of drums: 'The initial idea had been to wire myself – and my girlfriend at the time – with contact microphones and sensors. I wanted to trigger synth sounds from the sensors and record our heartbeats accelerating and perhaps synchronising, as we had sex.'

Although this didn't work out, the recordings with Eno signified 'the beginning of the next phase' for the band, Foxx recalls, as they acquired a

Roland TR-77 drum machine and an ARP Odyssey synthesizer for electric violinist Billy Currie. Their second album of 1977, *Ha!-Ha!-Ha!*, saw them reaching towards a unique voice with the elegiac electronics of 'Hiroshima Mon Amour' and the new-wave disco of 'The Man Who Dies Every Day'. But it was only on the Conny Plank-produced third album, *Systems of Romance*, that they perfected their grandiose European synth-rock sound – a sound that would become an eighties archetype and convince young new-wave singer Gary Numan to switch from guitar to electronics.

Despite its creative vigour, *Systems of Romance* was a commercial disappointment and Foxx wouldn't share in the mass-market success that Ultravox achieved in subsequent years. He left the band in 1979 to follow his own minimalist electronic visions and released his solo debut, *Metamatic*, the following year – a cold, harsh and lyrically Ballardian album that he described as 'a sort of synthpunk dub'. (One of the *Metamatic*-era tracks he released as a B-side, 'Mr No', has also been cited as proto-electro).

As well as absorbing Eno's ideas of the studio as instrument, Foxx had witnessed Lee Perry mixing a Bob Marley session at a studio in London and came to believe dub was 'at least equal to Kraftwerk and European electronics as a seminal force'. Released a couple of months before *Metamatic*, Public Image Ltd's *Metal Box*, with Jah Wobble's reverberant basslines and Keith Levene's sheared-metal guitar and sleeting synth sounds, also explored dub techniques, which would exert a growing influence over post-punk rock in the early eighties.

Foxx says *Metamatic* was an attempt to 'discard any and all American blues references' and reflect a specifically British environment. 'My own real experience is a wilderness of factory towns, ruined countryside, isolation, concrete, motorways, factories, housing estates, cinemas – and the mystical strangeness emerging at times out of all this,' he explains. 'It was addressing our situation at that moment – magic-brutalist music, tailored by Burton's. I set out to make it strictly minimal – eight tracks on tape and no more. Three instruments and a couple of effects boxes and that was it.

'I wanted to make a kind of music that would be British, but looking over to Europe, rather than to America. It had to sound like a kind of music that would have happened if America had never existed. I also imagined a mysterious neon jukebox in a future European motorway café – what would it play?'

Gary Numan performing at the Granada Theatre in Chicago, October 1980. ©Paul Natkin/Getty Images.

The Coming of Gary Numan

'I couldn't play for shit. And that wasn't what I was interested in. I was interested in trying to find sounds that people hadn't heard before – that I hadn't heard before.'

Gary Numan

One evening in May 1979, 19-year-old singer Gary Numan and his young band Tubeway Army made their dramatic first appearance on the BBC's prime-time TV chart show, *Top of the Pops*. The song, 'Are 'Friends' Electric?', would become the first post-punk electro-pop single to reach number one in the British charts, awakening the music business to the commercial potential of this emerging genre.

It was one of the coldest, starkest hits in British pop history – an alienated sound-sketch that lacked any conventional hook or chorus, with Numan's mannered, aloof vocal informed by his own sense of social disconnection. On *Top of the Pops*, he moved like a mechanised marionette, clad in his black Tubeway Army uniform, his pale, disdainful eyes also marked out in black. With his black-costumed band behind him lit by flashes of white light, he looked astonishing.

Born Gary Webb to a working-class family in London, Numan had grown up feeling he was a somehow a man apart. A specialist told him that he had Asperger's syndrome, which is characterised by difficulties with social communication and interaction, and which compounded his sense of being unique, other, *alien*. He would use these feelings to make his music special. At secondary school he got into T. Rex and then David Bowie, dyed his hair and had his ear pierced; his classmates taunted him for being gay, although he wasn't. When Bowie's *Station to Station* tour came to London, Numan was in the audience, in white shirt and waistcoat with slicked-back blond and orange hair. He'd started to style himself a persona.

His stage name was adapted from a listing he saw in the *Yellow Pages* telephone directory for Neumann Kitchen Appliances. But although he was using ideas for lyrics that he picked up from SF writers like Ballard, Philip K. Dick and Isaac Asimov, his band, Tubeway Army, were a relatively conventional new-wave outfit – until Numan had his first encounter with a synthesizer.

'I discovered it by accident because I had gone to the studio to make a conventional album,' he recalls. 'I'd never seen a real synthesizer before. I'd never even touched a keyboard before I made that first album. Never. I didn't have a piano at home. I didn't know a single chord.' When he pressed a key on the MiniMoog, the sound that blasted out was so powerful that it seemed to shake the room – and all his perceptions. 'I just hit one note and it was like this huge sonic attack. It completely blew me away. I felt like this what I was had been looking for.

'What turned me on was the fact that it was all about the *sound*. I used to say that sometimes one note will do, you just need one note because it's the *sound* that matters, and how that sound evolves and what you can do with it. If you've got a really interesting sound, you don't need to have loads of different notes going on, one note can conjure up all sorts of thoughts and images and feelings in your mind, it can create a sense of menace, a sense of power – it doesn't have to be always dark, but it usually is for me.'

Numan immediately decided to replace some guitar parts on the Tubeway Army album with synth sounds and told his record company he was abandoning punk, which he declared was 'at the end of its time'.

He acknowledges that on this first album, he was in transition between the punk of the recent past and the electronic future. 'Essentially, I was grafting on a new layer of sound to something that was fairly conventional.' Influenced by

Ultravox's shift towards electronics with *Systems of Romance* the previous year, the second Tubeway Army album, *Replicas*, which featured 'Are 'Friends' Electric?' and the saturnine SF drones of 'Down in the Park', represented his complete break with his past.

Whitening his face with make-up, bleaching his hair blond and using his own awkwardness to define a unique posture, Numan created a powerful image he then sought to inhabit. 'I was getting terrible stage fright, really terrible, and I needed to find a way of dealing with it. So I created a persona that I could hide behind, so I could become this other character, this person who wasn't nervous, who was absolutely as confident as you could possibly be and knew exactly what he was doing, while underneath all that is me, who isn't confident at all and doesn't know what he's doing and is painfully aware of that,' he explains.

Numan followed *Replicas* with his first solo album, *The Pleasure Principle*, distilling his dystopian android pop to its vital essence with some of his most gloriously glacial synth lines – 'Cars', 'Films', 'Conversation', all immaculately highlighting his unusual songcraft. 'Are 'Friends' Electric?' and 'Cars' don't have conventional choruses. 'Cars' doesn't really have one at all,' he says. 'It wasn't deliberate, you know, I didn't think, "Oh, I'm going to try to write songs back to front to other people." That was just what came out. And I used to be quite embarrassed by those differences. I didn't sit there being proud of it and thinking how different I was and what a breath of fresh air I was, I just felt really awkward all the time.

'So I used to struggle with that and I hated my voice, and was aware that it was different but never tried to sing differently, just never quite liked what I was doing. Fucking hell, man, I was very confused for a very, very long time.'

Numan was Britain's first electronic pop star and he was both loved and hated for it. After *Replicas*, his own replicas started to proliferate – the 'Numanoids'. When he gazed out from the stage, he saw scores of clones staring back at him. Simultaneously, he was treated abysmally by the British music press – mocked for the artifice of his image, his mannered voice and awkward character, satirised for his enthusiasms for flying planes and buying sports cars, condemned for his very un-punk desire to be a star and put on a show for his fans.

Numan found the criticism hurtful and difficult to comprehend; he remained unsure for years afterwards about whether journalists disliked him or his music. 'There was a great deal of hostility towards electronic music when I first started,' he explains. 'The music was very, very different and the way I presented it was quite different. My whole image was sullen and moody. There was no smiling, and I do have Asperger's so when I talked about things it was done in a way that wasn't "normal", I guess – I hate that word.

'I'm not very good at manipulating or adapting what I say to suit people, I just blurt it all out. And I was just blurting out all this stuff that I wanted to be famous, I wanted to be a pop star. And I never saw anything bad in that, I never saw ambition as being a bad thing. But coming on the back of the punk movement, I think it was seen as a bad thing because punk was seen as being anti-hero and anti-popstar, although I don't think it was actually, because so many of them became huge pop stars.'

Numan's importance to British electronic music history, as a connector between the post-punk new wave and electro-pop, would be completely reappraised in the 21st century. In America however, particularly among progressive Black musicians who knew little of parochial, class-based British snobbery, his status as a futurist icon was never in doubt.

Prince was one of several influential Black artists who loved Numan. 'There are people still trying to work out what a genius he was,' Prince once said.[38] Afrika Bambaataa credited Numan as a major influence on the New York electro sound, alongside Kraftwerk. 'Man he was dope. So important to us. When we heard that single, 'Are 'Friends' Electric?' it was like the aliens had landed in The Bronx,' Bambaataa said. 'Numan was the inspiration. He's a hero.'[39]

Such tributes showed how UK post-punk electronic records caused unexpected reverberations in the US, making a significant impact on the sound of early electro, techno and house music. 'Alleys of Your Mind', the debut single from Detroit innovators Juan Atkins and Rik Davis' proto-techno band Cybotron, was sonically indebted to Ultravox's 1980 track 'Mr X', while its flipside sounded like it was influenced by Orchestral Manoeuvres in the Dark. Davis said he loved what he called the 'techno-rock' that British bands like Ultravox were making.[40]

Numan only heard Bambaataa's story in 2004, when the two men collaborated on a cover version of his song 'Metal'. 'It was years afterwards and I wish I'd known about it at the time, it would have helped to balance all the shit I was getting in England. It would have really helped,' he acknowledges. 'It lifted my spirits when he told me. It made me feel good.'

Thomas Dolby and Landscape Get Scientific

'I like the early fog of innovation, where you know it's exciting but you don't really know why.'
Thomas Dolby[41]

From Numan's electric 'Friends' onwards, science would be a key theme for early electro-pop, as it had been for electronic music from the post-war period onwards. Some electro-pop players even styled themselves as techie visionaries, like Thomas Dolby, who featured 'mad scientist' TV personality Magnus Pyke on his hit 'She Blinded Me with Science', and whose song 'Windpower' was an early pop tribute to sustainable energy; 'an alternative technology anthem', [42] he called it.

Dolby's eclectic career as a recording artist and later as an internet-era tech entrepreneur 'on a constant quest to explore new worlds',[43] as he once put it, revolved around the nexus of music and technology at points of great change in both spheres. 'What interests me is plunging in where there's uncertainty,' he said.[44] This son of a professor, who later became a professor of the arts himself, recounted in his autobiography how he found the first synth he ever owned in a dumpster around the back of the EMS shop in London – a Transcendent 2000 kit designed for home assembly. Dolby and his soldering iron soon got it making noises.

Dolby was a key figure in bringing electronic sounds into mainstream rock music in the early eighties – as a young session player, he worked on UK metal band Def Leppard's *Pyromania* album (credited under the parodic name 'Booker T. Boffin') and created the contemplative synth intro for Foreigner's soft-rock power ballad 'Waiting for a Girl Like You', which the US band approved even if they thought its dreamy, ambient tones sounded like 'massage music', [45] according to Dolby.

At that point, American rockers often believed that synths were for wimps, so Dolby was effectively part of an experiment in exploring a new sonic language for them. 'There were no preconceptions of what the keyboards would sound like on their records. So I got into the studio with them, and it was a challenge,' he recalled. 'I had to introduce an alien element into that music.'[46] (He wasn't the only British electronic star to influence American rock; when bearded boogie monsters ZZ Top saw Orchestral Manoeuvres in the Dark play in 1980, they were so impressed that they decided to start using synths and drum machines on their own records).

Dolby also produced and played on records for musicians as diverse as Prefab Sprout, Joni Mitchell and George Clinton. Prefab Sprout's *Steve McQueen* was lauded as a classic; Mitchell's *Dog Eat Dog* wasn't. 'The album was quite electronic, and I think that her fans didn't receive the album well and they [wanted] someone to pin the blame on, and that was me,' Dolby acknowledged.[47]

His own albums were complex, cleverly crafted, at times introspective and thoughtful, at others irrepressibly effervescent and a little silly. He said he wanted to bring 'some kind of warmth or humanity to electronic music',[48] as imagery of computer-age alienation and future dystopias had become a cliché. More than many, he also worked to make electronic music's visions of a digital future real – in the early 1990s, he set up a Silicon Valley music software company that went on to create audio tools for websites and a microsynthesizer for mobile phones that allowed them to play polyphonic musical ringtones.

The music press sometimes mocked performers like Dolby as 'brainiacs' and 'eggheads' – stereotypes that Booker T. Boffin himself seemed to have a lot of fun sending up – but it was clear that electronic music did offer a platform for the technically adept to flourish. Landscape, best-known for their chirpy hit 'Einstein a Go-Go', also had an inventor in their ranks, drummer Richard James Burgess, who was involved in developing the hexagonal Simmons electronic drums, which became a staple of 1980s pop with their distinctive look and sound.

Landscape's members came from a musically-tutored jazz background rather than being Kraftwerk imitators or self-schooled electro-punks, although they did sometimes dress rather bizarrely in skintight black plastic or vibrantly-coloured jumpsuits, complementing their playfully clever, herky-jerky pop. 'People described us as looking like the bar band in *Star Wars* and I don't think that's unfair, we were pretty weird-looking back then,' laughs Burgess.

Their sleeve of their first single, 'European Man', saw probably the first use of the acronym 'EDM' for electronic dance music, which would not come into vogue in the US until the 21st century. 'The catalogue number is EDM1 and on the back it says: "Electronic dance music – EDM – computer programmed to perfection for your listening pleasure",' notes Burgess.

Landscape were genuinely fascinated by technology; Burgess had been one of around just 200 people in the world to buy a Roland MC-8 Microcomposer, a hugely expensive early sequencing unit that went on the market in 1977, while his bandmate John L. Walters had a Lyricon, an early electronic wind instrument. They even went on the BBC's popular science show *Tomorrow's World* in 1979 to demonstrate how they could process traditional instruments electronically. Addressing the TV audience, the presenter marvelled at the possibilities: 'Technology with its synthesizers, phasers, flangers, echo chambers and mixers has given the rock artist an entirely new palette of sounds.'[49]

But it was when Burgess heard a young DJ called Rusty Egan in a nightclub in Soho that he realised how electronic music could also become the soundtrack to a culture. 'What he'd done, which was in my mind genius, was he'd found every single track that fitted together to create a sort of sonic picture that he could visualise in his mind,' Burgess marvels. 'For me it was like: *Now I totally get it.* I understood where all this was going.' The club night was called the Blitz.

Blitz and Some Bizzare, New Romantics and Futurists
'The New Romantic movement of the late seventies was pivotal in creating a platform for what happened in the eighties. A lot of the electronic music that was played at clubs like the Blitz, as naive as some of it was, you could hear it filtered through into pop music in the eighties.'
Princess Julia, DJ and journalist

One of them was a bisexual dandy from a Welsh mining town who was desperate for *fame, fame, fame, fame*. The other was an entrepreneurial musician who had tuned into developments in continental Europe and heard the electronic future coming. Together, they became instigators of a scene that would help to shape the 1980s synth-pop movement.

Steve Strange had been known as Stephen Harrington until he reinvented himself, as he would also encourage others to do; his friend, club-runner Chris Sullivan, recalled how he 'created this being, "Steve Strange", who was his "art".'[50] Strange and DJ Rusty Egan started what they called a Bowie Night on Tuesdays at a little club called Billy's in London's Soho in 1978, drawing a mixture of fashion students, working-class chancers, stylists and hairdressers, all bored with what punk had become and still in love with the Thin White Duke.

'People stood in the Soho rain in gold braid and pill box hats, waiting to get in. Cossacks and queens mingled happily as narcissism ran riot,' Strange wrote in his autobiography. 'All these people were dressed like royalty, while in reality they were just ex-punks running up the clothes on their mum's sewing machines at home in the suburbs or living in the nearby squats.'[51]

For Mark Moore, a teenager who was going out clubbing for the first time, this hedonistic confection of gay, straight and polysexual was a revelation: 'It felt to me like the crowd were people who had been punks but had got sick of the uniformity of punk, in both the way people were dressing and the way people were making music. So it was almost like a rebellion against that, keeping a certain punk integrity but just going back to the original idea of punk, which was to be individual, rather than being a Sid Vicious clone.'

In February 1979, Egan and Strange relocated the club to Blitz, a World War II-themed wine bar in Covent Garden, which would retrospectively become known as the birthplace of the New Romantics. Strange argued they should have been called 'the cult with no name', but at the time, they were just known as the Blitz Kids, if anything at all: young individualists of various sexual persuasions who delighted in defying sartorial norms.

On the dancefloor were 'lads in breeches and frilly shirts, white stockings and ballet pumps, girls as Left Bank whores or stiletto-heeled vamps dressed for cocktails in a Berlin cabaret, wicked witches, kohl-eyed ghouls, futuristic man machines,'[52] journalist David Johnson later recalled. Strange created a stage on which they could perform; leading by example, he encouraged them to aspire to be original; dare to be different. Like him, they could escape social conventions and transform themselves into whoever they wanted to be.

Egan had travelled to Berlin and Düsseldorf and brought back crucial records like Gina X Performance's mighty 'No GDM', which he combined in the mix with the new post-punk DIY electronic music now being made by innovators like The Human League, Ultravox and The Normal; the Bowie Night name was dropped. Egan was unusual in post-war British youth culture for looking towards to Europe, and most specifically to Germany, for inspiration. Even though Britain had voted to join the European Economic Community in 1973, pop-cultural influences from mainland Europe were rarely imported and few European records reached the UK charts (Kraftwerk's 'Autobahn' in 1975 and Space's 'Magic Fly' in 1977 being notable exceptions). 'Rusty Egan was a fantastic DJ, he doesn't get enough credit. What he did was very futuristic, playing Kraftwerk and Yellow Magic Orchestra, test pressings by Visage, the original Ultravox, Telex,' says Mark Moore, who within a few years would become a celebrated DJ himself.

Blitz club founder and Visage frontman Steve Strange (centre) in London, July 1981. ©Brian Cooke/Getty Images.

While Egan's selections helped to define a post-punk electronic soundworld, the Blitz clubbers styled up glamorous images that would soon filter into the mainstream. This new pop-fashion hybrid would be hugely influential on the popular culture of the early eighties and make stars out of some of the club's regulars, including Strange and Egan themselves.

Both men were members of Visage, a band put together by Egan and singer Midge Ure, who would later replace John Foxx in Ultravox and finally push the band to pop success with the grandiloquent 'Vienna'. Visage's line-up also included Ultravox keyboard player Billy Currie and various members of Magazine. With decadent, Euro-tinged electronic disco tracks like 'The Damned Don't Cry' and 'The Anvil', they channelled some of the flamboyant energies of the clubs that Strange and Egan were running. Their biggest hit, 'Fade to Grey', with its shuttling synth riff and chilly atmospherics, also became an influence on early Detroit techno.

The other major band to emerge from the Blitz scene was Spandau Ballet, who were initially produced by Landscape's Richard James Burgess and wanted their synth-embellished white funk to resemble the music Egan played. 'We'd discussed it at the club,' the band's songwriter Gary Kemp remembered. 'Our future sound had to be like the one we heard every Tuesday night.'[53] Other Blitz clubbers created more eccentric sounds, like

Rexy, an off-kilter electronic duo featuring the deliciously deadpan vocals of fashion student Rex Nayman, who made one album of alluring song-sketches, *Running out of Time*, then disappeared into obscurity for four decades before returning with a follow-up that included a poignant tribute to the club where they met, recorded after Strange's death in 2015.

Billy's and Blitz showed how clubs could operate as incubators for new sounds and inspirations for new projects, as well as connectors for like minds seeking creative collaborators. 'These little clubs were like an experimental platform for people to say, "Right, we can actually make this sort of music ourselves",' says Princess Julia, who worked with Strange and appeared in Visage's 'Fade to Grey' video. 'The clubs were a catalyst for the people that were going to the clubs to start creating music that then became the soundtrack to the clubs.'

In a period of political tumult, rising unemployment and Cold War anxieties as Margaret Thatcher's right-wing government came to power, the Blitz Kids represented a colourful diversion for frivolity-seeking media. Coverage spread rapidly from the new youth magazines of the post-punk era, *The Face* and *i-D*, into the tabloid mainstream. 'They listen to loud, repetitive electronic music by cult bands,' the *Daily Mirror* reported. 'They dance using a mesmeric mixture of mime and robot movements.'[54]

David Bowie offered Blitz the ultimate publicity boost when he recruited Strange and three other regulars to appear in the video for 'Ashes to Ashes', which brilliantly mirrored back the sounds and images that had been partially copied from him in the first place. But the rock press was often dismissive about what one *Melody Maker* journalist called a 'narcissistic little scene' with 'depressingly sterile' music.[55] The Blitz Kids were portrayed as superficial and materialistic, unashamedly craving celebrity. But there was also an undercurrent of homophobia to the dislike of the New Romantics; while they may have been pure hedonists, they implicitly challenged social norms with their in-your-face, gender-fluid fashion styles. For men, wearing make-up in public was a serious taboo that could provoke violence. 'In such intolerant times, the way we all looked was extremely dangerous,'[56] Gary Kemp noted.

Outside London, the courageous minority who dressed to transgress were taking similar risks. 'If you dressed like a New Romantic, if you looked different, you would get called a poof or a fag. You were a target for ridicule at the very least or aggression at the worst,' says DJ Paulette, who began her glittering career in nightlife as a teenage dancer in the Roxy Room at Pips in Manchester, a club where post-punk misfits, Bowie freaks and proto-goths gathered.

By 1979, there were increasing numbers of British electronic musicians making records – not only better-known names like Gary Numan and Ultravox, but also completely out-there recordings from experimental bands like Storm Bugs and Metabolist, as well as humorous oddities like Blah Blah Blah's preposterously over-the-top squaddie satire 'In the Army'. Some of the early synth-pop records were ridiculously po-faced or insufferably quirky, and the singers often sounded like talent-night Bryan Ferry impersonators or anglicised versions of Iggy Pop circa *The Idiot*, but it was clear that some kind of movement was beginning to coalesce.

One of its animateurs would be Stevo Pearce, a working-class teenager from Dagenham in Essex who had started what he called a Sci-Fi Disco at London's Chelsea Drugstore; his photocopied flyer promised 'the weirdest sounds ever heard this side of Venus'. Stevo, as this excitable eccentric was simply known, described the electronic music he liked 'Futurist'; he saw it as less pop than the Blitz soundtrack and closer to industrial noise. Egan described him as an outsider: 'He was dyslexic, he was scruffy, he was not a cool Blitz kid.' But he also had irrepressible urge to evangelise for the music he loved, Egan added: 'He was incredible.'[57]

Up and down the country in 1980, a new British synth-pop narrative began to emerge amid the aftershocks of punk, as clubs that were running Bowie and Roxy nights or playing post-punk alternative music started showcasing electronic tracks as well. 'At one room at Pips [in Manchester] you'd get Siouxsie and the Banshees, Killing Joke and Bauhaus, in another you'd get Bowie and Roxy Music but also the new electronic records – Gary Numan, John Foxx, early Human League, Cabaret Voltaire,' says DJ Paulette. Clubs also started launching dedicated Futurist or New Romantic nights, from places like The Warehouse in Leeds, where Soft Cell's Marc Almond was one of the DJs, to Birmingham's Rum Runner, which nurtured Duran Duran.

Steve Proctor witnessed the emergence of Futurist clubbing as a DJ at Cagneys in Liverpool. 'When we started, we were doing Roxy-Bowie nights and the music was anything post-punk, anything electronic or different, and those nights evolved into what we called the Futurist scene,' says Proctor, who later went on to play at formative acid house clubs like Shoom. 'By the end of 1980, we were already hard into electronic dance music, which was like the new punk to me: it was experimental, it was independent, anyone could make a record.'

After *Sounds* started publishing Stevo's 'Futurist chart', listing his DJ selections, musicians began sending him tapes of unreleased material and self-financed 7-inch singles, so he decided to set up his own record label, the deliberately misspelt Some Bizzare, and assemble a compilation. The *Some Bizzare Album*, released at the start of 1981, was a snapshot of a genre taking shape. It included future stars Soft Cell, Depeche Mode, The The and Blancmange, plus cold-wave electro-pop from The Fast Set and Naked Lunch, experimental tracks from Neu Electrikk and Blah Blah Blah, and an indie band with a synth, B Movie. The compilation helped to define a Futurist musical style: offbeat pop produced on cheap electronic equipment – the sort of music that would become incredibly popular as soon as it became less offbeat and less cheaply produced.

Stevo was a maverick disruptor like Sex Pistols manager Malcolm McLaren; he sought to provoke controversy and sensation for the sake of publicity. 'Stevo was bonkers, but his intentions were good,' says Neil Arthur of Blancmange. He signed uncompromising bands to his Some Bizzare label, then convinced big record labels to finance their albums while preserving their artistic independence, relocating progressive art into a mainstream context. 'He collected eccentric bands that didn't fit the mould, and then licensed them to major labels. After the success of electronic-based bands like The Human League and OMD, record-company A&R men were looking for other synth-based new sounds, and Stevo tapped into that,' recalled Marc Almond, whose Soft Cell were signed by Stevo and then licensed to a major.[58]

This uncommon entrepreneur went on to sign up and then license a remarkable array of nonconformist musicians – Cabaret Voltaire, Coil, Psychic TV, Einstürzende Neubauten, Test Dept and even Agnes Bernelle, the former wife of sixties musique concrète experimentalist Desmond Leslie. 'The aim of Some Bizzare is to get the innovators deserved positions of recognition,'[59] he declared.

And for a few splendid years, as electronic music moved from the post-punk fringes of the late seventies into the mainstream pop arena of the eighties, he succeeded.

Soft Cell pose for a promotional photo in 1981. ©Pictorial Press Ltd/Alamy.

5

JUST CAN'T GET ENOUGH

Synth-Pop and Art-Rock

Soft Cell and the New Electronic Pop
'It was more than just pop music. We were definitely influenced by the punk attitude, as well as by Kraftwerk, who were like the electronic Beatles to people like us.'
Dave Ball

IN A SHIMMER OF SILVERY BANGLES and studded wristbands and a flicker of dark eyes traced out in kohl, the imp of the perverse and his besuited accomplice beckoned the early-evening audience of millions into their cabinet of decadent delights.

It was August 1981, and Marc Almond and Dave Ball were making their debut appearance on BBC One's prime-time TV chart show *Top of the Pops* with a performance of 'Tainted Love' that would provoke both outrage and adoration. As Almond, louche and brazenly queer, reconceptualised Gloria Jones' bittersweet Northern Soul banger as a transgressive anthem, Ball's minimalist electronic backdrop with its plink-plink syndrums and bouncing Korg bass made it sound immaculately modern.

'Tainted Love' made the link between queerness and electronic music overt. With Soft Cell's *Top of the Pops* appearance, Almond said he was seeking to emulate the impact that Bowie's extraordinary performance of 'Starman' on the BBC chart show had made on him back in 1972, when the outlandishly-garbed androgyne showed off his white nail polish and purple eyeshadow as he draped his arm around the shoulder of his golden-catsuited guitarist.

As a lonely gay teenager growing up amid the homophobic claustrophobia of a provincial town, this televised vision of an alternative sexuality which defied all socially-accepted sartorial norms made Almond feel he was not so isolated. In his autobiography, he wrote that he wanted to make teenagers 'squirm and blush', just as he had while watching Bowie: 'I felt like a Pied Piper for all the outsiders, for the unconventional, for the rejected and misunderstood, for the unattractive.'[1]

Almond's performance was all the more astonishing because it didn't conform to the camp stereotype projected by TV comedy figures of the time like John Inman or Larry Grayson, as he pointed out: 'I was something else – something insidious, dangerous, corrupting and sexual…'[2] Ball claims that after the broadcast, furious parents started calling the BBC to complain that Soft Cell were corrupting their innocent youngsters; he also believes their appearance made a deeply positive impact on lonely and isolated gay teenagers, just as Bowie had done for Almond: 'A lot of young gay men said to me that seeing Soft Cell, I knew I wasn't the only one.'

'Tainted Love' was one of the records that heralded the start of British synth-pop's imperial phase. But it was far from being the first UK-made electronic number one since the emergence of a post-punk electro-pop scene in 1978. Gary Numan, with Tubeway Army and solo, had topped the charts twice in 1979; The Buggles' 'Video Killed the Radio Star' also reached number one that year, while M's bouncy new wave-disco hybrid 'Pop Muzik' – with synthesizer played by John Lewis, sometime musical partner of the BBC Radiophonic Workshop's Brian Hodgson – got to number two. Electronic pop songs were still often perceived as novelty records at this point, but this was changing rapidly.

By early 1980, John Foxx was optimistically telling *Record Mirror* that 'some people have predicted that the synthesizer will be to the eighties like the guitar was to the sixties'.[3] Musicologist Joanna Demers has argued that the start of the eighties saw a turning point for electronic music, as the technology became progressively cheaper and easier to use. 'For most of the previous decade, synthesizers were expensive and bulky, and the few artists who had access to them were either successful rock stars or academic composers at research universities,' she wrote. 'The reasonably priced Korgs and Casios that flooded the market came with "patches" or preset materials, meaning that synthesizer users no longer had to know how to program their instruments. Early-1980s synthesizers were also lighter and smaller and therefore more portable.'[4]

The technologically-enhanced society envisaged by Kraftwerk's *Computer World* in 1981 was arriving; the early eighties saw the rise of arcade videogames and cheap home-computers like the ZX Spectrum and the Commodore 64, introducing computer graphics and 8-bit bleep music into young people's lives, while the BBC Micro brought programming into schools as part of a mass computer-literacy initiative. (Aphex Twin Richard James, who was a schoolboy when Sinclair Research first marketed the Spectrum in 1982, once said he always wanted to make his music sound like 'a danceable version of a Spectrum game'[5]). Even that early-eighties cultural paragon of British patriotism, Hugh Hudson's film *Chariots of Fire*, had an electronic score, albeit written by a Greek, Vangelis Papathanassiou.

New technology came onto the market constantly as the decade progressed, continually getting cheaper and more user-friendly. This was the era that moved to the beat of drum machines like the Linn LM-1, which debuted in 1980 with its programmable, sampled acoustic drum sounds, used liberally on albums like The Human League's *Dare*. The Linn and Oberheim DMX drum machines, as well as FM synthesizers like the Yamaha DX7, with its wealth of distinctive preset sounds, and the Fairlight, Synclavier and Emulator digital sampling synths combined to create the glossily artificial sounds that immediately came to signify 'eighties pop' and define the canon of classic songs played incessantly on the radio ever since.

In the early months of 1981, hits like 'Vienna', 'Fade to Grey' and 'Einstein a Go-Go' showed how the spiky, post-punk DIY electronic stylings of the years since 1978 had mutated into something that could be consumed as pop by a wider public. And because British pop moved so fast, by this time synth hits were not only made by musicians who came from the post-punk underground; there was also showbiz family progeny Kim Wilde with 'Kids in America' and The Korgis, former members of prog band Stackridge, with 'Everybody's Got to Learn Sometime'. When 'Tainted Love' and The Human League's 'Don't You Want Me' became Britain's best-selling singles of 1981, it confirmed that electronic music had moved conclusively from the post-war classical avant-garde into the pop-cultural mainstream.

Synth-pop would become one of the key cultural signifiers of the early eighties years of seemingly contradictory realities: a time of bright colours and grim politics; of technologically-modernised music but also of rising unemployment, manufacturing decline, inner-city riots, industrial strife, anti-nuclear demonstrations, IRA bombings and war with Argentina over the Falkland Islands. Synth-pop's stylistic genderfluidity was also at odds with the traditionalist moral values promoted by Margaret Thatcher's Conservative government. It wasn't just sonically progressive; by spotlighting openly gay performers, it implicitly promoted tolerance and a vision of a less prejudiced future.

Synth-pop's emergence as a major commercial force began when bands like The Human League, Blancmange and Vice Versa left behind the gawky weirdness and esoteric tinkering of their post-punk years and made their music more radio-friendly as they shifted from independent to major record companies and the New Romantic scene exploded out of the clubs. Journalist Dave Rimmer, who wrote for *Smash Hits* magazine, the mass-selling journal of eighties pop, noted how bands started to 'abandon any pretence at sonic experimentalism in favour of using new technology and electronic sounds to craft what were essentially good old-fashioned pop songs.'[6]

Blancmange had started out in the aftermath of punk 'making noises and trying to express ourselves' using tape loops, borrowed instruments and 'a weird Woolworths-type organ', according to singer Neil Arthur. But just a year after getting a song on Stevo Pearce's *Some Bizzare Album*, they had an international pop hit with 'Living on the Ceiling' and were having their sexually-charged electro-disco track 'Feel Me' remixed for the clubs by American DJ John Luongo. The culture was moving fast. 'It was a shock,' Arthur recalls; the duo had never really seen themselves as being part of the post-Blitz movement at all. 'Were we ever synth-pop? We used synthesizers and created pop music, so maybe. But were we Futurists? No, that was something that Stevo conjured up and I wanted nothing to do with it whatsoever. New Romantics? Absolutely fucking not.'

Soft Cell also graduated rapidly from the *Some Bizzare Album* to a much wider audience. Following on from original New York electro-punk band Suicide and quirky Los Angeles siblings Sparks, Marc Almond and Dave Ball set the template for the British synth-pop duo with their combination of charismatic singer and poker-faced keyboard player. Both men were from coastal towns in the northwest, Southport and Blackpool; Almond once described them as 'an industrial futuristic seaside cabaret act',[7] a perverted version of the pierhead cabaret partnership of overwrought crooner and Bontempi organist.

Ball, the adopted son of a telephone engineer who became an electronics expert whilst serving in the RAF during World War II, had built his own mobile-disco system as a teenager and used to go out dancing to Northern Soul at clubs like the Blackpool Mecca and Wigan Casino; Almond, whose father was a violent, alcoholic ex-army lieutenant, was into Bowie and T. Rex. Almond was gay and Ball was straight, but were both interested in the dark, subversive fringes of electronic music, bands like Cabaret Voltaire and Throbbing Gristle, as well as having aesthetic tastes in common, according to the singer: 'We both shared a love of the bizarre, the kitsch and seedy.'[8]

They met at Leeds Polytechnic, where they were both studying art and Ball had started experimenting at the college music studio using a secondhand Korg synth and a Stylophone. 'I'd never met anyone like Marc,' he says. 'I'd never known a guy that wore make-up. I just found him fascinating.' One of the guest lecturers was eccentric musique concrète composer Ron Geesin, who gave a demonstration of tape editing and the creative manipulation of pre-recorded sounds. Ball agreed to provide soundtracks for Almond's 'explicit and narcissistic' performance-art pieces, which had names like 'Glamour in Squalor' and 'Twilights and Lowlifes' – themes the duo would explore more deeply in the coming years.

Their songs developed into lyrically sardonic 'pocket operas', as Almond described them, warped social commentaries about everyday weirdness. 'Live, we had Super-8 films and slides projected behind us, which The Human League were also doing; it was quite a common thing at that time, I think because the nature of a synth band makes you quite static,' Ball explains. 'If you're stood behind a synth, you don't really move that much, unless you've got one of those stupid synths that look like a guitar.'

'Memorabilia', their first 12-inch release, was mixed by Daniel Miller, with its electronic pulses and insistent bassline inspired by the disco records they had heard at The Warehouse in Leeds; it wasn't a big hit but would come to be regarded as one of the earliest British proto-house tracks. It was followed by 'Tainted Love', with its idiosyncratically percussive bleeps created by running a Synare synth-drum through producer Mike Thorne's delay unit – a sound that Almond said would haunt him for the rest of his career – and its glorious segue into a cover of The Supremes' Tamla Motown classic 'Where Did Our Love Go' on the 12-inch.

From the outset, Almond styled himself as a misfit aesthete, a bard of sleazy glamour. But he was criticised by the gay press as a 'closet case' for not coming out publicly; he later admitted he'd been afraid his career would be damaged in the virulently homophobic social environment of the early eighties, when even major stars like Freddie Mercury and Elton John didn't dare reveal the truth about their sexuality. Almond also thought it was more interesting to decline to be defined: 'Hadn't all the stars that I'd ever loved been sexually ambiguous, mysterious, enigmatic? I wanted to be like them,'[9] he said.

This equivocation didn't save him from abuse; he has recalled how journalists variously described him as slimy, creepy, ugly, beady-eyed, pathetic, snivelling, miserable and mincing. One called him a 'perverted pipsqueak' while another said he couldn't wait for a suicide attempt. This was partly due to the male-dominated rock media's disdain for electronic musicians who didn't have guitars and made music 'for gays', Almond believes. 'There was a sneeriness laced with a not always obvious homophobia.'[10]

A crucial moment for Soft Cell came when they travelled to New York in 1981 to record their first album, *Non-Stop Erotic Cabaret*. Out clubbing one night at Studio 54, Almond met a young woman who called herself Cindy Ecstasy and introduced him and Ball to MDMA. Seven years before 1988's acid house 'summer of love', *Non-Stop Erotic Cabaret* would be the first British record to be coloured by the drug, according to Almond: 'It became a whole album that was done all around ecstasy.'[11]

It was another development in the long and fascinating relationship between electronic music and consciousness-altering drugs, and it made a significant impact on Soft Cell's creative processes. 'The albums I did around that time probably wouldn't have been the same without ecstasy. The first three Soft Cell albums – *Non-Stop Erotic Cabaret*, *Non-Stop Ecstatic Dancing* and *The Art of Falling Apart* – were all really albums that were just done around ecstasy and the whole E feeling,'[12] Almond explained.

Non-Stop Erotic Cabaret was made relatively cheaply using Ball's Korg, a Roland TR-808 drum machine – the unit that would become a crucial element in electro, house and techno – and a Synclavier, an early digital synthesizer with sampling capabilities owned by producer Mike Thorne, who had brought electronic textures to art-school post-punk band Wire on their albums *Chairs Missing* and *154*. 'I thrived on change,' said Thorne, who was one of the first British producers to buy a Synclavier. 'Having grown up producing punk and progressive (such as Soft Machine), I was intrigued by synthesizers, like anyone at the time looking for new sounds.'[13]

With Thorne, Soft Cell developed what would become one of the most distinctive sounds in eighties pop. 'I had a Korg SB-100 Synthe-Bass, it had a very dirty sound, a very distinctive bass sound, and Mike Thorne had the Synclavier, so we had a kind of collision of cheap, dirty, analog sounds with what was then a state-of-the-art drum machine, the 808, and then these mad digital sounds from the Synclavier which no one had ever heard before, including us,' says Ball. 'I think that was the classic Soft Cell early eighties pop sound – a mixture of this very expensive digital technology and a very cheap and dirty bass end.'

Non-Stop Erotic Cabaret also revelled in the seedy underside of socially conservative Britain in songs like 'Sex Dwarf', with its title lifted from a tabloid headline: 'Sex dwarf lures hundred disco dollies to life of vice.' In an example of life imitating art that imitated life, the video for the song – partly shot in a Soho brothel and featuring a naked trans person, Almond in fetishwear and Ball wearing a leather apron and wielding a chainsaw – was condemned as obscene by the tabloids, sparking a police raid on their management's office. 'I think we were transgressive and a bit naughty, poking fun with a tongue in cheek,' says Ball. 'We were always quite intrigued by political scandals – the Profumo affair, [disgraced MP] Jeremy Thorpe – and the whole idea of the hypocrisy behind the veneer of respectability of the establishment, who were basically the most corrupt and sleazy of all.'

Their subsequent release, *Non-Stop Ecstatic Dancing*, also produced by Thorne, was one of the first remix albums made by a white British band, although re-versioning existing material had long been commonplace in reggae. The album's sound was even more directly influenced by MDMA; Ball says it was intended to encapsulate the atmosphere of the clubs, music and drugs they had experienced in New York. Cindy Ecstasy's rap on the remodelled 'Memorabilia' preached the delights of taking a pill and surrendering to its empathic effects, a message enhanced by Thorne's psychotropically echoing sonic treatments. Almond called it 'the first ecstasy dance track' – not that anyone in Britain realised at the time. 'Nobody knew what we were talking about at all,' says Ball. 'When we got back to London, nobody had ever heard of ecstasy.'

Soft Cell's New York experience was just one of the factors that contributed to their unique vision, alongside northern glam and post-punk culture, performance art, queer sleaze, trash media and industrial experimentalism. But the massive success of 'Tainted Love' meant they were now a pop group, so pop songs were expected of them. Almond and Ball found this hard to deal with; they purposefully made their next albums of that period, *The Art of Falling Apart* and *This Last Night in Sodom*, darker, moodier and more difficult to consume. 'We never set out to be a pop band,' says Ball. 'It's just that first album just happened to sound like pop with very catchy songs, but then after that, we didn't really want to be pop anymore because we hated doing those stupid pop programmes like [children's TV show] *Tiswas* and those stupid pop magazines, and we just deliberately, wilfully wanted to sound dark in order to get away.'

In 1984, they decided to split. 'I think we were probably both doing too many substances,' Ball acknowledges. 'We were both a bit fucked up and didn't really know what the hell we were doing... It was sort of like being in a car with a foot on the floor and no steering wheel – it was bound to end.'

The Human League and Heaven 17

'I'd grown up with pop music, and I loved pop music... I really wanted to be in a pop band with our photos on the front cover.'
Phil Oakey[14]

In 1981, Britain's first big synth-pop year, Phil Oakey's dream came true: four huge hits for The Human League, culminating in their immaculate mini-drama 'Don't You Want Me', which sparkled festively at number one for a month over Christmas and New Year. Like Soft Cell, The Human League's roots were in arty alternative circles where people like Bowie, Burroughs and Ballard were idols; a review of one of their early gigs in *NME* in 1978 described their sound as 'experimental disco muzak for the humorous of heart'.[15] But they were always determined that their experiments would eventually lead to the pop charts, rather than stranding them on the avant-garde periphery. 'I like commercial music, and we certainly wanted The Human League to be commercial,' asserted Oakey.[16]

After their *Reproduction* and *Travelogue* albums, both artistically intriguing but relatively commercially unsuccessful, the band split in two, as singer Oakey and Human League visuals operator Adrian Wright parted ways with

The Human League in 1982. ©Pictorial Press Ltd/Alamy.

the band's synthesizer players, Martyn Ware and Ian Craig Marsh. Oakey and Wright continued as The Human League; seeking a purer pop sound, they made the audacious decision to replace the synthmen with two 17-year-old school students they met at a Futurist disco in Sheffield – Joanne Catherall and Susan Ann Sulley, who were complete musical amateurs and joined as dancer-singers – plus two professional musicians as keyboard players, Ian Burden and Jo Callis.

Catherall and Sulley were initially mocked and subjected to sexist insults. 'This man burst into Suzanne's dressing room and said, "I *hate* you, I think you are rubbish. You can't sing and you can't dance. I don't know why they had to recruit two such stupid girls",' Catherall told *Record Mirror*.[17] But their untutored vocals gave the music genuine charm by capturing the feeling of ordinary teenagers living the pop dream.

Forty years later, Sulley recalled that when 'Don't You Want Me' topped the charts, she thought to herself: 'This doesn't happen to schoolgirls from Sheffield… When I hear it on the radio today, I still wish I'd sung it better, but I was an ordinary girl doing her best and I think that resonated.'[18] Indeed, it was the combination of guileless enthusiasm and melodic nous, of northern working-class nightclub chic and art-pop acuity, plus producer Martin Rushent's deft programming of Linn drums and

Roland MC-8 MicroComposer, which made The Human League's third album, *Dare*, such a powerful statement of pop modernism, and such a commercial success.

In interviews, the band sought to distance themselves from rock orthodoxy, with Oakey talking about his love of ABBA and how they resisted their record company's urging to 'get a proper drummer' instead of a drum machine. 'I get sick of seeing these groups of four men. Four middle-class white young men,'[19] he said. In case their position was in any doubt, Wright explained helpfully: 'I hate rock.'[20] Oakey's image also added a tantalising element of genderfluidity. With his red lipstick, high heels, women's blouses and asymmetrical haircut reputedly copied from a young woman he saw on a bus, his ambiguous look put the questioning of identity on prime-time television, at a point in time when men who went out wearing conspicuous make-up and dangly earrings like Oakey risked physical attack.

Perhaps the ultimate embodiment of The Human League's anti-rock stance was their 1982 remix album *Love and Dancing*, a masterpiece of reimagination assembled by Martin Rushent and issued under the name of The League Unlimited Orchestra. Like Soft Cell's *Non-Stop Ecstatic Dancing* remix album, which was released a couple of weeks earlier, it was partly inspired by New York culture. But while Almond and Ball had been entranced by MDMA, Rushent was motivated by hearing hip-hop DJ Grandmaster Flash cutting up beats and thinking he could do something similar at his studio in Berkshire. Playing the multitrack tape of the *Dare* album through the mixing desk and manipulating the sound with an Eventide Harmonizer unit, delays and phasers, Rushent created new sequences and then spliced the best sections together manually. 'There were thousands of edits on the master and it took forever to do,'[21] he said.

Martyn Ware and Ian Craig Marsh took a more circuitous route to pop success than their former Human League colleagues. After the split, they initially set up what they described as a production company called the British Electric Foundation (B.E.F.). 'I wanted it to be like a conceptual art project so I thought wouldn't it be great if you could make it sound like this is an organisation that has existed forever and that you just never noticed it before,' explains Ware. Its first release was a cassette-only release of quirkily atmospheric electronic instrumentals called *Music for Stowaways*, intended to be played on the recently-introduced Sony Walkman (initially called the Stowaway in the UK). They also started a band with singer Glenn Gregory, named Heaven 17 after a fictional pop group in Anthony Burgess's dystopian novel *A Clockwork Orange*.

Ware said he was desperate for Heaven 17's first album, *Penthouse and Pavement*, to be a bigger hit than anything The Human League released because of the acrimony surrounding the breakup. 'To say we were motivated is an understatement,' he recalls. 'One of the things we said to ourselves was that we are going to be the most directly pop thing you could imagine – all that stuff about, "Oh, we want to be cool outsiders," went in the bin. So we were going to dress stylishly, do stylish videos, keep it electronically flavoured but with influences from Black American dance music, using things like funk bass guitar. We wanted to move away from the minimalist thing into a kind of a brave-sounding pop.'

They were also happy to play with the social dichotomies of the times. On the cover of *Penthouse and Pavement*, the trio ironically styled themselves as sharp-suited corporate executives, aspirational Thatcherite heroes – 'Play to Win', one of the tracks urged. As prime minister, Conservative leader Margaret Thatcher advanced a political philosophy that was anti-welfare state, anti-union, pro-boss and pro-profit, styling herself as the champion of 'hard-working families', industrious small business owners and ambitious entrepreneurs; those who aspired to create wealth and status for themselves. Many musicians, as instinctive non-conformists, were ideologically anti-Thatcher, although at the same time they were self-reliant individualists seeking 'independence' and 'freedom', concepts that Thatcherites said they prized.

Despite the album cover image however, Heaven 17 were leftists, like most electronic musicians from northern Britain. 'Anybody who reads the lyrics must know that there's a huge amount of socialist thought going into a lot of the subject matter,' Ware insists. "This is Mine' [from their third album] is practically a socialist manifesto in disguise, about allying yourself with other people, and of course we had a song that was actually banned by the BBC for its politics.' The corporation declined to play Heaven 17's first single, '(We Don't Need This) Fascist Groove Thang', because its lawyers feared that the electro-funk track libelled US President Ronald Reagan by calling him a fascist.

The peak electoral year for Thatcher's Conservative government was 1983, when it was returned to office in a landslide victory, heralding the most politically divisive period of the decade. It was also a peak year for bright and shiny eighties electronic pop, as exemplified by hits like Eurythmics' 'Sweet Dreams (Are Made of This)', Thompson Twins' 'Hold Me Now' and Heaven 17's melodramatic tour de force 'Temptation'.

Ware and Marsh had honed their pop strategies with the previous year's British Electric Foundation album, *Music of Quality & Distinction (Volume One)*, a set of cover versions of vintage hits by singers including Billy Mackenzie of The Associates, Sandie Shaw and Gary Glitter. The album was credited with instigating the commercial resurgence of Tina Turner; Ware and Marsh would go on to produce some of the American R&B star's solo tracks. By 1983, when they released Heaven 17's second album, *The Luxury Gap*, they had developed a sound that would come to be regarded as definitive mid-eighties electro-pop, including songs like 'Temptation' and the more moodily emotional 'Let Me Go' with its acidic bassline, one of the first pop records to feature the Roland TB-303.

'By this time we had the tools to make classic pop music and the budget to hire session players, orchestras and so on because the record company believed in our hit potential,' says Ware. 'We weren't worried about our credibility, because we thought we'd pretty much established that with the early Human League and with B.E.F. So we had nothing to prove. It was time to take the brakes off.'

Depeche Mode, Perpetual Futurists

'You have to take risks… you can't be safe all the time.'
Dave Gahan[22]

It's an enduring irony that the band that went on to make some of the greatest electronic pop records of their era were initially seen by critics as lightweights, second-rate latecomers, gawkily-dressed teenagers from the unfashionable Essex town of Basildon; wimps. 'Depeche Mode are inoffensive fledglings, wide-eyed and fluffy-haired... earnest and endearing, young, glowing and sweet,'[23] an *NME* reviewer wrote in 1981, the year that the band's main songwriter, Vince Clarke, quit after their first album was released.

It was thought they would flounder without Clarke, but the opposite happened. Over the years that followed, with Martin Gore taking over the lead songwriting role, Depeche Mode started to explore new sampling techniques, harder beats, more dramatic melodies and deeper lyrical themes – masochism, guilt, betrayal, redemption. Decades later, they were still making powerful new music when many of their contemporaries were playing nostalgia tours and back-to-the-eighties themed festivals.

Depeche Mode were a second-wave UK synth-pop group, formed after Gary Numan's first number one hit. Founding members Clarke and Andy Fletcher were churchgoing young Christians, but punk inspired them to form a band; Gary Numan and Orchestral Manoeuvres in the Dark then showed them they could make more interesting sounds cheaply. 'I realised that you could buy a synthesizer for a certain amount of money, and just by hitting one or two keys you could do things that sounded fantastic and contemporary,'[24] said Clarke. For singer Dave Gahan, Bowie also gestured towards another way of being. 'Bowie represented a way for me to get out of myself, and also to escape from where I was,' Gahan explained. 'Bowie gave me a hope that there was something else. This world that he seemed to be a part of – where was it? I wanted to find it.'[25]

By this point, Daniel Miller's Mute Records had established a reputation for innovative releases: Miller's own single as The Normal, techno-punky records by Fad Gadget and Deutsch Amerikanische Freundschaft (D.A.F.), plus Silicon Teens, a fake teenage electro-pop group that was actually Miller with his Korg. When he saw Depeche Mode for the first time in 1980 at a pub in London's East End, he found his dream of a teen synth band come to life: four young innocents in High Street New Romantic clobber with their little synths mounted on beer crates and a lead singer holding a light that he shone upwards onto his face, in an attempt to cast shadows that would make him look mysterious.

Miller was impressed by their functional methodology. 'They had three very simple synths, basically the three cheapest you could buy at that time – all monophonic, no presets – and a little Boss drum machine, and I thought what they created with that, live, with that very kind of minimal equipment, was really outstanding,' he says. These weren't art-school students who worshipped Throbbing Gristle or Can, but Essex boys making pop music with electronic instruments; ingenues in eyeliner, happy to be called Futurists.

The Mute founder became Depeche Mode's record-label boss, producer and musical mentor. 'The songs were written, pretty much, but he helped us with sounds because we were completely clueless. We'd never seen a sequencer, and we'd never been into a professional recording studio before. It was all new, and he was our guide,' recalled Clarke. 'The artists on Mute, especially in the early days, they were his children.'[26] The Basildon boys responded by delivering seventeen Top 10 albums for Mute over the four decades that followed.

Early singles like 'New Life' and 'Just Can't Get Enough' pulsated with youthful optimism but were scorned by some reviewers as tinkly and trite. By contrast, when Clarke left the band and started Yazoo with R&B-loving ex-punk singer Alison Moyet, the duo attracted instant acclaim for their fusion of soulful vocals and minimal but evocative electronic settings – even though Moyet initially declared that she was a musical traditionalist who 'can't accept the fact of blues with synthesizers at all'.[27]

As Miller pointed out, Moyet's boldly assertive image 'didn't fit the typecast female pop star image' of the time.[28] Combined with Clarke's chilly synths, her passionate contralto also set Yazoo apart; few others apart from Eurythmics were fashioning such a distinctively British electronic soul sound at that point. 'Only You' was one of the most emotionally powerful ballads of the period, while 'Situation' became a proto-house classic in US clubs. Moyet's effervescent laughter, echoing across the start of the song, would be sampled scores of times, reappearing as a vivacious motif in records as diverse as Rhythim is Rhythim's Detroit techno classic 'The Dance' and Los Del Rio's international novelty hit 'Macarena'.

Yazoo's brilliant trajectory was brief. They only recorded two albums together before they split in 1983; Moyet became a solo star while Clarke went on to form yet another hugely successful synth-pop band, Erasure. 'You don't need talent to play a synthesiser and make electronic music,' he once said, perhaps sarcastically.[29] But this unostentatious artist-technician certainly had a creative gift: the enduring ability to construct electronic pop songs that made people happy.

Around the same time as Yazoo were breaking up, Depeche Mode were beginning to surprise some of their critics with their increasingly adventurous approach to technology and songwriting on their third album, *Construction Time Again*. Miller had bought a Synclavier digital synthesizer, and its sampling facility gave the band access to sounds that few others had. 'We were very into pushing the technology as far as we could,' he says of their collaboration. 'Generally we tried to create all the sounds from scratch, which is more interesting and much more fun, whether it was a drum sound or a bass.' Miller always insisted that Depeche Mode were 'a Futurist band, not a New Romantic band'. Now they were proving it.

With engineer-producer Gareth Jones, they would take tape recorders to a scrapyard and a disused railway depot near the east London studio where they were recording and capture the sounds of hammers and sticks clanking on metal pipes or banging on corrugated iron. The best recordings were sampled into the Synclavier and used as percussion noise. 'We made a conscious decision to become harder musically. So we thought, "What sounds really hard and nasty?" – and of course we decided on metal,' explained synth player Alan Wilder.[30]

Ideas were adopted from German metal-bashing industrial band Einstürzende Neubauten, Gore admitted: 'I was at their ICA [Institute of Contemporary Arts] date [in London], when they did the metal concerto, and the power and the excitement of it was brilliant. What we're doing, though, is using the ideas in a different context, in the context of pop.' Gahan said he couldn't understand why other bands used the new sampling technology to emulate traditional instruments: 'If you're going to spend that amount of money hiring a piece of equipment, then why not explore it?'[31]

Construction Time Again was mixed at Hansa Studios in Berlin, near the Wall in the western part of the then-divided Cold War city, where the band also explored sleazy bars and gay clubs 'because they had the best vibe and music',[32] said Wilder. '[Berlin] was a place full of artists and people interested in alternative lifestyles, and it's a 24-hour city,' Miller told the band's biographer, Steve Malins. 'It was a very sexual place. It had a sense of eroticism, adventure and excitement.'[33]

Inspired by Berlin's fetish clubs, Gore started wearing rubber and leatherwear, as well as bondage harnesses that exposed his nipples, although he still resembled a peroxide-quiffed cherub. 'I suddenly discovered all this freedom,' he said. 'It was a big turning point for me.'[34] Channelling their Berlin experiences, Depeche Mode's fourth album, *Some Great Reward*, introduced darker, more sexualised atmospheres, although it didn't stop S&M-themed single 'Master and Servant' becoming a pop hit.

Depeche Mode developed their sampling techniques yet further on the *Black Celebration* album in 1986, generating new sounds to avoid synth presets, using samples of struck springs to create guitar parts or hitting the end of a Hoover tube to build bass notes, feeding the sounds through guitar amplifiers to transform them again. 'We had this theory at the time that every sound must be different, and you must never use the same sound twice,'[35] recalled Andy Fletcher. They also started to use remixers, commissioning reggae producer Adrian Sherwood to add dubbed-out esoterica to their 12-inch releases.

What followed was a brace of albums whose sonic ambition has rarely been equalled in British electronic pop: *Music for the Masses* in 1987, followed by the magisterial *Violator* in 1990. 'Never Let Me Down Again', the first single from *Music for the Masses*, signalled the band's intent with its swooning rush of a chorus and lyrics that seemed to simultaneously suggest both homoeroticism and narcotic euphoria; its follow-up, 'Behind the Wheel' was ambiguously sexual and hedonistic. *Violator* was even better, a drift through Gore's obsessions with guilt and redemption, sexual obsession and self-consciousness set to an obsidian-sheen production by Flood, with mixing by New York disco veteran François Kevorkian that sounded as futuristic as some of the best techno records of the time.

By this time, Depeche Mode's influence was not only being felt in the mainly white 'alternative' dance clubs of Europe and the US, but also with some young Black Americans. Many British electronic pop records were popular with cutting-edge Black DJs in the US – Afrika Bambaataa loved Gary Numan's 'Are 'Friends' Electric?', Larry Levan loved Yazoo's 'Situation', Ron Hardy loved Visage's 'Frequency 7' – and as a consequence, new underground dance genres like Chicago house and Detroit techno incorporated ideas from British electronic bands like Depeche Mode, often to their surprise.

When they visited Detroit in 1988 and met some of the Black techno innovators who admired them, they were completely bemused. 'We can't create dance music, and I don't think we've ever really tried. We honestly wouldn't know where to start,'[36] Gore said. Fletcher recalled how they were welcomed with open-hearted enthusiasm at the Majestic and Music Institute dance clubs: 'We were just mobbed by beautiful black people, young girls and boys. It was kind of weird – we always thought we were the whitest of the white,'[37] he said.

But for Detroit techno producer Kevin Saunderson, there was no confusion about the band's appeal: Depeche Mode's sound was clean, electronic, beat-heavy – and exotic: 'It's real progressive dance, and had this feeling that was *sooo* European.'[38]

Joy Division, New Order and the Electronic Side of Factory

'Most people who listen to Joy Division today never got to see us live so they've got no idea that we actually sounded nothing like the records.'
Stephen Morris

Back in 1979, Joy Division were making an album that would have a huge emotional impact on their generation; an album that used electronic textures and studio experimentation to create a groundbreaking piece of post-punk rock music. The only problem with *Unknown Pleasures* was that the band weren't completely sure that they actually liked how it sounded.

During the recording process, their raw live sound was relocated into imaginary sonic environments created using guitarist Bernard Sumner's glacial sweeps of synthesizer, Stephen Morris's synth-drum sounds and the unconventional techniques of Factory Records' in-house producer Martin Hannett, which involved the extensive use of reverberation, echo and effects created by Hannett's beloved Marshall Time Modulator and AMS Digital Delay boxes.

Like Bowie's Berlin Trilogy, Hannett's work for Joy Division expanded the sonic vocabulary of rock music. 'What Martin did with Joy Division was he put it in a place that didn't really exist anywhere, and it certainly didn't exist in *our* heads,' says Morris. But the band often felt that his reinterpretations lacked their raw live power. 'We had an idea about what it should sound like – we'd have done it more like The Stooges. But Martin gave it an atmosphere, using the studio as an instrument and all these effects and delay lines to process the drums.'

While they were making *Unknown Pleasures*, Hannett didn't explain much to the band about what he was doing to their music, or why. 'Martin was very, very important to the sound of Joy Division,' says Morris. 'But unfortunately, he wasn't really the most communicative of people – sometimes I wonder if he knew what the idea in his head was, or whether he was actually just making it up and seeing what happened.'

Nevertheless, Morris enjoyed playing with the new technology. 'When I first got a syndrum, I found I could just twiddle a few knobs and get a wild and interesting sound out of it without knowing what the hell I was doing. Helicopters! Machine guns! Lasers!' he exclaims. Sumner had built his monophonic analog synth from a kit – a cheap, British-produced unit called the Powertran Transcendent 2000, designed by a former technician at EMS, purchased by mail order after he saw an advertisement in hobbyist magazine *Electronics Today*. Adverts for the synth kit offered it for 'only £168.50 + VAT!' Sumner said he started getting interested in electronic instruments when singer Ian Curtis introduced him to Kraftwerk: 'He used to play *Trans-Europe Express* before we went onstage, and I loved it.'[39]

Despite some of their reservations about Hannett's eccentric approach to recording, Sumner and Morris got more deeply involved in his experiments on Joy Division's second studio album, *Closer*, the last they would make before Curtis committed suicide in May 1980. The Moroderesque rhythm on 'These Days' was created by feeding a guitar signal through a synthesizer, while the horror-movie effects on 'Atrocity Exhibition' came from a Synare drum synth fed through a fuzz pedal. The increasing emphasis on the artificial wasn't universally welcomed, however: Sumner said Curtis felt that the extensive use of synths on *Closer* 'made it sound like fucking Genesis'.[40]

After the shock of Curtis's suicide and the band's subsequent reinvention as New Order, their initial concerts were a rather dour contrast to the darkly thrilling energies of Joy Division's performances, as the band struggled to establish a new identity without their singer. 'We had to change, we were in a state of not knowing what we were going to do next,' says Morris. They invited his partner, Gillian Gilbert, to join the band on keyboards, shifting the orientation of their sound further towards the synthetic, changing the way they constructed their music as well as altering the gender balance. 'You cannot underestimate the sudden shock and the change that bringing a female into what was sort of an all-lads club,' recalls Morris. 'It was difficult for her, she had to put up with the misogyny and all that fucking male bullshit, but it was what she wanted to do.'

In Sumner's autobiography, he describes the emergence of New Order's individual sound as a move out of darkness. 'Our music had become so incredibly dark and cold, we couldn't really get any darker or colder,'[41] he explained. Speaking to author Richard King, the guitarist also credited cannabis and LSD for opening his ears to electronic dance music. 'I guess for a long time after Ian [Curtis] died I was really depressed and sad,' he said. 'Then I started smoking draw and I found when I was smoking draw that electronic music sounded great, and I started taking acid. Electro music: 'E=MC2' by Giorgio Moroder, Donna Summer albums, early Italian disco records – it had a wonderful effect on me.'[42]

New Order's self-produced third single, 'Everything's Gone Green', started to establish their own blend of post-punk rock and electronic dance-pop. Morris said the record was the result of a chance experiment – the rhythmic chattering that emerged when a Boss Dr. Rhythm analog drum machine was plugged into an ARP Quadra synthesizer, just to see what happened. 'It went "dakka-dakka-dakka-dakka-dakka" and we thought, "This sounds brilliant! It sounds like Giorgio Moroder, let's just do a track just like this!'" he recalls. 'It was a happy accident. There were lots of happy accidents at the time because the gear was very, very limited in what you could do with it. But it seemed magic.'

The sound reflected the band's enthusiasm for the energy and groove of the early electro tracks they heard while gigging in the US. Sumner also said he was inspired by European electronic dance records sent to the band from Berlin by their record label Factory's representative in Germany, Mark Reeder, and cassette tapes of New York dance radio station Kiss FM: 'We all thought New York sounded like the future.'[43]

The ideas that they filtered out of New York and continental Europe into 1983's 'Blue Monday', their 12-inch masterpiece, were many and various: Morris has cited the Italo-disco classic 'Dirty Talk' by Klein & M.B.O., which was a dancefloor favourite at electro nights at Manchester's Legend club, and Donna Summer's 'Our Love', whose unusual rat-a-tat bass-drum punctuation New Order imitated. Sumner has also mentioned influences ranging from US electro and Sylvester's gay anthem 'You Make Me Feel (Mighty Real)' to the clubs they visited in New York like the Fun House and the Paradise Garage. (The oft-repeated suggestion that they plagiarised the tune from Mancunian novelty electro-punk band Gerry and the Holograms' self-titled debut single has been denied, however).

For the recording of 'Blue Monday', they also had some crucial new electronic kit – a programmable Oberheim DMX digital drum machine, whose punchy beats would become synonymous with hip-hop in the eighties, and an E-mu Emulator, a digital sampling synthesizer. They used the Emulator to lift the distinctive choir chords from Kraftwerk's 'Uranium', which were themselves samples of a choir that the German band had taken from a Vako Orchestron, an obscure 1970s keyboard instrument that replayed sounds prerecorded on optical discs. There was also another happy accident: an unintentionally brilliant, out-of-sync melody line created by Gilbert when she was manually programming the song from notes on paper; she said she 'accidentally left a note out, which skewed the melody'.[44] It sounded great. 'When we heard it, we were like, "It's wrong – but in a really good way,"' says Morris.

Adding to the chain of sampling and resampling involved in the creation of the record – a theme that would become increasingly common in electronic music as the eighties continued – 'Blue Monday' itself would be reused as the basis for hi-NRG maestro Bobby O's production of American drag performer Divine's song 'Love Reaction', and would also reverberate through early Detroit techno tracks like Kreem's 'Triangle of Love', produced by Kevin Saunderson and Juan Atkins.

The huge success of 'Blue Monday', with Peter Saville's cover artwork based on an Emulator floppy disk, highlighted how independent rock music was changing as it adapted to the possibilities of technology and the 12-inch vinyl format. Synth-pop bands like Soft Cell, Depeche Mode and Blancmange, as well as mainstream stars like Queen and Billy Idol, were already exploiting the creative and commercial possibilities of the 12-inch by having extended remixes commissioned with heavier drums and more dubbed-out noises to boost their dancefloor impact.

Blitz club instigator Rusty Egan was among the first UK club DJs to get involved, remixing French cosmic disco band Space and the cult Afro-electronic track 'Burundi Black' in 1981; the following year he also remixed Madonna's debut single, 'Everybody'. Blitz regulars Spandau Ballet were one of the first bands to have an entire record remodelled, with the box set of 12-inch remixes of their *Diamond* album by Richard James Burgess in 1982, while producers Mike Hedges and Martin Rushent were also creating extended mixes for alternative rock bands like Siouxsie and the Banshees and Altered Images. It was a trend that was set to intensify as the decade continued.

Initially, however, there was no remix of 'Blue Monday'. When Greg Wilson, a DJ at Factory's Haçienda club, asked New Order's Peter Hook if he could rework it, the bass player said no: 'I told him to fuck off, thinking it was the most disgusting thing anyone had ever suggested – why should we let someone tamper with our work?'[45]

Despite Hook's initially hostile attitude to remixology, New Order decided to make a collaborative record in New York with Arthur Baker, who had produced Afrika Bambaataa and the Soul Sonic Force's 'Planet Rock', the track that helped to define the electro genre. Baker was a non-musician who had a Roland TR-808 drum machine, a talented keyboard-playing co-producer, John Robie, and a pragmatic attitude. When confronted with 'hours and hours of rambling jams' recorded by New Order while they were trying to come up with a song, Baker decided to scrap most of the material. 'He just went: "No, I can't listen to that",' says Morris. 'Because Arthur was a DJ, he said: "I just want that specific bit, *just that bit* – just play those two bars over and over and over." And that was how 'Confusion' started, really. We built it from just an 808 riff, which was basically from Arthur's file of 808 riffs.'

New Order's 'Confusion' single wasn't Factory Records' only dalliance with electro. Sumner and A Certain Ratio's drummer Donald Johnson also produced and remixed a series of records for the label that made them key figures in the crossover between punk-funk, electro and soul that was happening in Manchester at the time, including 52nd Street's 'Cool as Ice' and psychedelic post-punk band Section 25's iridescent, trancelike 'Looking from a Hilltop (Megamix)'.

Sumner and Johnson brought a warmth and grooviness that contrasted with the wintry productions of Martin Hannett. 'We did the complete opposite of what Martin did. He wanted everything to be clean and accurate so he could work with the sound, but we wanted more humanity,' Johnson explains. 'We were trying to create these hybrids, we wanted to mash things up, like the music we soaked up in New York every time I was there with A Certain Ratio, from Sugar Hill to 'Planet Rock' to Talking Heads and Lou Reed.'

Live recordings from the period also testify that Section 25 had started using the wild, flaring acid noise generated by the Roland TB-303, even before many Chicago acid house records. Singer Larry Cassidy was characteristically forthright about his band's shift from post-punk experimentalism into a kind of electronically-inflected dance-rock: 'You can't be a punk all your life,'[46] he declared.

Factory's most wholeheartedly electronic band were Quando Quango, who were also produced by Sumner and Johnson and whose line-up included future DJ star Mike Pickering and future professor of sonic culture Hillegonda Rietveld. Pickering, who used to publish the fanzine *Modern Drugs* with Martin Fry (later of Vice Versa and ABC), formed the band with Rietveld in her hometown, Rotterdam. She said that when Vice Versa came to the Dutch port city to record their 'Stiylagi' single, she became intrigued by how the Sheffield group were using synthesizers. 'So ironically, we started making electronic music at the point when Vice Versa picked up the guitar and became ABC,' she says.

Relocating to Manchester when Pickering was appointed creative director of Factory Records's new club, the Haçienda, Quando Quango started recording singles for the label – left-field electro-pop and 808-driven alternative dance records like 'Go Exciting' and 'Love Tempo'. Their sound was unusual in the UK at the time because they drew on Rietveld's desire to emulate minimalist electro-punk bands like D.A.F. and Suicide, as well as on Pickering's love of Black American dance music and Northern Soul. 'It was actually quite a good strong combination because it had some kind of poptasticness with lots of weird sounds,' says Rietveld.

But while Quando Quango were seen in Britain as an odd post-punk group, their music connected with some of the more adventurous DJs at New York dance clubs who had a taste for what Rietveld describes as 'European import weirdness'. 'Larry Levan and Mark Kamins loved the 'Love Tempo' record, much to our astonishment,' confirms Pickering.

Like New Order, Quando Quango operated for a brief but significant period as cultural couriers between New York and their hometown, bringing fresh ideas direct from Manhattan to Manchester. Kamins remixed 'Love Tempo' and Quando Quango played at Levan's club, the Paradise Garage, making a crucial connection for Pickering, who quickly started to implement what he had learned: 'When they were putting the DJ booth in the Haçienda, they started putting in a built-in microphone and I said, "I don't want a microphone." And they said, "How's the DJ going to talk to the audience?" And I was like, "Through the decks, that's how the DJ talks to the audience," because I'd seen it in New York – the DJs just mixing records, not talking.'

The Haçienda provided a social forum that nurtured creative talent in the city for fifteen years but operated chaotically and had to be sustained by more than a million pounds of investment from New Order, who effectively became patrons of the city's musical scene. But despite the financial losses, Stephen Morris believed that ultimately, it was worthwhile: 'That money made a lot of people very happy, it helped to make something that in some small way changed the way the world worked and the way people thought,' he wrote in his autobiography. 'That is priceless.'[47]

As for Quando Quango, they split up after one album when Pickering and Rietveld's relationship ended. Rietveld only realised years later that records like 'Love Tempo' had made a serious impact on some of the creators of house music when she travelled to Chicago to research her PhD thesis about the genre. 'People I talked to in Chicago just thought it was quite wild and different,' she says. 'When I interviewed Vince Lawrence, who claims to have recorded the first house record, 'On and On', he said that he heard 'Love Tempo' when he was about sixteen and felt very inspired by it and thought, "Wow, if that is possible, then I want to try making a record".'

Over in Liverpool, meanwhile, another band that attracted admirers far from home was also creating wild and different music: Pink Industry, who mapped out territory between electronic dance music and indie dream-pop. Their singer was Jayne Casey, a cultural instigator who would continue to be a key figure in the rave era, when she worked as head of communications for Liverpool 'superclub' Cream, and then as artistic director for various cultural institutions in the city. An admiring profile in the *Liverpool Echo* once described her as an 'eternal non-conformist' with an 'uncanny zeitgeist instinct'.[48]

Casey became a face on the local alternative scene while she was still a teenager, known for her keen wit, sharp mind and compelling shaven-headed image. In 1977, she joined Big in Japan, a short-lived punk band better known for its various members' subsequent careers than its own music, including Bill Drummond (later of The KLF), Holly Johnson (Frankie Goes to Hollywood), Budgie (The Slits, Siouxsie and the Banshees) and Dave Balfe (The Teardrop Explodes), amongst others.

After the demise of her post-punk group Pink Military, Casey formed Pink Industry with Ambrose Reynolds, a bassist who had been involved in an early incarnation of Frankie Goes to Hollywood. 'I wanted to get rid of drums and get rid of middle eights and let things just run and groove, just let those drum machines roll,' she recalls. 'Before I was working with musicians who were more from a rock background, so it could only go so far.'

Casey was also seeking a means of self-expression outside the gender stereotypes of the time. 'I think that's one of the reasons that I found electronic music. I was really interested in how to express myself as a woman and in electronic music, I found that freedom,' she reflects. 'I was young and I had a story that I wanted to tell, and it was a very sad story, and to set it against quite cold, industrial music worked perfectly.'

When Pink Industry started, Casey had recently had a baby. 'Things like that have a massive impact on women in music,' she says. 'I had to write around all these domestic things, I wrote the bassline for the first Pink Industry song 'Don't Let Go' while I was washing the dishes.' Seeking independence, Pink Industry recorded at home and released their three albums independently on their own Zulu label. With their minimalist settings, hazy melodies, ticking drum machines and Casey's intimate song-sketches, they initially sounded like fellow travellers of 4AD Records dream-pop bands like Cocteau Twins, but by the time of their *New Beginnings* album they had developed their own idiosyncratic strain of left-field, electronic dance music.

Pink Industry attracted a cult following in Brazil, where their electronic tracks were compiled on the album *New Naked Technology*, but they split in 1987, just before the dance music boom that might have granted them a wider listenership in the UK. 'We were out on a limb musically, working in the wilderness, not really selling many records,' explains Casey. 'It just seemed like it was time to end it.' Unexpectedly, however, some of the people who did like their music went on to play important roles in the British dance scene, among them DJ Andrew Weatherall. 'Even though we had such a small audience, that audience had gone on to be kids who created dance music,' Casey says. 'I found that absolutely fascinating.'

Trevor, Malcolm, Frankie and the Fairlight

'The only form of music that isn't conservative is pop music... It's whatever you can get normal people to buy.'
Trevor Horn[49]

Veteran British singer Dusty Springfield took to the dancefloor in 1979 with a synth-disco song called 'Baby Blue'. The same year, an obscure band called Chromium, whose players included future Art of Noise member Anne Dudley and future Hollywood soundtrack composer Hans Zimmer, put out a poppy sci-fi dance album called *Star to Star*. Also in 1979, a ludicrously catchy electro-pop song inspired by a J. G. Ballard short story about an opera singer rendered unemployable by new technology reached the top of the UK charts.

The song was 'Video Killed the Radio Star' by The Buggles and the link between all three records was producer Trevor Horn, a former jobbing musician who had played in British disco star Tina Charles' band and soaked up wisdom from her Indian-born producer, Biddu. Horn's first production had been a singalong record for Leicester City football club.

The Buggles were initially conceived as a kind of 'robot Beatles', Horn has said, and some of the traits that would make him perhaps the definitive British pop producer of the 1980s were already audible from their first record: the intensive production techniques, the love of technological novelty, the desire to create widescreen landscapes of sound and the (sometimes unapologetically cheesy) sense of fun. As pivotal moments in his musical development, Horn has cited an ear-opening LSD trip in his twenties – 'My paradigm for a record was always putting on a pair of headphones and getting lost in it; the record taking you on a journey' – as well as hearing Donna Summer's 'I Feel Love' and Kraftwerk's album *The Man-Machine*: 'A mechanised rhythm section... It sounded so new and exciting, so full of potential.'[50]

As with so many British electronic producers, another source of ideas was dub reggae. 'I loved how it was so brutal,' Horn wrote in his autobiography. 'How the producer would break down the sound, strip it to its raw elements. How everything would go through an echo unit and clank between the speakers. Most of my ideas for the 12-inch remixes I used to make in the 1980s came from those records.'[51]

His work, even more than most other producers of the 1980s, was defined by the new technological innovations coming onto the market and his adeptness at exploring their possibilities. He started out using basic string synths on the pop-disco records he produced in the late seventies as he couldn't afford real players – the same motivation that drove some of the original Chicago house music producers to use obsolete Roland drum machines to try to emulate disco, creating an entirely new genre in the process.

But the instrument that became synonymous with Horn's productions, and with the gleaming electronic pop sound of the mid-eighties, was Fairlight Instruments' Fairlight CMI (Computer Musical Instrument), generally regarded as the first commercially-available digital sampler. It went on the market in 1979, the year before New England Digital released its rival sampling synthesizer, the Synclavier. Press advertisements promoted the Fairlight as 'an entirely new concept in electronic musical instruments'.[52] Ads for the Synclavier were similarly effusive: 'Its patented digital method transcends "realism",'[53] one declared.

The advent of the Fairlight and the Synclavier marked a crucial shift in pop music away from natural sound recordings of songs performed on acoustic or electric instruments towards music partly or wholly constructed technologically, prefiguring the computer-based music of the following decades. By the early eighties, the music on some pop records had become so completely removed from natural sound that it 'resembled nothing that had been heard before', as musicologist Samantha Bennett noted in her history of recording techniques.[54]

'With Fairlight, the horizon didn't just broaden, it virtually disappeared,' said Horn, who was one of the first people in Britain to buy one. 'All you needed was an imagination.' Sounds could be stretched, layered, pitched up or pitched down; Horn said he used to stay awake at nights dreaming up new tricks to play with it: 'Quite a few times in the early 1980s, I would find myself

177

in a room with a record producer and I'd know what they were going to ask, and it would be this: "How the hell are you doing what you're doing? There's something going on and I can't figure out what it is." The answer was the Fairlight.'[55]

Fairlights and Synclaviers were hugely expensive, and few could afford them, initially giving producers like Horn an advantage. Whilst producing ABC's *The Lexicon of Love* album, Horn assembled a creative team that included keyboard player and arranger Anne Dudley, engineer Gary Langan and Fairlight programmer J. J. Jeczalik. 'J. J. was like a scientist. He didn't sample instruments. He sampled tennis matches, things falling over, small explosions. It gave me a whole new palette of colours,'[56] Horn later said.

Jeczalik took the view that that there was little to be gained creatively from using the Fairlight to parrot existing instruments. Whilst producing a session for Paul McCartney, George Martin had asked him to work up a horn section out of trombone samples. The result was unimpressive, and Martin grumbled disappointedly: 'That doesn't sound much like a horn section does it?' Jeczalik responded: 'Well, it's not. That's not what it is. It's a sample of trombone.'[57] Sampling synths couldn't provide a truly believable imitation of the 'real thing', but they could be used to generate other sounds entirely.

The first complete project that Horn worked on with Dudley, Langan and Jeczalik was *Duck Rock*, an album for Malcolm McLaren, the former Sex Pistols manager and pop-culture provocateur. Taking the punk ethic one step further, McLaren had decided to make a record even though he couldn't sing or play anything at all; Dudley described him as 'an artist with no visible signs of talent, no songs'.[58]

But McLaren did have ideas: on a trip to New York in 1981, he recognised the huge potential of hip-hop culture when he saw Afrika Bambaataa and DJ Jazzy Jay play a Zulu Nation show in The Bronx. McLaren loved the irreverent creative bricolage: 'It was extraordinary', he enthused, that scratch DJs were 'making music out of other people's music'[59] by cutting up records on turntables. (Theoretically, turntablism might be traced back to John Cage's use of gramophones in his 'Imaginary Landscape No. 1' in 1939, although it's hard to see any clear line from the avant-garde composer to hip-hop originators like DJ Kool Herc).

'Scratching is probably the newest urban folk music,'[60] McLaren declared. His prescient revelation came after the original punks had widened their horizons from three-chord thrash and discovered reggae, funk and hip-hop; The Clash were already incorporating rap into their music and playing gigs with Grandmaster Flash when McLaren saw the Zulu Nation show. Ever excited by the possibility of besmirching the British establishment, the former co-owner of the Sex and Seditionaries shops was thrilled that Bambaataa had taken his name from Bhambatha kaMancinza, a Zulu leader who led an uprising against the colonial administration in 1906. McLaren decided he should go to South Africa to record some Zulu musicians.

On the *Duck Rock* album, South African rhythms and vocals were mixed with samples of the Double Dutch female rope-skipping troupe from the US, a Mariachi band, Linn drums, Dudley's keyboards, banjo-picking hillbillies from Tennessee and New York hip-hop radio show duo the World's Famous Supreme Team – plus McLaren's stilted English 'rapping'. Inevitably there were allegations of cultural appropriation, but he denied being a neo-colonial exploiter. 'I didn't do the Doctor Livingstone bit and play the white man from across the sea,' he insisted. 'I want to demonstrate how these people live and dance. I want to be able to put across their ideas… I'm with all the dispossessed people of the world, not the gentlemen.'[61]

The tracks for *Duck Rock* were assembled by Horn and his team using the elements that musical flaneur McLaren had commissioned. On the album's keynote song, 'Buffalo Gals', which featured square-dance calls, hip-hop scratching and a heavy drum-machine beat, the problem was that McLaren could neither sing in tune nor rap in time, and Horn had to keep banging him on the chest during the recording to keep him on the beat. But the track proved to be unexpectedly influential; American jazzman Herbie Hancock even credited it as one of the inspirations for his electro bombshell 'Rockit', as it was the first time he heard a DJ scratching: 'I said, "What is that? I want to do something like that!"'[62]

J. J. Jeczalik said that the former Sex Pistols manager's unconventional attitude to making *Duck Rock* inspired him – along with Dudley, Langan, Horn and music journalist Paul Morley – to create Art of Noise, a Fairlight-powered electronic pop group named after Italian Futurist Luigi Russolo's 1913 manifesto *The Art of Noises*. 'His attitude was "well, why not?" rather than "you can't do that".' Jeczalik said of McLaren. 'He was always exploring mad avenues that nobody in their right mind would do, with the attitude that it didn't really matter how you did anything or what you did with it, as long as it was fun and interesting.'[63]

Art of Noise's first EP featured two of their most important recordings, the delectable 'Moments in Love' and 'Beat Box', a rhythm-and-sample track based on a drum loop left over from Horn's production of the *90125* album for prog-rockers Yes. As well as featuring unfeasibly large snares and kick-drum sounds, Art of Noise's music was playfully ironic and silly-headed, and its shiny, plasticised textures and cartoonish sonic interjections would prove hugely influential on music subsequently made for advertisements, TV signature tunes and idents in the eighties. Appropriately for records created from samples, 'Beat Box' and its follow-up, 'Close (to the Edit)', would also be sampled by scores of other artists for decades to come.

The *Into Battle with the Art of Noise* EP was the first release on ZTT, the label set up by Horn, his wife Jill Sinclair and Morley, its name taken from sound poem *Zang Tumb Tumb* by Futurist movement founder Filippo Marinetti. Dudley described what Art of Noise did as 'raiding the twentieth century', sampling any kind of sound source from Stravinsky to a Volkswagen car ignition. 'In other words, everything is available to us,' she explained. 'We just think, "Oh, this'll be fun, let's stick this in".'[64]

But nothing could have been more fun than ZTT's most famous signing, Frankie Goes to Hollywood. Frankie were a remarkable combination of queer energy, scallywag vulgarity, sonic adventurism, BDSM posturing, post-punk questing, electronic expertise, laddish bravado, Liverpudlian self-belief and awe-inspiringly colossal basslines. They were a cultural supernova, exploding out of obscurity to dominate the pop landscape of 1984 before crashing back to earth; a sensational story of pop genius and hubris.

Singer Holly Johnson was a young, working-class Bowie and Roxy fanatic who had started wearing make-up and dressing outrageously in his early teens. 'What have I done to deserve a walking freakshow for a son?'[65] his father once demanded to know. Out in Liverpool's gay bars, Johnson met like-minded teenagers Paul Rutherford (later Frankie's backing vocalist and dancer), Jayne Casey (later of Pink Industry) and Pete Burns (later of Dead or Alive). He soon left school and dedicated his life to being fabulous.

As they created Frankie Goes to Hollywood's image, Johnson and Rutherford decided to use leather and fetish imagery derived from the clubs they frequented. 'People wanted sex and spectacle,' Johnson asserted. 'We decided to incorporate the Mad Max warrior look with [gay erotic artist] Tom of Finland and create a kind of post-apocalypse, S&M punk look. We were bound to get attention and have lots of fun that way.'[66] At one early

Frankie gig, Johnson wore leather chaps with no underwear, his backside exposed with one arse-cheek painted pink and the other blue. Rutherford argued that they made an impact because their in-your-face homosexuality was authentic and honest. 'Why lie?'[67] he asked rhetorically.

The three other members of the band were straight Scouse scallies who overcompensated by constantly proclaiming their heterosexuality. 'We're not a gay band,' insisted guitarist Brian 'Nasher' Nash, arguing that Frankie 'just happen to be fronted' by two gay men.[68] But although the 'lads', as they called themselves, could be boorish, they weren't raging homophobes. 'Being gay is just part of life,'[69] Nash declared.

It took around two months for Horn and his studio colleagues to produce Frankie's first single, 'Relax', which was recorded and scrapped three times before it was finished. It was first played by the Frankie lads, then replayed by Ian Dury's band, The Blockheads, then a hybrid version was created. Finally, Horn completely reconstructed the track electronically without the band present at all. The result was immense – a massive bass charge locked to a compulsive metronomic kick. It was also hugely provocative, an exaltation of the male orgasm sung by an unashamedly gay man. With a splashy sound effect supplied by Horn that left little to the imagination, 'Relax' ejaculated gay sex into the living rooms of Britain.

It was Frankie's fuck-you interpretation of gay liberation activism, said Johnson. 'It came without a political edge. It said: This is the way it is. And if you don't like it, so what?' he asserted. 'It didn't come saying we're fighting for the right to be this way. It didn't ask for permission.'[70]

After BBC Radio 1 presenter Mike Read declared 'Relax' was 'overtly obscene', station controller Derek Chinnery issued a statement announcing that the BBC believed 'the lyrics are not suitable for a show with a family audience',[71] and it was removed from the corporation's daytime playlist. Aided by the publicity generated by the controversy, 'Relax' quickly rose to number one in the pop charts in January 1984, where it remained in salacious defiance for a month.

The band's second hit, 'Two Tribes', tapped into fears of nuclear war that had escalated after the Soviet Union invaded Afghanistan in 1979 and hardline anti-communist politician Ronald Reagan was elected US president the following year. When Britain agreed to host the US Air Force's cruise missiles with nuclear capacity, making the country a potential target for attack, protesters set up peace camps outside Royal Air Force bases at Greenham

Common and Molesworth and at the Faslane naval base on the Gare Loch. Hundreds of thousands of people joined Campaign for Nuclear Disarmament demonstrations as apocalypse anxiety reached new heights of intensity. In 1983, the Soviet authorities interpreted NATO's Able Archer exercises as preparations for a nuclear strike and temporarily readied their own nuclear warheads for launch. Armageddon had never seemed so close.

Frankie redrew the Cold War face-off as pop art. The intro to 'Two Tribes' was voiced in dramatically chilly style by actor Patrick Allen, the voice of the British government's 1970s *Protect and Survive* public information films, intended for broadcast if nuclear attack was deemed imminent; it even used some of the text from the films about the perils of an attack. 'Two Tribes' also had another powerful bassline, and although it was a song about the potential destruction of humanity, it was a rambunctious ball of fun that topped the charts for around two months.

'Frankiemania' became the pop-cultural phenomenon of the politically tense summer of 1984, in a country divided by the bitter political showdown of a nationwide miners' strike. The divisions played out culturally too, as teenage pop fans went crazy for the Liverpudlians' lubriciously homosexual electro-pop and wore T-shirts with slogans like 'Frankie Say Arm the Unemployed' – at the same time as a right-wing Conservative government was promulgating homophobic 'family values' and vowing welfare-benefit cuts for unemployed people.

Frankie's debut album, *Welcome to the Pleasuredome*, reportedly had a million advance orders before its release. Its title track was another Trevor Horn epic, the finest example yet of the cinematographic sound and dramatic sequencing he had been developing since his seventies disco productions, with a lyrical allusion to English Romantic poet Samuel Taylor Coleridge and another killer bassline. Parts of the album were as bold, irreverent, frivolous and hyperbolic as the men who made it, featuring some of the most sumptuously constructed electronic pop music ever pressed onto vinyl. But away from the peak moments, the weaker songs sounded worryingly like perfunctorily-conceived filler.

After the title track was released as a single, Frankie would only have one more Top 10 hit before they burned out in a spectacular conflagration of legal action and personal enmity. Their disappointing second album, *Liverpool*, suffered from a distinct lack of magic. It wasn't produced by Horn and featured members of the band actually playing their instruments, after they decided to turn back to rock and discard the grandiose synthetic treatments that made their hits so exciting. Years later, in his autobiography, Johnson belatedly mourned the loss of something special: 'We had created a new kind of dance music, and now we were abandoning it.'[72]

Nevertheless, Horn's vision of an utterly artificial dance music would endure, not least because ZTT's concept of repeatedly remixing a current release to maximise interest, boost sales and extend the record's life in the clubs and on the radio would become a standard music industry practice. With Frankie, Horn kept remixing the tracks until the idea of a 'definitive version' was meaningless. He then took the idea even further on Grace Jones' *Slave to the Rhythm*, an entire album of versions of the same song, an immaculate groove based on a Washington DC go-go percussion loop, constantly repeating, constantly changing, which Horn proudly confirmed bore little relation to 'performed' music: 'It's completely fabricated – the whole thing – and that's what makes it so interesting.'[73] And this, perhaps, was a definition of what Trevor Horn, and a certain type of electronic pop, was all about in the eighties.

In 1984, Horn was also asked to produce what became the biggest-selling synth-pop record in British history, the Band Aid charity single for victims of famine in Ethiopia, 'Do They Know It's Christmas?' He couldn't do it because his meticulous studio techniques would have meant spending several weeks on the production and the record needed to be made within days, to reach the seasonal market, so Midge Ure of Ultravox and Visage produced the record instead. (Horn remixed it for the 12-inch).

Despite its all-star vocal cast, 'Do They Know It's Christmas?' was a slight confection, played by Ure on synths augmented by a rhythm section. But neither its basic arrangement, nor its mawkish and naive lyrics, mattered at all. A total of 3.8 million copies were sold and it became part of the sentimental pantheon of British Christmas songs, endlessly replayed from year to year, a cultural artefact seemingly impervious to criticism or aesthetic judgment.

Its success concluded a year in which the best-selling singles were largely electronic, from Frankie's glorious hits to the synthetic soul-pop of 'Last Christmas' and 'Everything She Wants' by Wham!, Queen's 'Radio Ga Ga' and Phil Oakey's collaboration with Giorgio Moroder, 'Together in Electric Dreams': songs of glamorous escapism in times of political confrontation and hostility.

Bronski Beat, Imagination: Countering Conformity

'It is as impossible to imagine British gay culture without [Bronski Beat's] *The Age of Consent* as it is the plays of Oscar Wilde, the films of Derek Jarman and the agit-prop politics of Peter Tatchell.'
Paul Flynn, author of British LGBT cultural history *Good as You*[74]

In the mid-eighties synth-pop era, gay men were more visible in mainstream British culture than they ever had been. 'Music has helped society accept gay sexuality because of the weird creatures on TV– Boy George, Marilyn, Pete Burns and Freddie Mercury,'[75] Frankie Goes to Hollywood's Paul Rutherford somewhat optimistically suggested in 1984.

A reporter for the *Washington Post* even claimed that a new wave of politically conscious, sexually diverse pop acts was 'flourishing in a newly tolerant (or curious) atmosphere' in Britain. 'The word "gay", at least in the record biz, is no longer pop poison,'[76] he marvelled. The same year, Britain's first all-gay, politically-militant, electronic pop band had their first hit: Bronski Beat, a trio who were unambiguously *out* when some of the stars Rutherford cited were still in the closet.

While Frankie celebrated the libidinous hedonism of gay male nightlife, Bronski Beat highlighted the other side of the reality – social rejection, prejudice and violence. On their debut album, *The Age of Consent*, Jimmy Somerville's soaring falsetto delivered powerful messages about coming out and fighting back against gay-bashers and homophobes. Author Paul Flynn has written that when he heard *The Age of Consent* at the age of thirteen, it laid out for him, song by song, 'how to navigate life as a gay man, at a time when turning into one felt like it might be just about the most ostracising thing in the world.'[77]

The record's unquestionable passion, underpinned by pulsing electronic rhythms, helped to pull off the difficult feat of combining politics and dance music without sounding too banal or preachy. Somerville's own experience of growing up in Glasgow put raw honesty deep into songs like 'Smalltown Boy'. 'Most of my youth, I was traumatised and bullied. I was red-headed, short, very sensitive and obviously gay,'[78] he recalled. In London, he met telecommunications engineer Larry Steinbachek and his boyfriend, keyboard player Steve Bronski. Each was driven by politics as much as music and wanted more than the hedonistic gay club scene could offer. 'Heaven [nightclub] was trying to mirror the San Francisco idea of gay, but a bunch of us didn't fit in,'

Somerville said. 'We loved Talking Heads and Lou Reed as well as Donna Summer.'[79]

The Age of Consent was produced by Mike Thorne, whose work on Soft Cell's first two albums had made him one of UK synth-pop's leading architects. The record drew heavily on late seventies disco, which Somerville saw as an intrinsically political music because of its celebration of diversity, as well as Giorgio Moroder's synthetic treatments for Donna Summer. A cover version of 'I Feel Love' segued into John Leyton's 'Johnny Remember Me', a song originally produced by Joe Meek in an era when male homosexuality was illegal.

The album's inner sleeve listed the age of consent for gay men across Europe and provided contact numbers for legal advice helplines. With its pink-triangle graphic reclaiming the stigmatic symbol the Nazis had used to identify homosexuals in the concentration camps, it was a powerful statement at a time when British politicians were openly homophobic and tabloid media described AIDS as a 'gay plague'.

The Conservative government's health minister, Norman Fowler, later revealed that while creating the 'Don't Die of Prejudice' campaign in 1987, which sought to provide credible health information about HIV and AIDS, he encountered resistance from other ministers who considered homosexuality immoral. 'Many people treated the idea of gay sex with hostility and distaste, and thought that the victims of AIDS should be left to their fate,'[80] Fowler said.

Conservative parliamentarians' views were made even clearer when Thatcher's government brought in a piece of overtly anti-gay legislation, Section 28 of the Local Government Act 1988, which made it illegal for local authorities to publish any material that would 'promote homosexuality' or allow any teaching in educational establishments about 'the acceptability of homosexuality as a pretended family relationship', enabling the banning of a whole range of books in schools as well as the stigmatisation of gay people in general.

As committed activists, Bronski Beat criticised other gay pop stars who preferred to keep their sexuality private, arguing that when their community was under attack from the authorities and under threat from HIV and AIDS, it was their duty to take a stand. 'These people are after an easy life,' Somerville said at the time. 'They should be proud of what they are – they're just scared.'[81]

Away from the militancy of Bronski Beat and the bawdy provocations of Frankie Goes to Hollywood, synth-pop also provided a forum for experiments in gender nonconformity, as glam rock had done in the seventies. For a few fabulously dolled-up years, pop stars like The Human League's Phil Oakey, Dead or Alive's Pete Burns and Eurythmics' Annie Lennox defied gendered conventions on men wearing make-up and skirts or women wearing masculine suits and ties, explored new non-binary images and insisted on the right to represent themselves as they pleased.

Oakey explained that he was inspired by Bowie and by seeing Roxy Music take to the stage in Sheffield garbed in 'make-up, high heels and lurex'.[82] Lennox said she donned a man's suit because she wanted to defy sexist expectations that women singers should appear sexy. 'Ironically, a different kind of sexuality emerged from that,'[83] she noted.

Some of the most audacious sartorial images in eighties pop were created by a Black British electro-soul trio called Imagination – Leee John, Ashley Ingram and Errol Kennedy. Like Frankie Goes to Hollywood, they were openly sexual but also projected a distinct ambiguity. Singer John, a multi-talented trouper with a wicked falsetto who described himself as a 'vaudevillian' character, explained that the trio's gaudy, skin-revealing stage costumes were inspired by post-punk fashion and the London jazz-funk scene of the time as well as Parliament-Funkadelic, Grace Jones and Bowie: 'What you have to remember is that in the early eighties what you saw us wear on [*Top of the Pops*] was an extension of what was happening in the clubs. Everyone was trying to be unique.'[84]

Their first appearance on the BBC pop show, clad in metallic gold with John twirling bare-chested in a skirt and glittering headband and pouting at the camera, caused astonishment: 'They'd never seen a black group like us,' John said.[85] Journalist Marcus Barnes has argued that their image was part of a 'lineage of black flamboyance', but also challenged expectations about how Black British groups should look and act.

'For Imagination's musical trio, to buck against the stereotypical view of the virile, ultra masculine black male – presenting alternative masculinity with feminine attributes while still embracing their sexuality and flaunting their half naked physique – was powerful, setting a new stylistic and cultural standard for the black male performer,'[86] Barnes wrote.

Imagination wanted to make an instant impact, explains their drummer Errol Kennedy, a veteran of early Brit-funk bands Midnight Express and TFB

(Typical Funk Band). 'When we started Imagination, we were talking about wanting to do something new – we're going to have this new sound and this new look and we're going to be really outrageous,' he says. 'Everything we wore was specially made – the gold lamé suits and the hot pants. We wanted to take everything to the next level. We were also wanting to do something new for black music, because at that time, record companies weren't really investing in black artists.'

The band's producers, Steve Jolley and Tony Swain, created a phantasmagorical backdrop of Moog basslines, drifting synths and twinkling keyboard melodies. When their debut single, 'Body Talk', was released in April 1981, before press coverage started to focus on the sexual suggestiveness of their performances and the shiny snugness of their costumes, the *NME* published an ecstatic review, naming it single of the week alongside Taana Gardner's Paradise Garage classic 'Heartbeat': 'The Imagination disc is simply out of this world; a more *dis*embodied piece of music you could not hope to find,' enthused journalist Barney Hoskyns.[87]

Imagination's brilliant *Night Dubbing* remix album in 1983 was the equal of some of the critically acclaimed material released by US labels like Prelude and West End Records at the time. Psychedelically dubbed-out, handclap-echoing, Larry Levan-style reworks including a deliciously lissom take on 'Just an Illusion' and Levan's own remodelling of 'Changes'. 'We had included 'Changes' in the shows that we were doing at the Paradise Garage and Studio 54 [in New York], and Larry Levan really fell in love with that track and did us that fabulous mix,' explains Kennedy. 'So that started us off doing *Night Dubbing*, his mix became the guideline for the remixes we then did with Steve [Jolley] and Tony [Swain] for the album.'

Imagination were one of the few all-Black British groups in eighties electronic pop, a genre that was distinctly white, with a few exceptions like Barry Adamson of Visage. John was proud that Imagination managed to get on the covers of teen-pop magazines when Black British groups were rarely granted such representation, deprived of the budgets and promotion that their white counterparts received: 'I think there's been a lot of institutional racism,'[88] he said. He also argued that the trio offered a glimmer of necessary escapism to the mid-eighties. 'The day to day politics were grim: riots, coal miners striking, mass unemployment,' he recalled. 'We needed some colour in the darkness of it all.'[89]

But most synth-pop was usually more colour than darkness; the miners' strike of 1984-85 – a clash between two visions of society that exemplified the political divisions of the Thatcher years, between right and left, individualism and collectivism, bosses and unions, big business and communities – wasn't often directly reflected in the electronic music of the time.

Among the few records to address the strike was 'Soul Deep', a stirring electro-soul appeal for working-class solidarity with an insistent electronic bassline, instigated by The Style Council's Paul Weller and credited to The Council Collective, featuring a starry cast of soul singers. From further left-field came *Shoulder to Shoulder*, an album of raucous industrial metal-bashing tracks by Test Dept interspersed with comradely songs by the South Wales Striking Miners Choir, and 'Strike' by The Enemy Within, a cut-up of speeches by National Union of Mineworkers chief Arthur Scargill set to a battering hip-hop beat by producer Adrian Sherwood and drummer Keith LeBlanc. The name adopted by Sherwood and LeBlanc appropriated Thatcher's description of the miners' leaders and socialist politicians as Britain's 'enemy within'. From even further out, Hawkwind singer Robert Calvert recorded an electronic concept album called *Freq* that was inspired by the dispute, featuring spiky industrial pop songs like 'Picket Line' interspersed with field recordings of striking pitmen and union activists.

Pet Shop Boys' Love Letters to Pop
'The Pet Shop Boys came along to make fabulous records, we didn't come along to be politicians, or to be positive role models.'
Neil Tennant[90]

If any electronic pop band in the eighties managed to be simultaneously colourful and sombre, hedonistic and politically aware, it was the Pet Shop Boys. They had the eloquence to obliquely reflect the turmoils of their times – and of course, they also made fabulous records. Indeed, the Pet Shop Boys could perhaps be judged the most significant of all the British synth-pop bands, for their immaculate taste in electronic disco records and their adeptness at adapting the most appropriate bits for themselves; for their wry, socially observational, often elegantly humorous lyrics; for their look – so English, while so subversive of 'Englishness' – and most of all for their completely uncynical pop sensibilities. As singer Neil Tennant once said: 'We appreciate the real ecstatic response that a really good pop or dance record can generate.'[91]

Tennant was working as a journalist for pop magazine *Smash Hits* in 1981 when he decided to buy a Korg synthesizer; he met keyboard player Chris Lowe in a shop when he went to get a lead for it. They started recording together, as well as going out to London clubs like Heaven, a gay venue that was crucial to a whole range of developments in electronic dance music throughout the eighties. At the time, Heaven's main DJ was hi-NRG mastermixer Ian Levine and the club had a state-of-the-art sound system with a spectacular lighting rig, perfect for getting lost in the groove. 'That's a very, very powerful thing, just going in, the main dancefloor at Heaven – lasers and lights and these pulsating sequencers, it's a very heady atmosphere,' [92] Tennant would recall.

One Heaven favourite was 'Passion' by The Flirts, produced by Bobby Orlando, and its hard electronic sound became the template for what Tennant and Lowe thought the Pet Shop Boys should be. 'One of the things we always liked about Bobby O is that we thought he sounded like punk disco,'[93] Tennant explained. Their initial aim was to make a record with Bobby O in New York that people could buy on 12-inch import at Record Shack, a shop in London known for specialising in hi-NRG releases.

All of this happened. Their debut, 'West End Girls', was produced by Orlando (and engineered by Steve Jerome, a former member of Hot Butter, who made early Moog hit 'Popcorn' in 1972), and it became available on import at Record Shack. The song itself was deliciously moody, the first of many Pet Shop Boys records about the magical possibilities of the city at night. Its decidedly English rapped lyrics picked up on phrases from everyday conversations, accentuating its feeling of locality and reflecting the nocturnal world that Tennant and Lowe moved through in London. But although the Bobby O version was a club hit, it was only after they recorded a lusher, more atmospheric version with producer Stephen Hague for their debut album *Please* that it became a number one single.

The songs on *Please* introduced another key Pet Shop Boys theme, escape – from suburban ennui, from constrained circumstances – as well as another of Tennant's lyrical proclivities, knowing humour. 'Let's Make Lots of Money', a satire on Thatcherite greed and the flaunting of wealth that had suddenly become socially acceptable in the eighties, was 'meant to be provocative', said Tennant: 'It's meant for everyone to hate it: here's this nauseating synth duo singing a song called "let's make lots of money".'[94] 'Tonight is Forever' was the first of many Pet Shop Boys songs evoking a sense of ecstatic disco melancholia; a song about clubbers surviving on the dole and living to go dancing to Heaven – 'a life of living at night', as Lowe put it, while 'I Want a Lover' and 'Later Tonight' were about sex and sleaze, end-of-the night pick-ups and impossible yearnings.[95]

'I see us in the cultural tradition of, say, Joe Orton and Noel Coward, in that I think we're serious and comic and lighthearted and sentimental and brittle,' Tennant once said. 'Like middle-class playwrights we're *of* the middle class but totally *against* it… We slag off suburbia but we both come from suburbia.'[96] This wasn't very rock'n'roll, and indeed the duo seemed to enjoy any opportunity they got to express disdain for rock's traditionalist values of macho 'authenticity'. 'We're not about being "real",' Tennant asserted. Asked at a press conference if they ever used any guitars on stage, Lowe responded disdainfully: 'Don't be *ridiculous*.'[97]

Tennant said that they wanted to make 'disco music with un-disco lyrics'.[98] Their second album, *Actually*, fulfilled this aspiration as it constructed a shadow drama of the Thatcher years – the transactional relationship in 'Rent', the avaricious traders on the London financial markets and the public-utility privatisations in 'Shopping', and the abandonment to destitution of 'King's Cross'. Most personally, Tennant said 'It Couldn't Happen Here' was about a friend who was diagnosed with HIV, and about 'how AIDS affected the gay community, and the way people reacted to the gay community and suggested it was almost as though the gay community had been too visible and had themselves to blame'.[99] But as ever there was brightness too: the uprush of sheer joy that was 'Heart' and the grandiose, twisted fervour of 'It's A Sin'.

Where the Pet Shop Boys also excelled, probably because of their deep and genuine feelings for the dancefloor, was in their use of remixers. Commissioning mixes from innovators like Shep Pettibone, Arthur Baker and Frankie Knuckles showed they had a vision of the coming wave of the late eighties and nineties, when electronic dance music would dominate pop. Indeed, Lowe said he was unhappy recording their fourth album, *Behaviour*, in Germany in 1990 because he felt he was missing out on the rave explosion. 'It was possibly the most exciting time in English culture ever including the sixties, and we were in Munich,'[100] he lamented.

Japan, Simple Minds and Other Art-Rock Adventurers

'We felt we were musically apart from everything that was going on at the time.'

Richard Barbieri, Japan

Paul McCartney's musique concrète experiments had played a vital role in bringing electronic music into the pop arena, and the former Beatle was still only 37 years old in 1980 when he returned to his outer limits with a solo electronic album, *McCartney II*. In words reminiscent of his interviews for the sixties underground press, he explained that he wanted to 'experiment with anything, any little noise'; to explore in 'total freedom'.[101]

Rock critics didn't much like the ex-Beatle's eccentric post-punk record, which McCartney later described as a descendant of 'Tomorrow Never Knows' and a precursor to his 1990s electronic work as The Fireman with former Killing Joke bassist, Orb collaborator and Goa trance instigator Martin 'Youth' Glover. But *McCartney II* went on to gain cult status; of its various curios, 'Check My Machine' was a hit on Brazil's samba-rock scene while 'Temporary Secretary' came to be considered a Balearic classic.

McCartney was one of many rockers from the pre-punk era who had a go at electronic pop in the eighties – Thin Lizzy frontman Phil Lynott recorded the lyrically dubious 'Yellow Pearl' with Ultravox's Midge Ure and Billy Currie, while guitarist Bill Nelson from art-rock band Be-Bop Deluxe launched his electronically-textured new wave project Red Noise. Of all the seventies veterans exploring electronic music, Hawkwind's Robert Calvert spun the furthest out, as might have been expected, staging his own sci-fi noir 'electronic musical', *The Kid from Silicon Gulch*, at a London theatre in 1981. It featured an electro-punky soundtrack and starred Calvert as a Chandler-esque private eye of the computer age. But the most entertainingly over-the-top were ELO, who followed their discofied *Discovery* with the luxuriantly-arranged synth-prog concept album *Time*.

For some bands however, synthesizers were simply a stopgap measure while they waited to become popular enough to secure a budget for real strings, horns and choirs. Talk Talk used synths on their classic album *It's My Life*, even though singer Mark Hollis said he hated them: 'Synthesisers were really only a means to an end,' he asserted. 'All they've enabled us to do is go some way towards reproducing organic sounds when we haven't been able to afford the real thing.'[102]

But the new technology thrilled rock musicians who understood it as a tool to develop their own, very specific sonic vocabularies. The early eighties saw new forms of art-rock emerge as artists like Peter Gabriel, Kate Bush and Japan produced complex and fascinating records that drew from pop, prog, new wave and non-Western music, but existed somewhere beyond all of them.

Japan in particular were a band whose music – reflective and anomic, with stylised hints of intellectual sophistication and sexual ambiguity – was destined never to fit in to the politicised post-punk environment or the hedonistic New Romantic scene. Their first two albums in 1978 sounded like post-glam rock, drawing on the same kind of Bowie and Roxy Music sources as early Ultravox!.

'It was a kind of a new wave thing – angular gritty guitars, a little bit punky,' recalls synthesizer player Richard Barbieri. 'But we weren't interested in English punk at all. Absolutely hated it. We loved American punk – bands like Television, Talking Heads – because there was an intellect behind it.'

Barbieri also liked what Brian Eno had achieved as a non-musician bringing electronics into a rock band context: 'I started introducing raw sounds, a lot of white noise and frequency modulation, as dynamic effects,' he says. 'What I was doing was taking abstract sound and putting it in the context of a song.'

The band found their unique voice after they collaborated with Giorgio Moroder on the swaggering electronic disco-rock track 'Life in Tokyo'; their *Quiet Life* and *Gentlemen Take Polaroids* albums moved towards a lush and funky art-pop coloured by David Sylvian's languid, Ferryesque vocals, Mick Karn's sensual fretless bass playing and Barbieri's atmospheric synth phrasings. '*Quiet Life* was a huge change – David's voice changed completely, the sound changed completely,' notes Barbieri. 'A lot of the tracks are sequencer-driven, it was more textural, it wasn't as harsh.'

Quiet Life sounded like a New Romantic record before Duran Duran or Spandau Ballet had even released an album. By the time they had, Japan had moved on. Their masterwork was to be their final studio set, 1981's *Tin Drum*, which was characterised by its delicate minimalist arrangements, diaphanous touches of electronic sound and pointillist rhythms. Recorded without a lead guitarist, it not only sounded utterly *un*-rock but entirely unlike anything else being made by bands of their generation.

'*Tin Drum* is a musical statement – completely not of its time and just out there on its own. I think whether people like the music or not, or whether they're great songs or not, anyone who hears that album is always pretty stunned by the sonics,' argues Barbieri. 'It's all analog synths but we were either making new sounds or trying to impersonate acoustic instruments with the synthesizers. The biggest influence during *Tin Drum* was Stockhausen. If you listen to 'Ghosts', it's just full of Stockhausen kind of sounds.'

Barbieri said they felt no musical kinship with the synth-pop bands with whom they were bracketed at the time. 'We were already onto something else. We weren't listening to our contemporaries, we weren't listening to Gary Numan or Human League or Depeche Mode,' he explains. 'David would be listening to Stockhausen and Frank Sinatra albums. Mick would be listening to Arabic music and Turkish pop music. I was listening to world music. And that's what *Tin Drum* is, really. You can see the influences – world music, electronic music, abstract music.'

After Japan split up in 1982, Sylvian would further explore abstract musical forms that existed beyond pop. On his first solo album, *Brilliant Trees*, he collaborated with Jon Hassell, the master of the electronically-processed trumpet, Japanese composer Ryuichi Sakamoto and former Can bassist and noisemaker Holger Czukay, who added taped sounds using an old IBM dictaphone he found in a dustbin outside a factory and then customised.

Sylvian went on to make two important ambient albums with Czukay in the late eighties, *Plight & Premonition* and *Flux + Mutability*, whose dreamlike driftings and brooding moods were to recur as tropes in some of the post-acid house ambient tracks of the nineties. Both records had the feeling of lightness, almost immateriality, that often permeated Sylvian's work. 'I'm interested in the idea of music as a sense of place that doesn't exactly exist in the world but it exists in the imagination of the listener or the writer,'[103] he explained.

Like Japan, several British bands of the period developed their music in the long shadow of Bowie's Berlin Trilogy and Eno-era Roxy Music, as well as the work of Can, Neu! and Kraftwerk, looking towards Europe rather than the United States for sonics and symbolism; away from the 'authenticity' of rock and towards the theatrical artifice and cool detachment of an imagined continental noir aesthetic. But it was a band of working-class youths from Glasgow called Simple Minds who would most fiercely express their ardour for this idealised Europe and the romantic sense of freedom aroused by travel, as they sought to create a music free from rock'n'roll cliché.

For Simple Minds' singer Jim Kerr, a pivotal moment came when he heard Donna Summer's 'I Feel Love' in 1977 while the band were still playing punk rock under the name Johnny and the Self Abusers. Kerr was buzzing on cheap wine and speed, and when a DJ put on the metronomic disco anthem, he was transfixed. 'We need to get a synth,' he thought. 'Punk's finished.'[104]

Simple Minds recruited Mick MacNeil, who grew up playing Scottish traditional music on the accordion and was gigging with a covers band on the Glasgow club circuit, but had begun experimenting with processing his accordion sound through a phaser pedal and a Cry Baby wah-wah to modify its tone. 'You would think an accordion was trebly enough, try it with a Cry Baby screaming – people would be bleeding at the ears,' MacNeil laughs.

He had been intrigued by the synth sounds on Hawkwind records and Chicory Tip's 'Son of My Father', and had bought himself a monophonic Korg 770, which in turn brought him together with Simple Minds. 'I don't think they were actually looking for a keyboard player as such – just any guy with a synth would do. And I was the guy, the only guy who had one.'

Bowie, and the cultural references that swirled around him, represented another key input for Simple Minds, as Kerr explained: 'Back then, if you read a Bowie album review there would be references in it to some German sculptor or art movement, and you'd be like, "I've got to check this out!"'[105] Ideas adapted from Bowie and Kraftwerk helped them leap free from punk's restrictions on their second album, *Real to Real Cacophony*.

For MacNeil, supporting new-wave art-rock band Magazine was another important moment: 'Hearing [keyboard player] Dave Formula, that sound that he got, made me realise that you can create your own noise here, you don't have to copy anyone, you can start from scratch. Their guitarist John McGeoch, who used a lot of [effects] pedals, also influenced Charlie [Burchill] with some of his guitar sounds. Not unlike ourselves, the keyboard and the guitar were intertwined, all operating in the same space, you couldn't always tell them apart. Plus me and Charlie were always trying to try to outdo each other with pedals, echoes and reverb.'

All Simple Minds' inputs came together with imperious power on their third album, 1980's *Empires and Dance*, a mixture of European electronics, scratchy post-punk guitars, motorik rhythms and filmic textures, with Kerr tracing out suitably oblique and allusive lyrics, a disconnected outsider journeying across a stylised, history-burdened continent. 'It's not defined, but it's a travelogue. The person seeing this stuff is a bit ambivalent. It's voyeuristic,' he told the band's biographer Graeme Thomson. 'It broods but it is somehow glamorous too.'[106]

The double album that followed, *Sons and Fascination/Sister Feelings Call*, an ambitious set of electronically-inflected punk-funk songs and cinematic trance-rock instrumentals produced by former Gong guitarist Steve Hillage, showed how Simple Minds had developed an entirely novel interpretation of alternative rock. Hillage recalled that during the recording sessions, they were listening to Chic as well as Neu!, La Düsseldorf and Peter Gabriel; dance music had become another significant input.

Drummer Brian McGee would come up with beat patterns by imitating disco records, recalls MacNeil: 'When we were sitting writing music, he would put headphones on and he would play his own music on his Walkman, and play along with that, so he was listening to Donna Summer and Giorgio Moroder and Diana Ross and he had all this going in his head and we were just playing along with this drummer who was playing along with the disco music. But it also meant that he was like playing along with a metronome and it was really solid.'

The melodic grandeur and kinetic power of 'Themes for Great Cites' made it the double album's highlight. But despite its haughty magnificence, it was a song with modest origins, says MacNeil: 'It was actually created with Charlie and I in my bedroom at my mum's house. And it used to be called 'Do You Want Anything from the Van?' because an ice-cream van was outside the house and I copied the tune that was playing from the van and just started playing it on top of the track.' Its frozen dessert-derived melody and compulsive bassline were recycled several times in the house era, most exhilaratingly when combined with a Latin freestyle rhythm and a Queen sample on Corporation of One's 'The Real Life', an anthem on the early rave scene.

The next Simple Minds album, *New Gold Dream (81-82-83-84)*, perfected their widescreen dance-rock sound and provided them with their pop breakthrough, 'Promised You a Miracle'. It was based on a funky groove adapted from the disco track 'Too Through' by Bad Girls, which new drummer Kenny Hyslop had taped from a DJ mastermix show on New York's Kiss FM. 'It really broke us into a whole new commercial market and made us think, well, actually we can write a pop song now,' says MacNeil. 'You need to grow, you need to get on, and that was the door opening really for us.' It was a door that opened into pop stardom and stadium anthems; Simple Minds' arty Europhile phase was coming to an end.

At a time when post-punk musicians were intensively seeking new sounds, the Glaswegians weren't the only band to experiment with synthesizers: Magazine, Public Image Ltd, former Penetration singer Pauline Murray with the Invisible Girls and Paul Haig of Josef K all made hybrid electronic records; before them all came The Stranglers, whose keyboard player Dave Greenfield used a Minimoog from their first album in 1977 onwards to add a proggy vibe to their gruff and sleazy rock.

There was also Generation X bassist Tony James's Suicide-meets-Moroder electro-trash band Sigue Sigue Sputnik and Buzzcocks singer Pete Shelley's

Martin Rushent-produced synth-pop album *Homosapien*, from which the title track was reportedly shunned by daytime radio playlisters because of gay sex allusions. (Shelley had long been fascinated by electronic music; in 1974, he had made a primitive oscillator-noise album called *Sky Yen*).

Various post-punk bands used drum machines at some points in their careers instead of human drummers, including Echo & the Bunnymen, Young Marble Giants, The Sisters of Mercy and The Durutti Column. But there were also musicians who did not come from the bohemian fringes and simply wanted to use the new technology to make pop music. Among them were husband-and-wife duo the Techno Twins, whose peculiar debut album *Technostalgia* in 1981 featured electronic covers of 1930s and 1940s standards, including the Marlene Dietrich classic 'Falling in Love Again' – although the pair are largely remembered for their use of the word 'techno' before it became a well-established dance music genre.

Peter Gabriel, Kate Bush and ORCH5

'I find that a lot of rock rhythms don't make me want to dance any more.'
Peter Gabriel[107]

Peter Gabriel was standing in a scrapyard, clutching a big hammer. 'One, two, three, four,' he intoned, then brought it down on a car windscreen with a satisfying crunch while a sound engineer recorded the moment of impact.

This was a scene from a 1982 ITV *South Bank Show* that documented how the former Genesis singer was one of the first rock stars to realise the potential of sampling technology to transform the way music could be made, and one of the first to own a Fairlight CMI in Britain. The programme showed Gabriel shattering the discarded windscreen, smashing a television and blowing through a metal pipe, then playing back the sounds at different pitches on the Fairlight's keyboard as he made his third self-titled solo album (informally known as 'Melt').

The record was a mixture of serrated post-punk and arty post-prog, chilly white synth-funk and dark, doomy rock. Gabriel used it to explore themes of psychological disturbance, criminal insanity and the madness of warmongering, as well as to highlight the murder of anti-apartheid activist Steve Biko by the South African police. His American record company

Kate Bush performing at the Concertgebouw in Amsterdam, 1979. ©Gijsbert Hanekroot/Alamy.

Atlantic rejected the record – 'they thought the album was too esoteric and called it commercial suicide,'[108] he said.

They were wrong: the first single from the album, 'Games Without Frontiers', with its processed guitar, synthetic bass, electronic percussion and anti-nationalist lyrics, was a big hit, while 'Biko' became one of the most politically effective protest songs in eighties rock, raising the profile of the anti-apartheid movement within pop culture and helping to inspire the Artists United Against Apartheid campaign.

Another influential aspect of the 'Melt' album was a specific studio innovation, the bombastic percussive impact achieved by using noise-gated reverb on Phil Collins' drums, which inspired amazement at the time, just as the processed kit on Bowie's *Low* had in 1977. It was a sound technique that Collins would go on to use on his hit 'In the Air Tonight', and it became an eighties pop archetype.

The ITV documentary showed Gabriel replicating rhythms from a suitcase of recordings of non-Western music using a Linn drum machine, a fascination that also led to his creation of the WOMAD festival and Real World record label to promote non-Western musicians. He was sensitive to allegations of cultural appropriation, insisting that rock performers must always be conscious of their music's roots in African cultures, but also argued that cross-pollination was a legitimate creative force: 'Whether it is Picasso in the twenties or music of any form, artists have always plundered things that excite them. That's what keeps music and art alive,'[109] he argued. As sampling became more widespread, this was an issue that would excite much more debate in the years to come.

On Gabriel's 'Melt' album, the '*jeux sans frontières*' phrase from 'Games Without Frontiers' was voiced by Kate Bush, a young singer who had become the first woman to top the UK charts with a self-written song, her debut single 'Wuthering Heights'. Bush was a unique figure in British popular music who developed a gloriously esoteric sound that was partly melodic pop, partly mystical neo-folk, partly hippie prog, partly art-rock, partly theatrical melodrama and partly something else that was utterly indefinable. 'It's not important to me that people understand me,'[110] she said.

During the sessions with Gabriel, Bush was introduced to the sampling possibilities of the Fairlight and became intrigued by the possibilities of using the sounds of the natural world as compositional elements, opening up new ways of realising her ideas. 'What attracts me to the Fairlight is its ability to create very human, animal emotional sounds that don't actually sound like a machine,'[111] she explained.

Bush used the Fairlight for the first time on her third studio album, *Never for Ever*, in 1980, programmed for her by Landscape's Richard James Burgess and John L. Walters. Burgess was impressed. 'She's a visionary, there's no question about that. I was not a Kate Bush fan until I did those sessions with her. And I've got to say after several days spent working with her, I don't think there's any musician or artist that I have more admiration for in terms of creativity and vision,' he says. 'She really ran the sessions, creatively speaking – she is definitely one of the great producers, in my opinion.'

Burgess recalls how they smashed glasses from the studio kitchen for the samples used on 'Babooshka' and used real guns owned by Bush's family for the rifle-cocking rhythm on 'Army Dreamers'. 'They have a farm and so there's different weapons there, so her brother Paddy brought them into the studio and we basically cocked them all and recorded them into the Fairlight. And then you map them out onto the keyboard and then play a combination of them, changing the pitch by going up or down the keyboard.

'The interesting thing is that with the Fairlight, you're not trying to emulate a real instrument; it has a very distinctive quality – to me, that was exciting and Kate got that right away,' Burgess continues. 'If she wanted an instrument playing on her record, she would have got someone to play that instrument. But she realised that when you put it into a Fairlight, you got something completely different, you got a new instrument. And most people did not get that for the first couple of years the Fairlight was out. What they were looking for was a way of playing trombone on a keyboard. If you want a trombone, hire a trombone player, because the sound you will get is this really weird thing that happens when you put a trombone into the Fairlight.'

Not only was Bush using cutting-edge technology, she also co-produced the album and would produce the next one, *The Dreaming*, by herself – taking full charge of the production process at a time when few women had such power. 'The most important thing seemed to be that I had control,' she explained. 'Because one of the worst things that can happen to one's product – that terrible word – is that you become manipulated.'[112]

Although she declined to define herself as a feminist, Bush played mischievously with gender roles in her lyrics and sang openly about her own sexual desires. 'You can't really separate sex from music,' she insisted. 'Especially modern music. It's so full of sexual energy.'[113] She described herself as apolitical, but some of her songs were informed by contemporary issues: the claustrophobically intense 'Breathing', on the *Never for Ever* album, about an unborn baby's fear of atomic fallout, was one of the great anti-nuclear records of the synth-pop era, alongside 'Two Tribes', 'Enola Gay' and Young Marble Giants' fragile, minimalist 'Final Day'. It's hard to gauge exactly how much the threat of atomic apocalypse influenced the music made in the early eighties, but in retrospect the pervasive sense of unease certainly seemed to permeate records like 'Breathing' and Orchestral Manoeuvres in the Dark's *Dazzle Ships* album, with its crepuscular atmospheres and samples of Eastern Bloc radio broadcasts.

Bush's fifth studio album, *Hounds of Love*, represented a creative peak and the intense, sensual, lithely rhythmic 'Running Up That Hill', with its Fairlight melody and rolling Linn Drum groove, Bush's feverish entreaties and ecstatic cries of abandon, was its most delicious, delirious moment. Perhaps more than any other of her songs, it encapsulated a feeling that Bush said she was trying to achieve: 'a sense of moving away from boundaries that you can't in real life. Like a dancer is always trying to fly, really – to do something that's just not possible.'[114]

Bush also said she wanted to use technology to incorporate arcane sounds as well as novel textures into her music, to 'apply the future to nostalgia', as she put it. The playful title track from her 1982 album *The Dreaming* was a good example, with its didgeridoo drone and a repeated sample of a punchy orchestral flourish. However, the use of the orchestral sound cast her unwittingly in a much wider story about how samples took on unpredictable lives of their own once the original sound from which they were derived was digitised and made available for use and reuse.

The low-resolution, 8-bit sound file containing the orchestral stab that Bush used was named ORCH5 and had been included on one of the floppy discs of samples provided to Fairlight CMI purchasers. The sound, a tiny excerpt from a recorded performance of Russian classical composer Igor Stravinsky's orchestral score for the 1910 ballet *The Firebird*, had initially been digitised by musician David Vorhaus, who had been a member of late-sixties musique concrète psych-rock band White Noise with the BBC Radiophonic Workshop's Delia Derbyshire and Brian Hodgson.

Vorhaus says he was staying with Fairlight developer Peter Vogel in Sydney when he found the Stravinsky record while flicking through his host's collection and decided to sample it. 'It was very hard to tell how something was going to work on a Fairlight because 8-bit is a pretty gross representation of the real sound. But in this case, it worked – it actually perhaps added to the sound and the sound is amazing in the first place,' he explains. 'Instead of degrading it, like the Fairlight did to almost everything else, when the sound was turned into 8-bit, it kind of pushed it further.'

As well as being used by Kate Bush, ORCH5 was deployed in 1982 on Afrika Bambaataa's 'Planet Rock', the disembodied orchestral fragment giving the electro-funk track a science-fiction movie feel. The sample became 'the classical ghost in the hip-hop machine',[115] as musicologist Robert Fink put it. This spectral blast from Stravinsky's score was so compellingly emphatic that ORCH5 was also used on hundreds of other recordings in the decades that followed, from hardcore hip-hop and Latin freestyle to hi-NRG, house and mainstream pop: Mantronix and Freeez, Michael Jackson and Prince, U2 and the Pet Shop Boys, Milli Vanilli and The Smiths.

Asked more than four decades later what he thinks about the long, strange artistic life of the sample that he digitised, the laidback Vorhaus replies simply: 'Well, I'm surprised.'

The Last Days of the Radiophonic Workshop

'People say, "Oh, you made history." The thing about making history, you're living your life and you're doing the job you enjoy doing. You have no sense of creating history, you're just living in your own time.'
Brian Hodgson, BBC Radiophonic Workshop

The BBC Radiophonic Workshop started using digital sampling after acquiring a Fairlight in 1981, signalling the impending end of the tape-splicing era. 'It was a watershed moment,' Peter Howell wrote in his memoir, *Radiophonic Times*. 'We would no longer need to use John Baker and Delia Derbyshire's methods... for music requiring short samples, the Fairlight would do the job in a fraction of the time.'[116]

Coincidentally, the Fairlight had a distant connection to the Workshop: one of its creators, Kim Ryrie, once said that 'the *Doctor Who* music and sounds were his inspiration for getting into the industry',[117] according to Brian Hodgson. Nevertheless, as late as 1985, some Workshop producers were still using tape loops, although Hodgson cautioned: 'The composers are no longer the experimental wizards. There isn't time for the old-style experimentalism and there isn't time for self-indulgence. When there wasn't the equipment, you had to work that way, but now that the equipment is here, there's no excuse for doing anything the hard way.'[118]

Soundtracks for *Doctor Who*, with its signature tune brightly remodelled for the eighties in a synth-and-vocoder treatment by Howell, continued to be creative highlights for the Workshop in the eighties, alongside Paddy

Kingsland's music for the TV adaptation of *The Hitchhiker's Guide to the Galaxy* and Elizabeth Parker's compositions for *Blake's 7* and David Attenborough-presented nature series *The Living Planet*. Parker says her aim was to make electronic music more emotional. 'I wanted to get more heart into it, to make it more soft, more warm,' she reflects. 'At the Workshop, there was a definite move away from the abstract electronic stuff in the eighties, Paddy Kingsland and Roger Lim were using real sounds, guitars and session musicians. It was certainly getting less pure.'

The Workshop's commissions began to decline after new BBC procedures allowed producers to go outside the Corporation to buy soundtracks more cheaply from the independent suppliers who proliferated with the spread of digital recording and ever-cheaper music technology.

'There were a lot of other studios where they'd got the same equipment or similar equipment and everything also started to sound a bit the same,' says Parker. 'It just had the feeling of presets. Presets were just too easy to use and everybody had them, and lots of people had the same presets. Think how far removed that was from the times of John Baker and Delia Derbyshire. So once you start sounding the same as everybody else outside and they are much cheaper – well, that was the beginning of the end.'

While some fine electronic music was composed in the Workshop's final years, commissions had dwindled by the mid-nineties and the unit became a luxury that the BBC thought it could no longer afford. In 1998, after four decades of bringing musique concrète and electronic sound into the living rooms of Britain, the Workshop was finished as a creative unit.

'Two large skips arrived outside BBC Maida Vale, and all the tapes from our library were removed to the main BBC archive in a pantechnicon,' recalled Howell. 'It was April 1st, the 40th anniversary of the Workshop's opening.'[119]

The Workshop's final composition was completed by Parker. 'I was the last actual composer there,' she recalls. 'I'd done a deal to buy a bit of the equipment because I was setting up on my own. So I got myself together, got the stuff that I'd bought, got into a rented van, handed over the key and walked out. And that was it.

'I was really sad when I left – it was just awful, you know. But it certainly had run its course, without a doubt. We were no longer unique.'

The Aba Shanti-I sound system at the Notting Hill Carnival, London.
©PYMCA/Avalon/Getty Images.

6

COUGHING UP FIRE

Dub Reggae and Sound Systems

The Roots and Culture of Sound Systems

'What we did in sound systems was we created alternative public arenas where *we* were in control. These were our sanctuaries.'
William 'Lez' Henry, sound system MC, academic and author of What the Deejay Said

WHEN VINCENT FORBES ARRIVED IN BRITAIN as a stowaway on a boat from Jamaica in 1954, he found a country that was dreary, cold and unwelcoming to newcomers from the imperial colonies of the Caribbean. London was often subsumed under heavy fog, while the skies of the industrial cities of the North were grimy with pollution; prejudice was omnipresent. Forbes found himself a place to live in the then-dilapidated west London neighbourhood of Notting Hill, where slum landlords exploited immigrants who couldn't find more salubrious accommodation because of the colour of their skin. He got work as a railway-engine cleaner and went out looking for some fun.

Back in Kingston, Forbes was known as Duke Vin; he was a selector, playing records at parties for Jamaican sound system operator Tom Wong, alias The Great Sebastian. Like thousands of other recently arrived Jamaicans, Forbes found the entertainment options in his new home city completely inadequate: 'I look around and see what's up. I said, "Boy, the country is dead." Nowhere a sound, nowhere to go.'[1]

The Caribbean expatriate parties he did manage to find were being held in people's homes, with the records played on domestic radiograms that didn't have the volume and power he craved. So in 1955, the year after he arrived, Forbes bought his own sound equipment. 'I couldn't find nowhere to go for a dance, so I start my own sound system,' he explained. 'I made the first sound system in the country.'[2]

The British Nationality Act 1948 gave citizens of Commonwealth countries the right to live and work in the UK, and tens of thousands of people from the Caribbean colonies began to exercise this right as British citizens each year. As the legislation was going through parliament, the passenger liner HMT Empire Windrush brought one of the first big groups of around 800 West Indian immigrants to Britain. They arrived seeking work and prosperity in an alien country where only around 75,000 Black and Asian people lived; where the chauvinism of empire remained strong and the white majority maintained a firm belief in their own racial superiority. The new arrivals inevitably encountered suspicion and hostility – and crucially, for young sensation-seekers like Duke Vin, they were sometimes barred from dancehalls, clubs and other entertainment venues.

Despite all this, the post-war immigrants who became known as the Windrush generation and their descendants would have a transformative effect on British culture and identity, and Duke Vin's decision to set up his own sound system proved to be one of the most significant initiatives in the popular music of what would soon be an increasingly multicultural country.

Reggae sound systems were to become crucial vectors of influence for electronic sound and bass culture in Britain, spreading alternative ideas of how music could be constructed, how it could be heard and what it could mean. Sound systems were much more than just a collection of speakers and amplifiers; in his book *Sound Bodies*, Julian Henriques described them as 'vehicles for cultural expression, vessels for identity and pleasure, economic engines, commercial ventures, instruments for musical production, institutions for artists' training, multimedia communication systems, test-beds for technological innovation, laboratories for sonic science.'[3] They nurtured creative talent and showed how playing records could be a performance in itself, long before the superstar DJs of house and techno.

Sound systems also operated as independent cultural institutions, providing autonomous social and creative spaces that young Black people could unite around amid the pervasive alienation of living in a racist society. As dub poet Linton Kwesi Johnson said: 'These things gave us a sense of our own identity, made us feel that we had something going for ourselves that made us proud and strong and independent.'[4]

One of Duke Vin's fellow stowaways on the boat from Jamaica to the UK was Wilbert Campbell, also known as Count Suckle. After Vin started his sound system, Count Suckle established the second Jamaican-style 'set' in the country, both of them playing R&B, and later ska, at shebeens and house parties held illegally due to racist door policies at London's clubs and dancehalls. 'So many places in London wouldn't let black men in,' Jah Vego, who was a selector on Duke Vin's sound system, told author Lloyd Bradley. 'So we have to do our own thing, keeping dances in houses, in basements, in the shebeens.'[5]

But these makeshift dance spaces were constantly at risk of being busted by police who didn't like large groups of Black youths gathering for any reason. Duke Vin was often harassed and his equipment vandalised. 'One inspector told me that if I played my sound system in his area, he would get me ten years in prison,' he said. 'Another policeman take a shovel and mash my speaker, saying, "We don't want this thing in this country." And all the while them young white girls and guys love the music: "We've never heard anything like this before".'[6]

Police harassment of reggae dances continued into the 1970s and beyond. Celebrated sound system operator Lloyd Coxsone, who ran Sir Coxsone Sound, told London Weekend Television in 1976: 'Wherever I play, there's always the police. Because it's a reggae dance, the police come and break down the house and mash up everything.'[7]

Violent racists also targeted sound system dances. Count Suckle recalled that in 1958, white youths laid siege to a house party while he was playing, throwing petrol bombs and shouting: 'Burn them! Send them back home!'[8] The same year, after attacks on West Indian immigrants became increasingly frequent, riots erupted in Notting Hill and in the St Ann's area of Nottingham.

But the demand for sound was unstoppable. Year by year, as sound systems proliferated in Black communities around the country, bigger speakers were constructed, more powerful amplifiers acquired, bass weight intensified. Even in the early years, Jah Vego recalled that when Duke Vin went to get some gear built, the electrical engineer was amazed at how much power and bass he wanted: 'My God, where are they going to play that?' he exclaimed. 'That will kill people!'[9]

The acquisition of stupendous audio firepower had a very specific purpose, journalist Colin McGlashan wrote in an unusually perceptive newspaper article for *The Sunday Times* in 1973: 'The point isn't volume, but the amplification of the bass until it sounds like the world's biggest drum, until it becomes music you can feel. You feel it in your feet, in the vibrations of a Coke tin with an unlicensed shot of Scotch inside, you feel it through your partner's body. The first time you hear it, it's unbelievable, unbearable, oh my God!'[10] Tactile bass weight would later become one of the central features of British electronic dance music; one of many sonic passions that it inherited from reggae sound systems.

Sound system selectors prided themselves on exclusive pre-releases from Jamaica cut onto one-off acetate discs – dub plates – or unique 'specials', personalised versions of tunes revoiced for the sound system itself, prefiguring the remix culture of dance music that developed in the 1980s, when any track was considered malleable and subject to endless reinterpretation. 'To be a reputable sound system, to be recognised, you had to have exclusive material that only you had access to, exclusives that would make people go, "Did you hear that version?"' explains Dennis 'Blackbeard' Bovell of Jah Sufferer sound system.

Sound system crews worked as collectives, each individual making their contribution – the owner and manager, the equipment builders, the box boys who lugged the gear, the selector who played the tunes and the deejays toasting on the microphone. (Confusingly for outsiders, sound system MCs or toasters were also known as deejays, while the DJs were called selectors). The idea of the creative collective would prove hugely influential on UK dance music crews in the eighties and nineties. But running a sound system was hard work – maintaining and repairing the equipment, transporting and carrying the huge speaker boxes, often for meagre reward. '[You need] a young team of men who are ambitious, record crazy and have young ideas,'[12] said Lloyd Coxsone. It was a vocation for the hardcore. The 1981 documentary *Sound Business* depicted young men obsessed with the nature and possibilities of sound. 'This is my life. I am in sound totally, you know? I am in sound; I run a sound,'[12] Coxsone said in the film.

It was an obsession that took root early. Mikey Dread of Channel One, the son of a sound system operator from Jamaica who took over the running of his father's set in the late seventies, recalls how he started to build his own equipment while still at school in London. 'I grew up from childhood with amplifiers in the house, [speaker] boxes in the house, I grew up with turntables and cables, I grew up knowing about sound systems like Duke Vin and Count Shelley and Admiral Ken, so that's what I wanted to do,' he says. 'Everybody was making their own stuff in them days – it was all handbuilt. It was like a trade and a way of life at the same time.'

In the seventies and eighties, reggae and its culture of spirituality and heavy bass also came to embody the spirit of young Black British resistance. Linton Kwesi Johnson, who at various points was a journalist, a member of the British Black Panthers and the dubwise poet-chronicler of the Afro-Caribbean experience in the UK, explained in an article he wrote in 1976 that the music gained its power from the experience of slavery: 'It is a music that is at once violent and awesome, forceful and mighty, aggressive and cathartic,' he said. 'It is the *spiritual expression* of the *historical experience* of the Afro-Jamaican.'[13] Reggae was rebel music, the defiant sound of the oppressed, but also a joyous noise of celebration, Johnson said.

'It's about more than resistance, it's about transcendence as well,' explains William 'Lez' Henry, alias Lezlee Lyrics, a Black British author, social anthropologist and sometime deejay with Saxon Studio International, one of the country's most important sound systems. The use of Jamaican patois and Rastafarian rhetoric by toasters in the UK promoted solidarity in a country where Black history was untaught and representations of Black people in the media were often negative. 'You had music and lyricism that crossed the spectrum of what the Black experience was, from a UK perspective,' says Henry, who also ran his own Ghettotone system. 'It was about community, 100 per cent. There's an African word for it, *ubuntu*, which means "I am what I am because of who we all are".'

Like many UK deejays, Henry sometimes used his London accent as well as patois, and his verses depicted the realities of the environment in which he lived. 'My lyrics were about a Black British experience, or the experience of a Black person in Britain of African ancestry. I spoke about London – why am I going to talk about Jamaica when I ain't even been there? I couldn't talk about picking mangoes on the way to the dance or something like that. How could I? I was living in Lewisham.'

The seventies and early eighties were crisis times for Black British youth; times of repression and riots, crackdowns and fightbacks. The 1976 Race Relations Act outlawed racial discrimination, but an overwhelmingly white police force disproportionately arrested Black people; blues dances and sound system parties were often seen by the police as incidents of suspected disorder, to be dealt with as potential crime scenes rather than cultural events. On television, there was racist humour in programmes like *Love Thy Neighbour* and *The Black and White Minstrel Show*. In politics, the far-right, pro-repatriation National Front was gaining in popularity and Conservative Party leader Margaret Thatcher was trolling for anti-immigrant votes, declaring in 1978 that 'people are really rather afraid that this country might be rather swamped by people with a different culture'.[14]

Dancehall deejay Macka B (Christopher MacFarlane), recalled growing up as the son of Jamaican immigrant parents in Wolverhampton, where their member of parliament was the racist politician Enoch Powell, whose inflammatory 'Rivers of Blood' speech in the late sixties had predicted that Black immigration to the UK would cause a violent reckoning. Macka B argued that reggae culture was a unifying force that clarified Black youths' sense of injustice and focused their will to resist. 'We realised what we were up against and who the real enemy was,' he explained. 'We were the first generation to really fight against certain things.'[15]

The crisis times became a golden age for sound systems with their messages about identity and community; times when Black British youth 'created a living history that challenged their negative depiction',[16] Henry wrote in his book about the culture, *What the Deejay Said*. During this period, reggae dances were held in all kinds of legal and illegal venues – church halls, community centres, youth clubs, unoccupied houses and people's own homes and basements, wherever a sound could 'string up' and let the bass shake the foundations.

The dub poet and writer Benjamin Zephaniah, who started his career as a guest toaster on Birmingham's heaviest sound system, Quaker City, recalled that when he first went to a dance, it was a revelation. 'This is where I first encountered people who were feeling as I was about where we lived, how we lived, and how we listened to music,' Zephaniah wrote.

There was an unspoken collective feeling that this culture was something that they owned, he said. 'It was created by us, and not by record companies. It was inspired by our elders but it was now. It was social, political and musical.'[17] Some of the music made in Britain by innovative producers like Dennis Bovell and Mad Professor would reflect this potent synthesis of communal resistance and exultation.

Dennis Bovell, Jah Shaka and Saxon Sound International
'Some people might dream mentally, but I get my dreams through my ears.'
Jah Shaka[18]

In December 1974, a distinctly unusual song reached the top ten of the British pop charts. Actually it was hardly a song at all – a few phrases wreathed in trippy echo, a fractured rhythm, fragments of guitar and a ludicrously catchy refrain that schoolchildren adored: 'Skanga! Skanga! Skanga! Skanga!' Rupie Edwards' 'Ire Feelings' was one of the records that introduced dub stylings to the mainstream British public, even though many of them probably thought it was just a wacky novelty record.

The history of dub went back to the sixties in Jamaica, when instrumental versions of tracks were created for deejays to chat over at sound system dances. In the early seventies, producers started remixing these instrumental versions, foregrounding the drums and bass and adding effects – EQ filter sweeps, echo and reverb, using the mixing desk as a creative tool to produce new tracks that sometimes bore little resemblance to the original sonic material. With their adventurous use of recording technology and sound-manipulation techniques, early dub producers like King Tubby and Lee 'Scratch' Perry established remixing as a Jamaican sci-fi art form, disassembling songs and reconstituting them as hallucinatory phantasms. (They were also being financially prudent, extracting the most value out of each recording).

The sound of dub mimicked and enhanced the temporal and sonic distortion of the senses created by strong marijuana, recalibrating perceptions and firing the listener into a surrealistic landscape of drifting sonic fragments – 'ghosts in the mix, duppies in the machine', as cultural academic Louis Chude-Sokei described them. More than a sound, dub was 'a strategy or, as many would argue, a world view, a way of hearing',[19] Chude-Sokei suggested.

In Britain, one of the first to put dub versions on vinyl was sound system operator Lloyd Coxsone. His album *King of the Dub Rock*, credited to Sir Coxson Sound and released in 1975, included tracks by Jamaican artists like

Augustus Pablo and Delroy Wilson, and also a dub called 'Many Moods of Coxson' – a rework of 15-year-old British schoolgirl singer Louisa Mark's early lovers' rock hit, 'Caught in a Lie'. The instrumental track for Mark's song had been laid down by UK reggae band Matumbi, whose guitarist, Jah Sufferer sound system operator Dennis Bovell, would go on to become one of the most influential dub producers in the country.

As well as being one of the first lovers' rock productions, 'Caught in a Lie' was one of the first UK reggae records to use a Moog synthesizer. Bovell, who had once been a member of a prog rock band called Stonehenge, said it was a serendipitous accident; he only started playing the synth in the studio to impress a visiting star from Jamaica. 'Being a fan of people like Rick Wakeman, Yes, Deep Purple and King Crimson, I was no stranger to that kind of sound and I wanted to have that sound in reggae. And that was my chance,' he recalls.

'While I was in the studio, [Jamaican bassist] Robbie Shakespeare was present and I was doing a bit of showing off with the Moog: "I bet you don't have one of these in your studio in Jamaica!" I put the tape on and I played the Moog, and Lloydie Coxsone went: "Did you record that? Keep it in, that sounds new, that sounds good." And that became my arrangement of that song.' He had used his love of prog to enhance a record from an ostensibly incompatible genre; the kind of cross-fertilisation for which he would become renowned.

Bovell was born in Barbados and joined his parents in Britain at the age of twelve after his father got a job working for London Transport and his mother decided to train as a nurse. He started creating his own 'versions' while he was still a schoolboy. 'The school had a studio meant for making sound effects for the drama group so it had a couple of quarter-inch Ferrograph tape recorders, and that's when I began experimenting with loops, because I'd been reading that The Beatles and George Martin had been making loops. So the first loop I actually made, I helped myself to a few bars of a very popular reggae tune, 'Young, Gifted and Black' by Bob and Marcia,' he says.

Bovell used Matumbi's recordings as raw material for dubs that he played on the Jah Sufferer sound system. 'That was our little secret because we didn't have money to fly to Jamaica and avail ourselves of the latest King Tubby's dubs and all that. That came later. But to get off the ground, I made our own,' he explains. 'It was most definitely a DIY job. And it gave us the satisfaction that no one else had those versions.'

While working with Jah Sufferer, Bovell also experienced first-hand the kind of aggressively racist policing that fuelled discontent and alienation among Black British youths in the seventies. In 1974, he was arrested during a raid on a Jah Sufferer dance in Cricklewood in north London and spent six months in prison for 'causing an affray' after police accused him of inciting the crowd to attack them.

When he was eventually cleared on appeal, he went back to making his own dub productions, like The 4th Street Orchestra's *Leggo! Ah-Fe-We-Dis* and *Ah Who Seh? Go-Deh!*, with covers designed to look like Jamaican imports, which were considered more 'credible' than British releases. 'It was widely thought that reggae couldn't amount to much if it was recorded in the UK. I was hell-bent on proving that wrong,' says Bovell. He also continued to play with Matumbi and registered a historical landmark when the band headlined the first gig ever staged by the Rock Against Racism campaign, in east London in November 1976.

Bovell was a studio engineer too; he worked on the 1978 debut album for roots reggae band Creation Rebel, the first production by a young Englishman called Adrian Sherwood, who would become one of the country's most influential dub producers and independent record-label operators. He also worked for Japanese electronic producer Ryuichi Sakamoto on his *B-2 Unit* album, which included the proto-electro track 'Riot in Lagos'. 'I was a big Yellow Magic Orchestra fan, and to hear that the boss had summoned me to do some dub on his new creation – oh, *that* was an accolade,' says Bovell. 'Once he finished recording it, Ryuichi said to me: "Do your thing." So I mashed it up. I've realised it was actually the first Japanese electronic dub album – made in 1980.'

Bovell's influence was felt way beyond reggae; his album productions for audaciously inventive post-punk bands like The Slits (*Cut*) and The Pop Group (*Y*) offered new possibilities for rock music at the end of the seventies, when dub was permeating white listeners' consciousness through punks' infatuation with reggae, Rock Against Racism concerts, DJ John Peel's eclectic broadcasts on BBC Radio 1, releases by key Jamaican artists on Virgin Records' Frontline reggae label and dub poet Linton Kwesi Johnson's powerful recordings, also produced by Bovell.

Punk and post-punk bands like The Clash, Public Image Ltd, Killing Joke and The Ruts all experimented with dub techniques or reggae basslines at a time when taking a stand against racism felt vitally urgent because of the rise of the National Front and the use of racist rhetoric by Conservative politicians. The punks were enraptured by reggae's sense of apocalyptic dread and its damnatory lyrical reportage on the wickedness and iniquities of Babylon, and awed by its revelation of deeper sonic dimensions.

'Nothing prepared me for the shock of listening to dub, especially through big custom made 22″ speaker cabs. There was the bass taking up most of the signal, resonating deep into my solar plexus, the core of my being. All the big plate reverbs and tape echoes, especially the long decaying halftime ones, conveyed a sense of inner space,' said Public Image Ltd bassist Jah Wobble. 'Most of all I was fascinated by the bass lines… the sheer physicality of the experience set it apart from any other.'[20]

'Our music is roots and culture. It's a spiritual music, it sends out a message and it gives you some upliftment,' says Mikey Dread of Channel One. But when dub was embraced and imitated by white Britons and disconnected from its Afro-Caribbean social context, it inevitably lost some of the religiopolitical charge it carried as a very specific articulation of Black resistance. Dub became a 'sound' – although a hugely influential one and a crucial factor in the development of genres like ambient, jungle, drum and bass, dubstep and most subsequent British-made electronic dance music. 'Dub changed the way people listen to music and it changed the way people conceive music and compose music,' argues Bovell.

To remixers seeking to trip out listeners' minds, dub's wild reverberations were irresistible; to producers like Brian Eno, its disorientating atmospherics and creative use of space were fascinating strategies to be explored. Eno adored how dub engineers used 24-track technology to creatively *subtract* rather than to add. 'When I heard my first dub record I was tempted to give up, really. I thought it was so advanced, electronic music was kids' play compared to it,'[21] he said.

In 1980, Bovell worked on the soundtrack for Franco Rosso's film *Babylon*, a drama about the tribulations of a young sound system crew as they faced off against racist thugs and violent cops in south London, while preparing for a showpiece soundclash with the mighty Jah Shaka – the greatest sound system operator of his era. Chris Menges' brooding cinematography sketched an unforgiving landscape of dingy alleyways, railway arches and lock-ups, towerblocks and grimy convenience shops; for the young soundboys, their music represented defiance, transcendence and release from what one of the characters called a 'dirty, corrupted and wicked' society.

The climactic scene in a crepuscular dancehall full of stepping dreads featured a cameo from Shaka, dropping his earthshaking mix of Johnny Clarke's 'Babylon', unleashing squalls of electric noise from his dub siren that swirl upwards into the smoke and gloom, snares crackling like automatic gunfire as the police try to break down the doors and the deejay declaims a vow to 'chant down Babylon oppression'. It was a prescient vision: the year after the film was released, riots erupted in Brixton, Moss Side in Manchester, Toxteth in Liverpool and other inner-city districts around the country as Black youths rose up and released their fury about oppressive police stop-and-search tactics and systemic racism.

Jah Shaka was born Neville Powell to devout Christian parents in 1948 and first played music as a child in church. His family emigrated from Jamaica to London in the fifties, a time when Black people were 'rated like you were not a human being',[22] he once recalled. Taking his name from the 19th-century African warrior king Shaka Zulu, his sound system rose to prominence in the seventies with its fervent steppers rhythms, cavernous bass, spooked FX and devout rootsman chanting. His mastery of bass and treble manipulation and radical use of delay effects created a soundworld that was profoundly disorientating but also full of joy and celestial vibrations.

'Shaka sound is based on a principle, not just equipment,' he declared.[23] Inspired by liberation activists like Malcolm X, Martin Luther King and Angela Davis, as well as by Rastafarian deity Haile Selassie and Pan-African nationalist leader Marcus Garvey, Shaka saw music as a source of political expression and spiritual resilience that had sustained and unified Black people not only since the arrival of the Windrush generation from the Caribbean, but since their forced removal from Africa as slaves; it transmitted vital messages from history as well as yearnings for salvation. 'The music itself is what kept the people [together] through the struggles, through slavery, kept the spirits alive,'[24] he said in an interview not long before his death in 2023.

He would often play on through the night for seven, eight, nine hours at a stretch, going deep into a trance. 'That's the force of music,' he declared. 'It's a feeling created by God himself.'[25] At a dance in 1981, music journalist Vivien Goldman watched astounded as Shaka triggered 'sheets of energy' from the speakers and dreadlocked youths stepped and leaped around the dancehall. Shaka's belief in his cause inspired dedication; a crew of young men gave themselves to the task of carrying his huge soundboxes.

215

Jah Shaka performing at the Albany Empire in London, February 1988. ©David Corio/Getty Images.

'Money doesn't even come into it,' one of them told Goldman. 'It's a message we're carrying, not just a sound.'[26]

The music released under Shaka's own name was full of primal vitality: fearsome rumbles of bass, twinkles of melody, chirruping syndrums and unearthly wails from his dub siren, which he fed through a tape loop-based echo unit, stretching out long trails of chirr and scree. He launched his *Commandments of Dub* album series in 1980, kicking off with the mighty 'Verse 1'. Raging with cosmic sound effects, with Shaka himself on bass, its eerie sirens would be liberally sampled on nineties jungle tracks.

Shaka's themes were ancient and spiritual, but his methods were modern; by the third in the series, 1984's *Lion's Share of Dub*, he was incorporating unconventional synth textures and electronic drum sounds. The ninth *Commandments* album, 1989's drum machine-driven *Coronation Dub*, created as UK roots reggae started to go digital, was completely electronic and utterly sublime.

Lez Henry, who used to lug speaker boxes for Shaka's sound when he was a teenager, has argued that he and other sound systems created an 'autonomous space'[27] temporarily liberated from the domination of the white oppressor. But like soundmen before and afterwards, Shaka would be targeted by authorities who could not comprehend his culture. In 1975, *Race Today* magazine reported how police officers busted one of his dances in Brockley in south London: 'The police proceeded to kick, punch and truncheon people indiscriminately. Not content, they went on to wreck £400 of equipment with their truncheons.'[28]

Shaka was a dominant force in UK roots reggae for decades, but equally influential on the dancehall side of sound system culture was Saxon Sound International, which nurtured some of Britain's most famous reggae deejays like Tippa Irie, Smiley Culture, Papa Levi, Maxi Priest and Peter King, who developed the tongue-twisting 'fast chat' MC style sometimes also known as 'rapid rapping'.

Tapes of Saxon sessions from the 1980s testify to the irreverent creativity of their lyricism and the frenzied excitement of their dances, with the MCs delivering mind-boggling streams of convoluted rhetoric, ranging through exaggerated boasts and political declamations to fearsome putdowns of rivals, religious imprecations, lairy slackness, loopy witticisms and impassioned urgings in Jamaican patois or Cockney slang to hype up the crowd. Their followers responded by setting off airhorns and blowing whistles in a manic counterpoint to the sub-bass detonations from the speaker, creating a powerful synthesis of lyrical eloquence, compulsive rhythms and pure noise. Saxon MC Daddy Colonel said that the sound system was the only outlet they had to express themselves freely as young Black men in a racist society: '[So] we channelled everything into our music… we channelled all of our energy, our thoughts, our creativity, our vision.'[29]

Some sound systems became known for their colossal bass power, like Jah Tubbys or Quaker City. Saxon was known for its creatively untouchable crew of MCs. 'We were the reggae hitmakers because we had the artists,' said selector Trevor Sax. 'We had the MCs and we had the dubs and we had the togetherness.'[30] One of their best-known deejays, Smiley Culture, took fast chat into the UK pop charts with 'Cockney Translation', his tribute to Black British youths' London-Jamaican hybrid dialect, while another, Papa Levi, made the first UK deejay record to become a number one in Jamaica with 'Mi God Mi King'. 'We created our style and our own identity and people from the Caribbean couldn't believe that we were from England,'[31] said Tippa Irie.

Like Shaka's dub sirens, Saxon's MCs and the system's noise effects from their sound tapes and *Coughing Up Fire* live album were widely sampled in nineties jungle records; their lyrical originality also gained them respect among New York rappers, as well as in Jamaica. 'What Saxon did first and foremost was they revolutionised the way people performed on the mike as British MCs,' says Lez Henry. 'Saxon made English accents acceptable, they basically kicked that door open that led to rap and grime and drill.'

Saxon's renown spread through the alternative communication networks that developed around reggae sound system culture. In the eighties, cassette recordings of dances from Jamaica, known as 'yard tapes', as well as session tapes from British sound systems, were widely recopied and exchanged around the UK, updating listeners on the latest sonic developments as well as what deejays were chatting about Jamaican life and politics; transmitting cultural messages eagerly received by Black British youths, but hidden from and largely incomprehensible to the white majority.

As a teenager in Bristol, rapper Tricky cherished Saxon Sound International tapes that he managed to acquire. 'They would make a cassette in London, then that cassette would go all around England. You'd get a tape off someone, then you'd pass it on to someone else,' he explained. 'We'd constantly listen to those tapes, full of the latest early-eighties dancehall rhythms from Jamaica, with them chatting over the top.'[32]

Pirate radio stations were another vital independent medium for reggae in Britain, as they would be later for house, techno, jungle and UK garage. Britain's first Black-owned pirate, Dread Broadcasting Corporation, went on air in 1980. Founder Lepke (Leroy Anderson, Rita Marley's brother) described the station as a public service broadcaster, even though it was illegal: 'We exist because there is a need – a public demand – for a Black music station.'[33] 'Our format allows us to play music that would otherwise never be heard publicly,' explained the station's best-known presenter, Ranking Miss P. 'The point is to show that a Black person can actually get up and own and control something.'[34]

The authorities often characterised unlicensed radio operators as criminals, endangering the public by interfering with legal stations' frequencies and disrupting communications channels used by critical services like air traffic control. But like Lepke and DBC, many pirates were idealistic enthusiasts who risked raids, equipment seizures, convictions, fines and even potential prison sentences to broadcast the music they loved.

'The people involved deserve more recognition for what they did in helping Britain move to a more open and diverse broadcasting system,'[35] Stephen Hebditch argued in his book *London's Pirate Pioneers*. From steppers rhythms to rave breakbeats and beyond, pirate stations sustained not only Black British performers but also electronic dance music in general, giving it a vital platform for development in the years before legal broadcasters started trying to represent non-mainstream cultures more adequately.

Mad Professor Goes Boom

'I wasn't trained, I taught myself audio engineering and I built my own studio and I started making records myself. So I didn't know if what I was doing was right or wrong.'
Neil Fraser

Mad Professor. ©Matt Anker/Avalon/Getty Images.

In 1985, the fifth and most psychedelic of Jah Shaka's *Commandments* series, *Jah Dub Creator*, was mixed in typically surrealistic style by British reggae's pre-eminent dub scientist, Neil Fraser, alias Mad Professor.

Born in Guyana in 1955, Fraser's obsession with audio technology began when he was a child and took apart his mother's radio to find out how the voices magically emanated from it. He had built his own radio and amplifier by the time he was 10. The young electronics adept's family then emigrated to Britain, where after leaving school, he found work as an audio-equipment repair technician. By his mid-twenties, he had built a mixing desk using a diagram from hobbyist electronics maven F. C. Judd's *Practical Electronics* magazine; the DIY technology advocate's influence resurfacing yet again in another genre of music. Fraser then set up his own recording studio, Ariwa Sounds, at his home in the south London suburbs.

'My idea was to make different-sounding records,' he says of his initial releases on his Ariwa label. 'I brought musicians into my studio which was in my front room, recorded the drummer and the bass, and then I started to play with those tracks. I used echo and reverb but I started to play with more feedback and phasers. A lot of my peers and contemporaries would not play with a lot of stereo, so I would go left and right, bringing things around the whole spectrum, left to right, front to back.

'That's why it sounded futuristic, because I was also using elements like harmonisers, pitch transposers and stuff that most engineers were using very moderately, and I was using them in a way that was quite over-the-top: *Boiiiiiink! Booooom!*'

In 1982, he started his long-running *Dub Me Crazy* album series, which became a showcase for his ability to twist sound into bizarre and unpredictable shapes. He followed this with his politically conscious *Black Liberation Dub* series, which he describes as 'a way to remind people we need to be Black and proud like James Brown would have said in the sixties'. With his phased drum machines, treated horns, digital synthetics and echoing fragments of lyrics about slavery and colonialism, Fraser fashioned a militant strain of sonic Afrofuturism: 'Freedom Must Be Taken', one of his track titles declared.

The fabulous cartoon art of his album sleeves depicted the mild-mannered, bespectacled Fraser as a comic book superhero of dub, a techno-sorcerer with the power to bend sound to his will. As he points out, dub foreshadowed dance music's remix culture in turning producers into star attractions: 'It was the start of the engineers being artists.'

As well as his own records, Fraser produced ten albums with Lee 'Scratch' Perry after the extraordinary Jamaican relocated to London in the eighties. He also issued a wealth of lovers' rock recordings and took commissions from reggae-loving post-punk bands like his dub remodelling of Ruts DC's album *Rhythm Collision*, although his greatest non-reggae work – his alchemical transformation of Massive Attack's *Protection*, remixed as *No Protection* – was to come later.

In the mid-eighties, dub producers were sometimes commissioned by rock musicians who were searching for the perfect echo; Island Records' in-house producer, Paul 'Groucho' Smykle, worked on material for post-punk bands like Big Audio Dynamite and Colourbox as well as classic dub albums like Black Uhuru's *The Dub Factor* and Sly and Robbie's *A Dub Experience*. Smykle, the son of Jamaican immigrants who ran a weekend shebeen at their house after they emigrated to the UK in the fifties, would also use any downtime at the Island studio to mix dubs for Jah Shaka.

Fraser made two dub albums with the spiritually-motivated Shaka, but in his own Mad Professor recordings, he avoided overt religiosity. He also actively promoted female artists who delivered feminist messages to reggae's male-dominated culture. 'We talked about topics most people would rather not talk about,' he said. 'A lot of men were using their position to exploit women sexually, in a very chauvinistic way.'[36]

One of his female artists was Sister Audrey (Audrey Litchmore), whose synthetic horn-driven 'English Girl' – released by Shaka's label in 1982 – recounted how the promises of prosperity made to the Windrush arrivals of the 1950s had turned to disappointment for their children's generation, who were being told by politicians like Thatcher that they had 'swamped' the country and taken what rightfully belonged to Britain's whites. 'There were people who'd been brought into that country and thought they were part of the country and then realised they're not,'[37] Sister Audrey explained.

Another Mad Professor production was feminist deejay Ranking Ann's powerful first album, *A Slice of English Toast*. Ranking Ann – Ann Swinton from Croydon – was one of the first female sound system toasters in Britain to make a record. Few women had prominent roles with sound systems at that point; among the exceptions were deejays like Sister Audrey and Sista Culcha, the Nzinga Soundz duo and Valerie 'Lady V' Robinson, who ran V Rocket in Nottingham and often used to travel to Jamaica to cut dubs for her sound system at studios like King Jammy's and Channel One. 'It was amazing,' Robinson recalled as she looked back on her eighties experiences. 'But it wasn't easy.'[38]

Ranking Ann started out toasting on her brother's Black Rock sound when she was a teenager in the late seventies, although male deejays were sometimes reluctant to let her have the microphone. 'Back in those days, guys would turn around and look, see that I'm a young girl and just basically ignore me,' she recalls. 'But every now and again, every once in a while, they would give me the mike. I was quite shy at that time but I found my voice when I was chatting.'

Songs like her debut, 'Liberated Woman', vented her anger and frustration about men 'trying to control women and not respecting them as individuals'. Her feminist stance was unusual in reggae in the early eighties; she says she was once threatened at a deejay competition because of her lyrics and described as 'a ranting housewife strutting up and down the stage' by one reviewer.

Her track 'Black Rock Posse' was her response to such attempts to belittle her: a defiantly celebratory tale of grabbing the mike at a sound system dance and then demanding she be served a Babycham, a vodka martini and then a Cinzano Bianco. For her, sound systems were the cultural heart of the Black British community. 'They brought people together in a very positive way and they created a feeling of excitement because they were pushing new tunes and educating us about what music was out there,' she explains. 'For a lot of people who had Jamaican roots but were born in this country, we were also being educated about Jamaican culture, which was so refreshing compared to what was going on in England, which was quite a grey place in the seventies.

'Back then there was something very, very special about reggae music. It was giving people a sense of togetherness and a sense of justice. It was speaking of fighting for your rights, but it was also speaking of love.'

Adrian Sherwood, On-U Sound, Mark Stewart and Tackhead

'Dennis Bovell put it very well, he said that dub is the time of the engineer. When the musicians have finished their job, the engineer deconstructs it and creates another picture altogether.'
Adrian Sherwood

It was such an unlikely combination of disparate personalities that perhaps only a producer with a taste for the highly unconventional, living in a city where cultures had long intermingled and cross-fertilised, would have thought of putting them together on record.

Jamaican musicians Style Scott, Eskimo Fox, Crucial Tony and Lizard Logan from toaster Prince Far I's former backing band Creation Rebel, Ari Up from The Slits and Public Image Ltd guitarist Keith Levene – a mixture of roots reggae and post-punk, Caribbean and British, virtuosos and autodidacts – were united in a studio in London in 1981 to make an album overseen by a young white Englishman who had been a dub connoisseur since he was a boy. The record, *Threat to Creation*, credited to Creation Rebel/New Age Steppers, was a sparse, heavy, psychedelic affair, one of so many delightfully demented dub recordings produced by Adrian Sherwood and his rotating collectives of Jamaican players and British mavericks in the eighties.

As a teenager, Sherwood had worked as a promoter and distributor of Jamaican singles, co-founded independent reggae label Carib Gems aged 18 and then set up Hitrun Records to release roots tunes by Jamaican musicians, many of whom would record for him after he established the label for which he became best known: On-U Sound.

Independent ska and reggae labels had proliferated in Britain from the 1960s onwards – years before Rough Trade, Factory, Mute and the post-punk independent boom – supplying Jamaican tunes to specialist shops in cities with large Black communities. One of the earliest, Blue Beat, was founded in 1960, releasing R&B and ska; it was an imprint of Melodisc, which had started putting out calypso, mento and jazz in London as far back as 1947. Others followed, most notably Chris Blackwell's Island Records, Sonny Roberts' Planetone, which was possibly the first Black-owned label in the UK, and later fellow Jamaican Lee Gopthall's Trojan and Chris Cracknell and Chris Sedgwick's Greensleeves.

At On-U Sound, Sherwood drew around him many unique and esoteric talents who appeared and reappeared under various names and aliases: New Age Steppers, African Head Charge, Singers and Players, Dub Syndicate, Tackhead. At some point this sprawling collective included Keith LeBlanc, Skip McDonald and Doug Wimbish, former members of the house band at early New York hip-hop label Sugar Hill Records, as well as Jamaicans Bim Sherman and Deadly Headley, the Creation Rebel and Roots Radics rhythm sections, post-punk diva Annie Anxiety Bandez, ex-Psychic TV electronic savant David Harrow, and Lana/Alan Pellay, a former drag performer from Grimsby who once recorded a hi-NRG hit called 'Pistol in My Pocket'. Another idiosyncratic presence at On-U's London studio was Sherwood's inspiration, Lee Perry, for whom he produced a series of albums.

Sherwood's style of production was based on solid reggae grooves but incorporated harsh noise, African percussion, spoken word snippets and electronic inflections that might equally have appeared in recordings by industrial musicians like Cabaret Voltaire (whose album *Code* he produced). His sound also picked up on the non-musicianly strategies of post-punk bands and the fierce energy of hip-hop.

'The Jamaican producers like Lee Perry would all pride themselves on having their own identifiable sound. I soon started realising by being in the studio a lot more that by using a couple of techniques that I liked, like flying things through speakers and remiking them and then using certain reverbs and certain EQs and certain distortions, I'd started formulating something that people started recognising as "my sound",' Sherwood explains. 'I didn't want my music to be too cold, I wanted a bit of charm and a bit of mischief and a bit of fun in the productions. Something to mess it up a bit. That's what I learned from Lee Perry. Lee was all about creating mischief and creating magic.'

Sherwood describes some of the records he produced as 'designer dub' – music designed as a work of dub from the beginning. 'Which isn't actually what dub was when it started, because it all used to be versions of songs,' he points out. 'Although a lot of people make dub records from scratch now, originally all those great albums of Lee Perry, Joe Gibbs, Errol Thompson and all that, they were derived from songs.'

Perhaps inevitably, given his unwillingness to stay close to established templates, his productions were sometimes criticised as inauthentic by reggae purists. 'The purists were never going to like On-U Sound, it was too unconventional,' he says. It was also too English. 'Doing English reggae, you know, it was kind of frowned upon by the reggae fraternity, for them it's got to be from Jamaica, that was the real deal and ours was like a pale imitation. So there was no point, in my mind, copying what was coming from Jamaica.'

A Jamaican dub tradition that Sherwood did cherish was versioning – remaking killer rhythm tracks multiple times with a variety of different vocalists; creative recycling. 'It still to this day fascinates me, like all reggae fans – if you've got a good rhythm, you want to hear twenty versions of that rhythm,' he says. 'It's like an art form, you know, a great rhythm. I could never understand why other genres didn't do this – have a big hit with a great track and then just take the artists off, put another couple of artists on it and just reinterpret it. That is effectively a remix, but remixes for me all come from what Jamaicans call *version*.'

Some of On-U's wildest and most wayward albums were made by African Head Charge, Sherwood's smoke-breathing, psychedelic dub ensemble led by Ghanaian percussionist Bonjo Iyabinghi Noah. As drummer Eskimo Fox put it: 'Those were extreme, extreme records.'[39]

Equally extreme were the records that Sherwood made with Mark Stewart, former vocalist with The Pop Group, Britain's original punk-funk free-jazz noise-fusion outfit, whose agonised, almost feral intonational style was memorably described by writer Mark Fisher as 'a gaggle of incantations, yelps and howls'.[40] Stewart loved to exaggerate the strangeness of his voice by putting it through effects pedals and overloading the distortion; he once said he got some of his ideas from jazz player Eddie Harris, who used a Varitone pickup and effects unit on his saxophone and sometimes vocalised through the horn and manipulated the sound with a wah-wah pedal.

Stewart had been obsessed by dub since hearing the heavily-manipulated flipside mix of reggae hit 'Feel Like Making Love' by Elizabeth Archer and the Equators when he was a schoolboy in Bristol. He used to walk to school to save his bus fare to spend on reggae records, then play truant on Fridays to wait for the latest releases to be delivered to his local record shop.

A political radical with a deep interest in techniques of social control, information warfare and the villainies of capitalism, Stewart brought the ideas of Burroughs and Gysin to the On-U collective, using extreme juxtapositions like they were cut-ups in an attempt to disrupt conventional sonic narratives. 'Nothing is sacred and dub's deconstruction of the so-called real is how my mind works anyway, with filters, delayed gratification, multiple dimensions, weird science and para or hypernormal shit. I see dub as a kind of skeleton key to reality,'[41] he once said. (He wasn't always so earnest about his work: 'I go on about plunderphonics, but sometimes it's more like blunderphonics,' he quipped during an interview for this book before his death in 2023).

Stewart was responsible for making On-U Sound's connection with the former Sugar Hill players LeBlanc, McDonald and Wimbish after he heard LeBlanc's track 'No Sell Out', a cut-up of speeches made by Black Muslim activist Malcolm X that was one of the first combinations of hip-hop beats and spoken-word samples used in place of a lead vocal. The albums that Stewart made with LeBlanc, McDonald and Wimbish took the sounds made by one of the world's great rhythm sections and layered them with clamorous samples and caustic effects; their use of metallic hip-hop beats and brutally treated vocals was a clear influence on the music later made by artists like Nine Inch Nails.

'I made [1985 album] *As the Veneer of Democracy Starts to Fade* on fairly decent equipment, then I went back to Bristol and I had a cheap Sanyo double-cassette machine and just kept on cutting up bits of it, dubbing and dubbing until it just kind of overloaded,' Stewart recalled. 'Somehow people like Trent Reznor and Ministry picked up on that. I thought I was like making proper heavy dance beats, right? But they called what I was doing "industrial-strength hip-hop".'

Sherwood said that Stewart would go to Jah Shaka dances and tape them, but because the sound system was so loud, the recordings came out overloaded and distorted; Stewart thought this was brilliant and said he wanted his own records to sound similar. 'I thought at first he was taking the piss with his live Shaka tapes, but he wasn't, he was deadly serious,'[41] Sherwood marvelled.

Stewart explained that he had adored wild effects since childhood. 'When I was about 6 or 7 I had Action Man records with helicopter sounds and explosions on them. I just used to love noises like that,' he said. 'Then I remember at the youth club, they played 'Rock On' by David Essex, which has got an incredible dubby production, and then 'Skanga' by Rupie Edwards, one after the other, and those two things together blew my head.

'Then it was hip-hop – two turntables and a microphone and double-cassette boomboxes. It changed me and all my mates. I was in The Pop Group and we were in New York when hip-hop was really starting, and I went to a few block parties and [graffiti artist] Keith Haring was drawing, and we heard [New York radio stations] Kiss FM and WBLS and brought these tapes back to Bristol and everyone copied them.' Recipients of these NYC hip-hop tapes included some of the young men who would later play crucial roles in Massive Attack and Soul II Soul.

LeBlanc, McDonald and Wimbish agreed to come to the UK and deploy their talents with Sherwood's On-U Sound collective because of the freedom they were offered as musicians, and because they admired how the English dub producer used the studio as an experimental tool. 'He was like a person playing an instrument, and he was using frequencies that no one would even touch here in the US – shit felt like it was coming out of the floor, coming out of the ceiling. And what really caught my ear was that he made chords with the bass drums,' says LeBlanc, remembering how he watched Sherwood at the mixing desk at the first time. 'That's the reason we ended up working with Adrian – every day we were breaking ground.'

LeBlanc and Sherwood would experiment with an Oberheim DMX drum machine, layering quadruple bass-drum kicks to create colossal detonations and triggering samples from an AMS delay unit – sounds that ended up on Le Blanc's exhilarating *Major Malfunction* album. 'I played drums, so the only thing that really interested me with a DMX was doing stuff a drummer could never do,' explains LeBlanc. 'Most people were trying to get a drum track out of it, I was trying to stretch it out of shape, make it do shit like getting a tom-tom to sound like a huge jackhammer drill. We certainly weren't using the equipment the way people intended it to be used, let's put it that way. We were technological anarchists.'

The three Americans became the Maffia, Mark Stewart's band from his second album onwards, and also recorded with Sherwood as Fats Comet and as Tackhead, developing a style that incorporated prodigious basslines and head-battering hip-hop beats programmed on LeBlanc's DMX, embellished with politically subversive samples and wild guitar solos. They also played live with Stewart as the Maffia and as Tackhead Sound System, with Sherwood live-treating the sound from the mixing desk.

'My whole drum set was wired with sensors, and I was triggering samples live. Doug got himself a [foot-controlled] MIDI step pedal and he had it hooked up to an [Akai] S900 sampler and Skip had a keyboard, so basically we would play our instruments and trigger shit live at the same time,' says LeBlanc. 'I'd have a percussion loop on the DMX so the tempo would be spot-on and Adrian could set the delay speeds and dub it live.' With Stewart on the microphone, raging vengefully like a disharmonious Cassandra drowning in a sea of echo, it was a shockingly intense experience: the funk militant. 'Tackhead at the time was such a violent force, a very daunting little crew,' says Sherwood. 'I was very competitive, I always wanted to go in, make the loudest noise you'd ever heard and completely mash the place up.'

Tackhead Sound System also toured with MC Gary Clail, a former building-site labourer from Bristol who sometimes performed with his head swathed in bandages. Clail was another singular character who got involved in the On-U collective via Stewart; he claimed to have started his performing career at blues dances 'singing Irish rebel songs over the top of reggae beats'.[43] He once described his declamatory vocal style as 'Bristolian MCing – half-

Irish grown up in a black area... It sounds like a hod carrier who's got this kind of rhythm.'[44]

Although the concept of the burly Clail ranting political slogans in a West Country accent over beats laid down by one of America's funkiest rhythm sections seemed bizarre, it was a potent mixture. Completely unexpectedly, he would go on to have some of the greatest chart successes of all the On-U Sound crew, with music that strayed furthest from the label's reggae roots.

Digital Dub and UK Steppers

'There can never be a point where you can go too far with dub.'
Dennis Bovell[45]

As long as the genre has existed, reggae producers have adopted and adapted new technology for their own specific purposes. Lee Perry and The Wailers' Aston 'Family Man' Barrett are often credited as the first people to use a drum machine in reggae, back in 1971 on the Bob Marley song 'Rainbow Country'. The drummer Sly Dunbar was another electronic innovator in Jamaica, integrating syndrums, a Roland TR-808 and a Simmons electronic kit into productions he worked on with Robbie Shakespeare in the mid-eighties. But it was Wayne Smith's 'Under Mi Sleng Teng', with its insistent bassline generated by a Casiotone MT-40 keyboard, that heralded the digital dancehall era in reggae in 1985, sparking hundreds of imitative versions as the music turned decisively towards the electronic.

While digital dancehall was often a profane party music, some productions coming out of studios in Kingston pointed towards the possibilities of a new, high-tech roots sound – an idea that was embraced by followers of Jah Shaka's sound system in Britain. Shaka kept the spiritual roots vibe alive in the UK in the mid-eighties dancehall-dominated era when productions that suited his singularly committed style had dwindled, until his British acolytes started to bring him their new, drum machine-driven roots tunes to play from dub plates.

One of the records to suggest the style that became known as UK steppers was Sound Iration's 'Seventh Seal', recorded in 1988 by a duo that included Kiss FM pirate radio DJ Nick Raphael, one of the founders of Manasseh sound system. For Manasseh, a group of young white reggae enthusiasts, Shaka carried the standard. 'He was number one. Definitely,' says Raphael. 'He was unique in that he was playing pure, heavyweight, minor-key, spiritual roots music all night long. When Manasseh started in 1985, I would say hardly any other sound system was doing that.'

Dread and Fred's muscular 'Warriors Stance', with its ultra-synthetic beatbox-and-synth-horns sound, was another formative digital steppers record, made by two brothers from Bedford and released on Shaka's label in 1989. The *Sound Iration in Dub* album also highlighted how the new sound was evolving. 'The tempo of the music changed, it was faster than classic roots and the basslines sounded different because they were all played on keyboards,' explains Raphael.

Access to cheaper home-recording technology was a key factor, Raphael says. 'The whole UK steppers thing is partly about the beginning of home studios, the democratising effect that had. You could make a record and it didn't matter if it wasn't the best musicians in town, if it rocked the crowd, it rocked the crowd and nobody could argue with that. And it *did* rock the crowd, because it came with this new feel that was rock solid because it was quantised [aligned into perfect tempo technologically].'

Another landmark digital roots release in 1989 was *The Disciples*, an album made for Shaka's label by Russ and Lol Bell-Brown, two English reggae fans from Surrey. As The Disciples, they recorded four albums for the revered sound system operator, beginning with *Deliverance*, the sixth record in his *Commandments of Dub* series. They were even given their name by Shaka. 'We were happy with that, because we always saw it as we were disciples of Shaka – and not just him alone, the sound system and the scene too,' says Russ Bell-Brown.

The brothers initially started to make tracks at home, then made the connection with their hero by cutting a dub plate and taking it to his Rastafarian arts and crafts shop in London's New Cross. 'Shaka just said, "Give me anything else you've got, do me four mixes and come to the next dance." And that was our initiation,' recalls Bell-Brown.

The dance they attended the following week had a huge impact on the way they made music. 'It was quite awesome, really, for two white guys that lived out in the suburbs,' Bell-Brown says. 'I remember the first tune came on and I could hear the spit and crackle of the tops, then the mid-range comes in, then suddenly the bass was just tearing into me, it just felt so intense that I was standing there thinking, "How am I going to be able to breathe now?"

'There was one particular track that I remember him playing, a solid steppers roots by Johnny Clarke, but when Shaka played it at the dance, suddenly you realise that it's made for *this* environment, *here* – it's *made for the dance*. In that intense atmosphere, with that heavy sound system, suddenly the basslines made a lot more sense. So that became the focus for my own original basslines.'

When Shaka embraced a heavily synthetic sound on his 1989 album *Coronation Dub*, it delighted devotees like Bell-Brown, who said he loved the 'staccato, rigid, in-your-face rhythms'. This basic drum-machine-and-synth template would also define the sound of many other British roots musicians, like Alpha and Omega and Zion Train, who emerged around the end of the eighties. 'Most of us that started at that time, like Alpha and Omega and Dub Judah and Sound Iration, we used drum machines through necessity,' says Bell-Brown. 'But that gives the music a certain vibe. And once you start using drum machines, you ask, do we need to use live bass? And then you find that digital bass has a different feel so it makes you build rhythms in a different way.'

Like other forms of electronic dance music that were nurtured within self-sustaining scenes, UK digital steppers developed through a process of creative interchange between its protagonists. Techniques and ideas were shared or copied, individual innovations reworked and improved upon, as musicians and producers collaborated or competed with each other to push the sound forward.

A new wave of UK roots sound systems also emerged – Manasseh, Iration Steppas and Jah Warrior among them – playing spiritual roots tunes and digital steppers rhythms to audiences that gradually became much more racially mixed than the crowds of hardcore Rastas who leaped and pranced in militant Zulu warrior style at Shaka dances in the seventies. With each year that passed, white dub fans got involved in the UK scene in increasing numbers. 'The most predominant change you can see is a change of nations coming into the dances,' acknowledged Aba Shanti-I, who ran one of the best loved of the new-school sound systems. 'In the seventies and eighties it was predominantly black people that would go to these sort of gatherings.'[46]

Aba Shanti-I was the name adopted by a London deejay and devout Rastafarian called Joseph Smith. At the time, he was working as a disc-cutting engineer for Jah Tubbys, the veteran London-based sound system, equipment vendor and vinyl-mastering studio, where he was mastering many of the new steppers tracks. The desire to spread the message of Rastafari and promote this upsurge of roots creativity were among the inspirations for him to start his own sound system. 'We needed somebody to champion what we were doing in the UK,' he explained. 'Aba Shanti was the voice of the UK artists.'[47]

His brother Blood Shanti, who produced digital roots tracks for their Aba Shanti-I record label, argued that the tough electronic steppers sounds that developed in the UK inevitably reflected the fact that they came from chilly Britain, not sunny Jamaica. 'We've been born here and we must create our own sound forms,' he said. 'When we create music we reflect and echo what we see all around us... I know that some Jamaican musicians see our music here as too hard and harsh, but we're in a concrete jungle, you overstand, and I can only express myself from the way I live.'[48]

This harder UK digital steppers sound would hit a creative peak in the early nineties with tracks like the majestic 'Prowling Lion' by The Disciples and 'High Rise Vibrations', a full-on synth-dub assault embellished with acid squelches and ecstatic house pianos by sound system duo Iration Steppas. Growing up in Leeds, where riots erupted in 1981 inflamed by racism and youth unemployment, Iration Steppas' founder Mark Iration (Mark Millington) had been a dub aficionado since his youth but also loved Chicago house. His first release was a dubwise house track, 'Ital's Anthem', released under the name Ital Rockers, the name of his previous sound system.

One of Millington's earliest gigs as Iration Steppas was with Jah Shaka in Leeds; a tape of the session highlights the origins of his mutant strain of electronic dub. Before the Shaka dance, he recorded a series of tracks with Leeds comrades The Rootsman and Bunnington Judah specifically for the night. 'We spent a week building some fresh tunes to do damage,' he recalls. 'Of course we took it seriously – Shaka was an idol, he was a big man. I was just a little boy, I was nobody, I was just starting off.'

Firing through a series of his own Iration Steppas specials in a fierce roots-rave style, Millington conjured a hurricane of whirling echoes, phased rhythms, crazed screams, chattering snares and fragmented piano chords, peaking with a gloriously bonkers technoid reinterpretation of Shaka anthem 'Kunta Kinte'. 'Keep up the good work,' Shaka told him after the dance ended.

He did. With Iration Steppas, Millington went on to introduce rave synth sounds to UK steppers grooves, creating a homemade fusion of digital dub and techno inflections that he called 'Year 3000 style', even though some of his more conservative roots peers disapproved. 'We got a lot of flak, but we influenced a lot of people too,' he asserts.

He also caused controversy among traditionalists by playing specials from DAT tapes instead of dub plates because he couldn't afford to cut acetate discs all the time; this allowed him to stay up all night before a dance building tunes at home on his Atari computer, drum machine and synth, and then play them out that evening.

He explains that he wanted to develop a sound that looked to the future as well as respecting the past, as innovators like King Tubby and his hero Shaka had done before him: 'When Shaka started using effects and echoes and sirens, he evolutioned the whole sound system scene by actually having the guts to make that kind of noise. Then everybody started to copy him.' So it was time for the music to evolve again. 'Dub was just going in one direction – it was just drums, bass and a bit of flute and horns here and there. It had got samey, it needed to change. So because I liked the house music and hip-hop, I fused it all with the dub,' he says.

'I've always wanted to do things differently, you know? When you do make things different, at first people think you're mad. But then it opens doors for other people to start inventing too.

'The old music still lives on, but the new music has to keep moving forward.'

British rapper Newtrament (Bertram Johnson) on the back of a truck on Euston Road, London, June 1983. ©David Corio/Getty Images.

7

TEARIN' DOWN THE AVENUE

Electro and Hip-Hop

B-Boys, Buffalo Gals and the Rise of Electro
'1982 was the year when the funk warped out into hyperspace.'
David Toop, author of Rap Attack[1]

IT WAS AN UNLIKELY CATALYST INDEED. A 36-year-old white Englishman, former punk band manager and clothes shop owner with a wonky sense of rhythm and an unconventional manner of speech, looning around Times Square in a hillbilly hat to a pounding hip-hop rhythm with fashion models square dancing in Vivienne Westwood couture, New York graffiti artist Dondi spraypainting a piece, the Rock Steady Crew breakdancing and a DJ scratching with a 7-inch single.

For some British teenagers, the promotional video for Malcolm McLaren's single 'Buffalo Gals', based on what the former Sex Pistols manager had seen at a Zulu Nation show in The Bronx, was a revelatory introduction to the key elements of hip-hop culture. The video became a formative influence on the UK's emerging electro and breakdance scene after it was shown on BBC chart show *Top of the Pops* in December 1982. 'It was like wow, scratching, breakdancing, rapping, graffiti all in one video,' recalled George Evelyn, then a schoolboy in Leeds, later to form Nightmares on Wax. 'I remember going to school the morning after *Top of the Pops*, that Friday morning, and everyone was trying to break and pop in the school yard.'[2]

'When I first saw people doing those moves, spinning on their heads, I couldn't believe it,' said Benji Reid, who became a member of Manchester breakdance crew Broken Glass. 'It was the first time you had seen a physical depiction of the culture. You got to see the dancers doing headspins, backspins. It showed us the moves.'[3] Winston Hazel from Sheffield, who would become a pioneering DJ, saw the video for the first time at a jazz-funk all-dayer event: 'Everyone was crowding round, trying to work out how this guy was spinning on his head. After the 'Buffalo Gals' video, everyone started to practice what they'd just seen. By the next all-dayer, breakdancing exploded.' In Bristol, Adrian Thaws, later better-known under the alias Tricky, was watching too: 'Malcolm McLaren looked like an idiot to me, but the little kids body-popping and the little girls in the dresses with the black make-up across their eyes – to me, they were the coolest ever.'[4]

Wild Style, Charlie Ahearn's 1983 feature film about New York graffiti artists, which featured hip-hop instigators like Grandmaster Flash, was another catalyst for the UK scene. 'When I saw that, it was, "I could do that, I could breakdance, I could spray paint, I could rap, I could DJ, I could learn how to do it",' Kirk Thompson, later to become drum and bass DJ Krust, told Joe Muggs and Brian Stevens in their book *Bass, Mids, Tops*. 'You'd have a piece of lino and you'd hassle your mum to get you a tracksuit and white gloves and you were a breakdancer. Then you'd nick some spray cans and you're a graffiti artist. You write a few rhymes and you're a rapper. Finally, you take your mum's gramophone player with the tape deck and the turntable and you switch the button between tape and record and now you're a DJ because now you can learn how to scratch.'[5]

After seeing the film, Thompson and his friends in Bristol formed a crew called Fresh 4. Within a few years, they would be among the instigators of a very British hip-hop-derived sound, alongside Massive Attack, whose 3D (Robert del Naja), a renowned graffiti artist as a teenager, recalled how all the early players on the Bristol scene turned out to watch *Wild Style* when it came out: 'We went down to see it three or four times in a row, just trying to absorb everything.'[6] All over the country, groups of teenagers formed breakdance crews and would gather in squares and parks, roll out a piece of lino and battle each other for choreographic supremacy. Many of these tracksuit-clad enthusiasts, like George Evelyn and Winston Hazel, went on to play important roles in British electronic dance music.

Hip-hop had already been familiar in Britain for several years by this point; The Sugarhill Gang's 'Rapper's Delight' had even reached number three in the UK pop charts in 1979. But now the more adventurous British DJs were also championing the ultra-synthetic sound of electro. Tracks like Afrika Bambaataa's 'Planet Rock', with its spindly Roland TR-808 drum-machine pattern, synthetic bass blurts and melody purloined from Kraftwerk, made perfect sense to a generation growing up with the frenetic bleeping of videogames like Pac-Man, Space Invaders, Galaxian and Asteroids.

Greg Wilson, a DJ who was playing the latest imports from the US at his nights at Legend in Manchester and the Wigan Pier club, describes electro as dance music's missing link because it took over from jazz-funk in non-mainstream British clubs and foreshadowed the electronic dance culture of the late eighties. 'It was just so exciting – the studios were being really experimental, dub ideas were being brought in by remixers and this whole electro-funk period was kind of moving things into what was going to be the future, which was house, techno and hip-hop,' Wilson explains.

Electro had multinational, multiethnic roots; it was created by Black, white and Latinx artists and producers in the US but drew from European synth-pop as well as Black American funk – another precursor was Cat Stevens' freaky 1977 electro-boogie oddity 'Was Dog a Doughnut' – while its sound palette was shaped by Japanese technology. 'Electro was such an open-minded thing – you had Bambaataa in The Bronx playing stuff like Yellow Magic Orchestra and Gary Numan, and obviously that would then influence what he did,' says Wilson.

Influences were bounced back and forth across the Atlantic in a kind of intercontinental, cross-cultural feedback loop; electro fed into the proto-techno being made by Cybotron in Detroit in the early eighties, which was significantly influenced by European electronic musicians like Ultravox and Kraftwerk. Electro records also helped to propagate the idea of including dub mixes and skeletal 'bonus beats' tracks for DJs to manipulate – more building blocks for the electronic dance music that would follow.

Electro emerged at a time when the some of the more progressive British DJs were starting to mix between tracks instead of talking on the microphone; its metronomic minimalism was perfect for steady segues.

Wilson credits Greg James, an American who moved to Britain to play at London's Studio-54-style mixed-gay Embassy Club in 1978, as being perhaps the first to introduce the novel concept of continuous, beat-matched mixing in the UK. Other early advocates of mixing in British clubs were hi-NRG don Ian Levine and Froggy (Steve Howlett), one of the so-called 'Soul Mafia' DJs who played at funk all-dayers and huge weekender events around southeast England in the post-disco era. Froggy had become convinced that mixing was the future when he visited New York clubs like the Paradise Garage, where he watched Larry Levan synching up two records to create an entirely new narrative.

Mixing was also championed by James Hamilton, the disco columnist for pop magazine *Record Mirror*, known for his idiosyncratic descriptions of records and his then-innovative listing of beats-per-minute counts in his reviews ('thumpily striding 121 BPM galloper'). Hamilton was involved in putting together one of the first mixed compilation albums in the UK, 1979's *Instant Replays*, which was supplied to DJs by CBS Records as a promotional tool for its disco output.

But initially at least, most British DJs weren't much interested in mixing and, like a lot of electronic music genres in their early stages of development, electro also met some resistance – jazz-funk and soul purists insisted it wasn't 'real music' because it was made by machines. 'I was seen as a bit of a heretic,' recalls Wilson. 'They were telling me I was ruining the scene by playing these records. But the people who did like it were the younger Black audience. They loved it.' *The Face* magazine later reported that the soul scene was 'riven into war zones' by the arrival of electro, with white traditionalists sneering – radio DJ Robbie Vincent called it 'that electro shit'[7] – while musically progressive Black youths embraced it.

Kermit Leveridge, one of the young dancers who was a regular at Wilson's nights in Manchester and would become part of the Broken Glass breakdance crew, argues that the Black youths who were into electro were the cultural innovators at the time. 'We weren't following trends, we were actually creating trends,' he says. 'We used to go to Legend to hear Greg playing electro and do fusion dancing, quick footwork to the electro tracks. Then hip-hop and breakdancing started coming in and it just opened up a whole new dimension. Some people that couldn't breakdance got into graffiti. Some people got into DJing. Some people got into rap, some people got into fashion. So there was this *whole fucking explosion* of creativity.'

Electro remained a largely underground subculture in the UK until a savvy entrepreneur called Morgan Khan launched his *Street Sounds Electro* series of albums in 1983, compiling tracks from import 12-inches onto budget-price compilations mixed by DJs like Herbie Laidley of the Mastermind sound system and warehouse-party instigators Noel and Maurice Watson. Khan was a dance music-loving Anglo-Indian promoter who had helped turn 'Rapper's Delight' into a UK hit and released Imagination's first single on his own label. He was also involved in releasing *Calibre Cuts*, an intriguing cut-up mix album of soul and disco tracks that was issued in 1980, the year before the 'The Adventures of Grandmaster Flash on the Wheels of Steel' brought turntable collage to a mass audience and showed how the DJ had become a new kind of musician.

Khan noticed that the best electro tracks being played in the clubs were only available on expensive 12-inch imports. UK record companies at the time didn't take dance music seriously and usually didn't see Black musicians as worthy of long-term investment, Khan said: 'There was a racist attitude to Black music: it wasn't "serious" music.'[8] So he flew to the US and made deals to license tracks for the *Street Sounds Electro* series, which would later become *Street Sounds Hip Hop* as the decade progressed.

The *Street Sounds* compilations played a central role in popularising electro in Britain, particularly outside the major cities. 'They introduced so many people to the music. They were the albums that sold the music to the suburbs,' says Wilson. 'A lot of them were selling on cassettes, because they were ghettoblaster albums, mixed records, which was totally unusual at the time – it was a perfect accompaniment for the crews to roll the lino out and start busking. If you look at a lot of those British dance musicians who were making stuff in the later eighties, you can guarantee that they got started on those electro albums from Morgan Khan.'

In 1984, Khan decided he wanted to release an album of UK-made electro, but at that point little had been made in Britain apart from Newtrament's politically-conscious 'London Bridge is Falling Down' and 'Confused Beats' by New Order, an electro mix on the B-side of the Factory band's Arthur Baker-produced 'Confusion'. So Khan turned to Wilson and musicians Martin Jackson, formerly the drummer with post-punk group Magazine, and Andy Connell, the keyboard player with A Certain Ratio. 'Morgan wanted it to look like there's this thriving UK electro scene, so he wanted us to use pseudonyms,' says Wilson. Using a Linn Drum and an Emulator, Connell,

Jackson and Wilson recorded all the tracks for *Street Sounds Electro UK* under various names except one, which was written by Herbie Laidley with New York scratch DJ Whizkid and credited to The Rapologists.

'We literally made it up as we went along,' says Wilson. 'It was a kind of madcap project that was maybe too quirky and odd for the Black scene and too Black for the white scene, but it became a cult thing, loads of kids grew up with that album and adored it. It was certainly like a precursor for that whole British approach to dance music, that spirit of "Let's just go in the studio and make something up".'

One of the tracks, 'Style of the Street', which was credited to Broken Glass, Manchester's top breakdance crew, featured a rap by Kermit Leveridge, who would go on to co-found the Ruthless Rap Assassins and Black Grape. (Years later, the track was sampled by The Prodigy in their song 'Girls'). Wilson had become the Broken Glass crew's manager and when he was booked to play electro each week at the Haçienda, they would dance on stage to his sets.

Some journalists were intrigued by the role played in the project by Wilson, a DJ and apparent non-musician; at that point in Britain, DJs were often depicted in the music media as rather naff figures with big egos but little discernible talent. 'It was years before things like Coldcut and Bomb the Bass happened – although [Northern Soul and hi-NRG DJ] Ian Levine had been already making records since the seventies, so I can't take much credit there,' Wilson says.

Apart from Khan's Street Sounds label, one of the few other sources of UK-made electro was Jive Records, which released a couple of albums of purpose-built tracks for DJs recorded by The Willesden Dodgers, a group of in-house engineers and musicians at Battery Studios in northwest London's Willesden area. *Jive Rhythm Trax* and *Jive Scratch Trax* were sets of stripped-down electro and hip-hop breaks, all simply named after their BPM counts – precursors to the raw beat tracks and 'DJ tools' of the house era.

The impulse for the records was entirely mercantile, explains one of the Willesden Dodgers, Pete Q. Harris. South African businessman Clive Calder, co-founder of Jive's parent company, the Zomba Group, wanted to break into the emerging hip-hop market and was encouraging his engineers to imitate the freshest sounds. 'We were trying to make money as producers and so we were listening to the latest, best tracks, as we were directed to by Clive, who was very, very in touch with what was going on,' Harris says. 'He would bring in maybe twenty, thirty tracks on cassette, stuff that was either about to break big or was big, tracks that he believed that it was possible to either emulate or get close to.'

Some of The Willesden Dodgers' tracks were created to resemble specific electro hits – '122 BPM' had distinct hints of Afrika Bambaataa and Kraftwerk, for example – but not enough to be legally actionable, explains Harris. 'Those are very closely inspired by but not breaches of copyright of those original tracks. They were not designed for commercial consumption or to be played on radio, they are essentially beats for jocks to scratch to. The DJ was an integral part of early hip-hop and the rapper needed to have a breakbeat to work to. So there were plenty of exposed kick drums, snares and hi-hats, with minimal actual music going on.'

'122 BPM' in particular has been sampled repeatedly by hip-hop and dance-pop producers over the decades; *Jive Rhythm Trax* and *Jive Scratch Trax* became cult classics, to Harris's wry amusement. 'I don't think we were trying to break new ground or being inventive musically by being minimalist, we were just trying to make things that people could use as a tool,' he said. 'They weren't meant to be standalone artistic works because there were no lyrics and not really any melodies, although there may have been a floaty Roland synthesized arpeggio and a doomy kind of chord from time to time. They were meant to be useful.'

As Jive Records sought to deepen its involvement in hip-hop, Harris and fellow Willesden Dodger Nigel Green also worked on the eponymous debut album for US rap group Whodini. But the standout track on the record, 'Magic's Wand', was actually produced by a young British synth player called Thomas Dolby. However, Dolby has insisted that any claim that he played a major role in early hip-hop history is 'quite tenuous' as he programmed the infectious tune in London and never even met the American rappers: 'My beats were sent over on floppy disks to New York and loaded into a Fairlight there and they added a rap over the top.'[9]

Electronic Dancers: TW Funk Masters, Freeez

'Electronic music can't stay still for long. It keeps moving.'
John Rocca, Freeez

Before synth-pop, electro and electronic soul tracks made with synths and drum machines by UK Black musicians like Phil Fearon and Loose Ends, Brit-funk bands had already been deploying new technology to cosmic effect;

multiracial crew Atmosfear released a series of synth-spangled jazz-funk tracks, including their dubwise futurist landmark 'Dancing in Outer Space' in 1979.

The following year, soul and funk DJ Tony Williams, who also hosted a reggae show on BBC Radio London, put together a band that became known as the TW Funk Masters to make a track for the clubs inspired by The Sugarhill Gang's 'Rappers Delight'. But the players he booked were reggae musicians and the sessions were mixed by UK dub specialist Mark Angelo Lusardi, and their instrumental, 'Love Money', turned out like a kind of Caribbean-inflected disco-dub, all syndrums and cascading echoes.

'Love Money' became a classic at New York clubs like the Paradise Garage – 'black lights, white shirts, feather clips and a room full of people just losing their minds.... still love this song to this day,'[10] reads one comment from a Paradise Garage veteran on YouTube. Its style had a powerful impact on NY remixers like François Kevorkian and Larry Levan as they started to employ dub techniques when they remodelled recordings.

Kevorkian said that hearing 'Love Money', a dance record that had 'all those big reverbs, those stops, those crazy effects where a piano comes in, cuts off and decays', was a revelation. 'I started going in the studio and playing with tape delays and all kinds of crazy regeneration effects,'[11] he recalled. Londoner Tony Williams had helped to change the sound of New York dance music – although he was unaware of this for years afterwards. 'Wow, you mean to tell me that this record is bigger than I even thought it was?'[12] he exclaimed when Greg Wilson informed him how significant 'Love Money' had been. As if that wasn't enough, on the other side of his record was a vocal version of the song, '(Money) No Love', with a rap by Williams' friend Bo Kool – one of the very first British tracks to feature rapping.

British electronic dance music's development was repeatedly swayed by creative interchanges between the UK and the US. In 1983, another British jazz-funk band, Freeez, had their sound transformed completely when they travelled to New York to record with Arthur Baker, the hot electro talent of the moment after producing 'Planet Rock' for Bambaataa. (Immediately after working with Freeez, Baker would make 'Confusion' with New Order).

'Basically he just felt a bit sorry for us,' says Freeez mainman John Rocca. 'He listened to our demos, which we did in London, and they were all a bit crap. But he said, "Look, I'll produce your album, but we're going to write a whole new set of tracks here in New York".' Rocca arrived in New York as hip-hop culture was booming and he recalls seeing breakdance showdowns on the streets, graffiti-bombed trains rolling into subway stations and B-boys carrying boomboxes playing the freshest electro mixes.

Baker and his keyboard player, John Robie, came up with an effervescent combination of 808 beats, synth and glockenspiel to create the chiming ice-cream van sound for a track they named 'I.O.U'. Baker then asked Rocca, who hadn't been Freeez's vocalist up to that point, to sing it. 'Arthur was really into those early eighties electronic bands – Yazoo, Human League and so on, and they've got these English voices, which is what I've got – but I didn't like it because I was into everything jazz, funk and soul, so my voice didn't appeal to me at all,' says Rocca. 'But he was the boss and he said: "You're going to do it".'

To Rocca's further dismay, Baker also insisted he sing 'I.O.U' falsetto, an idea inspired by what the American producer saw as UK synth-pop's subversion of gender stereotypes. 'Arthur said that Alison Moyet, a woman, was singing low. So he wanted to get me, a guy, to sing high. I didn't want to do it, I thought it was revolting, it just reminded me of the Bee Gees, which was something that back then I didn't like.' Baker's hunch worked out perfectly; Rocca's fragile, boyish voice gave the song a sense of masculine emotional vulnerability that provided a beguiling counterpoint to its tough machine rhythms. The five-vowel chorus was also sampled for a wild Emulator ad-lib played by Robie, credited on the record as a 'syllabic solo'.

'I.O.U' was an international hit and became one of the precursors to the relentlessly upbeat Latin freestyle sound. But despite its success, Rocca decided to go solo and left the Freeez name behind him. He kept the falsetto, however, and his distinctively delicate voice would go on to feature on a series of important club tracks in the US: 'I Want It to Be Real', again produced by Baker, and 'Move', produced by Chicago house pioneer Farley 'Jackmaster' Funk, both became proto-house classics on DJ mastermix shows broadcast by dance music radio stations in New York and Chicago.

During the rave era, Rocca went on to make some emotive house records as Midi Rain, but then dropped out of music to work in communications technology. When his back catalogue was rereleased as a compilation in the 2020s, it came accompanied by adulatory tributes from veteran US DJs like Junior Vasquez and Little Louie Vega, who lauded the recordings as New York dance classics.

Rocca wasn't the only Englishman to have an electro-fired international hit. There was also Paul Hardcastle, the curly-headed soulboy synthman best known for the 1985 anti-war track '19', a chirpy tribute to the teenage casualties of the US military campaign in Vietnam with processed vocal samples taken from a TV documentary and set to an 808-driven groove. Hardcastle explained that its stuttering 'n-n-n-n-nineteen' hook was created out of necessity because he was using 'an Emulator I with two seconds of sample time in it',[13] and the number 19 was the only part of the documentary's narration that made sense as such a short excerpt. It was another example of how astute producers could turn the limitations of technology to their own creative advantage.

Hybrid Beats: Cabaret Voltaire, Big Audio Dynamite

'I played samples because I couldn't fucking play anything else.'
Don Letts, Big Audio Dynamite

The new sounds of electro and the hip-hop art of turntablism, combined with the advent of the sampler and the introduction in 1983 of the new MIDI (Musical Instrument Digital Interface) technology, which enabled different types of machines made by different companies to link up and synchronise, opened up a new era for electronic music production. Excited by these innovations, by the compelling pulsations of electro-funk and by the possibilities offered by remixing, former punks and industrial experimentalists started to gravitate towards the dancefloor.

Among them were Cabaret Voltaire, who had become a duo after Chris Watson quit in 1981 to join the sound department of regional television broadcaster Tyne Tees. (He eventually became one of the world's most innovative wildlife and natural history sound-recordists). A remix by John Robie of 'Yashar', one of their last releases with Watson, helped open up a new direction; after his departure, Richard H. Kirk and Stephen Mallinder adopted a more beat-driven sound with less heavily-distorted vocals. By that point, said Kirk, 'the technological breakthroughs and the most radical music were both coming out of the dance scene.'[14]

The duo were listening to a lot of New York electro which, as working class ex-soulboys, they thought sounded much more adventurous than a lot of industrial music. 'Electro was great because it was a new generation playing with technology, fucking around with drum machines like we were,' says Mallinder. 'The early stuff that Bambaataa and other people were doing, using technology in an interesting way, with a groove, was really fascinating for us because the energy and the spontaneity and the visceral element of dance music was always massively part of what we were into.'

In interviews in 1984, Kirk set out the case that Black Americans were the leading innovators in popular music. 'Black music has always been very forward-looking: it's always embraced new technology as it's become available,' he explained. 'What's interesting is that it's getting more and more minimal: we've got to the stage now where they've pared it down to just rhythm box and vocals, with maybe a synth line with a delay on it here and there and a bit of Emulator or tapes.'[15] He said that he saw hip-hop as a kind of realisation of Gysin and Burroughs' cut-up techniques. 'To me Grandmaster Flash's 'Wheels of Steel' is pure Burroughs' *Electronic Revolution*.'[16]

Cabaret Voltaire signed with Some Bizzare supremo Stevo, who licensed them to a major label in 1983, as the synth-pop boom allowed various purveyors of electronic weirdness to come in from the margins. They went on to develop a kind of dark and subversive industrial electro-funk; music for a Burroughsian discotheque. Their mid-eighties albums, from *The Crackdown* to the Adrian Sherwood-produced *Code*, still vibrated with tension, menace and paranoid energy, but were illuminated by vivid hooks and underpinned by wrecking-ball rhythms.

Hip-hop was offering an array of creative cues and Big Audio Dynamite, the dance-rock band formed by guitarist Mick Jones after he left The Clash, were to interpret them in a completely different way. The multiracial quintet styled themselves as a gang of righteous dudes – *BAD!* – swashbuckling dandies with all the coolest records in their collections.

'Big Audio Dynamite was just a reflection of the multicultural way that London was going at that time and the sounds that we were tuned into – Jamaican basslines, the New York hip-hop beats that were coming out stateside, with UK rock'n'roll guitar all over it,' says Don Letts, the dreadlocked former Sex Pistols associate, filmmaker and reggae DJ who Jones recruited to select samples and co-write lyrics. 'It wasn't like, "OK, let's have a Black guy in the group, let's have a dread in the group." We were mates. Essentially we were working-class kids in a multicultural city who turned our combination of music and style into an art form.'

The Clash had long been interested in Black American dance music and in 1980, after hearing Grandmaster Flash and The Sugarhill Gang, the former punks recorded one of the first and best attempts by a white rock band to make a hip-hop-influenced record, 'The Magnificent Seven'. The flipside mix, a loose-limbed disco groove called 'The Magnificent Dance', became a favourite of New York DJs like Larry Levan. 'For us it was amazing because they'd picked up on this record, particularly the instrumental, and didn't know what type of group we were,'[17] said Jones.

Letts saw 'The Magnificent Dance' as a kind of antecedent to Big Audio Dynamite: 'One of the Black New York radio stations, WBLS, picked up on it and did a remix where they put in samples of Clint Eastwood in *Dirty Harry*, "Come on punk, make my day," and a bit of Bugs Bunny. I'm sure that that sowed some seeds in Mick's head with the whole sample and dialogue thing.'

Big Audio Dynamite's guitar-and-beatbox sound was a showcase for Jones' politically positive pop songwriting; Letts embellished it with excerpts of dialogue from spaghetti Westerns, comedy favourites and arthouse classics. 'Obviously I knew Holger Czukay was sampling stuff from FM radio back in the day [on the album *Movies*] and I knew Byrne and Eno's *Life in the Bush of Ghosts*. So I wouldn't say we originated it, I'd say that we were the first to have commercial hits with it,' he says. 'And it was so early in the day that the lawyers didn't know what was going on and we got away with it. We sampled from the fucking best – from *Scarface* right through to Sergio Leone to the Ealing comedies and Nicolas Roeg, and we only got hammered for using a song from *West Side Story*.'

Big Audio Dynamite were one of the first bands to use samples while playing live, triggered by Letts, who remembered his parts by putting stickers on his keyboard. 'Paul Simonon couldn't play when he joined The Clash and used to have coloured stickers on the frets of his bass to show him what to do,' he says. 'The difference between me and him is that Paul eventually got rid of his stickers. I never did and through my whole time with Big Audio Dynamite, when I was on stage I had coloured stickers on my fucking keyboard to know where to trigger the samples.'

UK Hip-Hop Finds Its Voice

'This decade we know will be remembered for when hip-hop came to the forefront. We know too that its influence will continue to be felt in the music forms of this age and those to come. No other music has the energy, excitement and exuberance of hip-hop, seemingly no other form carries so effectively the messages that have to be heard.'
DJ Mike Allen, writing in the programme for the UK Fresh '86 festival at Wembley Arena, London

Breakdancers at the Hip-Hop Jam festival at the Southbank Centre in London, September 1984. ©Kerstin Rodgers/Getty Images.

Filmed at a hip-hop convention under the neon disco lights of London's Hippodrome club in 1985, the documentary *Electro Rock* captures the scene in the capital at a point when it was still full of innocent enthusiasm. Breakdance crews costumed in garish synthetic fabrics – among them Broken Glass, the London All Stars and the Wolverhampton B-Boys, who included future drum and bass star Goldie – windmill and headspin to tough electro breaks, urged on by the fanatical cheers and whistles of a multiracial crowd of teenagers. Dreadlocked MC Dizzy Heights struts across the stage, urging 'all the breakers, the poppers, the lockers, the rockers' to dance harder: 'Give it what you got and don't stop!'[18]

In the years after Malcolm McLaren's 'Buffalo Gals' video and the release of *Wild Style*, hip-hop had developed into a major youth cult across the country. In London in the mid-eighties, breakdance crews, spraycan artists and fledgling rappers would come from all over the city to gather in the cobbled streets of Covent Garden every Saturday and paint pieces or show off their moves, among them future UK scene stars like the London Posse, Monie Love, Cookie Crew, Cutmaster Swift and DJ Pogo. 'Covent Garden was the training ground. The core of the early UK hip-hop scene started there,' says MC Duke (Anthony Hilaire), who was a teenage bodypopper.

'Everybody was looking to be part of something. Later so many of them got record deals.'

Hip-hop was inclusively low-tech, and it offered Duke and other Black British teenagers something to believe in; something that could be theirs. 'Hip-hop gave everybody a purpose and an identity,' he affirms. 'For me, hip-hop saved my life. I got kicked out of home onto the street when I was 14 years old. If it wasn't for hip-hop, I would have just kept going in jail like everybody else around me because it was normal in East London. But hip-hop grabbed hold of me and gave me knowledge and a purpose.'

Another of the Covent Garden breakdancers, Michael Henry, who became a renowned rapper under the name MC Mell'O', identified hip-hop as a grassroots Black arts movement that empowered young people and motivated them to become creatively active. 'You have to remember we were kids who'd grown up in the 1970s and early eighties in inner-city Britain under Margaret Thatcher,' he explained. 'We were used to being told that things like the arts weren't for us black kids. The arts weren't for poor white working-class kids.'[19]

London's first hip-hop club night, The Language Lab, had already started operating in 1982, launched by members of Brit-funk band Funkapolitan after they witnessed Grandmaster Flash cutting up breaks while supporting The Clash. Another scene animateur, Tim Westwood, an influential DJ on the pirate station LWR, later began running Saturday lunchtime hip-hop jams in 1984 at Spats club in Soho, giving the young Covent Garden crews their own space to dance.

The subculture was growing steadily, but it was only when hip-hop heads came together for major events that it became clear how big it had become. In Birmingham, the organisers of Thriller in the Park – the UK's first outdoor hip-hop festival, one baking-hot afternoon in August 1984 at Cannon Hill Park – were amazed when over a thousand people unexpectedly turned up to dance and be entertained by breakers dressed up as zombies who emerged from behind two large tombstones to bust out a routine to Michael Jackson's 'Thriller'. The following month, even larger crowds turned out for the Hip-Hop Jam breakdance festival on London's South Bank, where Dizzy Heights and Family Quest were among the rappers performing.

As the first wave of UK hip-hop reached peak popularity, Street Sounds founder Morgan Khan's UK Fresh '86 event brought thousands of youths in Adidas tracksuits and Kangol hats to London's Wembley Arena for an all-day festival headlined by Afrika Bambaataa, Mantronix and Grandmaster

Flash. (Zulu Nation leader Bambaataa was seen as an important role model in the 1980s, although his legacy was later called into question by allegations of sexual abuse, which he denied). The event showcased British breakdance crews and graffiti artists, but the only domestic rap group billed to perform was Family Quest, who had cut a couple of early UK electro tracks. Despite the enthusiasm for breakdancing and bodypopping, electro and hip-hop in Britain, and despite the efforts of pioneering UK rappers like Newtrament and Dizzy Heights, it took several years for a distinctively British interpretation of this particularly American musical genre to emerge.

Some of the first attempts at rap records in Britain were actually made by white pop and rock groups: 'The Magnificent Seven' by The Clash was followed in 1981 by Adam and the Ants' bizarre mixture of boisterous chanting and cod-Burundi drums, 'Ant Rap', then by pop duo Wham!'s 'Wham Rap!' the year afterwards. There was also a series of novelty rap records. In the seventies and eighties, new cultural phenomena from naked 'streaking' at sports tournaments to the craze for Citizens' Band radio were often celebrated by comedic tributes on vinyl, and the same happened with rap after The Sugarhill Gang's 'Rapper's Delight' was a hit. It was first parodied by Midlands DJ duo Allen & Blewitt's 'Chip Shop Wrapping' in 1980, followed by David Blair's jocular tribute to Geordie hedonism, 'Friday Neet (Gannin' te the Toon)', then by The Evasions' 'Wikka Wrap', a send-up of TV travelogue presenter Alan Whicker. All of them were set to loping funk grooves in session-player imitations of The Sugarhill Gang's style.

In an indication of how the music business operated in the early eighties, it seemed as though it was easier for a white rock band or a comedian to release a hip-hop record than it was for a Black British youth. One of the first genuine UK rappers to appear on vinyl was Dizzy Heights in 1982, although his seasonal single 'Christmas Wrapping' wasn't exactly hardcore hip-hop either.

Not all the early rap hits in the UK were lightweight, however. Politically-charged US tracks like Grandmaster Flash's 'The Message' and Gary Byrd's 'The Crown' also reached the Top 10. But because of its lyrical potential for comedic expression, rap seemed particularly attractive to creators of novelty songs. Comedian Kenny Everett's 'Snot Rap' and television puppet character Roland Rat's 'Rat Rapping' both became big sellers in 1983; atrocious efforts from 'rappers' as unlikely as Cockney entertainers Chas & Dave and the Liverpool football team would follow. Hip-hop was also appropriated for

TV advertising: the manufacturers of Weetabix launched an ad campaign in 1985 featuring a cartoon gang of tracksuit-wearing cereal biscuits. 'So now you know what's good for you, get on down with the Weetabix crew,' they rhymed as they bodypopped across a breakfast table.

While American hip-hop rapidly advanced, British rappers initially struggled in the mid-eighties to establish their own authentic voice and sonic aesthetics. The quest for a specifically British hip-hop realness can be tracked through the output of Music of Life, a London-based label set up by producer Simon Harris in 1986, which released records by many of the British rappers who emerged from the Covent Garden scene and the early London hip-hop clubs: MC Duke, Derek B, Demon Boyz, She Rockers, Hijack and Overlord X. The label's productions started out brash and Americanised but started to reach towards a British hardcore hip-hop style, with the Demon Boyz incorporating reggae chatting that referenced their background in sound system culture and Hijack raising the tempo and the intensity with fast and furious cuts and rhymes.

Music of Life's tougher releases fed into to the late-eighties, pre-jungle sound that later became known as Britcore, with its speeded-up breakbeats, frenzied scratches and forceful rhyming. The spacey, low-booming drum-machine groove of Derek B's 'Rock the Beat' was also repurposed as one of the rhythmic building blocks of the New Orleans bounce sound, highlighting again how electronic sounds could take on lives of their own, crossing continents and then reappearing in unpredicted contexts.

Many UK rappers started out by trying to imitate the US originators' intonation as well as their James Brown-derived beats, although they sometimes dropped touches of London slang into their rhymes. 'In the early days, everyone had a fake American accent,'[20] acknowledged the London Posse's Rodney P.

'As with every immigrant culture, it took a while for people to find their confidence,' explains journalist Vie Marshall, who covered early UK rap for *Hip-Hop Connection* magazine. 'All the rappers over here felt pretty much foreign everywhere – the culture and music they grew up with came from their parents' Caribbean or African backgrounds but the vast majority had never been to their parents' homeland; they felt foreign in Britain, the country they were born in or had been brought to at a very young age, and they were looking out to the most established and respected Black culture, the Black American culture, although that was also foreign to them. So generally, because we were the first generation of Black Britons, every day growing up we were trying to find an identity, trying to make something out of all these bits and pieces.'

British rappers, many of them little more than teenagers at the time, also came under pressure from record companies to lighten up their sound for the pop market. Monie Love and Cookie Crew made catchy singles that incorporated vintage soul and funk hooks to give them popular appeal without abandoning hip-hop scene credibility. But they tried to resist overt commercialisation because they saw themselves as part of a cultural community with shared principles and values rather than as entertainers building a career. 'I made a conscious decision: "I believe that I'm not going to make as much money as I probably could make",' recalled Monie Love (Simone Johnson), who went on to become part of Native Tongues, an Afrocentric collective of US hip-hop musicians that included Queen Latifah, the Jungle Brothers and De La Soul. 'I'm a culturalist,' she declared.[21]

She also refused to glam up her b-girl image to sell records. 'I wanted to be heard, I didn't want "pretty girl attention",' she said.[22] Cookie Crew's Susie Q (Susan Banfield) also said that they wanted to remain true to their hip-hop ideals: 'We weren't about to go and pimp ourselves out and show a bit of cleavage on stage; we wanted to show lyrically that we could stand next to [male rappers] and hold our own.'[23]

British hip-hop musicians made a major step forward when they grasped the confidence to use the influences they had absorbed from sound system culture as well as the experiences they had been through as children of the Windrush generation. A turning point for UK rap came with London Posse's 'Money Mad', which mixed hip-hop with dancehall rhythms. 'I was a reggae MC before so I still chat reggae lyrics but I do it in a rap style but in a Yardie accent and I use my own Cockney accent,' London Posse rapper Bionic explained at the time.[24]

Rodney P said reggae toasters like Tippa Irie and Smiley Culture from Saxon Sound International had shown them how an Anglo-Jamaican MCing style could authentically reflect a Black British identity: 'We took that mentality and said: "We're going to do that in hip-hop".'[25] Before too long, most UK rappers had abandoned the overt Americanisms. 'The majority of us went, "You know what, we're not copying them no more. We're not doing Yankee accents no more, it's fraudulent. Why can't we just rap in our own accents?"' recalls MC Duke.

In Manchester, brothers Anderson and Carson Hines and former Broken Glass breakdancer Kermit Leveridge were exploring similar ideas. As the Ruthless Rap Assassins, they had also started developing their own locally-accented variant of hip-hop. 'Being from Manchester, we had our slang, our street terms, so we'd slip those in,' says Leveridge. 'That's the beautiful thing about hip-hop, you can bring your own voice to it. It's part of the covenant of hip-hop to be as authentic as you possibly can.'

The Hines brothers used to have their own sound system called Ruffian Hi-Fi when they were teenagers, playing dub and lovers' rock at youth clubs. They met Leveridge while living in the Hulme Crescents, a condemned public-housing complex that had effectively been abandoned by the municipal council and became a haven for impoverished creatives and bohemians until it was finally demolished in 1994. 'Hulme was like a hotbed of radical thought and individuation – it was a kind of pirate utopia where anything went,' recalls Leveridge.

British hip-hop was initially heavily dependent on vintage funk samples, but Manchester hip-hop heads like the Ruthless Rap Assassins, MC Tunes and MC Buzz B were open to experimenting with textures from electronic music and rock as well. 'When we started, everybody else sounded American and they were all using James Brown loops, but we wanted to do everything different so we didn't just get classed as a typical rap band,' says Anderson Hines.

The introduction of overtly political lyrics to hip-hop by bands like Public Enemy also made Black British rappers more confident about telling their own stories of growing up in an institutionally racist, post-imperial country. 'Public Enemy, Queen Latifah, Jungle Brothers, Rakim – we were listening to them and it set off a bomb: people wanting to be knowledgeable as well as be part of the culture,' says MC Duke. The music played a key role in what MC Mell'O' described as an 'awakening' of a generation of British youths to ideas of Black power and self-reliance: 'We were seeing injustice around us and through our music we wanted to help awaken others and give people a message of strength and unity and empowerment.'[26]

Ruthless Rap Assassins' songs could be humorous – 'loads of self-deprecation and downright stupid shit,' as Leveridge puts it – but they also painted a vivid lyrical picture of life in Manchester as it was experienced by young Black men of their generation. 'All we had to do was look around ourselves and think about what was going on,' explains Hines.

In perhaps their best-known song, 'And It Wasn't a Dream', Hines' lyrics articulate the disappointments of the Windrush generation – the Rap Assassins' parents' generation – getting older but still waiting for the prosperity and respect they had been promised whilst living through years of discrimination after emigrating to the UK.

'My parents never talked to me about this,' says Hines. 'They never really said anything about their past, I think they went through such a lot of crap in those days that they didn't want to remember it. But I thought they should remember it, because we can learn from it. People need to know all this history.'

Mastermind, Soul II Soul, The Wild Bunch, Smith & Mighty

'We didn't want to be a band, Soul II Soul was a collective.'
Jazzie B[27]

When Jamaican sound system operators like Duke Vin and Count Suckle started holding their first dances after arriving in Britain in the fifties, they would play R&B records. In the sixties and seventies, sound systems championed ska and then reggae. But by the eighties, sound systems like Mastermind, Rapattack, Soul II Soul and Good Times, operated by second-generation Black British youths, were also playing soul, funk, hip-hop and electro.

'All of us in Mastermind came from a reggae background, but we all liked soul or disco, and what gave us the edge was that we used a reggae sound system to play non-reggae music,' says Mastermind DJ Dave Morrissey, better known as Dave VJ, who also got involved in making UK electro tracks with his partner Max LX as Hardrock Soul Movement.

Clubs in central London in the early eighties often had racist door policies that excluded Black youth; Dave VJ recalls 'various experiences of not being let into a club where white DJs were playing Black music'. The jazz-funk scene in the south-east was still dominated at that point by the white Soul Mafia 'jocks' and the main point of entry for aspiring Black DJs was through sound system culture, as Good Times DJ Norman Jay told author Lloyd Bradley: 'We needed to do this for ourselves.'[28] This meant holding illegal parties around London in empty buildings and warehouses – outlaw events that would provide musical inspiration for young producers and operate as testing grounds for new hybrid forms of dance music combining elements of the funk, soul, hip-hop and electro records played at the parties.

As it had done with reggae, pirate radio provided a vital outlet for the music of the warehouse-party scene. In the mid-eighties, stations like LWR, Solar and Kiss FM satisfied young Londoners' desires for funk, soul and hip-hop, music that legal broadcasters mainly ignored. 'What pirate radio did for the Black music scene was give us the opportunity to be playing records that you just couldn't hear on regular radio,' explains Dave VJ, who played for various London pirates including Kiss FM.

Founded in 1985, Kiss established a remarkable roster of presenters that included Jazzie B of Soul II Soul, Norman Jay and his brother Joey, Trevor Nelson, Manasseh, Jonathan More and Matt Black of Coldcut, as well as DJs who would play key roles in establishing the house and techno scenes in London: Paul 'Trouble' Anderson, Colin Faver, Steve Jackson, Danny Rampling, Judge Jules and Colin Dale. In the nineties, after winning a licence to broadcast legally, the station would be taken over by media company EMAP and its musical content softened up for commercial purposes, but for a few magnificent years Kiss genuinely lived up to its 'radical radio' motto.

Pirates like Kiss drew their strength from, and in turn promoted and nurtured, the musical community that grew around the club nights, warehouse parties, sound systems, specialist record shops and pirate radio stations that emerged from the funk, soul, hip-hop and house scenes in the mid-eighties. This was the era when a new kind of band also started to emerge: the DJ-led collective or crew whose roots were in the clubs and whose music was more studio-generated than live; who were informed by the plunderphonic culture of hip-hop turntablism and whose line-ups could be fluid, with collaborators coming in and out from project to project. Shaped by their time and cultural environment, collectives like these would offer their own, specifically British vision for dance music.

Emblematic of the sonic collective concept were Soul II Soul, funky dreads with Caribbean roots and a London attitude, a cult sound system crew who became pop hitmakers. Bandleader Jazzie B (Beresford Romeo) had been a sound boy since he was at school, when he started making his own equipment. 'In the woodwork class, everybody else made a chair or stool, we built speaker boxes,'[29] he said. Soul II Soul had ambition; they took their sound system out of the blues dances and community-centre gigs into West End venues and multiracial warehouse parties, bringing sound system style to London's fashion and art-school crowds as well as the soul and funk hardcore without compromising their ethics and aesthetics.

Black British academic Paul Gilroy has argued that Soul II Soul combined soul, reggae and hip-hop in an idiosyncratically British way, creating a sound that was 'not traceable back to an inferior copy, or a copy at any rate, of something that black Americans had done'.[30] Jazzie B's vision of cultural cross-pollination was the antithesis of Conservative government minister Norman Tebbit's 'cricket test': the idea that non-white communities who supported their country of origin in matches against British teams were not really integrated into society. Through music, the Soul II Soul DJ had developed a clear view of the enrichment made possible by multiple allegiances and the complexities of identity: Black, British, from the Caribbean, from London. 'There is no way this could have happened in any other part of the world,'[31] he said.

Soul II Soul's reggae-conscious, hip-hop-inflected street soul encapsulated his ideas and their songs 'Keep on Movin'' and 'Back to Life' provided the soundtrack to the summer of 1989, blasting from car stereos and sound systems across the country, amplifying the feeling that a new era in British musical culture had begun, and that it was truly glorious to be living through it.

Soul II Soul's debut album, *Club Classics Vol. One*, was co-produced by Nellee Hooper, a former member of the Wild Bunch crew from Bristol, another collective whose impact on British music would resonate through the decades that followed. Hip-hop journalist Malu Halasa described Bristol at the time as a city where 'musically, anything can happen';[32] where genres and cultures intermingled to create unforeseen hybrids. This was already evident in the late seventies from the music made by nonconformist post-punk funk and jazz-influenced groups like The Pop Group, Rip Rig & Panic and Maximum Joy, with whom Hooper once played percussion, but Bristol also had a strong reggae tradition with bands like Talisman and Black Roots.

Reggae culture was a crucial factor in shaping the music that was made in the city, said Daddy G (Grant Marshall), one of the Wild Bunch DJs who later formed Massive Attack. As a child, his mother and father used to host dances at their house: 'When my parents came over in the late fifties from Barbados and there was a lot of West Indians in Bristol, there wasn't anywhere for them to go,' he explained. 'So they made their own parties.'[33] Punk also made a serious impact on him as a teenager. He was fascinated by the commingling of punk rock and reggae encouraged by bands like The Clash and DJs like Don Letts, who played Jamaican imports at London punk club The Roxy. 'I used to dream of being a DJ like Don Letts. I loved the way that he integrated reggae into the punk scene,'[34] he said.

It was a sonic interrelationship that also affected another Wild Bunch and Massive Attack member, rapper and graffiti artist 3D, who said he was 'awakened' to Black dance music by The Clash: 'They introduced me, as a young punk, to reggae and dub music. In 1981, tracks such as 'Radio Clash' and 'The Magnificent Seven' also put me on to rap and funk.'[35]

A cheap and scruffy basement bar called The Dug Out on the edge of Bristol's ethnically-mixed St Paul's area became one of the crucibles of the city's cultural-hybrid scene in the early eighties, where hip-hop, soul, electro, reggae and post-punk dance sounds were mixed and mashed up. 'The Dug Out was quite grimy and dirty, but the music and the cross-section of people was great,' recalls Wild Bunch DJ Milo Johnson. 'It was like a club for misfits, very eclectic – down the road is the biggest hospital in Bristol so you used to get some of the staff nurses and doctors going there after their shift, you'd get artists and actors, punks, all the old-school Bristol musicians like The Pop Group, Pigbag, Maximum Joy, then you had the Black community in St Paul's too. People also used come down from London who were affiliated with Mark Stewart – Neneh Cherry and Sean Oliver and so on.'

'As everyone was on the dole, most people went there: punks, rastas, soul boys, jazz people, all those polymerisations in that club, people exchanging ideas,'[36] said Rob Smith, another Bristol musician who hung out there. Johnson and the rest of the Wild Bunch crew – Daddy G, Nellee Hooper, 3D and Willie Wee (Claude Williams) – played at The Dug Out regularly. An evocative black-and-white photograph from the time, taken by Bristol scene chronicler Beezer, shows them clustered intently around the Dug Out decks with Nellee Hooper mixing, Willie Wee rapping and a baby-faced, leather-jacketed 3D holding a mike, ready to join the fray. 'We were like a sound system as a collective but without the hardware,' says Johnson.

The Dug Out wasn't the only outlet for The Wild Bunch and other hip-hop-inspired musicians in Bristol; there were also illegal warehouse jams, house parties and one-off nights in clubs and community centres, as well as the annual St Paul's Carnival. The Wild Bunch were forging important connections outside the city too, playing with Soul II Soul and Newtrament at early hip-hop events in London, linking up with hip-hop heads in New York and Tokyo.

Daddy G, 3D and Mushroom of Massive Attack. ©Mick Hutson/Getty Images.

Early Wild Bunch recordings like 'Tearin' Down the Avenue' saw them developing their own take on hip-hop. But their decision to cover Burt Bacharach and Hal David's winsome sixties pop song 'The Look of Love' proved to be a critical moment, both for them and for music in Bristol. It incorporated sounds they loved from the scenes that shaped them, but transformed them into something entirely different: partly hip-hop, partly lovers' rock, partly soul, all delivered with a punkily irreverent attitude.

'If there is a Bristol sound, it started with the Wild Bunch and 'The Look of Love',' insisted 3D. 'That was the first lovers' hip-hop track with a song over a heavy beat, minimal shit, you know?'[37] The track also referenced the well-established tradition of Jamaican singers cutting reggae covers of white pop hits, from Elvis to The Beatles to country and western songs; Bob Marley once even covered The Archies' bubblegum classic 'Sugar Sugar'. As a reggae aficionado, Daddy G was well aware of the phenomenon: 'I've got [a reggae version of Sandie Shaw's hit] 'Puppet on a String' by Ken Boothe, an old Studio One record – and old Cliff Richard covers and stuff like that,'[38] he once said.

While making 'The Look of Love', they wanted to use the punishing Def Jam-style drum sound that was in vogue at the time, Johnson explains: 'the really heavy kick for the bottom end rather than a regular bass guitar or synth.'

They decided to drive the track with a funky breakbeat from 'The Jam' by Graham Central Station, which they used to play in their Wild Bunch DJ sets. But the record company was nervous about the legality of pirating the break, 'so we rewrote the beat on a drum machine using that 808 tom [sound] transposed down to make that heavy kick,' Johnson recalls. A couple of years later, when Hooper worked with Jazzie B on Soul II Soul's *Club Classics Vol. One*, he would use the same Graham Central Station beat on 'Back to Life'. 'The formula of using Bacharach and David songs on a hip-hop beat would be used by other Bristol acts after that also,' adds Johnson.

The style was further developed by a breakbeat-driven cover version of soul anthem 'Any Love' by Rufus and Chaka Khan, cut by Daddy G and the Smith & Mighty production duo with vocals from Carlton McCarthy and excerpts of rap from 3D and Tricky Kid (later simply known as Tricky). A distinctive sound was coalescing, one that combined plaintively soulful melodies, hazy hip-hop rhythms, roots vibrations and smoke-filled lyrical reveries; what would later be categorised as 'trip-hop'.

'Any Love' was self-released by Daddy G in 1988 under the name Massive Attack – the name that he, 3D and Mushroom would then use for their album *Blue Lines*, which brought together many of the influences from their Wild Bunch days and beyond. Like Soul II Soul's *Club Classics Vol. One* and Tricky's subsequent solo debut album, *Maxinquaye*, Massive Attack's *Blue Lines* was a remarkable exposition of the creative potential of multicultural cross-fertilisation and the enduring legacy of sound system culture and the early UK hip-hop scene.

Tricky appeared on *Blue Lines*, but he always seemed destined to follow his own path. He had grown up in a mixed-race, working-class family in one of the most impoverished districts of Bristol; as a teenager he was into 2-Tone and Saxon Sound International before discovering hip-hop. 'My peers are Terry Hall of the Specials and Rakim,'[39] he declared. It was all of these inputs, plus a surreal sense of humour and a substantial amount of weed, that gave Tricky his unconventional perspective and made him one of the most unique voices in British music, 'a dub wise, black punk rocker on a future-primitive soundtrip',[40] as American writer Greg Tate once described him.

Tricky's recording career began when he was befriended by On-U Sound maverick Mark Stewart, the former Pop Group singer who was a vital tastemaker on the Bristol scene and had evangelised for the early hip-hop tracks he brought back on record and cassette from New York. 'In Bristol, he was the one that everyone was looking to and influenced by – this punk-rocky indie sound with heavy dub effects and electronics,'[41] explained Ray Mighty of Smith & Mighty. Stewart encouraged Tricky to record his first song with singer Martina Topley-Bird, 'Aftermath'; Massive Attack didn't want to use it, so Tricky pressed up 500 copies himself. Soon he had his own record deal.

One of his first live performances had been at a gig by Smith & Mighty; they were playing a version of Erik Satie's 'Gymnopédie No. 1' when Stewart urged the young Tricky onto the stage to chat over it. (Stewart also recorded a wracked vocal over the Satie piano figure and released it as 'This Is Stranger Than Love'). Like Stewart, Smith & Mighty were a connecting factor that linked many Bristol musicians together. Their roots were in reggae: Rob Smith used to play in local reggae band Restriction, who once recorded a 12-inch with Mad Professor, while Ray Mighty operated a sound system. They began experimenting together using drum machines and synths at their little studio at Smith's flat in the St Paul's district, 'playing around with cheap bits of equipment, ending up getting a lot out of it 'cause you were limited by it,'[42] Smith explained.

Smith & Mighty's first two singles on their own Three Stripe label – 'Walk On' and 'Anyone Who Had a Heart', both Bacharach and David covers – established their style: heavy basslines, clattering breakbeats and drum machines, chiming piano lines combined with off-kilter melodic counterpoints and charmingly naive, lovers' rock-style vocals. Reggae was at the core of the music they made, even when they were doing house and rave tracks, Smith declared: 'It's dance music from a reggae perspective, a British perspective.'[43] House music actually reminded him of a steppers groove, he added.

The duo's studio in St Paul's operated as an incubator for young talents like Fresh 4 and rap trio 3PM. 'They were the mentors,' said Flynn of Fresh 4, whose lovers' hip-hop cover of Rose Royce's 'Wishing on a Star', produced by Smith & Mighty, became a Top 10 hit in 1989. 'They were very open-minded and accessible and they wanted people to come into their studio and make music.'[44] They would also invite drum and bass producers like Roni Size to record for free when they were starting out, mentoring Bristol's next creative generation.

Alongside collectives like the Wild Bunch and Soul II Soul, Smith & Mighty helped to nurture a British bass-centric sound that drew on American and Jamaican styles but had a multicultural flair that was very much the UK's own. It was a sonic synthesis that would form the basis for a lot of the most vital electronic dance music that would be made over the subsequent decades. But Smith & Mighty would never receive the same mass recognition as Bristol peers like Massive Attack and Tricky. Media-shy and self-effacing, they preferred to remain on the margins, recording non-commercial tracks for independent labels, committed to the cult of bass.

'Who knows why things happen the way they do?' Smith mused, several decades after their first release. 'Remaining underground was probably the right thing for us. Everyone has their own path and I'm really happy and grateful about mine… Life has been very sweet and continues to be.'[45]

Cosey Fanni Tutti and Chris Carter, 1982. Photo courtesy of Chris and Cosey.

8

UNNATURAL HISTORY

Experimentalists, Industrialists and Noise-Musicians

Chris and Cosey, Psychic TV and Coil
'We always kept hold of our freedom. We made sure we were never obligated to anyone.'
Cosey Fanni Tutti

IT WAS 23 JUNE 1981, and Throbbing Gristle had already played their last concert when they mailed out a postcard to their contacts with an announcement bordered in black like a funeral notice: 'The Mission is Terminated.' But for the band's four members, the end represented another beginning; new missions were already underway that would confirm their status as some of the world's most musically influential non-musicians.

Cosey Fanni Tutti and Chris Carter, whose incipient relationship was one of the reasons for the Throbbing Gristle split, remember it as a traumatic time. 'It was like a divorce, you know, you take one side or the other. A lot of people we used to know stopped being in contact,' recalls Carter. 'We were ostracised, basically,' says Tutti. 'But that in a way just opened the door to fresh air. We made new friends and new music.'

Their brilliant first three albums as Chris and Cosey, *Heartbeat, Trance* and *Songs of Love and Lust*, saw them leave behind Genesis P-Orridge's maleficent grotesquerie and establish a more personal, sensuous style. One of their most delicate pieces, 'October (Love Song)', was about the secret moment their affair started, when Carter took Tutti's hand on an escalator at Charing Cross underground station on the way to Throbbing Gristle's performance at the *Prostitution* exhibition at the ICA in October 1976.

From the outset, Chris and Cosey's music seemed to reveal a previously hidden emotional domain. 'I think we'd suppressed the feelings that we had inside for so long and it all came out in the music, these emotions that were so strong and intense,' says Tutti. 'And I was pregnant, so suddenly there was a whole new life opening up, like there was with the music. There was still a dark undertone and you could still hear a bit of TG in it, but ultimately we were saying that we are these people that can actually be decent to one another and love one another.'

Out of the shadow of P-Orridge, Tutti could further define her own identity as an artist. In 1983 she published a booklet called *Time to Tell*, documenting what she thought about the intimate spectacles she had staged with avant-garde collective COUM Transmissions and her use of her sex industry work as a stripper and model for porn magazines as source material for her contributions to Throbbing Gristle. Accompanied by a one-sided cassette of her mysterious, unsettling ambient music, *Time to Tell* was a courageous statement of intent, highlighting again how electronic music could operate as a platform for unorthodox artistic ideas.

Its release came at a time in the early eighties when a subculture of low-budget, do-it-yourself experimental and industrial music inspired by Throbbing Gristle and Cabaret Voltaire was at its peak; a thriving cottage industry of tiny independent labels issuing short-run vinyl releases and cassettes with homemade artwork and photocopied covers. The music, sometimes recorded with the most rudimentary equipment, could be uncompromisingly noisy, insufferably quirky or downright bizarre, and its creators sometimes had little more ambition than to be noticed by like-minded others. Tapes were often swapped by post in an informal system of mutual exchange.

This subcultural movement co-existed with the mainstream synth-pop of the eighties; its adherents often saw their music as a radical alternative to electronic bands who they thought had 'sold out' by adopting more commercial strategies. Although it remained obscure to outsiders, partly because the themes explored were often dark and the recordings often 'difficult' – in other words, almost unlistenable to all but the most committed consumers of weirdness – the movement provided a support network for nonconformists like Chris and Cosey to thrive.

Chris and Cosey's music was more melodic and rhythmically propulsive than a lot of Throbbing Gristle's output, picking up on the directions offered by TG electro-disco moments like 'United' and 'Hot on the Heels of Love', although Carter and Tutti didn't completely abandon abrasive atonality and unnerving atmospherics. They also started using Roland's TB-303 bass machine and TR-808 drum computer, two of the formative sound sources for the house and techno music that would emerge from Chicago and Detroit in the mid-eighties; as early as 1981, 'Bust Stop' on their debut album *Heartbeat* was already sounding like proto-acid house.

Unlike Cabaret Voltaire, they weren't much interested in exploring the possibilities of New York electro, but they ended up making some wonderfully warped dance records anyway. Tracks like 'Love Cuts' became favourites of DJ Laurent, a French hippie whose hypnotic sets soundtracked the full-moon party scene in Goa and helped to inspire the LSD-charged sound that would become known as psytrance – showing how the legacy of the industrial subculture would continue to exert an influence in the techno era. The 12-inch mix of 'Exotika' from their fourth album in 1987 was another Goa favourite; its euphoric Eurodance stylings made it their biggest hit. 'We were quite shocked because we'd got into something melodic almost without expecting to,' says Tutti. 'We'd accidentally hit our sweet spot.'

In the aftermath of Throbbing Gristle's demise, the band's influence would become greater than it ever was when they were together, but all four of them took new directions as they sought to escape the artistic confinement of industrial clichés. P-Orridge's next initiative was launched in an eerie howl of Tibetan thighbone trumpets, clanking bells and urgent declamations – '*Wake up, now!*' – at The Final Academy, a four-day convocation that brought hundreds of industrial-culture devotees to Brixton's Ritzy Cinema in 1982 to hear readings by William Burroughs and Brion Gysin as well as performances by Cabaret Voltaire, funky experimentalists 23 Skidoo and uncompromising noise ensemble Last Few Days.

P-Orridge's new 'band', Psychic TV, which initially involved TG comrade Peter Christopherson and acolytes like Geff Rushton and David Tibet, was a kind of avant-rock collective that came with its own magickal-sect-cum-fan-club, Thee Temple ov Psychick Youth. Their first album, *Force the Hand of Chance*, was a peculiar mixture of warped ballads and curdled psychedelic pop combined with lush orchestral settings and P-Orridge's disturbed/disturbing singing. It concluded with 'Message from the Temple', a promotional bulletin for the Psychick Youth organisation and its commingling of ideas of sex magick and sigilism from British occultists Aleister Crowley and Austin Osman Spare. Temple followers signified themselves with their Tibetan monk-style Psychick Youth shaved-head-plus-ponytail haircuts and tattoos of the organisation's triple-barred cross symbol.

But although the Temple claimed to be challenging structures of control, it had a dominant individual as leader figure, P-Orridge, and soon developed into a 'cult of personality',[1] according to Christopherson. Disillusioned, he left Psychic TV to concentrate on Coil, his new band with his partner Geff Rushton, who would rename himself John Balance (and even later Jhonn Balance). Typically for the post-punk era, when ideas were often seen as being as important as music, they announced the project in 1983 with a manifesto: 'Electricity and elementals. Atonal noise, and brutal poetry,'[2] it promised. Before the two men's deaths in 2010 and 2004 respectively, they would repeatedly deliver what they had pledged.

As *Guardian* journalist Richard Smith noted in his obituary for Balance, Coil were the 'first resolutely queer group',[3] delighting in transgressive imagery, hallucinogenic drugs, occult practices and the energies generated by homosexual copulation. Christopherson believed that being gay gave him an insight that was artistically crucial: 'I think that gay people have the advantage in that when they realise they're gay it's tangible proof that the world is not the way it's represented.'[4] At a time when most gay and lesbian pop musicians were still hiding their sexuality from the public, Coil unapologetically and imaginatively used it as a vital part of their aesthetic; the sleeve notes for their first album *How to Destroy Angels* described it as 'ritual music for the accumulation of male sexual energy'.

Balance had suffered an unsettled childhood and a troubled time at school, where his classmates nicknamed him 'Weird' and the headmaster wrote to his parents to alert them that their son was 'unhealthily obsessed with the occult and supernatural'.[5] As a teenager, he ran his own industrial fanzine, *Stabmental*, and corresponded with Throbbing Gristle by post.

Balance's taste for the esoteric and Christopherson's fascination with new technology were central to Coil's work. 'How Coil actually sounds is often a function of the state of the technology at that time,'[6] Christopherson told author David Keenan. Stephen Thrower, who was a member of the band in the period from *Scatology* to *Love's Secret Domain*, recalls how Christopherson, who was relatively affluent because of his work as a graphic designer and video director, would hire in an expensive Fairlight then stay up all night cutting samples. 'Sleazy had an enormous amount of technical knowledge, he was an early adopter on everything, he was the first person I knew who had a computer, he learned how to use the Fairlight and programming technology; he was the one that could be bothered to read the entire manual,' Thrower says.

On 1986's *Horse Rotorvator*, the samples used by Christopherson ranged from grasshopper sounds recorded at an ancient Mayan temple, where humans were once ritually sacrificed, to the squeals of a young boy playing and a reversed, pitched-down and looped excerpt from Stravinsky's *The Rite of Spring*. These were coupled with jarringly artificial Fairlight brass and strings, and clanking synthetic percussion as well as real instruments, in an attempt to achieve what Christopherson called a '"big movie theatre" ambience'[7] for the record.

Coil created their own mysterious, magical sonic language that drew from Christopherson's industrial heritage and technological inquisitiveness but also from medieval choral music, offbeat psychedelia, avant-garde electro-acoustic music and, towards the end of the eighties, house and techno as well. 'With Coil, there was a very broad, wide-ranging curiosity about sound – what happens if you bring this sound and this apparently totally dichotomous other sound together? What kind of sparks will fly if you collide them?' says Thrower.

Their music could be melancholy and intimate, comedic or unsettling, but it could also rage like a fearsome threshing noise machine, as on *Horse Rotorvator* – a record released in 1986, during the AIDS epidemic, which expressed the fear and anger that they were feeling. 'As a gay man at the time, you couldn't fail to be aware that the dominant culture wanted you out, wanted you dead. You were being scorned and attacked in the tabloid press and treated as lepers or disease carriers and the agents of your own misfortune and potentially the people who are going to infect "normal" people,' explains Thrower. 'People were dying and friends getting sick and at the same time, as a young man, you've got up to two completely contrasting and contradictory things happening in your life – the excitement of becoming involved in sexual activity, but just as you start to taste the fruits of liberation, there's poison in the air, so it's very difficult and inevitably leads to some introspection and a great deal of anxiety and dread and horror. And so the darkness, the heaviness of that album came quite naturally from the life that all gay people were living at that time.'

Coil's extraordinary cover of Soft Cell's 'Tainted Love', a benefit single to help fund counselling for people with HIV and AIDS, turned the song into a harrowing representation of grief and desperation. 'Maybe it wasn't activist in the same sense that you would get the Gang of Four doing a song about the evils of capitalism or Mark Stewart lacerating international arms dealers, but nonetheless, there was a political dimension – any statement that you made about being gay at the time was a political statement,' argues Thrower. 'I think at the time, there was just us and Bronski Beat who were "out" gay bands – all the other prominent figures, all the other figures in alternative music and pop culture who were gay, were either studiously avoiding discussing it or were actively denying it.'

Later in the eighties, Christopherson and Balance both got caught up in the chemical passions of the ecstasy-charged acid house scene. The sense of abandon, of disorientation to the point of oblivion that was central to the ecstatic club experience, also filtered through into Coil's music as the two men embraced its chaos and licentious madness. Dedicated seekers of delirium, the further out they spun, the more powerful their music became, like despatches from a deeply drugged subconscious.

MDMA and LSD were not just hedonic indulgences for Coil, they were integral parts of their creative process. 'Drugs were very important, inescapably important,' says Thrower. 'People talk about getting out of it – well, you can be looking for a way of getting out of a structure, out of a trap, out of a set of rules. And so drugs can throw the doors wide open and you can find all sorts of ways of getting out – suddenly there are no locked buildings and you can get out into the sky. So yes, they can be hugely, hugely valuable and exciting – until at some point, they're not anymore.'

Thrower recalls that when they were recording the track 'Chaostrophy' for *Love's Secret Domain*, Christopherson had written a 'beautiful pastoral melody' that they decided should be played on real instruments rather than a Fairlight and asked arranger Billy McGee, who had worked a lot with their friend Marc Almond, to score it for a string ensemble. 'Billy did the most beautiful arrangement, it was like a Douglas Sirk [Hollywood melodrama] soundtrack or something, with incredible strings and cor anglais. And then when we were in the studio, Sleazy was high and he went into a very strange sort of wormhole and totally distorted the entire piece in a phenomenal way and turned it into this monstrous electrical storm. And I think that journey from this classical beauty to this terrifying storm couldn't have been taken if he'd not been heavily soaked in otherworldly chemicals. It was the fact that he could fly very, very deep into the heart of a storm in his mind's eye with whatever he was taking at the time. The sheer scale and depth of the transformation he exerted on that piece, I think was an example of drugs and creativity riding lockstep with each other in a very interesting way.'

But while narcotics helped to shape Coil's unique vision, the amount of substances that Balance was consuming caused him to drink increasing amounts of alcohol to get through the comedowns. It was his alcoholism that eventually led to the fall that killed him at the age of 42, Christopherson believed.

After Balance's death, Christopherson completed the last Coil studio album, *The Ape of Naples*, in tribute to his lost partner. Its remarkable concluding song, 'Going Up', pulled off the seemingly impossible feat of combining a melody that sounded like one of 17th-century baroque composer Johann Pachelbel's minor-key chaconnes with the theme song from 1970s TV sitcom *Are You Being Served?* – whose lyrics list the floors in a department store as though described by a lift operator – to create an exquisitely poignant electronic meditation on death and the transition beyond the body. Six years later, Christopherson would die too, but Coil's reputation and influence would continue to grow.

Among the friends and relatives gathered in mourning at Balance's funeral in 2004 was another vital figure in the post-industrial underground scene who, like the Coil singer, had originated within Throbbing Gristle's soundworld but developed his own unique vision. David Tibet is a genuine English musical original and a scholar of the sacred and the magickal; he was known as David Michael Bunting until given his pseudonym by Genesis P-Orridge because of his fascination with Eastern mysticism. He made his early recorded appearances blowing forlorn moans from a Tibetan thighbone trumpet on Psychic TV's *Themes* record and on 23 Skidoo's mesmerising ethno-industrial album *The Culling is Coming*, one side of which was a spectacularly uncompromising live performance using 'instruments' like gas cylinders, metal sheets, beer kegs and tapes of voices and found sounds.

Tibet's work with his own project, Current 93, was initially based on loops and electronics; his first album, *Nature Unveiled*, was a heavy experience, full of doomy classical samples, sinister choirs, baleful voices and harsh squeals, with titles like 'Christ's First Howling' and 'Ach Golgotha (Maldoror Is Dead)' indicating that it was far from easy listening. 'I was trying to make a truly majestic and apocalyptic album,' he explains. 'It's not a Black Mass, but it is a literally diabolical record in some ways.'[8]

Tibet was known for sharing his industrial peers' intense fascination with Aleister Crowley, but as he began to focus more on his Christianity, the occultist fell from his favour somewhat; at one point he even made a synth-pop novelty record called 'Crowleymass' to satirise 'tedious' Crowley worshippers who used to write letters to him. Unfortunately, the joke backfired, Tibet recalled: 'We started to get even more letters saying, "How cunning of you to use the pop disco dance form to spread the Great Beast's ideas".'[9]

Working with Steven Stapleton of Nurse with Wound, Tibet went on to further develop Current 93's intense and hallucinatory electro-acoustic style, weaving together anguished incantations and disorientating loops on albums like *Dogs Blood Rising* and *Live at Bar Maldoror*. But as the eighties progressed, he left electronic noise behind and switched to a kind of arcane neo-folk style – one of many musicians who were inspired by Throbbing Gristle and the industrial scene but took their ideas in different directions.

Eventually, bands like Nine Inch Nails, Ministry and Rammstein would use the genre's sonic signifiers as the basis to create a mass-market industrial rock, keeping some of the shock tactics, abjection and aggression but incorporating cyberpunk tropes and losing a lot of the arty playfulness and absurdist humour, as well the ramshackle DIY aesthetics.

One of the most interesting diversions from the genre was explored by Lustmord, the alias of Welsh musician Brian Williams, whose early albums like *Paradise Disowned* and *Heresy* used brooding drones and ominous chimes, disembodied horn sounds and rumbling incantations derived from Tibetan Buddhist rituals and Gregorian chant. 'I'm an atheist but I've always liked the intensity and the power of religious music,' Williams explained.[10]

Lustmord's recordings, some of them made in crypts, caves or slaughterhouses, helped to shape the post-industrial 'dark ambient' genre. Williams deplored the fact that industrial music eventually became an established stylistic formula: 'Just as punk wasn't about sounding like The Clash, industrial wasn't about sounding like Throbbing Gristle or Nine Inch Nails, it was about ideas. So I never get people who just wanted to repeat this stuff.'[11]

Like fellow industrialists Trent Reznor of Nine Inch Nails and Graeme Revell of SPK, Williams also achieved some success as a sound designer and composer for Hollywood movies, a tribute to the genre's ability to conjure sinister atmospherics. Or as Williams put it himself: 'I get a phonecall and they're telling me the hero's in hell, his children are in hell, and can I give them some sound for that? And it's like yeah, OK, piece of piss, that's what I do.'[12]

Whitehouse and Power Electronics

'The main goal for me is to take the audience to a place they haven't been before, whether they like it or not.'
William Bennett, Whitehouse[13]

When Throbbing Gristle ceased to exist, some of their admirers headed deeper into the dark passages that they had signposted. In 1982, the creator of some of the most confrontational and misanthropically obnoxious industrial recordings, William Bennett of Whitehouse, announced in his sleeve notes for his *Psychopathia Sexualis* album what would become a new subgenre: 'power electronics'.

Whitehouse's music was a combination of ear-shredding feedback, shrieking synths, sheets of white noise, subsonic bass frequencies and screamed vocals, with no hint of conventional melody or rhythm: an antisocial cacophony, all intended to provoke a reaction – revulsion, hatred, anger, pain. Bennett said he wanted to use sonic extremism as a liberating force to overcome what he called 'internal programming' – to 'dismantle [people's] personality, access their vulnerability, tap into this vast ocean of possibility this person has, where anything is possible, where anything can be thought of'.[14]

Bennett started Whitehouse in 1980, when he was still a teenager. Before that, he had played guitar with post-punk band Essential Logic and recorded under the name Come with Daniel Miller of The Normal, who was using the pseudonym Dr Death. Come released a punky album of guitar thrash and synth blurts, *Rampton* – named after a high-security psychiatric hospital, with a cover image depicting a semi-naked woman bound with rope – but Bennett wanted to go much further into extreme noise and imagery. He acquired what he described as 'an uncontrollably vicious beast of a synthesizer',[15] a Wasp capable of producing ear-shredding frequencies, and set out to create a music that was far more uncomfortable than anything recorded by Throbbing

Gristle, who he believed had abandoned their aesthetic courage when they recorded the more melodic *20 Jazz Funk Greats*. 'Why are they trying to make music?'[16] he asked.

Unusually for the industrial scene, Bennett could actually play an instrument, but he decided to disown his proficiency and make a horrible racket instead. Whitehouse's debut album *Birthdeath Experience* was full of pestiferously buzzing drones and discordant synth screeches, with Bennett's belligerent yelling cranked up to overload.

Whitehouse's name was chosen as a reference to a British pornographic magazine of the same title and to well-known conservative moral campaigner Mary Whitehouse. Their early albums created an archetypal template that would continue to obsess power electronics practitioners for decades to come: Nazi atrocities (*Buchenwald*), serial killers (*Dedicated to Peter Kürten, Sadist and Mass Slayer*), sexual violence and torture.

Bennett insisted he was not a fascist or a woman-hater, but simply advocated total artistic liberty. 'You'll hear many claims to being adventuresome and edgy and risky and so forth, yet in truth rare are those prepared to confront danger and do something with it, and fewer still resisting the temptation for rationalisation,'[17] he declared. He refused to contextualise or provide any critical interpretation of his use of extremist imagery, leaving it open for some of the power electronics bands that came after him to interpret the style as a glorification of fascistic, sadistic and misogynistic brutalities. (Bizarrely for those who saw him as a monomaniacal provocateur, Bennett later gained renown as a DJ playing Italo-disco and then as a producer of African percussion-influenced electronic dance music under the name Cut Hands).

Whitehouse's admirers insisted that Bennett's power electronics records were confronting the ugliness and barbarity in humanity because they didn't aestheticise cruelty, but represented it sonically in its true form, making it almost unlistenably horrific. Paradoxically, there was also a sense of perversely self-deprecating humour about the relentless awfulness of Whitehouse's themes and their almost self-parodic sexual fixations. 'We were aware of a certain ridiculousness about it but were deadly serious,'[18] said longterm Whitehouse member Philip Best, who also recorded as Consumer Electronics.

The severity of Whitehouse's vision inspired others to emulate them in the early eighties – bands with names like Sutcliffe Jügend, Con-Dom, Ramleh, Skullflower and The Grey Wolves, whose music also sought to push beyond the boundaries of the sonically and politically unpalatable. *Fight Your Own War*, an anthology of writing about power electronics, asserted that this genre of angrily ranting white men had roots in Italian Futurist Luigi Russolo's ideas of noise-music that 'strives to amalgamate the most dissonant, strange and harsh sounds', French avant-gardist Antonin Artaud's vision of a confrontational Theatre of Cruelty and the violent, taboo-smashing performances of the Vienna Actionists, as well as Throbbing Gristle's industrial music. Noise musician Davy Walklett, who recorded as Milovan Srdenovic, even claimed in the book that it was possible to enjoy 'the ludicrous absurdity of guys screaming filth and hate-speak over washes of electronic shite'.[19] As *Fight Your Own War* documented, from the eighties onwards, the power electronics scene spread way beyond the UK, uniting an informal network of people who loved what was intentionally the ugliest electronic music possible.

The Incredibly Strange World of Nurse with Wound

'I love absurdity. I love Surrealism, I love Dada, I love quirk, I love comedy.'
Steven Stapleton

In 1978, a 21-year-old aficionado of German psychedelic rock and free improvisation called Steven Stapleton went into a recording studio in London with two friends, Heman Pathak and John Fothergill. They took a guitar, an organ and some percussion, plus some toys and bits of metal and other bric-a-brac; the studio also had a synth and a piano. None of the trio could really play an instrument, they had never rehearsed together, they only had a vague idea of what kind of music they wanted to make, and they only had a day's studio time.

'We had decided to use anything whatsoever as our sound sources. We loved avant-garde music and we loved the [free improvisation] stuff coming out of the London Musicians' Collective where anything went – people like Han Bennink and percussionists like that who just would use anything,' explains Stapleton. 'We didn't think we would ever press or release the record, it was just an adventure.'

Stapleton saw it as a direct descendant of the late-sixties era of avant-garde experimentation. 'It was just about making sounds that were interesting regardless of their musical worth – as John Cage says, you don't have to call it music if you don't want to,' he says. By the end of the session, they had what they thought was an album's worth of material and decided to issue it themselves on their own United Dairies label. The record, *Chance Meeting on a Dissecting Table of a Sewing Machine and an Umbrella*, its title taken from the Comte de Lautréamont's *The Songs of Maldoror*, was credited to Nurse with Wound. Its cover was an unsettling black-and-white S&M image of a leather-clad dominatrix and her naked male supplicants, and supplied with the record was a list of 291 adventurous musicians and bands: a pointer to the further reaches of weirdness. 'Step out of the space provided,' it urged. Compiled at a time when such music was little documented in the UK, the 'Nurse with Wound list' has since come to be seen as a visionary rollcall of left-field sonic artists.

The record itself was a challenging mixture of untutored improv and musique concrète, a kind of descendant of Jean Dubuffet's *Musique Brut*, bizarre cacophonic recordings that the French painter made in 1961 using instruments he had no idea how to play. (Dubuffet was one of the names on the Nurse with Wound list). A review in *Sounds* said that with its 'scrapings, tinkles, boinks, plunks and any other otherworldly sounds',[20] it made Krautrock band Faust's freeform *The Faust Tapes* sound like a Rodgers and Hammerstein musical in comparison. Stapleton thought they would struggle to shift the entire edition of 500 copies, but instead it sold out quickly; there were clearly like minds out there. He would go on to work as Nurse with Wound, to widespread acclaim, for decades to come.

Nurse with Wound recordings were largely electro-acoustic collages rather than pieces of electronic music. 'I seldom use synthesizers and I don't like a lot of electronic keyboards. I prefer acoustic sounds that are then manipulated,' Stapleton says. He describes himself as a technophobe: 'I've never turned on a computer. I hate technology. The only technology I have is this phone.' He preferred the maximum amount of spontaneity when recording and liked to utilise any noise-making device that came to hand. 'Whatever was in the studio, I would use.'

Musician and studio operator Colin Potter, who has collaborated on many Nurse with Wound albums, recalls one incident when Stapleton spotted a hand-crank siren in his studio that Potter had borrowed to make some sound effects for a World War II museum; it was immediately incorporated into the Nurse with Wound recording. 'Steve has an incredible ear for something that is unique or unusual,' Potter explains. 'He would have an initial plan but then pick up on an unusual sound and go off on a tangent through that accidental discovery. Several albums were produced like that.'

Stapleton has often expressed frustration that Nurse with Wound were classified as an industrial band because their debut album was noisy and had a 'dark' cover, and because he was 'around the scene' in the eighties, collaborating with figures from the industrial milieu like David Tibet, William Bennett of Whitehouse and John Balance of Coil. He prefers to describe his music as a kind of surrealist sound-art that celebrates the absurd and incongruous and is more closely related to the freakier fringes of German psychedelic rock, which itself was connected to the classical avant-garde and free jazz. 'I see my music as a continuation of some of the more outlandish Krautrock of the early seventies. It's the music I've always loved,' he says.

As a teenager, Stapleton bought the Amon Düül album *Psychedelic Underground* and became so excited that he travelled to Germany with his friend Pathak to find the source of the music and meet the players. During the trip, he stayed with Neu! producer Conny Plank, watched Floh de Cologne record an album and worked as a roadie for Guru Guru and others. He even went to rural Wümme to visit Faust, but they weren't there and he had to sleep rough in a bus shelter.

But unlike the German *kosmische* musicians and the industrial bands that followed in the wake of Throbbing Gristle, Nurse with Wound's music had little connection with 'rock'. Instead, it was a kind of shape-shifting bricolage – part Faustian ruckus, part Stockhausen circa 'Gesang der Jünglinge', part ludicrous *Goon Show* Radiophonic effects, part harsh post-AMM free improv, part La Monte Young minimalism, part Fluxus impishness and a whole load of other nonsense too.

Stapleton's recordings in the eighties could be disturbing, funny, delicate, annoying; they ranged from the deeply unsettling *Homotopy to Marie* to the glowing, cyclic feedback-loop drones of *Soliloquy for Lilith* and the parodic easy-listening oddness of *The Sylvie and Babs Hi-Fi Companion*. 'Every recording I did was totally different, not only just with the sounds, but I tried to vary the recording process and the people I had in the studio with me as much as I possibly could every time. Really just to keep it fresh, because I'm not a professional musician – if I'm anything, I'm an artist who works with sound,' he says. He once described Nurse with Wound as 'purveyors of sinister whimsy to the wretched'; this very English surrealist certainly succeeded in raising self-indulgence to a high art.

In 1985, Nurse With Wound's United Dairies label released *The Inevitable Chrystal Belle Scrodd Record*, a wonderfully peculiar album by Stapleton's then partner and musical collaborator Diana Rogerson under the pseudonym Chrystal Belle Scrodd; a woman he once described as 'the most absurd, vile, disgusting, highly charged, erotic, beautiful balance of parodies of extremes of human nature I've ever come across'.[21] Rogerson, whose music inhabited a perverse and bizarre world somewhere between Nurse with Wound's phantasmagorical electro-acoustic soundscapes and spiky post-punk rock, was a genuinely original voice. Although industrial musicians often used sexual content in their work to explore issues of oppression, violence and censorship, it was mostly from a male perspective and often tended towards the puerile and sexist. (Genesis P-Orridge's ex-wife, Alaura O'Dell, said that despite industrial music's pretensions to be radical, 'it was still the white-male narrative'.[22]) Like Cosey Fanni Tutti, Rogerson was an exception.

Rogerson and her friend Jill Westwood had previously been involved a short-lived and highly obscure performance group called Fistfuck, who used BDSM symbolism and an extreme noise soundtrack inspired by Whitehouse to project images of female dominance. Dressed in leather and latex and wielding whips, they assaulted and humiliated male submissives on stage in sadomasochistic performances inspired by their experiences on London's fetish nightclub scene. By experimenting with dominatrix personas, Westwood says she was seeking to challenge gender stereotypes and to play with ideas of power, intimacy and trust through theatrically ritualised violence. 'People looked transfixed, mesmerised by it all really, we could feel that as we were strutting up and down looking a bit scary,' she recalls. 'I guess we stood out at the time because we were women and it really wasn't usual at all for that to be happening.'

Westwood and the other members of the amorphous grouping around Fistfuck would create discordant collages for each of the handful of performances that they did around 1983. 'We'd make sound pieces from synthesizers or tape loops and the aim was really to make something really quite unbearable. We would also be doing a bit of screaming or howling – it was about arresting the audience, giving an experience that was quite shocking and frightening to shake people out of their comfort zone,' Westwood says. She went on to work as an artist and art psychotherapist, while Rogerson remained an esoteric but fascinating voice on Britain's noise-music underground, making a series of thrillingly odd records that fitted in nowhere. 'Even within outsiders I was an outsider,'[23] Rogerson once said.

Nurse with Wound's collaborators constituted a catalogue of the weird and dissentient, from Rogerson and Tibet to Satie-inspired pianist and soundscaper Robert Haigh, who released several wintry, elegiac albums under the name Sema in the eighties. Full of unearthly noises and lambent piano tones, they were obscure at the time but later came to be regarded as classics of industrial ambience.

Haigh was also one of several musicians from the industrial scene who would resurface in the rave era; in the early 1990s, he became fascinated by the British techno records being released on the Warp label, hearing 'a direct connection with certain innovative post-punk outfits, like Cabaret Voltaire, 23 Skidoo and Daniel Miller'. A DJ then told him how he had made a breakbeat hardcore track using a cheap Amiga computer with free software, which Haigh said 'really appealed to my post-punk DIY ethos'.[24] So he bought his own Amiga and reinvented himself as Omni Trio, making euphoric, piano-spangled breakbeat anthems like 'Renegade Snares', one of the tracks that exemplified the future-gazing early period of drum and bass.

Stapleton's United Dairies label also released *Rapid Eye Movements*, a startling album of tape-collage works by Irish electro-acoustic composer Roger Doyle, issued under the name Operating Theatre. But Doyle wasn't the only connecting point between post-punk experimentalism and the classical avant-garde. Colin Potter, who ran his own tape label ICR and operated a cassette-copying service for experimental bands, as well as working with Nurse with Wound, released several albums by electro-acoustic composer and sonic artist Trevor Wishart. The records included Wishart's powerful 1970s work *Red Bird: A Political Prisoner's Dream*, which used pre-computer audio-transformation techniques to incorporate human voices and animal sounds into a dramatic piece of musique concrète that explored ideas of freedom and the deprivation of liberty.

Potter had studied in the early seventies at York University, which was one of the first British educational institutions to have its own electronic music studio and electronic arts society; he was able to borrow a EMS Synthi A and to experiment by making tape loops. He also attended lectures by avant-garde luminaries like Wishart and Richard Orton, who co-founded the electronic music ensemble Gentle Fire with Hugh Davies. The York University electronic music studio was a thriving laboratory for new ideas and even had its own record label, which released pieces by Wishart and Orton on the compilation album *Electronic Music from York*. It also released Wishart's *Machine*, a musique concrète piece that mixed improvising choirs with factory sounds and machine loops, and *Journey into Space*, a sprawling collage combining noisy free improvisation with tape manipulation and snippets of audio from field recordings and NASA's Apollo moon mission.

One of the York University students who contributed sounds to *Journey into Space*, Jonty Harrison, went on to become a respected composer himself – part of a cerebral and highly academicised British electro-acoustic music culture nurtured by adventurous music departments and encompassing figures as diverse as Denis Smalley, known for his spectromorphological analysis of sounds, and the spiritually inspired Jonathan Harvey.

On his hallucinatory epic *Red Bird*, Wishart says he tried to effect 'transformations of birds into machines and voices into machines and animals into birds and all kinds of things like that', but although his composition was almost psychotropically mind-altering, he felt he was limited by the technical capabilities of the university's studio. 'There are things you could do in the analog studio, like editing, speed changing, mixing and things. But if you want to do really sophisticated things like turn a swarm of bees into a voice or vice versa, you can only do that with a computer,' he explains. 'So getting into the computer was kind of natural for me because my other big love in life is mathematics. I read books of really, really hard maths for fun.'

His subsequent *Vox Cycle*, a series composed over several years in the mid-eighties, explored his interest in using computer technology to transform the human voice and the sounds of the natural world. He was also involved in creating not-for-profit sound-processing software made available to other composers as a transformational tool; while most pop musicians were still using cheaper analog equipment, most British electro-acoustic composers had already moved into the computer era in the eighties.

Wishart says that using computers enabled him to design sonic landscapes that could not otherwise have existed. 'The computer made it possible to do the things I've imagined; to metamorphose sound,' he explains. 'So you no longer were restricted to an instrument, you could change anything into anything else. Instead of just morphing your materials from a major key to a minor key, you could now morph from trumpets to elephants. You could do whatever you wanted to do.'

DIY Noisemakers and the Cassette Underground

'There were all these outsiders, people on the outside doing their thing, who would find each other.'
Brian Williams, Lustmord[25]

'A compilation of difficult music' was the subtitle of a compilation released in 1983 that included Nurse with Wound, Chris and Cosey, Coil and various lesser-known bands associated with the industrial genre. *The Elephant Table Album* grew out of journalist Dave Henderson's 'Wild Planet' columns for *Sounds*; Henderson had noticed there were increasing numbers of experimental and electronic musicians, non-musicians and anti-musicians involved in making challenging, largely amateur recordings that were often released on cassette with self-designed, Xeroxed sleeves, sometimes in editions of fewer than 100, and distributed by post via an informal network of mutual contacts rather than being pressed on vinyl and sold in shops.

'Underground, free-form, experimental, avant-garde, industrial, call it what you will, but there's a blossoming sub-structure of groups around the world who are attempting to produce music that is ultimately different,'[26] Henderson enthused in his introductory 'Wild Planet' article. He documented bands and individuals all around the country making histrionic industrial noise, sub-Soft Cell electro-pop and abrasive, minimalist synth tracks created with basic drum machines like the Boss Dr. Rhythm, WEM Copicat echo units and excerpts of news broadcasts and film soundtracks taped from TV and radio.

The 'Wild Planet' columns were inspired by the release of *Rising from the Red Sand*, a cassette series issued by Whitstable-based Third Mind Records that Henderson saw as an exemplar of this amorphous independent network. Some of the individuals and bands who were featured on the *Rising from the Red Sand* compilations and others like them had been enabled by the availability of increasingly affordable electronic technology, particularly when it had been discarded by its initial users and was being sold even more cheaply secondhand. They were further boosted by the possibilities of making low-budget four-track recordings direct to cassette at home using the Tascam Portastudio, a relatively inexpensive unit that went on the market at the turn of the eighties and prefigured the home-recording boom. Other bands on the tape scene were even more lo-fi, with no pretensions to orthodox sound values, content to use anything from guitars and drums to household implements to make an abstract racket that they could record onto a cassette and call an 'album'.

'Punk had a great impact on people's idea of what could be described as "music" as well as the way this music could be distributed,' explains Colin Potter. 'I think there were a lot of people, myself included, who weren't brilliant musicians, they weren't technically adept, didn't even have decent equipment, but they really stretched what they had. It was a triumph of ambition over ability – the audio equivalent of naive art or something like that.'

Cassettes were a crucial platform for this DIY industrial noise-music subculture; they were cheap to buy, cheap to send by post and could be recorded over and reused. Just as on the reggae scene, where sound system 'yard tapes' from Jamaica brought the latest sonic innovations to West Indian diaspora communities, informal tape-swapping spread knowledge and information that nurtured the scene.

Throbbing Gristle had actively encouraged the tape-exchange phenomenon by soliciting strange cassette recordings via their Industrial Records newsletter. The cassette format encouraged experimentation in music – efforts that ended in failure were not expensive – and allowed DIY musicians to run their own production and distribution enterprises on a small, amateur scale, while also serving to erase the boundaries between producers and consumers. Musicians could release their own recordings of whatever sound they could make, without needing to use pressing plants, record labels or shops, completely outside the established music industry.

'Suddenly, people realised they could produce and distribute their own music – to use a cliché, they seized the means of production,' says Potter. 'The cassette medium became a way of not just messing about for your own amusement or with a few friends, but getting your music into the hands of other people.'

The primary motivation was creative satisfaction; for many people involved, particularly when they were starting out, it was the only way to be heard. 'This was the only outlet we had at the time. We couldn't really get gigs. At that point nobody was going to put on the sort of material that we did,' recalls Nigel Ayers of experimental duo Nocturnal Emissions, who started out by issuing a cassette compilation with a homemade, black-and-white photocopied cover on their own Sterile label in 1980, including an ear-bashing contribution by Geff Rushton (aka John Balance, pre-Coil) under the name Murderwerkers.

Few home-produced cassette albums were big sellers. Potter recalls that for some of the more popular compilation releases of post-industrial bands from well-known cassette labels like Third Mind, Adventures in Reality, Audion and Mirage, he might be asked to make several thousand copies, but with the more obscure releases, he would only copy 'fifty or a hundred' tapes over a period of months.

This was music that could never really be commodified because it didn't have enough potential listeners; it represented the scruffy, dissonant counterpart to the glossily produced pop that dominated the period. 'Besides happily recording in lo-fi, the common denominator between these artists is a rejection of eighties excess,' said a review of a retrospective cassette-culture compilation album in *The Wire*. Cassette musicians were refuseniks, 'uninterested in the dominant Anglo-American continuum'[27] and content to make scrappy, ugly music.

Because such music was inherently unpopular, the network that grew up around it was necessarily small-scale and personally rooted. As well as the addresses published on record sleeves, contact information was published by fanzines and by *CLEM* (*Contact List of Electronic Music*), a Canada-based contact magazine for amateur music makers and tape exchangers. Industrial music fans also regularly wrote to each other, exchanging ideas and cassettes by post, further developing what writer Mark Fisher described as a 'collaborative infrastructure'[28] that foreshadowed internet-era file-sharing.

'In that DIY independent scene around that time, people really did share a great deal of information. Sometimes bands were even putting their home addresses on the record covers – it seems unthinkable now. So you just wrote letters to them and such was the culture at the time, people did actually reply,' says Stephen Thrower of Coil, who started corresponding by post with Throbbing Gristle, Nurse with Wound and others when he was a teenager in Yorkshire.

Nigel Ayers says Nocturnal Emissions would respond to anyone who wrote to them. 'Very soon, we had contacts all over the world. People were always putting together these compilation cassettes of people they'd met that way, just on a small scale.'

Cassette compilations like the *Rising from the Red Sand* series and others would often include similar contributors – Nurse with Wound, Legendary Pink Dots, Attrition and post-industrial ethno-ambient explorers O Yuki Conjugate; groups that would continue to produce unconventional music on the margins for decades to come. Others were relatively short-lived, like Storm Bugs, a duo who self-released various cassettes and a couple of 7-inches made using secondhand reel-to-reel recorders bought at a flea market with a delay system copied from the back cover of Eno's *Discreet Music*, basic musique concrète techniques picked up from Terence Dwyer's book, *Composing with*

Tape Recorders, and vinyl records cut with a scalpel to create locked grooves – all combined with ordinary instruments.

Cassette releases were perfect for such unusual sounds, but the tape scene also provided a home for more conventionally melodic electronic musicians whose styles were seen as uncommercial by record labels. By the early eighties, the 'Berlin School' *kosmische* style of Tangerine Dream, Klaus Schulze and Ash Ra Tempel had fallen out of fashion in post-punk Britain, and the British synthesizer musicians who admired and sought to emulate the Germans – so-called 'synthesists' like Mark Shreeve, Ian Boddy, Paul Nagle, Ron Berry and Carl Matthews – all had to release some of their albums of cosmic electronics on cassette. Some of the synthesists' recordings were issued by Mirage, the cassette label run by the Bristol-based magazine of the same name, one of several electronic music fanzines of the era that included *Face Out*, *Neumusik* and *Aura*. Cassette fanzine *INKEY$* even organised an annual UK Electronica Festival, whose inaugural event in Milton Keynes in 1983 featured Chris and Cosey, various members of Hawkwind and several of the synthesists.

Cassette culture provided an outlet for various outsider artists who could never have conformed to the demands of the music business, like analog noise musician Paul Kelday, the creator of the kind of sounds summed up by one of his album titles, *Negative Hallucination*. From the mid-seventies onwards, Kelday made mysterious, abstract, electronic pieces full of tenebrous drones, spectral effects and warped signal tones, releasing them himself on cassettes with naive, hand-drawn inserts. He was virtually unknown at the time, but years later, recordings by Kelday and other obscure cassette-only albums by lo-fi British bands, like Solid Space's *Space Museum* and Oppenheimer Analysis's *New Mexico*, would become cult items that were lovingly rereleased by archive labels.

Muslimgauze, Bourbonese Qualk, Nocturnal Emissions

'I think we saw ourselves as being a sort of underground cell of resistance.'
Nigel Ayers, Nocturnal Emissions

The outsider artist who would posthumously come to be regarded by some as the enigmatic genius of the cassette culture era was Bryn Jones, who recorded as E.g Oblique Graph and then as Muslimgauze. Jones was remarkably prolific, making almost 200 Muslimgauze albums before his death in 1999,

Bourbonese Qualk playing live in Prague in 1987. Photo courtesy of Simon Crab.

many of them expressing his support for Palestinian liberation and Muslims' struggles against oppression. The first Muslimgauze album, 1983's *Kabul*, was informed by the Soviet Union's invasion of Afghanistan, while the titles of albums like *The Rape of Palestine* and *Hebron Massacre* were self-explanatory.

Despite the brutality and suffering that motivated him, Jones's curious, hypnotic music was often exquisitely delicate. He used drum machines, synths, Arabic percussion, looped breakbeats, samples of Islamic music and excerpts of TV newscasts and political speeches to assemble ethno-industrial sketches full of tension and uncertainty, compulsion and disruption, dream-state ambience and chimerical melody. 'Muslimgauze have never touched a computer/sampler. I use old equipment in a rough way. You use the same equipment as all the others; you all sound the same,' he explained in one fanzine interview. 'I use old cassettes/reel tapes/old equipment and I hope Muslimgauze sound unique.'[29]

Jones' albums certainly looked unique, decorated with radical Islamic imagery, like *Salaam Alekum, Bastard* with its cover image of hooded jihadi fighters, and *Hamas Arc*, which featured a photograph of women in chadors firing pistols. He wasn't a Muslim, didn't speak Arabic and had never been to the Middle East, but said he had been deeply affected by watching news of

Israel's invasion of Lebanon in 1982. 'Muslimgauze will never condemn any act of direct action the PLO [Palestinian Liberation Organisation] or Hamas feels is necessary to free all occupied territories,' he wrote in the sleevenotes for his album *Maroon*. 'Living in a democracy and able to vote, you cannot judge those unable to do so.'[30]

Some commentators accused him of applauding terrorism and justifying suicide bombings; others argued that Jones glorified violence in the Middle East in the same way as some industrial bands iconised serial killers and sexual aggressors: the provocative posturing of disaffected young men. 'He was interested in antagonising people, shocking people using images and sounds that are transgressive,' says Simon Crab of Bourbonese Qualk, who released one of Jones' early albums. Musically, Jones was similarly controversial. Some critics argued that he used Arabic samples without any understanding of what they meant, appropriating elements of Middle Eastern cultures as exotica for an 'alternative' Western audience.

But Ibrahim Khider, author of the book *Muslimgauze: Chasing the Shadow of Bryn Jones*, said he believed Jones was essentially an anti-colonialist who had 'realised the manner in which Great Britain acquired her wealth and power, and how this very colonialism is still at the root of Muslim-world conflicts'.[31] Others saw what he did as utterly compelling art. 'At its finest, Bryn Jones's music emits a dark, dislocative power, a sonic illustration of what Freud meant by "the uncanny",'[32] argued cultural commentator Jace Clayton.

Jones himself did not live long enough to read such accolades; he died at the age of 37, reportedly of complications from a rare blood infection. An isolated, painfully introverted figure – 'He wanted to talk, but he couldn't really do it,' Crab recalls – Jones was still living with his parents and making some of his music in his bedroom at the time of his death. He left no partner or children, just a huge cache of recordings that were released posthumously for years afterwards.

As Muslimgauze's output indicated, the mid-eighties were a politically-charged period in popular culture, as the Conservative Prime Minister Margaret Thatcher's rule became increasingly divisive, sparking a series of major outbreaks of social discontent: strikes, mass demonstrations, direct-action protests, riots. Some of the industrial bands associated with the cassette scene were involved in these protests; as activist-musicians, they were much closer in outlook to the anarchist punk collective Crass than they were to the ideologically ambiguous Throbbing Gristle.

In the febrile political environment of the Thatcher years, the proselytising of Crass and other anarcho-punk bands helped nurture a new anarchist subculture in the UK. As well as anti-nuclear peace camps, Hunt Saboteurs Association protests against blood sports, Animal Liberation Front raids on animal-testing laboratories and support campaigns for striking mineworkers, the squatters' movement was one of the focal points for anarchist activists who believed seizing and occupying uninhabited property was a righteous strike back against exploitation by capitalist rentiers. Squatting was also popular among impecunious left-field musicians and artists seeking rent-free accommodation, industrial outfits SPK and Lustmord among them. At this point, many independent musicians were unemployed through choice – welfare benefits were sometimes seen as a kind of informal arts grant to subsist on whilst doing something more creative than a 'normal' job.

In the winter of 1984, members of the post-punk electro-acoustic band Bourbonese Qualk occupied a former ambulance station on south London's Old Kent Road, beginning an experiment in practical anarchism by setting up a cultural centre inside the abandoned five-storey building where radical ideas could be developed and put into practice. They renovated the premises and created a performance space, an illegal bar, artists' studios, facilities for photographers and filmmakers, a local HQ for an alternative 'estate agency' called the Squatters Network, a screenprinting facility and a recording studio and office for Bourbonese Qualk's Recloose Organisation label. They also lived onsite in the midst of all the creative chaos going on around them.

The Old Ambulance Station became the coordination centre for some of the anti-capitalist, anti-militarist Stop the City demonstrations that disrupted London's financial institutions in the mid-eighties. But the squat infuriated local thugs and skinheads, furious that anarchists had set up an encampment in their neighbourhood, and the squatters sometimes had to physically repulse attacks on the building.

Bourbonese Qualk's releases also promoted their self-help, self-sufficiency, pro-squatting outlook and their belief that music had a vital role to play in movements for social justice. 'We saw ourselves at war with Thatcherite free market capitalism, and music and sound and noise was part of that,' explains the band's co-founder Simon Crab.

Musically, they were sonic bricoleurs in the spirit of Faust, Cabaret Voltaire and This Heat; their music was scrappy and abrasive, a kind of trashcan industrial punk-funk. Using a cheap Casio VL-1 synth, a Roland TR-808, tape loops and wayward vocals, sometimes heavily treated in a Mark Stewart style, as well as more traditional guitars and drums, it was often confrontational but sometimes unexpectedly melodic. Rough tape edits created jarring juxtapositions. 'This was totally intentional,' says Crab. 'Our ethos from the beginning was to provoke the audience, so one way of doing that would be to cut from something noisy into something that's very soft and vice versa and have unexpected jumps and jolts in the music, have the wrong titles for tracks and locked grooves just to play with the medium.'

Bourbonese Qualk neither wanted nor could afford to use a proper recording studio, choosing to make their music with whatever equipment they could assemble at the Old Ambulance Station. 'Because we pretty much lived in the recording studio, we just kept on recording, experimenting and erasing, mixing stuff up and splicing stuff together over maybe a year, and then we would stick the bits we liked together to make an album,' explains Crab. 'We used to process tape trying different chemicals – the ultimate was when I ate some of the tape to see what the digestive process did with my vocals on it and it had a really interesting effect. You couldn't do that in a studio, could you?'

Crab was disparaging about much industrial music, scenting the malodour of fascism in certain noise bands' use of imagery. But Bourbonese Qualk were friendly with Nocturnal Emissions, who were also connected to the squatter-activist community in south London. Nocturnal Emissions at that point were a duo, Nigel Ayers and Caroline K (Caroline Kaye Walters), who had been running their Sterile Records label out of a squatted house from 1979 onwards. Former art student Ayers had been involved in the Mail Art scene and saw Nocturnal Emissions as an anti-capitalist sound-art activist project that delivered messages of dissent. In his book *Electronic Resistance*, he explained how their music developed against the backdrop of the 'ideological battle'[33] being waged by the Thatcher government against trade unions and independent community groups.

The duo's initial set-up was distinctly low-tech. 'At the start, we just had cassette decks and a synth,' recalls Ayers. 'The first record was largely recorded onto cassette. It was very much like field recording – live improvisations, probably edited together quite crudely.' Like various other bands on the industrial scene, Nocturnal Emissions would also produce manifestos and photocopied collages that they distributed by post to anyone who contacted them, as well as their irregular magazine *Network News*, and would make experimental Super-8 films to project at gigs. Artwork for the band's records combined disturbing pictures of military massacres, photographs of human deformities and surgical procedures from medical literature, grotesque laboratory experiments on animals and pornographic images to expose and challenge what they saw as the hidden crimes and hypocrisies of Western society, concealed behind the mendacious façade of 'normality'.

Early albums – like the stark and disruptive *Fruiting Body* or *Drowning in a Sea of Bliss*, with its shearing noise and distressing cover image of a lab-test monkey – were intentionally traumatic. 'It was harrowing stuff because it was meant to make a point,' says Ayers. 'I think the research and the obsessions and the ideas that we were looking at then shaped the music. There was definitely a raw anger going on because it wasn't just about one poor monkey, it was the entire population being manipulated – on mainstream TV, you had the Miss World contest and blatant homophobia and racism being broadcast.' A flyer for a gig in London in May 1982 described Nocturnal Emissions' performances as 'attacks' that use 'perceptual bombardment, calculated to bypass rational processes to directly address the unconscious part of the mind' – to bypass 'pre-programmed obedient consumer responses'[34] and force listeners to become active and make their own choices.

By 1983 however, Nocturnal Emissions had tired of the conventions of the industrial genre. 'Images of death have just become like a style and it doesn't have any meaning anymore because it's so clichéd,'[35] Caroline K said. Ayers believes that some industrial bands were simply posturing as transgressors without any substance beneath their slogans. 'I didn't see that what they were doing was in any way connected with any sort of revolutionary social engagement, which I think was happening in DIY culture and the squat culture,' he argues. 'It was like a comic book pose that they were using, stupid, obvious and with a total lack of empathy; like an incel fantasy – porn and fascism. Meanwhile, we were going on marches against the National Front.'

The band's sound was also mutating, taking in fresh inputs as they started to develop their own raw and spiky strain of low-budget industrial dance music. Ayers had been collecting Morgan Khan's *Street Sounds* compilation series and Nocturnal Emissions' 1983 album *Viral Shedding* was their first to use electro beats – the track 'No Separation' sounded like an unlikely combination of Crass and Tackhead – while *Songs of Love and Revolution*, made during the miners' strike, was a fabulously twisted electro-pop record. In 1987, they decided to close their Sterile label and launch a new one, Earthly Delights, taking a more explicitly melodic direction. The first release was Caroline K's remarkable solo album, *Now Wait for Last Year*, a collection of dark ambient dronescapes and poignant electronic laments. It was followed by more records from Nocturnal Emissions, by this time an Ayers solo project that increasingly explored ideas of paganism, shamanism and magic.

Portion Control, 400 Blows, Nitzer Ebb and 'Funky Alternatives'
'That whole era was the beginning of a process – the post-punk period bleeding into the dance music culture.'
Tony Thorpe, 400 Blows

As the eighties progressed, the creative significance of electro and hip-hop became increasingly clear to some British industrial musicians who decided extreme noise had become an artistic dead-end and started to base their sound on heavy electronic rhythms. Records like D.A.F.'s 'Der Mussolini', 'Planet Rock' co-producer John Robie's mix of Cabaret Voltaire's 'Yashar' and SPK's 'Metal Dance' helped define a more rhythmic iteration of industrial music that retained its nonconformist aura but was less sonically intimidating. It was this style that would gain increasing popularity in the US via college radio and alternative dance clubs, opening the way towards the subsequent success of Nine Inch Nails, Ministry and Marilyn Manson.

The London electronic trio Portion Control were one of the first bands on the DIY cassette scene to use rhythm as their focal point. With their harsh, sequenced riffs and raucous vocals, they saw themselves as electronic punks, years before The Prodigy. 'We'd grown up listening to punk, so our idea of song structure was very much verse-chorus and we wanted to keep that punk edge, although our ethos was electronics,' explains co-founder John Whybrew.

On their 1982 breakthrough album *I Staggered Mentally*, Portion Control were one of the first industrial bands to use the Roland TB-303, which later in the decade would provide the squelching basslines for acid house. They also bought an early sound sampling system, the Greengate DS:3, which worked with an Apple II computer and was marketed by a Hemel Hempstead-based company as a budget alternative to the Fairlight. 'It was 8-bit, tiny sampling times, but we could start to see the potential to sample and sequence found sounds into our music,' says Whybrew. 'There was also a big influence from Mad Professor and all those effects in dub records, so we started to embrace some of those techniques as well.'

Nitzer Ebb performing at the University of London Student Union, 1989. ©Martyn Goodacre/Getty Images.

They sometimes found the sounds made by the machines they were using were not hard or weird enough for their punkish tastes, however. '*I Staggered Mentally* has got a sort of dystopian feel, it's meant to be an uncomfortable record. So to make those machines dystopian and uncomfortable took some effort,' says Whybrew. 'So we would do things like put the drum machine through an amp and re-record the output or record the drum machine at double speed and then slow the tape down by half to change the sound to make it a bit more aggressive, a bit more edgy and powerful, because a lot of those early drum machines sounded really tame.'

Portion Control remained committed to their own distinctive vision and never made a mainstream pop breakthrough, even though tracks like 1985's 'The Great Divide', which sounded like the missing link between Depeche Mode and Chicago house, were catchy enough. Their sound was also one of the formative examples of electronic body music, the heavily-sequenced, musclebound hetero-electro style that would be fully defined by Belgian band Front 242 and Nitzer Ebb from Chelmsford.

Nitzer Ebb's music shuddered and roared with menacing intensity, but they also loved James Brown and gay disco. 'Our first exposure to electronic music was from funk and soul bands and not from white Europeans with synthesizers,'[36] explained the band's electronics programmer, Bon Harris. Like records by Chris and Cosey, Cabaret Voltaire, Front Line Assembly, Front 242 and Portion Control, Nitzer Ebb's tracks would become favourites at Goa full-moon parties and implicit influences on the development of psytrance, while their propulsive evocation of militaristic ardour, 'Join in the Chant', unexpectedly became an anthem at London's acid house clubs in 1988.

By the mid-eighties, the dancefloor – as a musical inspiration and as an arena for which music could be purpose-built – was becoming increasingly important to left-field bands. Compilation album series like *Funky Alternatives* and *Heavy Duty Breaks* focused on the nexus between white post-industrial music and Black electro-funk, featuring groups like Portion Control, Nocturnal Emissions, 23 Skidoo and 400 Blows – all mixing ritualistic and avant-garde elements of the industrial sound with the rhythmic innovations of electro and hip-hop, with varying degrees of flair or ineptitude. Some were also exploring dub; Colourbox covered the Augustus Pablo classic 'Baby I Love You So', while 400 Blows collaborated with Mad Professor on 'Declaration of Intent'.

400 Blows were Black sound system DJ Tony Thorpe and white post-punk musician Andrew Beer; a cross-cultural soundclash of a band. 'I was a soul boy, I started out as a DJ playing funk, disco and reggae. Andrew's music was all weird, punky, obscure,' explains Thorpe. 'We had totally different record collections so we were learning from each other. Listen to our albums – bits of industrial, bits of funk; it was all over the place really.'

Thorpe says he saw the *Funky Alternatives* albums that he and Beer compiled as a post-punk version of the *Street Sounds* series: a budget introduction to a hybrid almost-genre. 'There was a kind of open-mindedness to sound at that time,' he says. 'People took elements from other genres but did their own thing with them. They weren't really following anyone else, they were just playing their own game – they didn't really know what they were doing or where they were going, but it wasn't contrived or controlled.' (Thorpe would keep on exploring new hybrids in the 1990s, producing one of the earliest UK dub-house records, The Moody Boys' *Journey into Dubland*, with Jimmy Cauty of The KLF).

The first *Heavy Duty Breaks* compilation in 1985 was accompanied by a fast-moving DJ mix with juddering samples and snippets from TV broadcasts, produced by former Killing Joke bassist Youth and mixed by Eddie Richards, who was resident DJ alongside Colin Faver at Camden Palace – the New

York-style superclub hosted by New Romantic kingpins Steve Strange and Rusty Egan where they played electro, Italo-disco and synth-pop, and would soon start playing early house music.

Serendipitously, Richards owned a Greengate sampler. 'I got a bunch of records from the artists and I just sampled little bits of them into the Greengate – you could only sample short bits at that time and they were quite crunchy because they were only 8-bit. Then we went into the studio and dropped them into the mix,' he says. 'It was something new at the time, a kind of DJ mix with samples, done with indie bands.'

The ideas being explored on the *Heavy Duty Breaks* and *Funky Alternatives* records represented tentative attempts to create a new strain of British electronic dance music. There wasn't a mass audience for high-tempo electronic grooves embellished with samples quite yet, but it would soon come.

DJ Dave Dorrell (left) with M/A/R/R/S, 1987. Photo: Juergen Teller.

9
PUMP UP THE VOLUME
Samplemania, Hi-NRG and Dance-Pop

M/A/R/R/S and Bomb the Bass

'It's like William Gibson says, the street finds its own uses for technology.'
Dave Dorrell, DJ and member of M/A/R/R/S

IT WAS A RECORD THAT WAS BASED ON OTHER RECORDS, some of which were also based on some other records. It was full of joyous enthusiasm and opened minds to new ways of thinking about how to make music. It raised all sorts of questions about authenticity and originality and appropriation, encouraged all sorts of imitators and became the focus of costly litigation. It was hailed as the bold statement of a new artistic vanguard and condemned as a cynical rip-off.

'Pump Up the Volume' was emblematic of its time – 1987, that feverish year in British pop music, when stealing bits of other people's songs and using them to create your own seemed like a novel and possibly even revolutionary idea; a time when hip-hop and house became major influences on mainstream pop; when remixes became ubiquitous and when nightclub DJs started to become stars. Although it wasn't the first British sample-based dance track, or the first pop hit in which UK DJs played a major role, its success meant that many others would follow.

For a record so positive and upbeat, the making of 'Pump Up the Volume' was wracked with discontent. Ivo Watts-Russell, the head of independent label 4AD, had brought the bands Colourbox and A.R. Kane together to make some kind of collaborative alternative dance record, but they didn't gel creatively or personally, and each band ended up creating their own track with minimal input from the other. For their track, Martyn and Steve Young of Colourbox came up with a low-slung, undulating groove and wanted to layer some hip-hop cutting and scratching over it. They called Dave Dorrell, a London club DJ who had recently worked with Martyn Young on musical idents for the launch of MTV Europe. 'Martyn asked me to help so I went down to the studio with a bag of records and we played about a bit,' Dorrell recalls. 'The next day on the way to the studio I went into Soho and bought the new Eric B. & Rakim 12-inch, 'I Know You Got Soul', which had just arrived from the States on import. We flipped it over and on the other side of this wonderful new piece of vinyl was an acapella.

'We started to play through it, and then there it was: "Pump up the volume!" We were like, "Could that phrase work for us?" So Martyn ran the track and I just dropped the phrase in. *It worked.*'

Dorrell and his friend CJ Mackintosh, a skilful hip-hop DJ who won that year's DMC UK Mixing Championship, selected excerpts from Public Enemy, Trouble Funk, James Brown and a host of other soul and funk tracks and dropped them into Colourbox's propulsive rhythm to create a collage that fizzed with enthusiasm, picking up on ideas of musical bricolage from the records that Dorrell and Mackintosh played in the clubs. 'Grandmaster Flash's 'Adventures on the Wheels of Steel' was one inspiration, Double Dee and Steinski's 'Lessons 1, 2, 3' was another, and you already had people like Coldcut in Britain playing with the idea of making a musical narrative out of samples, so that was another,' explains Dorrell.

'Pump Up the Volume', credited to M/A/R/R/S, an acronym comprising the first-name initials of its creators, became an instant club favourite. Its freshness and irreverence then made it a pop hit too. 'When it first went into the charts at thirty-five, it made me laugh, but I didn't think it would go any further,' Mackintosh said. 'Then it went to eleven, then two, then one.'[1] But a brief snippet of a song they had purloined would cause them a problem. Pop production team Stock Aitken Waterman noticed that the M/A/R/R/S track used a few seconds of their song 'Roadblock' and issued an injunction. The lawsuit would turn the spotlight on the legality of sampling and whether the use of excerpts of other people's recordings constituted copyright infringement or creative 'fair use'.

Pete Waterman of SAW argued that using the sample was blatant theft. But critics accused him of hypocrisy as his production team relied on underground club tracks as creative source material, citing their imitation of the distinctive bassline from Colonel Abrams' 'Trapped' for their production of Rick Astley's hit 'Never Gonna Give You Up' – and their instant recycling of the bassline from 'Pump Up the Volume' itself in Pete Waterman and Phil Harding's remix of Sybil's 'My Love Is Guaranteed'. 'They fly over the latest fifty or so American dance imports, copy the basslines and chop and change the tunes around. Where's the creativity in that? Of course, when it's done to them it's a different story,' argued Danny Briottet of Renegade Soundwave, whose bass-heavy house track 'The Phantom' sampled The Clash's 'White Riot'. 'They should accept the fact that, because of the technology now available, musical performances have become raw material for other music.'[2]

Waterman acknowledged that his productions used samples: 'It's always legal, though,' he insisted – but he argued that pinching drum or bass sounds didn't contravene the law, only musical phrases that formed part of the 'integrity of the performance'.[3]

In the end, Watts-Russell decided to accept defeat and the M/A/R/R/S case was settled out of court, with 4AD making a payment to charity and a contribution to legal costs. But because there were so many samples in the record that hadn't been cleared before 'Pump Up the Volume' was released, Watts-Russell believed the legal problems could have been much worse. 'We should have been sued to fuck by everybody,' he said. 'We didn't get one fucking sample clearance for the original [version], that's how maverick it was.'[4]

Hip-hop had showed how new music could be assembled from existing sound sources, heralding a conceptual paradigm shift in music-making. The creation of records from sampled sound sources – 'plunderphonics' or 'sampledelia', as it was sometimes known at the time – seemed to be the sonic equivalent of visual arts innovations from the early 20th century: montage and collage techniques and the incorporation of found visuals into artists' canvases. But the M/A/R/R/S controversy raised a series of difficult questions: was making a record using samples a new form of art or just a new form of theft? 'Never before or since has a music technology development challenged notions of musical authenticity, reimagined musical instrumentation or transformed genre; the digital sampler confronted existing understandings of authentic musical performance, provoked legal and moral debates surrounding intellectual property and created divides in the western music and sound recording industries,'[5] wrote musicologist Samantha Bennett.

Most of the young electronic musicians who were using samples of others' music on their tracks took a liberal view of what should be permitted. 'You can't draw a line as to where people should stop. Everyone has their own view of where the line between plagiarism and creativity lies,'[6] said Martyn Young of M/A/R/R/S. Several decades later, Dave Dorrell says he still believes 'Pump Up the Volume' should never have been targeted. 'I'm totally in favour of an open-door approach to creativity and I think that means having the right to mess around with other people's work. Great things come out of it,' he argues. 'It's like Duchamp painting a moustache on the Mona Lisa and making a gag out of it, and also great art as far as I'm concerned, because sometimes you have to dare to be an iconoclast and break the frame. Shock, horror! Great. *Fucking great.* More of it, please.'

The sampling debate intensified as 1987 rolled into 1988, and the success of 'Pump Up the Volume' was followed by two other sample-based hits created by British DJs: Tim Simenon's Bomb the Bass, who reached number two in the UK charts with 'Beat Dis' in February 1988, and Mark Moore's S'Express, who went to number one with 'Theme from S'Express' in April.

Simenon was a teenage DJ of Malaysian descent who had been playing hip-hop and funk at the then-fashionable Wag Club in London's West End, whilst studying studio engineering by day and working part-time as a waiter. His friend James Horrocks was one of the founders of a new dance music record label, Rhythm King, backed by Daniel Miller's Mute Records. Seeking fresh talent from the London club scene, Rhythm King offered to pay for Simenon to go into a studio and cut a track with producer Pascal Gabriel, who had previously been involved in various post-punk electronic projects. 'So I went along with a bag of records to see what would happen,' says Simenon.

The track the duo made, 'Beat Dis', was a rushing torrent of samples from James Brown and Ennio Morricone to Prince and Afrika Bambaataa, with funk guitar taken from The Bar-Kays' 'Son of Shaft' and vocal inserts from old TV shows. '"Beat Dis' was really a collage of my favourite tunes and things that inspired me, like watching *Thunderbirds* as a kid – all that got scratched in,' Simenon explains.

He and Gabriel spent a lot of their studio time electronically dissecting and reassembling the track's sampled guitar hook: 'Elements of the wukka-wukka guitar had to be chopped up into parts so that it could be replayed in time, because that stuff had been recorded in the seventies, obviously by live musicians, and once we put down our [electronically precise] rhythm section, it sounded out of time. So we cut up the 'Son of Shaft' sample and then Pascal brilliantly replayed it.' Using three Akai 900S samplers, they created a patchwork of secondhand sounds over a synth bassline that pulsated with naive exuberance; what Simenon calls 'beginner's spirit'.

Simenon was one of a series of British DJs, most of them non-musicians, who decided to have a go at making records using turntables and the new sampling technology at around the same time in 1987 and 1988. For him, hip-hop was the key inspiration. 'Bomb the Bass wasn't hip-hop, but it had hip-hop roots. It was just really taking that kind of energy from New York that we had heard and read about, that culture of do-it-yourself music making where you would just have a basic beat and just slice sounds on top, and then putting a UK touch to it,' he says.

Initially, Simenon imagined he had made a track for underground dancefloors, not pop radio. 'In my mind, I thought we were just going to press up 500 copies or something of a 12-inch of 'Beat Dis' which I would have been playing in clubs. I didn't really consider what was going to happen after the studio, it was just like a couple of days of fun.' When it became a hit, effectively transforming him from a cult DJ into a pop star, the attention from music journalists who saw him as the radical young figurehead of the sampling generation made him distinctly uncomfortable: 'I think at the time I was quite naive about the world and life in general, and all of a sudden I was one of the faces of this new style of music and I just felt quite a lot of pressure having to talk about something that I was still trying to understand myself.'

He says the 'Beat Dis' sessions started out with no thought for money, contracts or legality, simply a spirit of 'Let's just try this, it sounds fucking great, why not?' But like M/A/R/R/S, he and Gabriel soon found that although they had relatively cheap technology that allowed them to use other people's music to make their own, it could come at a cost. American hip-hop label Sugar Hill Records demanded payback for the use of a sample of the Funky Four + 1. Other demands followed. '[Rhythm King] had to settle so many times that there was very little money left. We earned a fraction of what you would off a normal hit,' [7] Gabriel lamented.

297

Simenon also used several prominent samples in his fabulous co-production of Neneh Cherry's 'Buffalo Stance' later in 1988, including a snippet of Malcolm McLaren's 'Buffalo Gals' in tribute to his b-boy roots. But the consequences of what happened with his first record made him consider whether using so many excerpts of others' work – around twenty in 'Beat Dis' – was really worthwhile. 'As the Bomb the Bass project developed, we started saying, "OK, we're sampling your record but here's some money for it," or, "Here's a slice of the publishing [revenue]," which of course makes perfect sense because we were taking the inspiration from the people that made the original music. I was also using less and less samples and bringing in musicians to play things instead.' But even attempts to clear samples in advance could be tricky: Simenon wanted to use an excerpt from Pink Floyd's *Meddle* on his second album, but the band refused permission.

S'Express, The Beatmasters and Plunderphonic Pop

'In 1988, you constantly felt the future was arriving. Each time you'd go out to a club, you would hear something new and go, "Oh my God, what's this? This is amazing! This changes everything!" You were in a constant state of surprise at what you were hearing.'
Mark Moore, S'Express

The third of the great trilogy of sample-based hits that began with 'Pump Up the Volume' came in April 1988, when 'Theme from S'Express' reached number one in the British charts. Like 'Beat Dis', it was also a record created by a club DJ, Mark Moore, co-written by Pascal Gabriel and released by Rhythm King, but with some crucial differences. Irreverent, knowingly retro but simultaneously looking to the future, cheekily provocative but inclusively charming, wilfully absurd but sonically ingenious, it was one of the most original pop hits of the period.

Like Dave Dorrell, Moore had been excited by Double Dee and Steinski's 'Lessons' records, whose title British DJs took literally and studied seriously. Moore had the idea of making an upbeat sample track using hip-hop techniques, but with a house groove instead of a James Brown break and excerpts from disco records instead of vintage funk.

Samples in American hip-hop and dance records often functioned like citations of works that had resonance in Black or queer musical history, signifiers of community memory in cultures that struggled to survive on

Mark Moore of S'Express, 1988. ©Tim Roney/Getty Images.

the margins of an oppressive society. Moore said that with 'Theme from S'Express', he wanted to reference records like Yazoo's 'Don't Go' and the Peech Boys' 'Don't Make Me Wait' that carried meaning for him as a DJ in the mixed-gay clubs of London, 'almost like a homage'. All hustle and glitter, the song used the brassy hook from Rose Royce's disco classic 'Is It Love You're After?', the voice of performance artist Karen Finley shouting 'Suck me off!' and a sample of a hairspray aerosol for the hi-hat sound. 'It was a dance record, but it was also meant to be an experimental record,'[8] said Gabriel.

This was in keeping with Moore's character and the diverse interests that made him one of the most fascinating figures on the club scene of the era. The half-Korean Londoner had been a teenage punk who hung out at Malcolm McLaren and Vivienne Westwood's Seditionaries shop, danced to early electro-pop at Blitz, became one of the first DJs to play house music in London at the Asylum (later Pyramid) club, mixing it up with Hi-NRG and electro-pop; he would then go on to play at formative acid house clubs like Shoom in 1988. All these inputs fed into 'Theme from S'Express'. 'I wanted it to have a house music feel but I didn't want to copy other house music records, I wanted it to sound like a futuristic disco record,' he explains.

Moore styled S'Express as a kind of flamboyant collective of clubland characters, including singers Billie Ray Martin and Sonique and rapper E-Mix. When the acid house scene erupted in London, Moore was at its centre as DJ and recording artist, absorbing its ecstatic vibrations into his music. At one point, he befriended systems composer Philip Glass while he was in Britain staging one of his operas and took him out to a rave. 'Of course, everyone was doing drugs and we thought we'd better tell him,' Moore recalls. 'But he was just quite amused: "Oh, you think you're the only people who've ever taken drugs." So we gave him some and took him to the rave and he loved it. He wasn't so much dancing though, more head-nodding. He was so cool.'

Glass and collaborator Kurt Munkacsi returned the favour with a vivacious remix of S'Express's fizzy Sly Stone tribute, 'Hey Music Lover'. One of the unlikeliest collaborations ever to happen in electronic dance music, it was made even wilder by the fact that it sounded like the minimalist composer was having so much fun doing it. 'People were going, "This isn't a dance mix! What were you thinking?" But we wanted him to do what he does,' says Moore. 'For me, the whole thing I liked about remixing was going up avenues that you hadn't explored, rather than just being a tool to sell more records.'

Moore's other important collaboration around the same period was with producer William Orbit on Malcolm McLaren's track 'Deep in Vogue', which incorporated elements of New York ballroom culture a year before Madonna essayed her own homage with 'Vogue'. McLaren had seen a rough cut of Jennie Livingstone's powerful documentary *Paris is Burning* and loved the idea of dispossessed gay, trans, Black and Latinx youth irreverently reversioning haute couture concepts for their own purposes, just as he had been captivated by the rebellious spirit of hip-hop a few years earlier.

According to Moore, McLaren's track initially sounded like 'a live band on a cruise ship doing a cover version of [MFSB's ballroom anthem] 'Love is the Message' in a cocktail-jazzy kind of way'. Moore and Orbit transformed it into a deep house groove, but there was still something missing: 'We needed to make it sound like a Malcolm McLaren record and he was going, "I don't know what a Malcolm McLaren record sounds like, I've no idea." So we said, "Well, we think a Malcolm McLaren record has you kind of ranting or shouting or saying something."' McLaren then decided to recite a tribute to the legendary ballroom houses of New York, pirating the evocative phrasing from an article about the scene by journalist Chi Chi Valenti. 'And then it went to number one in the *Billboard* dance chart [in the US] and we thought, "Oh my God, how did that happen?"'

Orbit and Moore's remodelling of 'Deep in Vogue' showed how, by the late eighties, DJs were not only remixing records to make the groove hit harder in the clubs, but stripping them down, reassembling and sometimes re-producing them, retaining elements they thought would work functionally and aesthetically and adding new ones where necessary.

Back in the seventies, DJs had initially been commissioned as remixers by record labels simply because they understood what made people dance; they knew which parts of a track to extend, which to rearrange and which to remove altogether. After disco went mainstream in the US, remixes became increasingly commonplace; by 1978, even The Rolling Stones were getting an extended sleazed-out disco revamp of their song 'Miss You'. In the eighties, remixers then became cult figures in their own right and devotees would buy a record if an imaginative remixer like François Kevorkian or Larry Levan's name was on it, whoever the artist might be.

Remixes could work as commercial tools to sell extra copies of a record to completist fans; they could be audacious experiments like the Philip Glass rework of S'Express, or they could be canny rearrangements intended to highlight the pop elements of a song in order to get it onto the radio and into the charts. They could enhance the groove, or remove it altogether to leave pure, beatless ambience; they could be relatively faithful to the original or utterly mutilate it, as Aphex Twin would later become notorious for doing. But when remixes really worked, they took off from the original version into the realm of the sublime, transforming a song into a sonic artwork that might never have been conceived by the original artist.

Some British remixers became known for turning club tracks into pop hits, a talent highly valued by record companies. Among them were The Beatmasters, a trio of twentysomething clubbers who were labelmates with S'Express and Bomb the Bass at Rhythm King, the company that was channelling the energies of the London club scene of the late eighties into pop

301

music. The Beatmasters had started out making funky advertising jingles and idents for the frenetic new 'youth TV' programmes produced by Janet Street-Porter that came on air around that time – *Network 7* on Channel 4 and the *DEF II* strand on BBC2 – bringing the electronic sounds of the underground onto mainstream television.

'Suddenly there was a sort of explosion of quite creative adverts and youth TV shows so there was this need for some sort of hip jingles,' says one of the Beatmasters trio, Manda Glanfield. 'We were making these thirty-second collage things with loops and sounds chopped up, influenced by the music we were hearing at clubs and warehouse parties – hip-hop with lots of scratching, disco and the beginnings of house music.'

London clubland was operating as a kind of incubator for emerging talents in music and media, Glanfield recalls. 'Everybody was feeding off each other and just getting off on the energy of it, also fuelled by all the technology that suddenly became available,' she says. 'It was a very creative time and we were trying to inject some of that energy into these adverts just because it was fun.'

The Beatmasters were hitmakers from their first single in 1987, 'Rok da House', a collaboration with London rappers the Cookie Crew. As well as their own records, featuring enthusiastic mash-ups of the sounds they loved from the clubs, The Beatmasters became sought-after producers for other dance acts who wanted hits too. 'We had this pop sensibility, maybe because we'd done jingles. What we were known for was bringing the sound of the clubs and dance music to a 7-inch radio format, making that accessible, repeating all the hooks. We wanted to bring this fantastic music from the underground to the overground and let people hear it,' says Glanfield.

She describes herself as the 'techie' of the trio, programming sequencers, drum machines and samplers. She was also one of the few high-profile women producers in electronic dance music culture, which was overwhelmingly male-dominated despite its purported values of inclusivity.

'I had people around me really encouraging me and valuing my contribution, so obviously that helped and I wasn't that conscious of any gender bar, because people around me needed a techie musician and that happened to be me, and I happened to be female. So on the one hand, to me, it was no problem,' she recalls. 'But then on the other hand, every so often, I would look around me and think, "Where are all the other women?" And it did feel a bit lonely because there was no one else doing it.'

Coldcut, The JAMs – and Brian Eno (Again)

'We'll always find ways to work round the law. Whatever they develop, we'll develop faster... That's how music evolves, you take it, you mutate it, you make it your own.'
Coldcut, interviewed in 1987[9]

Sampling was initially the domain of high-level producers and musicians like Trevor Horn and Peter Gabriel, who could afford to buy Fairlights and Synclaviers. But as the eighties progressed, more affordable and user-friendly units like the Casio FZ1 and the Akai S612 and S900, both designed by former EMS electronics engineer David Cockerell, started to bring the technique to a much wider constituency.

'Everything about the S900 underlines how easy it is to use,'[10] raved specialist magazine *Electronics & Music Maker* when Akai released it in 1986. The Atari ST computer, with its built-in MIDI capability, also played a crucial role in the democratisation of electronic music-making by making it possible for people to sequence tracks at home using composition software like C-Lab Creator or Steinberg Pro-24. Much cheaper than a Fairlight and easier to use, the Atari ST was a machine that helped to shape the course of electronic dance music, although it never attained the revered status of Roland's 303, 808 or 909.

Coldcut's Matt Black and Jonathan More constructed many of their early tracks with the Atari ST, although these deft exponents of musical larceny initially used more basic equipment. Both pirate radio DJs on London's Kiss FM, Black and More released their first 12-inch in January 1987: 'Say Kids What Time is It?' was a rough cut-up of the kind of vintage funk and go-go breaks that were being played on London's warehouse party scene, cheekily laced with clips from movies like *The Jungle Book* and *Chitty Chitty Bang Bang*. Black said Coldcut took their cues from the BBC Radio 1's musically omnivorous presenter John Peel, 'who taught us that it was cool to be into a lot of different sorts of music,' and from the hip-hop techniques of turntable montage and real-time vinyl manipulation developed by Grandmaster Flash and collage duo Double Dee and Steinski.

'Say Kids What Time is It?' has been described as one of the first British sample records, although Coldcut didn't actually use a sampler when they made it. Black says the backing track was cut together on a cassette player using a pause-button editing technique he had developed, then the voice excepts and scratches were added on a four-track recorder and mixed down to cassette.

They decided to press up 500 copies without seeking legal permission from the copyright owners. 'We knew that Double Dee and Steinski's mixes had not been able to be released legally because they could not be cleared. So rather than fuck around trying to clear them, we just thought we'd just go for it,' Black recalls. Nevertheless, they decided to conceal their identities. 'We were worried that we would be arrested when we got to the pressing plant and that they would say, "Hey, your record's made up of other people's records, you can't do this." So we gave false names when we went to the pressing plant, but they didn't actually care less.' To further anonymise themselves, they used a soldering iron to melt out the matrix number that identified the UK pressing plant on each 12-inch so they could pretend the records were imports from the US.

Coldcut were not the only British DJs recording low-budget turntable collages at the time. Similarly inspired by Grandmaster Flash and Double Dee and Steinski was Norman Cook, the bassist with indie band The Housemartins, who would later adopt the alias Fatboy Slim. Cook was a hip-hop fanatic and 'The Finest Ingredients', his scratch-mix debut, was a jaunty swag-bag of funk, rock, film and TV fragments stitched together over an electronic beat and released under the name DJ Mega-Mix – his first step towards becoming one of the country's biggest DJ stars.

Coldcut's second 12-inch, 'Beats and Pieces', rolling along atop a looped drum pattern from Led Zeppelin's 'When the Levee Breaks' sped up from 33 to 45, was similarly packed with pirated extracts scratched into the mix. This time the duo booked a studio and worked with an engineer who went by the name of Raine Shine. 'There were not many female engineers around at that time and she also engineered the Vangelis *Blade Runner* soundtrack, so we were like, "Wow, this woman's amazing" – and she introduced us to the concept of a tape loop,' says Black. From these low-tech beginnings, they quickly graduated to arranging tracks with a Casio sampler and an Atari ST 1040 computer. 'That was really what advanced it over [using] records, that ability to compose [with the Atari],' confirms Black.

By early 1988, various other British DJs like Jazzie B, Nellee Hooper, Daddy G, Kid Batchelor, Mike Pickering, Graeme Park, Ian B and Eddie Richards were also making their own records, fired up by the creative energies pulsing through the clubs, enabled by cheaper and more accessible technology and informed by innovations in hip-hop and house music in the US. 'The UK would kind of funnel all this in and put it into our kind of blender machine,' says Black. 'And we were drinking on this intoxicating brew going, "Fuck, let's do this." And so a bunch of us did.' The 'Soul Mafia' DJ Froggy might arguably have preceded them back in 1985 when he released his 'Froggy Mix #1', a medley of James Brown extracts, while DSM's UK-made electro-funk track 'Warrior Groove' made use of comedy-posh English-accented vocal samples the same year, but now a whole new musical movement was coalescing.

At the time, Coldcut celebrated the anarchic freedom of sampling. 'Long live theft!' declared More in a 1988 interview with pop magazine *Record Mirror*, which enthusiastically asserted the duo were 'hip-hop punks' or even 'the Robin Hoods of pop'.[11] They certainly showed commitment to their cause: on the 12-inch of their hit 'Doctorin' the House', they included a 'theftapella' with all the samples they had used so other people could steal them too. 'That was very naughty really. 'Doctorin' the House' is chock full of samples, hardly any of which we cleared,' says Black. 'Putting them on the "theftapella" where they're nakedly exposed, we might as well have just given people a list saying: "Here you are, guys, sue us for all of these",' he laughs.

For their use of a four-word invocation from Dave and Ansel Collins' hit 'Double Barrel', Coldcut had to give away a significant amount of the publishing revenue. Nevertheless, Black recalls the early, unregulated sampling period as a joyful time: 'A disc jockey plays records, a DJ plays with records. And we were playing with records like a child plays on the beach. We were having fun.'

An even more twisted sense of fun was at play on 'All You Need Is Love', an inharmonious assembly of samples of The Beatles and 'Page 3' model-turned-pop-star Samantha Fox, Tackhead-style machine beats, a schmaltzy refrain and the wild ranting of a Scottish-accented 'rapper', released the same year as Coldcut's debut. It was credited to The JAMs, an acronym for The Justified Ancients of Mu Mu, a name adapted from Robert Shea and Robert Anton Wilson's *Illuminatus!* trilogy about secret societies and hidden conspiracies; the JAMs' 'pyramid ghettoblaster' logo also referenced the Eye of Providence used on the book's cover.

King Boy D and Rockman Rock were named as The JAMs' members; they were actually former rock band manager Bill Drummond and musician Jimmy Cauty, and their record signalled the beginning of one of the most

305

fascinating and bizarre creative interventions ever witnessed in British pop music. It would go on to involve a lawsuit from ABBA, a novelty mash-up of the *Doctor Who* theme, the making of several ecstatic rave anthems, a collaboration with country singer Tammy Wynette, the terrorising of a BRIT Awards ceremony and the burning of a million pounds.

ABBA threatened to sue over a sample of 'Dancing Queen' that was included in The JAMs' first album, *1987 (What the Fuck is Going On?)*, whose sleeve declared that the duo wanted to 'liberate these sounds from all copyright restrictions without prejudice'. The Swedes' writ caused the album to be withdrawn from sale and the remaining copies destroyed. Like Coldcut, Drummond and Cauty showed little respect for copyright law, but as they came from an indie rock background and weren't initially making music for club dancefloors, their targets for aesthetic thievery were more eclectic. As well as James Brown and Isaac Hayes' 'Theme from Shaft', the Sex Pistols, The Monkees and Whitney Houston all got mashed up into jarring, confrontational records that attempted to simulate the impact of hip-hop but actually sounded like a kind of pranksterish noise-art. 'Neither of us were DJs. We didn't know what the hell we were doing so it came out in a very British punk, white, ungroovy kind of way,'[12] Drummond said.

Tony Thorpe of 400 Blows, who later became a beatmaker and remixer for Cauty and Drummond's KLF, recalled hearing The JAMs on the radio for the first time and thinking: 'Oh my God, this is *awful*. But I was intrigued because they were using the worst samples possible and I wanted to find out more about these guys, because it was just so mad.' Like Dave Dorrell with M/A/R/R/S, Drummond made an art-world comparison, saying The JAMs were repurposing existing sounds as Andy Warhol had done with images: 'We're just doing musically what he did with Campbell's soup cans and pictures of Marilyn Monroe.'[13]

They were also enjoying themselves. In 1988, 'Doctorin' the Tardis' – their preposterous, flagrantly tacky combination of the *Doctor Who* signature tune, Gary Glitter's 'Rock and Roll Part 2' and The Sweet's glam anthem 'Blockbuster' – brought them a number-one hit under the name The Timelords. They then mythologised the incident by publishing *The Manual (How to Have a Number One the Easy Way)*, a book that not entirely satirically advised on how to make a pop smash from other people's music with the help of new technology, just as they had done. 'If you are already a musician sell your instrument,' it urged, counselling wannabe hitmakers to copy a groove from the latest hot American dance import and combine it with a singalong chorus, just like pop production trio Stock Aitken Waterman were doing at the time. But behind the ironic humour, *The Manual* was an entirely heartfelt manifesto for do-it-yourself creative independence in the sampling era: 'the future is ours,'[14] it declared optimistically.

The law regulating the performing and copying of music that was in place at the time of the ABBA lawsuit and the M/A/R/R/S case was the 1956 Copyright Act, which did not envisage the possibility of electronic sampling. 'It felt a bit like a creative free-for-all at the time,' recalls Manda Glanfield of The Beatmasters. 'It was just like, "Let's all pick what we can, isn't this great?" Hip-hop was a big influence on all this, with the drum loops and scratching, which was like the precursor to using samples. All these incredible artists like James Brown and his band the JBs were being sampled, but it was a bit of a grey area and I think everybody was a bit blind to it for a while.'

The fact that the Copyright Act did not specifically regulate the use of electronic samples created an area of uncertainty – was all sampling automatically a copyright breach, or could short samples be acceptable? Should everyone whose work was sampled be paid? If so, then how much? As hip-hop and dance music became increasingly sample-based, this was a question that began to interest record companies and their lawyers. *The Wall Street Journal* even reported that there was one Polygram Records executive who 'painstakingly listens to dozens of new recordings on other labels for traces of singer James Brown's trademark scream'.[15]

Legal challenges proliferated, particularly when recognisable sounds from famous musicians were sampled or when sample records like 'Pump Up the Volume' made it big in the pop charts, creating revenue that it was worth taking legal action to acquire. 'Our 'Say Kids What Time is It?' was it was so under the radar that Disney never found us for sampling [from *The Jungle Book*]. What could they really get for 500 copies anyway?' says Matt Black. 'But when you had the number one records, the lawyers sort of woke up and it's like, "OK, there's a juicy bit of new business for us here".'

When Coldcut used a vocal by popular Israeli singer Ofra Haza as the main hook in their light-fingered 'Seven Minutes of Madness' remix of Eric B. & Rakim's 'Paid in Full', which turned the US rappers' track into a firework display of samples, Haza demanded and received a substantial slice of the income. Coldcut only received a £700 fee for the remix, although it made European hits out of both the Eric B. & Rakim track and, as a consequence

307

of the exposure, Haza's original 'In Nin'alu'. (Eric B. & Rakim were initially aghast at the remix but later declared it 'dope'[16]).

Black believes the incident actually had a positive impact because it was one of the precedents that built up a legal framework for samples to be cleared: 'So out of a chaotic beginning where we were just doing whatever we liked, it was the Wild West, a framework enabled cooperation on sampling and I think it's worked out OK.'

In artistic terms, sampling removed sounds from their original context and injected them into a new one, often giving them new meaning and purpose. But was a sample a quotation, just as pieces of music throughout time had always quoted or referenced previous pieces of music, or the simple replication of something that already existed? Or was it something essentially new? British producer Stephen Hague suggested that sampling James Brown's idiosyncratic scream was like 'taking his personality'.[18] But musicologist Mark Katz has argued that when a sample is excerpted, digitised and then reconstituted as part of another piece of music, it is fundamentally transformed. 'A sample changes the moment it is relocated,' Katz wrote. 'Every 'Funky Drummer' sample, however recognisable, leads a distinct life in its new home.'[18]

Samples of real musicians' performances added a human vibrancy that could not be achieved by a machine at that point. Breakbeats taken from Black American funk tracks like James Brown's 'Funky Drummer', Lyn Collins' 'Think' and The Winstons' 'Amen, Brother' provided the groove for innumerable electronic dance tracks in the late eighties and early nineties, supplying the rhythmic foundations for entire genres like hardcore, jungle and drum and bass. Using Black American drummers' breaks also appealed to hip-hop-loving white indie bands who could electronically acquire the kind of grooves they were not able to generate themselves. This led to claims that some white musicians were unscrupulously appropriating and exploiting elements of Black performance, extracting them from their context in African-American history and using them as signifiers of 'funk' – often without paying. Others argued that music had always thrived through syncretism and cross-fertilisation, insisting that artistic freedom would be stifled by strict insistence on cultural purity and inflexibly interpreted ownership of styles of expression.

Controversies over the legitimacy of reuse or reinterpretation of other people's material were hardly new in the history of music in general, or electronic music in particular. On their album *My Life in the Bush of Ghosts* back in 1981, Brian Eno and David Byrne had employed the then-novel technique of using voices taped from the radio or excerpts of existing recordings of singers from around the world as their songs' lead vocals – US talk-show hosts and evangelist preachers, a Lebanese devotional singer and a group of Algerians chanting Koranic verses. The album's mixture of found sounds and funky drum loops was a powerful statement that Hank Shocklee of the Bomb Squad production unit described as an important influence on his own high-impact recordings with Public Enemy; Byrne and Eno 'opened my head up to new musical and, most importantly, non-musical experiences,'[19] Shocklee said.

Clearing the extracts used for *My Life in the Bush of Ghosts* proved time-consuming and arduous, as it was hardly common practice in the early eighties. A deceased American preacher's family objected to the use of one of her sermons, the Koranic chanting was removed from later editions of the album after complaints from an Islamic organisation, and Byrne and Eno only found out decades later that the Lebanese singer had never been told that the company she recorded for had given permission for her voice to be sampled.

On its release, *Rolling Stone* reviewer Jon Pareles described the record as 'an undeniably awesome feat of tape editing and rhythmic ingenuity'. But he cautioned, 'like most "found" art, it raises stubborn questions about context, manipulation and cultural imperialism.'[20] *Sounds* journalist Sandy Roberston confronted Eno when the album came out, asking how he felt about the criticism that 'taking black music and adding white boy quasi-intellectual lyrical concepts to it is imperialist.'[21] In response to such accusations, Eno has repeatedly argued that culture has always absorbed ideas from other places and peoples, although sources must be acknowledged and the proper respect shown. 'If you want to be purist about cultural imperialism, [I] would be reduced to English folk music of the 11th century as my source,'[22] he once said.

Matt Black of Coldcut makes a similar point. 'The history of art is the history of appropriation,' he argues, citing classical composers' use of folk melodies in their works. 'You can make a strong argument that no one really invents anything, but any artist is only building on what has gone before, we all have access to the cultural DNA pool of humanity. And arguably, that should be unfettered and encouraged, actually, which is how innovation takes place.'

What was clear was that by 1989, the entire history of recorded music was being seen as potential source material. Sample records had become an established pop genre and the people making them were not only fashionable club DJs anymore. In July that year, a beat-driven collage of Glenn Miller big-band tunes and fifties rock'n'roll called 'Swing the Mood' became the first of three sample-based number-one hits by Jive Bunny and the Mastermixers, a project led by a father-and-son duo from Rotherham.

The success of Jive Bunny's nostalgic medleys was not only a sign that the British public's love of novelty records remained strong, but that the sampling craze had gone mainstream. Indeed, the two top-selling singles of 1989, the first Jive Bunny release and Black Box's Italian piano screamer 'Ride on Time', were both based on other people's records. But amid a torrent of cash-in copycat tracks, the wearying overuse of certain samples and the increasing sense of familiarity with the style, the initial enthusiasm for overtly sample-heavy records started to wane. By the early nineties, what had so recently sounded like the music of the future was already beginning to feel a little dated.

Hi-NRG: Gay Disco Strikes Back
'Hi-NRG took disco music and reinvented it electronically.'
Ian Levine

At midnight, the lights went down, the music stopped and American actor Douglas Lambert stepped up to the microphone.

'In the beginning there was darkness, and God said let there be light, and there was light, and God said let there be man, and God created man,' Lambert intoned theatrically, before delivering the payoff: 'And man created Heaven.'[23]

Lasers sliced through the darkness, strafing the crowd below as the magnificent opening bars of Dan Hartman's disco anthem 'Relight My Fire' erupted from the speakers to screams of delight from hundreds of gay men packed onto the dancefloor.

This is how Ian Levine remembers the opening of Heaven, the London club where he was the resident DJ for a decade, from that first night in December 1979 onwards. With its powerful sound system and trippy lasers and strobes, Heaven was perhaps the greatest nightclub venue of its era in Britain. As an openly gay club, it also played a role in the struggle for emancipation, its

Hi-NRG singer Miquel Brown performing at Hero's nightclub in Manchester in 1983. ©Zoompics/Alamy.

founder Jeremy Norman argued: 'For gay men the dance floor was truly a place of liberation: a place where we could feel free to express our sexuality and the unity of our tribe,' he wrote in his autobiography. 'Gay guys have told me how their first visit to Heaven liberated them, making them realise that they were neither alone nor a freak but one with thousands of other like-minded souls.'[24]

Journalist Alkarim Jivani has pointed out that although gay pubs like the Coleherne in London and the Union in Manchester had operated since the 1950s, the emergence of clubs where hundreds of gay people could gather to carouse openly was much more than just an expression of hedonism: 'Dancing was a hugely symbolic activity – after all, innumerable gay meeting places had been prosecuted only a few years before because they had allowed members of the same sex to dance together.'[25]

Heaven would also operate as a cultural laboratory where sounds like acid house, hardcore and post-Eno ambient music were explored and refined – but above all, it was Britain's temple of hi-NRG, the gay electronic dance music of the eighties. Hi-NRG was a post-Moroder descendant of disco with pounding four-to-the-floor kickdrums, galloping basslines, arpeggiated synths and vocals that were part bittersweet sixties soul and part showtune melodrama, full of forbidden desires and sexual yearning, love and loss, come-ons and double entendres, usually delivered by bold and big-voiced women. It was garishly synthetic and sometimes irredeemably tawdry, as unfeasibly pumped-up as a Tom of Finland superman and as giddying as an amyl nitrate rush – but when it was good, it was glorious.

'These records are about liberation, freedom, physical pleasure,' said author Paul Burston, who was the gay and lesbian editor at *Time Out* magazine. Looking back on how the air at clubs like Heaven used to be thick with amyl fumes, he recalled Pet Shop Boys' Neil Tennant once describing the peak of a hi-NRG track as the 'poppers moment'. 'We all know what that is, the moment where the record soars and becomes hyper-sexualised,' Burston explained. 'It's the bit where everyone opens up their bottle and takes a snort.'[26]

Hi-NRG emerged after disco boomed and then seemed to bust in America in the late seventies and major record labels started to flee what had become an oversaturated and overcommercialised market. The genre's alleged demise was accelerated by the infamous 'Disco Demolition Night' at Comiskey Park in Chicago in July 1979, when a crate full of dance records was symbolically blown up in what resembled a homophobic and racist act of purgation. But although straight, white America declared disco dead in 1979, in the gay and Black clubs, the dance went on. To fulfil the continuing demand for new disco records that was no longer being satisfied by the major labels, gay DJs, musicians and producers in San Francisco, which at the time was the international capital of gay culture, began to set up new independent labels in 1980 and 1981 to serve the city's dancefloors.

Producers who cut tracks for gay-run independent labels like Moby Dick and Megatone did more than just copy the seventies disco sound; they mutated it, making it harder, faster, more electronic. Productions by Patrick Cowley in

San Francisco, Bobby Orlando in New York and Denis and Denyse LePage in Montreal helped to create the style that would become known as hi-NRG: brash, bright and throbbing with sexual vigour.

British producers were soon emulating their style, which music journalists also called 'Boystown' for a while. By 1982, *Record Mirror*, the only mainstream pop magazine in the UK that covered the genre seriously, was printing a weekly 'Boystown disco' chart; it was renamed the hi-NRG disco chart in 1984. The best-of-the year Boystown chart for 1983 in *Record Mirror* was topped by British singer Hazell Dean's wonderfully brazen 'Searchin''. Like a lot of UK Boystown, the track was made simply and cheaply. 'With one Prophet 5 synthesizer and a Linn Drum, I was able to make a record which in its field is now iconic, even though from my point of view, it's quite naive and simple,' recalls its producer, Ian Anthony Stephens. 'I feel I did much better records later, but never as successfully.'

Second on the *Record Mirror* Boystown chart for 1983 was Miquel Brown's 'So Many Men, So Little Time', produced by Heaven DJ Ian Levine. Born in Blackpool, Levine was a gay, Jewish lover of Motown who had earned his renown as a Northern Soul specialist, disco producer and one of the first DJs in Britain to mix records seamlessly. (He later also became known as one of Britain's most prominent and vociferous *Doctor Who* fanatics). Levine said he wrote 'So Many Men, So Little Time' after seeing a man wearing a T-shirt with the phrase printed on it in a Los Angeles club. But his involvement in electronic dance music initially began against his will.

'I never intended or wanted to make electronic music. *Ever*. I wanted to make disco,' he asserts. 'I'd made lots of disco records and had huge hits in the American disco charts, and I was in the middle of making three more disco albums in the middle of 1979 when the whole market collapsed and everyone turned on disco.'

Like other DJs on the gay scene in the UK, Levine filled the gap with imports from the San Francisco independent labels and from places like Italy and Canada. But he also convinced Record Shack, the London shop where he bought his vinyl to play at Heaven, to fund a hi-NRG record he would produce with Irish musician Fiachra Trench. 'Record Shack said that to make 'So Many Men, So Little Time', they'd only got a budget of two grand. So the only way to make a record with £2,000 was to use electronics not live musicians anymore. We only made electronic music because we couldn't afford strings and brass.'

This cheap and cheerful approach paid off. 'Record Shack budgeted that if we sold 10,000 records, we'd break even on our costs. We sold two million.' Levine was jubilant. 'After the world said "disco is dead", it came back in a new guise with a new name: hi-NRG,' he says. (Chicago DJ Frankie Knuckles would also describe house music, another electronic dance sound that evolved in gay clubs after the 'death' of disco, as 'disco's revenge').

Louis Niebur's book *Menergy* chronicles with poignancy how AIDS laid waste to the gay community in San Francisco in the early eighties, killing many of the scene's hi-NRG producers and musicians: people like Patrick Cowley and Sylvester, who had made some of the greatest electronic disco records together. This destruction of San Francisco's dance music infrastructure had the unexpected consequence of 'relocating the centre of high-energy music production to the UK',[27] Niebur wrote.

As in San Francisco, independent British hi-NRG record labels proliferated, with companies like Record Shack, Passion, Electricity, Proto and Fantasia providing the Boystown soundtrack for gay clubs all around the country – clubs that nurtured their own scene hits, many of which were rarely heard outside the gay community. 'There was a specialised gay disco scene, which meant you could make music for the hi-NRG market and it was guaranteed to get played in gay clubs,' explains Ian Anthony Stephens. 'I could release a record which would sell many thousands of copies and make money for everybody involved but never become widely known, because there were enough gay people and gay DJs buying the record for it to be successful in its field without anybody else ever hearing about it.'

Some of the top British hi-NRG producers – like Levine, Les McCutcheon and former Wigan Casino DJ Kev Roberts – came from the Northern Soul circuit and brought the upbeat positivity of its sound with them. 'The music's roots are in Motown rather than funk,' Levine said in a 1983 *Record Mirror* feature that hyped the 'new underground music scene' of 'Boystown disco'. 'What I was playing in the Northern Soul clubs was a progression of sixties music, it was the forerunner of modern Boystown.'[28] Indeed, Levine and Roberts cannily reworked a series of Northern Soul classics like The Tempos' 'Countdown (Here I Come)' as hi-NRG tracks for the gay clubs.

Levine says he was making records that were purpose-built for Heaven and for his favourite club, The Saint, the spectacularly decadent gay megadisco in New York that he adored. 'The Saint was just paradise and the music of The Saint was the most glorious ever made – romantic melodies built onto a disco beat,' he enthuses. In 1984, he distilled all his own creative essences into one utterly thrilling record, 'High Energy' by Evelyn Thomas – 'a song constructed specifically to be the anthem of the music which we all championed,'[28] he said. The musician he called his 'computer genius', Hans Zimmer, who went on to become the Oscar-winning composer of soundtracks for Hollywood films like *The Lion King*, programmed the Fairlight on 'High Energy', as he did on many of Levine's tracks, while a Linn Drum provided the beat. (Levine later said that he came to hate the sound of the Fairlight: 'Horribly electronic and soulless, but it was all the fashion at that time.'[29])

Highlighting the cross-pollination between hi-NRG and more mainstream electronic pop at the time, Levine explains how the compulsively escalating groove that powered 'High Energy' was partly inspired by a Trevor Horn production. 'I'd heard Frankie Goes to Hollywood's 'Relax' and I wanted to combine their rhythm with the rhythm of 'In the Navy' by the Village People – "We want you, we want you, we want you for a new recruit",' he explains, tapping out the beat.

Evelyn Thomas's powerful vocal was an example of how strong women's voices were highly prized by producers like Levine and Stephens. 'I think drama and melancholy is what you look for in hi-NRG, those dramatic female voices and the lyrics about meeting someone new or lost love, meant to appeal to gay men,' explains Stephens, who produced brilliant hi-NRG records for Angie Gold ('Eat You Up') and Swedish model Madleen Kane ('I'm No Angel' and 'Ecstasy').

Stephens argues that although hi-NRG's format was simple, it was unfairly derided as an inferior strain of dance music. 'The hi-NRG records were no less sophisticated than some of the house records that were coming out of Chicago in the eighties, which were just a bassline, a drum machine and maybe a top melodic line and a bit of vocal. But those records were considered cool and hi-NRG wasn't,' he argues. 'I always found it embarrassing to say I made hi-NRG records, I would try and say they were Eurodance records because I think people did look down on them – they thought hi-NRG was throwaway, disposable, machine-like, and that it didn't require any effort to make it. There's always been a snobbery about dance music in general and it was only the rave culture that made it into a mainstream thing and much more acceptable as an art form.'

As the eighties unfolded, AIDS began to wreak devastation on Britain's gay community, just as it had in San Francisco. The first fatality in the UK was recorded in 1981, when a 49-year-old man called John Eaddie died in London's Brompton Hospital. By the mid-eighties, many more gay men had died in Britain, including Douglas Lambert, the actor who delivered the effusive midnight oration at Heaven's opening night, and Terry Higgins, a *Hansard* reporter and DJ who worked as a barman at Heaven, and in whose name the Terrence Higgins Trust HIV-AIDS charity was founded. Also among the early casualties was John Lewis, who had made a couple of prog-synth albums with the BBC Radiophonic Workshop's Brian Hodgson under the name Wavemaker. Lewis had also played synth on M's electro-pop hit 'Pop Muzik' and recorded a hi-NRG track under the name Heat-X-Change. Before his death, he had been working for the BBC on the soundtrack for a season of *Doctor Who*, but was too ill to finish it.

As well as endemic homophobia, there was widespread ignorance about AIDS and how it could be contracted. It was portrayed by right-wing tabloids as the 'gay plague' and newspapers enthusiastically reported statements by religious conservatives like Greater Manchester Police chief constable James Anderton, who accused homosexuals of 'swirling around in a human cesspit of their own making'.[31] Even at the liberal BBC, Brian Hodgson recalls there was a 'major panic' among staff who feared that they could have been exposed to infection through the unfortunate Lewis.

The impact on the hi-NRG scene was dramatic. 'I often think that people don't understand the extent of the tragedy for gay men of my generation and just how many of our friends suffered and died,' said Heaven founder Jeremy Norman. 'Many of the boys that worked in my clubs were to die... I am never sure when a name from that era is mentioned if they are alive or dead.'[32] One of the fatalities was Levine's friend Shaun Buchanan, a young expatriate English DJ at The Saint who was known for his 'sleaze' selections, the downtempo tracks that would be played as the party eased into the morning hours. 'It was so very cruel,' Levine wrote in his privately published autobiography, recalling how Buchanan lost his looks and his hair as he wasted away. 'This was the most insufferably unbearable, dark time for all of us.'[33]

Singer Hazell Dean recalled going to sing at a club in Brighton that was usually packed with dancers and finding that the crowd had been decimated by AIDS or the fear of getting it: 'I walked into the room and there were a few people there but basically it was more or less empty.' But she and fellow British hi-NRG diva Kelly Marie refused to abandon the scene. 'We carried on, but a lot of people didn't, they wouldn't go into the clubs, they wouldn't do the shows.'[34]

Dean explained that she felt she owed a debt to the community because of the mutual affection she had felt since her debut performance at Heaven. 'I felt like a goddess walking onto that stage when I sang 'Searchin'' for the first time and there was always this almost like a love affair in a way, there was such great feeling and love and I wasn't going to throw all that away.' As the scale of the HIV-AIDS crisis became evident, she sang at benefit concerts and visited hospitals to sit with young men who were dying. 'It was heartbreaking, absolutely heartbreaking,' she said. 'To see those young guys... I was so upset...'[35]

As well as mourning, there was fury at the authorities' failure to respond adequately and at the homophobic hysteria in the media. 'We were shocked and angry,' said Jimmy Somerville, who had left Bronski Beat and was making electronic pop records with keyboard player Richard Coles as The Communards. Somerville became an impassioned advocate for the ACT UP movement, which staged direct-action protests to draw attention to the crisis and demand a proper public-health response. 'Richard and I were determined to bring the awareness of AIDS issues into the pop arena,' he said.[36]

The Communards were among the few pop musicians to reference the HIV-AIDS epidemic in their records, both directly and implicitly. Their ballad 'For a Friend' gave voice to the collective trauma of losing loved ones to the disease, while their hi-NRG cover version of 'Don't Leave Me This Way' channelled the spirit of 1970s disco, which Somerville saw as a music of joy and resilience for oppressed communities – a celebration of 'sexual freedom, hedonism and self-empowerment' in the face of adversity.[37]

Stock Aitken Waterman Seek Pop Perfection
'There's nothing wrong with making people happy.'
Pete Waterman

Although hi-NRG never really went mainstream in the US, where gay disco was despised by rock-loving straights, a lot of the most popular tracks – records by Hazell Dean, Evelyn Thomas, the Boys Town Gang and The Weather Girls – did become pop hits in the UK, as did records with hi-NRG inflections like New Order's 'Blue Monday' and Frankie Goes to Hollywood's 'Relax', both of which had pneumatic Boystown grooves. However, Bronski Beat and the Pet Shop Boys, who were genuinely part of gay culture in their own different ways, were among the very few to take hi-NRG seriously as a genre and to afford it the credit it deserved as a music of extraordinary brightness that lit up some of the darkest times.

Another hi-NRG track that became a chart hit, 'You Think You're a Man' by the fabulously grotesque US drag performer Divine, was made in London by an independent entrepreneur of Greek-Cypriot origin called Barry Evangeli, who ran Proto Records. He co-produced the record with the then little-known trio of Mike Stock, Matt Aitken and Pete Waterman. 'Divine had a two-fold career, as a very extreme and off-the-wall underground actor making independent films with [cult director] John Waters, and as a singer who'd had some underground hits in New York but never crossed over. I wanted to make Divine a crossover hit,' explains Evangeli.

With Divine's lascivious growl of a voice and Stock Aitken Waterman's priapic production, 'You Think You're a Man' was ludicrously over-the-top, but Evangeli never saw it as a novelty record intended to amuse or outrage. 'I was trying to make a great dance record with a great artist,' he says. 'I just loved Divine.'

He recalls that there was some nervousness among BBC executives when the twenty-one-stone singer was booked to perform the song on *Top of the Pops* in July 1984. But in the end, Divine toned down the lascivious camp for the programme's prime-time audience of millions – although the BBC still took flak for screening a performance by an unapologetically overweight man in a peroxide-blonde beehive wig and high heels bulging out of a way-too-tight, sparkly, silver dress slashed to the upper thigh on each side. 'Divine was perfect and didn't do anything suggestive or lewd, but I think they still had in the region of about 500 complaints because the audience weren't used to seeing a fat bloke in drag singing,' says Evangeli.

After Divine provided their first hit as producers, the Stock Aitken Waterman team would go on use hi-NRG as the basis for commercial dance hits that would dominate pop radio and mainstream nightclubs for the rest of the decade – although the genre itself would fade as house music and techno took over the gay clubs and its queer characteristics were assimilated into pop's sonic lexicon.

Pete Waterman was a working-class entrepreneur with a talent for spotting commercial opportunities and an abundance of self-confidence. He had worked on the railways, as a gravedigger and as a coalminer, as well as establishing himself as a DJ in his hometown Coventry, where he ran a record shop selling soul tunes and reggae imports from Jamaica. Waterman was responsible for signing Susan Cadogan's Lee Perry-produced song 'Hurt So Good' for the UK and making it a chart success, before working as a producer for Evangeli's independent label Proto, which released hi-NRG tracks by Hazell Dean as well as Divine.

Evangeli took him out to gay clubs like Heaven. 'The records they were playing were bloody dreadful,' Waterman recalls. 'They were cheap records – God, were they made cheaply! But I found them exciting. And so we knew there was a great market for them [on the gay scene] and we focused on 12-inches, we focused on what we knew we could sell. We knew we could make better records than these guys because our technology was better and we knew more about songs.'

Stock Aitken Waterman's first number-one hit, 'You Spin Me Right Round' by Dead or Alive, exemplified their initial hi-NRG-derived style: exuberant refrain, protrusive synthetic bassline, hard electronic drums and a Saturday-night-out-on-the-town feeling of hedonistic abandon. 'I just wanted a record that took your head off in a club, you know, where there were no real instruments on it but when you played it in a club, it would smash every window in the place and the door would fall off,' says Waterman.

He had recognised what would be popular in mainstream nightclubs across Britain – gay disco music straightened up for the pop market with slightly higher production values and choruses that anyone could sing along with. 'Our style was updated Motown – high-energy Motown,' he says. As the hits started coming, he came to see his production house as a contemporary British version of Motown's Hitsville USA studios, an unashamedly commercial enterprise making uncerebral pop for the masses; he even called his PWL studios the Hit Factory, while his PWL Records' slogan was 'The Sound of a Bright Young Britain'. 'We just loved pop music,' he declares.

The pop music Stock Aitken Waterman made for singers like Kylie Minogue and Jason Donovan was simple and cheerful, all shiny surfaces, uncomplicated emotions, major-key melodies and upbeat rhythms. It was also almost completely electronic. Waterman loved how technology put the producer in total control. 'The Linn Drum machine to me was like the greatest blessing, because suddenly it meant I didn't need a drummer,' he explains. 'And then I just thought, "Well, why have any conventional instruments? Why don't we just chuck them all out the window?"'

The producers at his PWL Studios used a Linn 9000 unit to programme their drums but usually replaced its sounds with samples; a Yamaha DX7 digital synth supplied most of the basslines while string and brass sounds came from a Fairlight, according to one of Waterman's crack engineer-mixers, Phil Harding. Later, they also used drum loops sampled from dance tracks. New technology was adopted with gleeful inventiveness, like the Publison Infernal Machine, a pitch-shifting sampler that they used to create the cheekily infectious 'tay-tay-tay-tay' vocal hook on Mel and Kim's hit 'Respectable'. Harding said that if a live bass guitar was ever recorded for a track, Waterman would often insist it be replaced by a synth bassline.

Like British record producers had done for decades, Stock Aitken Waterman used Black American music as source material. To keep their records fresh, they picked up new sounds from 12-inch imports and adapted them into their own productions. By 1987, house music was superseding hi-NRG as their primary influence, with Mel and Kim's 'Showing Out' owing an audible debt to Steve 'Silk' Hurley's Chicago anthem 'Jack Your Body'. Waterman says he was kept updated on developments in house music by BBC Radio 1 dance DJ Pete Tong, who also worked for London Records, the label of Stock Aitken Waterman-produced trio Bananarama: 'Pete Tong was coming down, playing us all these records out of Chicago, so we were at the cutting edge of what's going on.'

Harding recalled that after Tong convinced Waterman that house was the coming trend, he was ordered to 'sample some of the Chicago house beats and loops and stabs' for the Mel and Kim record. 'We got somewhere close to their sound, but with our UK commercial twist on it,' he said.[38]

Just as they had drunk deep of the vital essences of hi-NRG, Stock Aitken Waterman exploited all manner of other modish dancefloor idioms: elements of Latin freestyle, the Soul II Soul beat, glittering Italian house pianos, New York garage grooves, even a few acid house stylings. They also benefited from PWL Studios' team of bright young engineers, who were often out clubbing in London. 'They were quite wild and very creative, so they'd bring some records in and if we'd like a sound, they'd try and get that sound,' Waterman says. 'Sometimes we would use sounds from dub – we weren't making reggae records but we did like some of the effects that they used.'

Harding said it was 'a PWL custom to "plot" songs or productions from other successful or dance underground tracks that were around'. 'Plotting' songs, he explained, 'meant that you would "allow yourself to be influenced by" another song to write a new song in that style'. Often, two different songs might be used, perhaps taking the groove from one and the melody from another, 'so as to lead the originator and listener away from its origins'.[37]

Youth (Martin Glover), whose band Brilliant were produced by Waterman, recalled how it worked in practice: 'We'd be co-writing with them, starting a new song, and Pete Waterman would come in with a handful of New York import 12-inches with him, and he'd go to the record player and say, "Right, that's the fucking bassline!", and then he'd play another record and go, "That's the beat!"'[40]

This was pop distilled to its essence as commercial product and many rock journalists despised it. *NME* writer David Quantick even denounced Stock Aitken Waterman as 'the acceptable face of Thatcherism',[41] a savage insult at that time in British pop culture. Waterman says he detected 'an element of snobbery' in journalists' criticism: 'We made music for the public and they hated that.'

He also stresses that his PWL Records was just as much an independent label as Daniel Miller's Mute, with similarly uncompromising values in terms of artistic autonomy – just with a completely different approach to electronic music. Another PWL slogan described Stock Aitken Waterman's music as 'the soundtrack of a generation'. It was certainly the soundtrack to the late Thatcher years – by 1990, they had sold over 10,000,000 records and had more than a hundred chart hits in the UK.

But just a few months later, towards the end of 1990, the number ones stopped coming and the hit rate began to fall as their formula began to lose its mass appeal. Looking back several decades later, Waterman says he believes the trio's increasing wealth deadened their creative urges. 'The minute the big money started really rolling in, it spoilt it because we'd never done it for money,' he insists.

'It wasn't about money, it was about music – it was about writing a three-minute pop song that everybody loved.'

Forgemasters in Sheffield, 1989. ©David Bocking.

10

EMOTIONS ELECTRIC

House, Techno, Acid

The Foundations of UK House

'This was *our* music all of a sudden. It felt new and it had so much energy. It was also community music, because you could make it from home, so people that you knew were making it, and then it became really personal. Before, you'd have needed to know how to play an instrument, but with the electronic equipment, you could transmit that energy yourself.'

Winston Hazel, DJ and member of Forgemasters

WHEN MARSHALL JEFFERSON, FRANKIE KNUCKLES, Fingers Inc and Adonis brought their Chicago house sound to Britain for a club tour in March 1987, they encountered a curious mixture of bemusement and adulation. At some of the more mainstream venues, the audiences seemed disoriented by the fierce jacking power of a music that was still in its developmental phase. 'I saw a lot of wide eyes out in the crowd, like, what the hell is this, you know?' Jefferson recalled later. But when the Americans played the Haçienda in Manchester and Rock City in Nottingham, the dancers already knew the early Chicago house tracks well. The response was fanatical. 'They were losing their heads out there,'[1] Jefferson marvelled.

House music had originated in Chicago as an electronically-rendered, stripped-down descendant of disco a few years earlier, taking its name from DJ Frankie Knuckles' mainly Black and gay club The Warehouse. It wasn't completely unknown to the British public when Jefferson and his compatriots arrived in the UK. Farley 'Jackmaster' Funk and Daryl Pandy's 'Love Can't Turn Around' had been a Top 10 hit in September 1986 and Steve 'Silk' Hurley's 'Jack Your Body' even reached number one in January 1987. But as Jefferson saw for himself, it was in the north and Midlands where house had established itself most deeply, particularly at clubs that had adventurous music policies and multiethnic clienteles, the kind of places that would provide the environment for British reinterpretations of the music to flourish.

There are various claims for the title of the first British house record, but the hi-NRG producer Ian Levine insists it was 'On the House', a copycat Chicago-style record he made in 1986 with Hans Zimmer. Levine describes the song – a campy 'Love Can't Turn Around' reinterpretation that was credited to Midnight Sunrise with Nellie 'Mixmaster' Rush featuring Jackie Rawe – as part-tribute, part-parody. 'We all dressed as Chicago gangsters in the video, it was hysterical,' he says.

One of the precursors to house, Colonel Abrams' 'Trapped', was produced by Richard James Burgess, former drummer with UK synth-pop polymaths Landscape. Burgess made 'Trapped' with Abrams in New York using a simple synth-and-drum-machine set-up; it sounded relatively basic because it was originally intended to be a demo for the track, not the finished recording. 'I couldn't have guessed that was going to wind up being a proto-house track at all, I was just following my intuition,' says Burgess, who had absorbed ideas for the production from New York's clubs. 'I'd love to say, "Oh yeah, I was trying to create house music," but that wouldn't be true.'

When the first Chicago house tracks started to arrive in the UK on import in the mid-eighties, some listeners were perplexed by their unsophisticated minimalism. 'The early house was really raw, it was just made on a drum machine with some guy on a microphone saying "lose control" or whatever,' says DJ Eddie Richards, who started dropping tracks into the electronic sets that he and Colin Faver were playing at Camden Palace in London. 'People would ask, "Why are you playing this stuff? It's just a drum machine!" But to me, it was exciting, it was different.' Richards would soon start cutting his own house tracks – his spiritual deep-house tune 'Page 67', made with another UK instigator, Mr C (Richard West), was released in 1987.

Chicago house and Detroit techno producers had absorbed influences from British electro-pop, as well as from disco and from German and Italian electronic tracks; in dance music, ideas passed back and forth between continents, mutating and evolving in a continuous process of cultural diffusion. The American house and techno originators' use of relatively cheap and basic technology, particularly Roland's TR-808 and TR-909 drum machines and TB-303 bassline generator, became an inspiration for British musicians, just as fanzine urgings to learn three guitar chords then form a band had inspired young punks in the seventies.

By 1987, young producers all over the UK were making house records in various styles and with varying degrees of flair and competence: Chicago-derived jack-tracks from T-Cut-F and Groove (both from Nottingham), jazz funk-inflected textures from Hotline (from Huddersfield), upbeat dance-pop from Krush (Sheffield/Nottingham) and The Beatmasters (London). Some of them had been electro heads, breakdancers or jazz funk all-dayer devotees, others had come from the post-punk alternative scene. A few veterans of a previous multicultural dance craze, 2-Tone, also had a go at making house tunes: 'Faith, Hope and Charity' by FX was a rework of a Fun Boy Three song by a line-up including The Specials' Neville Staple, while 'Tired of Being Pushed Around' by Two Men, a Drum Machine and a Trumpet was made by ex-members of The Beat.

'Those early British house tracks had a kind of naive charm, with their Korg basslines, 808 and 909 drum machines and little riffs from analog synths,' says Graeme Park, a member of Groove and a DJ at The Garage in Nottingham, one of the first clubs in the country to embrace the house sound. In December 1987, the *NME* was already heralding what it called 'the British house boom', with journalist Simon Witter enthusing about a generation of 'young house addicts' trying to create a domestic version of the Chicago groove. Although many of these efforts were still derivative – Witter complained of 'weedy rhythm machines, plastic piano frills and a conspicuous lack of originality' – there were some significant exceptions.[2]

One of them involved Mike Pickering of Quando Quango, who had formed a new band, T-Coy, with salsa-loving percussionist Simon Topping, formerly of Factory Records punk-funk band A Certain Ratio. By this point, Pickering was DJing at the Haçienda's Nude Night every Friday with partner Martin Prendergast as MP2, championing the Chicago house sound but mixing up it with hip-hop and electronic soul; the era of 'house music all night long' was yet to come in British clubs. Topping would even play a segment of Latin records each week and young Black dancers from the Foot Patrol crew would show off their moves in a spectacular jazz-fusion style. 'It was more eclectic and creative in those days,' Pickering says. T-Coy's debut, 'Carino', a hypnotic house groove with cascading Latin-jazz piano and clattering timbales that Topping described as 'sort of a blend of Tito Puente and Adonis',[3] showed that UK house could add up to more than the sum of its American influences.

Another important trio of British house innovators who also released their debut in 1987 were Lawrence 'Kid' Batchelor, Keith Franklin and Leslie Lawrence, three young Londoners who called themselves Bang the Party; children of the Windrush generation who came from reggae, funk and hip-hop backgrounds. Batchelor had an elder brother who built speaker boxes for sound systems, but hip-hop had shown him how technology could transform music.

'What the DJs were doing creatively with the [Technics] SL-1200 turntables, what they were able to do with breakbeats using that technology, it was just so fresh, so innovative, so forward. Hip-hop changed the game for me,' he says. While he was still a teenager, Batchelor's former schoolmate Jazzie B gave him a start as a junior DJ on the Soul II Soul sound system, but he also managed to get guest slots with London's premier electronic dance music DJs at that point, Colin Faver and Eddie Richards at the Camden Palace.

Bang the Party's sound could be deliciously sensual, like their debut tracks 'I Feel Good All Over' and 'Jacques Theme' in 1987, or libidinously funky, like their dancefloor anthems 'Release Your Body' and 'Bang Bang You're Mine'. They recorded at Addis Ababa, one of London's few Black-owned studios, which was set up by Lagos-born Tony Addis after he fled political violence in Nigeria; Soul II Soul, Aswad and Jah Shaka also recorded there. 'Addis Ababa had been cultivated over years as a reggae studio with a lot of analog equipment. That's why although our music was house, although it was electronica, it always had that *heavy* Black influence, that *serious* blackness,' explains Batchelor.

Bang the Party's early recordings were also inspired by dancing to house music at clubs like The Lift, a mainly Black gay night at Stallions in Soho where Keith Franklin's brother Mel was a DJ. 'It was just off the hook in there, really advanced musically,' says Batchelor. 'When everyone else in London was listening to rare groove, I was listening to some serious jacking tunes, and it's from that experience we'd end up in the studio and put together some *wild house music.*

While T-Coy explored Latin stylings, Addis and Batchelor's label, Warriors Dance, added Caribbean and African elements to Chicago house sounds on tracks like the percussive trance-out 'Koro-Koro' by No Smoke or Bang the Party's 'Rubbadub' with its proto-jungle breakbeat, rolling percussion echoes and shearing metal noise. 'People started labelling it "tribal" but it was actually very early Afro-house,' argues Batchelor. 'Those tunes were coming from us young geezers just experimenting in the studio, coming out with sounds that were a twist on what was happening in London in particular because of the ethnic make-up of the city, inspired by the energies that were being created by the scenes we were involved in. The multiculti mix – it's a potent cocktail, isn't it?'

The Warriors Dance label's recordings were vital documents of their era in the capital, when DJs like Batchelor drew on the musical cultures that they grew up with in the UK to create British variants of house music. 'Pure, unadulterated Afro-futuristic music – that's what I was doing,' he says. 'A British version of Afrofuturism.'

Acid House and Rave Culture

'It was a unique time – a time of intense creativity, freedom, breaking boundaries.'
Lawrence Batchelor

'Acieeed!... Acieeeed!... Acieeeeed!... Acieeeeeed!' It was startling to hear them for the first time, these shrills of ecstatic abandon, screams of ardour for the sound of acid house, erupting across the dancefloor as a Roland TB-303 bassline started to bubble and squawk through the speakers. It was the spring of 1988 and the club was called Spectrum, the first large-scale acid house night in the capital, a self-proclaimed 'theatre of madness' that was packing out Heaven in London with hundreds of wild-eyed youths in Ibiza-influenced hippie-pirate chic – smiley-face T-shirts, baggy jeans, tie-dyed tops, beads and bandanas – *on a Monday night.*

'On one every Monday!' declared Spectrum's psychedelic eyeball flyer, using the idiom of the initiated, the ones who already knew what was invigorating the passions of this new cohort of electronic dance music devotees: 3,4-methylenedioxymethamphetamine, the drug better known as ecstasy. What would become known as 1988's 'Summer of Love' was already on the horizon, and the rise of the E-charged acid house scene was to open up a whole new chapter for electronic music in Britain.

While house music had been adopted by hardcore dancers in cities like Manchester, Sheffield and Nottingham when the first Chicago imports came in on labels like Trax and DJ International, it had initially caused divisions in London, where the underground clubs and thriving warehouse party scene were dominated by hip-hop and the vintage funk and soul styles collectively known as 'rare groove'. Like electro before it, house was sometimes dismissed as metronomic, soulless, anti-musical; at the time, homophobia was widespread and house was also derided as 'gay music'. London house pioneer Noel Watson recalled that when he and his brother Maurice started playing Chicago tracks at their club Delirium in 1987, hip-hop fans abused them and threw cans and bottles: 'Guys would come up to us and say: "Don't play that gay music or we'll come in there and beat you up!"'[4] Haçienda DJ Mike Pickering recounts a similar story of playing house in London and getting booed: 'Someone said to me, "Why are you playing this homo music?"'

The sheer otherworldliness of Chicago acid and Detroit techno tracks also astonished people. When DJ Dave Dorrell played Phuture's 'Acid Trax' at London's Raw club, 'people just stood there in shock', he remembers. But house also attracted committed partisans in London who believed fervently in the new sound and refused to stop playing it, like Mark Moore. 'Some people really didn't understand house at first, but when they started taking ecstasy, then they got it,' says Moore. 'I'm not saying you needed to take ecstasy to appreciate the music because you certainly didn't need to – but it was heard in a very different way when you were under the influence.'

By the summer of 1988, the atmosphere in London's clubs felt as if it had been electrified by the synergy of music and MDMA. At the club nights where ecstasy first proliferated in London, like Shoom, Spectrum and Future, DJs like Paul Oakenfold, Danny Rampling, Trevor Fung and Nancy Noise were initially mixing house with the kind of blissed-out European pop and indie-dance tracks that were collectively labelled Balearic, influenced by the eclectic, sun-dappled music they had heard DJ Alfredo playing at Amnesia in Ibiza the previous summer.

The beatific Balearic style became an enduring subgenre of dance music and would be reinterpreted with melodic eloquence by British musicians like A Man Called Adam. But fast and hypnotic house, techno and garage tracks from the US, and their European derivatives, would increasingly come to dominate the clubs as ecstasy surged across the country that summer, giving dancers a rush of chemical energy. 'Week by week it just kept getting even more intense,' recalls Jon Dasilva, one of the DJs at the Haçienda's midweek acid house night Hot, which started in July 1988.

The almost animalistic fervour for house and techno, the sheer energy rushing through a loved-up crowd synced to the beat at the peak of the night, was awe-inspiring to witness; ecstasy's empathogenic effects triggered powerful feelings of communal interconnection that amplified the emotional impact of the music. The acid house scene of 1988 may have had many precursors – the futurist club circuit, jazz-funk all-dayers, electro and hip-hop, reggae sound system dances – but for those who were involved at the time, it genuinely seemed like something extraordinary.

Oona King, a young clubber who felt this new energy transform the atmosphere that summer at the Haçienda, said that it 'felt like a triumph of collectivism'; something inclusive but also intimate. 'It wasn't about money, clothes, or status, it was about a shared physical and emotional experience,'[5] said King, who would later become a Labour Party MP. There were many stories of personal and collective transformation that year, many of them catalysed by MDMA. Journalist Sheryl Garratt described her experiences at London clubs like Shoom in utopian terms, as if everything had turned dayglo overnight. 'It felt like the barriers that had separated us were falling,' she wrote. 'Age, class, gender, sexuality... For a brief, heady time, we really were one nation under a groove.'[6]

From 1988 onwards, increasingly widespread consumption of MDMA caused a variety of side-effects for British electronic music, both immediate and long-term. As a drug that altered aural perceptions as well as physical sensations, ecstasy had a significant impact on the way electronic dance music was experienced and, as a consequence, on how it was made. Song structures disintegrated into fragments of lyric and dubbed-out sound effects; tracks extended into long, repetitive, trancelike grooves. The beat became *everything*; it had to go on.

House and techno tracks became longer, freakier and more rhythmically intense as the drug made dancers more receptive to unusual sonic textures and weird electronic noises. At the Haçienda, Jon Dasilva would embellish his mixes with acapellas and atmospheric excerpts from BBC sound effects records. 'It was exciting because people had their minds opened with the chemicals and the music you played could actually be very left-field – acid house was like house music's experimental wing,' he says.

MDMA also acted as an evangelising force that brought a mass audience of white British youth into what had previously been a subcultural dance music scene; this simultaneously boosted the market for house and techno records. Tim Raidl of Jack Trax, which licensed early Chicago and Detroit tracks for UK release, said the label was initially selling a couple of thousand copies a week. 'Then there was a sudden change when ecstasy came into the scene,' he told author Matt Anniss. 'Overnight we were selling 30,000 records a week. We couldn't keep up with demand.'[7] Another side-effect of this rapid popularisation was that increasing numbers of young producers started trying to make house and techno tracks themselves, some of them taking the music in unexpected directions.

The influx of newcomers was not universally welcomed, however. DJ Parrot (Richard Barratt), one of the early champions of house music in Sheffield, says that for the first couple of years, MDMA was 'an amazing thing, bringing a massive wave of energy and goodwill to dancers and producers' – but then the sheer number of younger converts arriving in the clubs transformed what had been a subcultural, multiracial scene into 'a huge mainstream business attracting a huge amount of mainstream people'.

As an indication of how the culture changed, DJ Greg Wilson cites a piece of footage filmed in 1986 at a party in Moss Side, Manchester: a crowd of Black youths jacking hard to Chicago house, cheering and blowing their whistles in sheer joy, two years before the ecstasy-inspired Summer of Love brought hordes of young white ravers onto the dancefloor. Wilson says these Black pioneers eventually got crowded out of the scene by the E-head novices; with little space left to really *dance* amid the sweat-soaked, arm-waving masses, 'they moved on and invented something new, as they've always done': styles like jungle, drum and bass, and UK garage.

But during 1988's Summer of Love and the first few years of the rave scene that followed it, an artistically fertile multi-ethnic musical culture flourished. Black British rave DJ Jumpin Jack Frost (Nigel Thompson), who would later become a key figure in drum and bass, recalled 'people from all kinds of backgrounds, colours, nationalities, all coming together… It was a revolution, a cultural explosion.'[8] Some of the most exciting clubs of the acid house period thrived on this diversity, like RIP (Revolution in Progress), a delirious sweatbox of a party that opened in the summer of 1988 at an old warehouse in Clink Street, near London Bridge, in a haze of dry ice, strobes, smiley-face graffiti, searing 303s and dancers utterly possessed by the rhythm.

'RIP was just totally dark, you couldn't see in front of you, sweat would be dripping off the ceiling, strobes flashing all the time – totally intense,' says Eddie Richards, who played there alongside Kid Batchelor of Bang the Party, Mr C and Shock sound system. As well as the DJs, there would sometimes be rappers, singers, drummers and even an occasional trumpeter, former Sade player Gordon Matthewman, blasting his horn through the clouds of artificial fog.

The fervid enthusiasms of the moment carried within them the earliest hints of new subgenres of house and techno. A photograph taken in the summer of 1988 by *Time Out* nightlife editor Dave Swindells, later published in his book *Acid House As It Happened*, showed future drum and bass kingpins Fabio (Fitzroy Heslop) and Grooverider (Raymond Bingham), two young party heads in bandanas, amid the seething crowd outside The Trip in central London, raving in the street to a soundtrack of car stereos and police sirens after the club shut at 3 a.m. The following year, Fabio and Grooverider would become resident DJs at Rage at Heaven, the club where they would assemble a high-velocity sonic narrative out of breakbeat house tracks and hard-riffing European techno – a style that became a formative influence on the emergence of hardcore and jungle.

Pirate radio stations also fuelled the growing demand for house and techno in 1988 and 1989. In London, Jazzy M had been broadcasting his *Jackin' Zone* selection on his show on LWR for several years, while Kiss FM had DJs like Paul 'Trouble' Anderson, Colin Faver, Colin Dale, Danny Rampling and Steve Jackson's show *The House That Jack Built*. Pirate broadcasters had proliferated in the eighties, confounding the authorities' efforts to shut them down. The Department of Trade and Industry increased the frequency of its raids on illegal stations from 97 in 1983 to over 300 in 1987, according to Stephen Hebditch's book *London's Pirate Pioneers*. In 1988, the acid house explosion pushed the figures even higher and there were 444 raids around the country. 'This was the year that the DTI lost control of the FM dial in London,'[9] Hebditch said.

Equipment to set up a new station could now be bought for less than £2,000, while transmitters were more reliable and easier to set up. 'Anyone wanting to start a station could now go to a handful of companies, set up by the engineers of long-departed stations, who would sell you the kit off the shelf and give you instructions on how to plug it together,'[10] Hebditch explained.

By 1989, the peak year for huge illegal raves like Sunrise, Energy, Biology and Back to the Future, dozens of pirate stations were broadcasting house music all day and all night long, seven days a week. The 1990 Broadcasting Act eventually signalled a crackdown, increasing penalties for broadcasting without a licence, but in the meantime, the pirates ruled the airwaves, providing a forum for new dance music that legal stations – with rare exceptions like Stu Allen's *Bus Diss* show on Piccadilly Radio in Manchester – were not offering.

Pirates like Centreforce, Fantasy, Sunrise and Dance FM also accelerated the development of the music in the UK by inspiring people to start making their own tracks. One of them was Peter Ford, a strikingly stick-thin, pale and cerebral musician who loved Marc Bolan as well as Marshall Jefferson. 'I was living a very basic life at the time, living in a bedsit, but I had pirate radio access,' he recalled. 'They played this kind of new electronic, abstract, body music, whatever you want to call it – acid – and I was off.'[11] Taking the name Baby Ford, he recorded 'Oochy Koochy', an acid-disco track with a speaker-punishing bassline that became an ecstasy anthem in London in 1988. His recordings then became increasingly adventurous, taking him deep into minimalistic experimental techno. 'It's music for parties,' he insisted. 'But parties with a twist.'[12]

House and techno provided the soundtrack for a mass youth movement in the UK, ensuring that electronic music would continue to be a dominant force in British pop culture for decades to come. But initially, the music remained strictly underground in its country of origin. Ford said that when he first went to play in the US in 1990, he was astonished that some people he met had 'never heard of house music, yet it was born in America'.[13]

The US originators of house and techno were amazed and occasionally baffled by the adoration their records generated in the UK, although they didn't always approve of the British reinterpretations. Some American musicians and DJs built international careers as a result of their sound's European popularity, but others were eclipsed by the Europeans who had embraced their music so passionately, creating a scene around it that grew increasingly detached from its origins as a musical expression of marginalised and oppressed communities. Just as Black American blues had been adopted and adapted by white musicians in the sixties and then commodified as rock music, house and techno became the basis for a globally popular entertainment format, but its originators were not always fully recognised or rewarded.

Back in 1988, however, this was still a music of the underground and the makers of British acid house records were still mainly cultural mavericks who liked strange sounds – people like 400 Blows' Tony Thorpe and Andrew Beer, who assembled a motley cast of obscure UK producers for their *Acid Beats* compilations. There was also Adrenalin M.O.D., an ethnically-mixed London trio whose few recordings vibrated with lysergic vigour, and Brian Dougans, later of Future Sound of London, who created the rabid riff-monster 'Stakker Humanoid' improbably championed by Pete Waterman on *The Hitman and Her*, a late-night TV show shot in rowdy, beer-drenched, high-street nightclubs.

Further out on the left-field fringes, Akin Fernandez's compellingly strange Irdial Discs label was releasing deranged acidic epics like Aqua Regia's 'Pump Up the LEDs to Red, Take Some Drugs and Shake Your Head'. But perhaps the most unlikely electronic dance music producer was Rob Davis, the guitarist from seventies glam-rock group Mud, who made Balearic-style tracks with Spectrum DJ Paul Oakenfold (and co-wrote 'Can't Get You Out of My Head' for Kylie Minogue).

DJs were now taking an increasingly central role in electronic music culture, as artistic creators as well as scene animateurs. Like the sample-record boom, many early acid track-makers were DJs, like Dave Lee (later known as Joey Negro), who was involved in making acidulated garage tracks with M-D-Emm, or RIP's Eddie Richards, who recorded a wild 303 romp called 'Acid Man' under the pseudonym Jolly Roger, using a suitably druggy sample from a Cheech & Chong skit.

In another example of how attempted imitation can inadvertently produce novel results, Richards said he was initially only trying to create a longer version of a Chicago acid track, 'Shout' by Jack Frost and the Circle Jerks, so he could play it in the clubs. His recollection of the process illustrates the makeshift nature of the techniques that some UK producers were using at the time: 'I tried to copy the acid line on my 303 and couldn't get it quite right – it was really similar, but it wasn't the same. I also couldn't figure out how to sync the 303 with my 909 drum machine. So basically I did it by ear and when it started drifting out of time, I stopped the tape and put in a sample where I'd stopped it.' His attempted copycat track unexpectedly became a hit.

'Acid Man' was one of the records reportedly banned by the BBC in the autumn of 1988 after a moral panic about drug-taking in acid house clubs, with right-wing tabloid *The Sun* revelling in its adopted role as the protector of vulnerable youngsters with a series of headlines like 'Acid house horror', 'Evil of ecstasy' and 'Girl drops dead at acid disco'. The BBC is said to have prohibited the playing of any record with the word 'acid' in its title or lyrics, including D-Mob's 'We Call It Acieed' and 'It's a Trip' by Children of the Night, which Conservative MP John Heddle claimed was an advertisement for drugs. 'Its explicit message is to encourage children to take the hallucinatory drug ecstasy,'[14] he asserted.

Emerging not long after the Conservative Party won its third consecutive term in office, acid house and rave culture thrived on human desires for collective activity and communal celebration that were not being fulfilled by the Thatcher government's creed of consumerist individualism. As raves brought together ever larger numbers of young people for illegal, drug-fuelled mass revels across Britain, they were seen as a threat to public order and to the welfare of the nation's youth. But despite the efforts of self-appointed moral guardians and the police crackdowns that followed, the scene continued to grow – soundtracked increasingly not only by US imports, but by British producers' reimaginings of American house, techno and garage styles.

A Guy Called Gerald and 808 State

'It might sound strange now, but at the time [in the late eighties] doing acid house music was really, really different. It was alternative.'
A Guy Called Gerald[15]

Gerald Simpson was a dancer. At night, the teenager from Manchester's Moss Side would go out dancing to the funk, soul and electro tunes he loved. After school, he and his brother would study contemporary dance and jazz moves at college. They were the only boys in the class.

A drummer used to come into the college to bang out rhythms for the dance students' warm-up sessions; Simpson bought a little drum machine so he could do the same at home, plugging it into his mother's Amstrad stereo system. 'I got intrigued by how I could programme this drum machine. It sounded like some of the electro stuff and I was thinking, "Wow, I could probably do 'Planet Rock'-type drums like on this",' he recalls. 'And I remember going to the [Manchester] Apollo and seeing Herbie Hancock with

A Guy Called Gerald and Graham Massey from 808 State playing live at Victoria Baths in Manchester, 1988. ©PYMCA/Avalon/Alamy.

Grand Mixer DST; I had heard the scratching on 'Rockit' but when I saw him doing it live, it really registered. So soon I was doing beats on this drum machine and scratching on my mum's Amstrad and recording it on tape.' He had also been enthused by hearing the Broken Glass track on the *Street Sounds UK Electro* compilation and realising Black youths from his hometown could get their music onto vinyl.

Simpson established his own hip-hop crew, Scratch Beatmasters, with a rapper named Nicky Lockett, alias MC Tunes. They started doing electro-funk jams in his mother's attic, inspired by the music he was hearing at clubs like Legend. He describes the crew as a 'b-boy sound system', inspired by the reggae collectives that he grew up around in Moss Side; they even built their own speaker boxes from wood lifted from building sites and components pilfered from a Maplin Electronics store. One of their gigs was at a Salvation Army centre in the Ancoats district, which had become a gathering point for local hip-hop fanatics and breakdancers because it had turntables, and where dexterous young DJ duo Andrew Barker and Darren Partington – who wore matching grey-and-maroon-striped Adidas tracksuits and called themselves The Spinmasters – would hold sessions.

The Scratch Beatmasters and The Spinmasters both appeared on a rough-and-ready hip-hop EP issued under the collective name of Hit Squad MCR, along with Martin Price – the co-owner of the Eastern Bloc record shop who had a background in left-field music – and Graham Massey of post-punk experimentalist band Biting Tongues, whose interest in electronic music dated back to seeing Hawkwind live in the 1970s and being excited by their 'untutored electronics'. In the years that followed, some of the most thrilling electronic music to come out of Manchester would be made by ex-members of the short-lived Hit Squad MCR crew.

As well as hip-hop, Simpson had started trying to emulate the acid house and Detroit techno tracks he heard Stu Allen playing on his Radio Piccadilly show. A cassette of his home recordings was given to Allen, who aired the tape on his show. 'I was calling myself DJ Ski when I was doing jams in the attic at my mum's house, then I changed my name to Jackmaster G. But what happened was the first time Stu Allen played my tunes, I hadn't put any name on the cassettes. So on the radio he said, "That was a tune sent in by a guy called Gerald." And from then on, I called myself A Guy Called Gerald.'

Simpson, Price and Massey also started to record together under the name 808 State, a tribute to the Roland TR-808 drum machine. The trio's disparate backgrounds in electro, jazz-funk, hip-hop and post-punk weirdness combined to make the spiky machine grooves of 808 State's first recordings, the *Quadrastate* EP and the *Newbuild* album, more unusual than many of the tracks being made by other British musicians who more closely mimicked the records coming out of Chicago and Detroit. Massey loved the wonky, atonal frequencies of acid house, a sound that was furthest from American dance music's R&B roots: 'I think acid house caught the imagination because it was its own little world, it was alien, it just sounded so twisted and so out-there that it really connected to people that had grown up on alternative music,' he says.

Massey's soprano saxophone-playing and a trilling sample of a Canadian loon bird also gave a retro-futuristic, Fourth World exotica sheen to 808 State's 'Pacific State', a track that eventually became so revered by ravers that it felt like 'writing the national anthem', Massey once said. 'I know it sounds like an ego thing but it wasn't, because it felt like that tune belonged to the whole culture,' he explained. 'Something that a whole collective of people put a new value on.'[16]

But the trio's partnership wouldn't last long. Simpson quit 808 State amid a dispute over the authorship of 'Pacific State', although he had already recorded the track that would establish him as one of Britain's pre-eminent producers of electronic dance music. 'Voodoo Ray' was a piece of cosmic wizardry that combined a clanging Roland SH-101 bassline, twittering acid melodies and the wordless ululations of singer Nicola Collier running forwards and backwards simultaneously. The title came from a sample of British comedian Peter Cook from his bawdy *Derek and Clive (Live)* album with Dudley Moore; according to Simpson, who had been a collector of spoken-word records since using them in his hip-hop mixes, Cook actually said 'voodoo rage' but his sampler cut off the ending of the second word because it didn't have enough memory.

He explained at the time that the record was made for his own nocturnal community, the young Black dancers who were early adopters of house in Manchester. "'Voodoo Ray' is based on the fusion house/jazz dancing of the Manchester dance crew Foot Patrol,'[17] he told the *NME* in 1988. A fan of Miles Davis and Chick Corea's electric jazz-fusion records, Simpson was seeking to give his records a mysterious, spectral feel. 'Spirit music,' he called it, channelling house, techno, electro-funk and what he describes as 'that inventive futuristic bug I caught from Chick Corea.'

'Voodoo Ray' became one of the most cherished UK-made house tracks. But even as Simpson was being hailed as the creator of an authentically British transmutation of house music and his record was inciting mania at raves in warehouses, aircraft hangars and open fields, he was still working at McDonald's in Manchester, living in a squat and giving interviews from telephone boxes.

In the years that followed, he would go on to create a 'British blacktronic Afrofuturism',[18] as Hillegonda Rietveld described it, with his feverish jungle releases on his own Juice Box label. 808 State, meanwhile, with The Spinmasters replacing Simpson, would go on to build heavy-riffing rave bangers like 'Cubik' and 'In Yer Face' and make one of the landmark British electronic albums of the rave era.

808 State's *90* was one of four remarkable albums released by British house musicians in 1990 that highlighted how sonically diverse the UK's fast-developing electronic dance music was becoming. Bang the Party's *Back to Prison* had a wickedly funky Afro-garage vibe, while Electribe 101's *Electribal Memories* was an impassioned electronic soul testament featuring the swooning, soaring voice of Billie Ray Martin. The Beloved's *Happiness* vividly reflected the indie-inflected Balearic beatitude and open-hearted,

ecstasy-charged positivity that the duo experienced at clubs like Shoom, from 'Up, Up and Away', which jubilantly evoked the MDMA rush, to 'The Sun Rising', a sublime exposition of what the album's sleeve notes called 'that 5 a.m. loving feeling'.

Their northwestern counterpart was *90*, encapsulating the joy and disorientation of being swept away by the communal euphoria of that glorious period while simultaneously referencing its roots with deftly chosen samples from synthetic soul and electro-funk records. The album's sonic aura came from the clubs but it deviated purposefully from acid house conventions. 'They used to play a lot of Latin music at the Haçienda and that was something that excited me, and I was trying to incorporate more complex rhythms into house music on album tracks like 'Cobra Bora' along with the ravey brass stabs and the keyboard sounds that echoed back to jazz fusion,' explains Massey.

Darren Partington said The Spinmasters' key concern at the time was that 808 State's music should not feel in any way like white indie music: 'It had to have soul and sound electro and dark.'[19] The Spinmasters would test-play new tracks from cassette to the hardcore ravers at the Thunderdome club in Manchester, and their dancefloor nous counterbalanced Massey and Price's experimental sensibilities: 'They stop us from being too self-indulgent,'[20] said Price.

'Pacific State', 'Cubik' and 'In Yer Face' were all Top 10 hits, and Massey says he loved getting deeply strange sounds into the pop mainstream: 'That's the thing I'm most proud of in a way, that it actually moved the music somewhere really new, and it just shows you that people are happy to listen to innovative music, like in the seventies when you had all the weird Bowie and Hawkwind and proggy stuff in the charts.'

Not everyone was convinced; an executive at Warner Brothers, their label ZTT's corporate parent, was appalled by the raucous 'Cubik', comparing it to a 'tuned fart'. (Even Massey once said that the song 'sounds like somebody shouting at you about Brutalist architecture'[21]). But for a few years there was a glorious feeling that 808 State were riding a wave of change, exploring new frontiers, cheered on by the adoring rave masses. 'We were very much feeding off what was going on around us because there was so much energy around,' Massey said. 'There was an atmosphere of "you can do it, you can do what you want." I just feel incredibly lucky to have been there at that point because music happens on a very personal level, but this happened on a collective consciousness level.'[22]

The rave scene's relentless appetite for ever wilder sounds and more hypnotic rhythms had pushed British house and techno producers beyond trying to copy what they heard on American house imports. 'I think everyone felt that at the time that a page had turned and the music had to reflect that, to have a sense of futurism,' says Massey. Because no restrictive conventions had yet been established, it seemed to be an open-access culture in which anyone could get involved and find a platform to express themselves creatively, bringing their own influences and ideas and playing with its musical paradigms as they desired.

This led to some very disparate characters getting involved in house and techno: ex-punks, soul boys, industrial music veterans, hip-hop heads and pop stars like Paul Weller, Martin Fry of ABC, Paul Rutherford of Frankie Goes to Hollywood, Norman Cook of The Housemartins and Boy George, who was involved in making the evocative 'Generations of Love' by Jesus Loves You and E-Zee Possee's pill-popping party banger 'Everything Starts with an E'.

Less unusual was the involvement of New Order, who as co-owners of the Haçienda witnessed the ecstasy upheaval right in front of their eyes. The band headed for Ibiza to do the initial recordings for their *Technique* album in the summer of 1988; perhaps predictably, the sessions on the hedonistic White Island were not massively productive as they spent most of their time flying high in the clubs. But their nights at Amnesia did inspire the ebullient acid-pop single 'Fine Time', which Peter Hook described as 'a declaration of the band's love'[23] for dance culture.

The summer of 1989 also saw various attempts to integrate live musicians and MCs with DJs to enhance the rave format. Among the clubs experimenting with hybrid performances was Confusion, which was one of the most intense experiences it was possible to have on a Sunday night in London: a boiling cauldron of bass, dry ice and fresh sweat, where DJ Kid Batchelor of Bang the Party tested out new sounds to the delight of his cheering, clapping dancers.

'I was mixing New York-style and of course I was playing all the dubs that we were producing in the studio for Warriors Dance before they were coming out, but what made the vibe so intense, what made it so *London*, was the two MCs, E-Mix and Noise, who would just vibe off the music I was playing – it was like they were cutting tunes live in the gig,' explains Batchelor. 'I was also introducing a Latin element from continental Europe, bringing over a lot of Italian DJs and records – bootlegs, I loved bootlegs!'

With the dub plates, exclusive tunes and MCs chatting and crooning on the microphone, the connection to reggae sound system culture was clear. 'It's a direct link – I would call it an umbilical cord,' agrees Batchelor. 'In London, because of the Caribbean communities and the Commonwealth histories, we have a particular melting pot and I was also adding that continental European side into the mix.'

Another creative development was the phenomenon of the 'keyboard wizards': flamboyantly garbed characters like former teen punk Adamski, ex-pub rocker Guru Josh and house-head Mr Monday, who played live electronic sets at clubs and illegal raves. Adamski's album *Liveanddirect* conveyed some of the frenzied energies of the peak rave year of 1989, while his single 'Killer', made with singer Seal, encapsulated the melancholies of the subsequent comedowns.

An outlaw party wasn't an easy environment in which to put on a technically elaborate show – Adamski (Adam Tinley) remembered 'lugging heavy keyboards over barbed wire fences and running through muddy fields with the police in pursuit'[24] – so the equipment had to be basic and the sound had to hit hard. But while the keyboard wizards' performances may have been rough-edged, they were the antecedents of the live electronic bands who would follow them in the 1990s: Orbital, Underworld, The Prodigy and The Chemical Brothers.

Adamski and Seal in London, 1990. ©Clare Muller/Getty Images.

The KLF, The Orb and 'Ambient House'

'When you come back from a rave at 8 a.m., the last thing you want to hear is more house music. You need something to come down to.'
Bill Drummond, The KLF[25]

It only operated for a few months and was only experienced by a few dozen people every Monday night in central London, but the chill-out room in the upstairs VIP bar at the Land of Oz night at Heaven made an impact that reverberated for years afterwards. The way that sonic prototypes were tested out there each week demonstrated yet again how nightclubs provided environments that stimulated the artistic development of electronic music in Britain.

DJ Paul Oakenfold, one of the acid house scene's instigators in London, began running the Land of Oz after his Spectrum night at the same venue closed to evade repercussions from a tabloid exposé about acid house and ecstasy-taking at Heaven in the autumn of 1988. Oakenfold invited Justified Ancients of Mu Mu prankster Jimmy Cauty and former Killing Joke roadie and dub fanatic Alex Paterson – who would soon start making records together as The Orb – to be the DJs in the upstairs bar and asked them to play anything but dance music.

Using multiple turntables, a DAT machine, a sampler and an echo unit, Cauty and Paterson looped grooves from hypnotic house tracks like 'Sueño Latino' and mixed them with German *kosmische* epics, ambient music by Eno and touches of reggae, plus birdsong, wave noises and babbling brooks from BBC sound-effects records. 'I saw it as a big joyride,' Paterson says. 'We were playing experimental music in the West End that we would normally have been playing in a squat.' Their quirky style was humorously psychedelic, a kind of stoner bricolage that would become the template for the music The Orb would go on make.

It would also inspire other DJs to begin their own experiments with chill-out rooms at house clubs. Mixmaster Morris (Morris Gould), a DJ with roots in post-punk DIY culture who became a central figure in the British ambient scene, was excited by how Cauty and Paterson would play records like *Tubular Bells* or *The Dark Side of the Moon* and 'sample them, layer sound effects over the top, and do all kinds of weird shit'. 'I asked Alex if I could play up there and he told me to fuck off. That's when I decided to do my own chill-out room,'[26] he said. The efforts of creative characters like Mixmaster Morris established an ambient subculture that would nurture a wealth of unconventional electronic musicians in the nineties – from Aphex Twin to The Black Dog, Plaid, B12, Autechre and Mira Calix – and build an audience for home-listening electronica.

Another album that Cauty and Paterson would play with was *Rainbow Dome Musick*, made by former Gong players Steve Hillage and Miquette Giraudy. One night, Hillage and Giraudy went down to the Land of Oz to see what was going on. 'I remember arriving and Alex Paterson was playing *Rainbow Dome Musick* – but with a beat under it,' Giraudy says. 'That was a beautiful surprise.'

Hillage claims to have seen electronic dance music would be the future way back in 1978, when he saw a DJ fill the dancefloor by playing Kraftwerk at a club in Plymouth. Ever interested in new psychedelic sounds, he also collaborated with electronic producer Malcolm Cecil of Tonto's Expanding Head Band on his *Motivation Radio* album, combining his glissando guitar style with funkier rhythms and synths including Cecil's colossal TONTO set-up. While the Steve Hillage Band were touring with a prototype Turbosound rig in the seventies, they also used to throw parties that he describes as 'prototype raves', where they would take magic mushrooms and get down to P-funk tracks by Parliament and Bootsy's Rubber Band. When Turbosound designer John Andrews started to provide rigs for some of the acid house raves, he urged Hillage to check out the emerging scene.

Sonic trippers like Hillage immediately tuned in to acid house, understanding it from their hippie perspective as a kind of technologically-enhanced psychedelia. 'We were very attracted to acid house because of the acid in it,' he quips. 'Basically, a lot of psychedelically-orientated people moved away from rock music into the developing electronic music scene in the eighties. We thought, "This is it, this is what we've been looking for."' As acid house and ecstasy brought hippie vibrations back to clubland, real hippies began to adapt the music to their psychedelic mindset. Hillage and Giraudy went on to start their own techno project, System 7, while another pair of hippie veterans, Merv Pepler and Joie Hinton, formerly of free-festival psychedelic-prog band Ozric Tentacles, founded synth-rave duo Eat Static.

The first single by The Orb, 'A Huge Ever Growing Pulsating Brain that Rules from the Centre of the Ultraworld', was a swirling mass of samples and effects that resembled Cauty and Paterson's Land of Oz sets, centred around a vocal from Minnie Riperton's 'Loving You' with a Floydian guitar figure, a choral drone from a Trevor Horn production for Grace Jones and a title copied from a piece that the BBC Radiophonic Workshop's Elizabeth Parker had composed for TV series *Blake's 7*.

Cauty soon left The Orb to concentrate on his increasingly rave-oriented work with Bill Drummond; the duo had dropped the Justified Ancients of Mu Mu name and were now calling themselves The KLF and making tranced-out warehouse party anthems like 'What Time Is Love?' and '3am Eternal'. They also put out an album called *Chill Out*, a sprawling mind-trip of a record intended to be an imaginary soundtrack to a journey though the American Deep South, with sound sources as diverse as Elvis Presley, 808 State, jazz clarinetist Acker Bilk, evangelist preachers, bleating sheep, Tuvan throat singers from Mongolia and a pedal-steel guitarist.

This was rambling, amorphous music for after-club smoking sessions and couchbound comedowns – Drummond described it as 'ambient house' in a tongue-in-cheek eighteen-point manifesto that he wrote to accompany the white-label promotional copies of the record. 'Ambient house only makes sense to those who made it to the furthest reaches of dance music in the last two years,' it declared. Self-deprecatingly, it added: 'Ambient house is just a Monday night clique in the VIP room at Heaven.'[27] Whatever, the name stuck. Ambient house had arrived.

'It was called ambient house because we didn't want anyone to call it New Age house or something tedious like that with a connection to [New Age record label] Wyndham Hill,' explained Paterson. 'It was taking dance music into your front room so you can listen to it, not just dance to it. It was also a major factor that everyone was taking ecstasy at this time as well. It opened people's minds.'

While The KLF would shift focus to make pop and then art in the years that followed, The Orb would turn ambient house into a career. In the process, they would also kindle renewed admiration for Brian Eno. In the seventies, when Eno released his pioneering ambient album *Music for Airports*, he recalled how he had 'buckets of critical abuse poured over my head' by rock critics who described it as dull, emotionless Muzak. 'Ambient didn't become a compliment until about 1990, actually, when The Orb took up the banner,'[28] he noted.

The Orb added their own flavours to the ambient style: absurdist Monty Python/Viv Stanshall-style humour, ganja-fired surrealism reminiscent of Lee Parry, drifting textures derived from spaced-out house tracks by Mr Fingers and Marshall Jefferson, plus an easy-going attitude to reusing other people's music. 'I'll sample away merrily until I'm caught out. But I don't take the obvious riffs,' says Paterson. 'We sampled Vangelis, but no one would even know that it was Vangelis because we detuned the whole thing, manipulated it and changed it.'

An admirer of Mad Professor, who he also sampled, Paterson transplanted ideas from dub reggae into ambient music and made the link between house and classical minimalism explicit by using the rippling guitar figures of Steve Reich's 'Electric Counterpoint' on The Orb's 'Little Fluffy Clouds'. 'Steve Reich was just totally blown away that someone had turned his piece of music into something completely different even though it was still his piece of music,' Paterson says.

Cauty, Drummond and Paterson were not the only alternative culture veterans who fell hard for acid house. Industrial instigator Genesis P-Orridge of Psychic TV and Richard Norris, editor of psychedelic fanzine *Bam Caruso*, got so excited when they heard the term that they decided to make their own acid house album together. The only issue was that neither of them really knew what acid house actually sounded like at that point. 'We just thought, "Acid house, brilliant, that means psychedelic dance music",' said Norris.

They went into in the studio for a couple of days with various collaborators including former Soft Cell synthesizer player Dave Ball and a load of records and films from which to extract samples, including Peter Fonda's dialogue from cult biker movie *The Wild Angels* – 'We wanna be free to do what we wanna do' – which was later used by Andrew Weatherall on his landmark indie-dance remix of Primal Scream's 'Loaded'. 'As they hadn't heard any acid house records, they just tried to imagine what it would sound like,' says Ball. 'I don't know what genre that album really is – it's not acid house, although it is psychedelic dance music, kind of.'

P-Orridge finally experienced some real acid house at Danny and Jenni Rampling's Shoom club in the summer of 1988. The former Throbbing Gristle provocateur loved 'the disorientation and the delirium'[29] of the communal rave experience, although this later turned to disillusionment when dance culture started to develop its own star system around the central figure of the DJ. While the album that P-Orridge and Norris made, *Jack the Tab*, was hardly a dancefloor landmark, it did get them featured in the music press, helping to facilitate house music's crossover into the indie arena as rock journalists also started turning on to MDMA and going out raving.

One of the first indie bands to realise acid house was the revolution they had been waiting for was The Shamen. The Scottish psychedelic rockers' experiences at London clubs like RIP convinced them immediately that their music needed radical change. '[RIP] struck me as a technologically and musically updated Acid Test, but with more emphasis on sexuality and syncopation,' said bandleader Colin Angus. 'At the time, it seemed like a prescient glimpse of the entertainment-form of the future. We were already en route to a more technologically based, rhythmic/psychedelic sound at that stage, but it helped point the way forward in terms of working with DJs, remixers, etc.'[30]

The Shamen recorded a collaboration with Chicago housemaster Bam Bam and recruited one of the RIP DJs, talented rapscallion and former milkman Mr C, as their MC. Of all the bands of their era, they would be the ones to most overtly exalt the pleasures of MDMA with their very, *very* naughty number-one hit 'Ebeneezer Goode'. They also helped to update the rock-gig format with their long-running Synergy tour, a rolling rave revue that combined live electronic performances with DJ sets, further expanding the white indie audience for house and techno.

British indie bands' interest in electronic techniques had been growing since the electro experiments of New Order, Cabaret Voltaire and Section 25 in the early eighties and then the post-industrial funk of Chakk, 23 Skidoo and 400 Blows. Rick Rubin's drum-heavy productions for Run-DMC and Beastie Boys, as well as The Bomb Squad's work for Public Enemy, also catalysed British bands like Age of Chance, Pop Will Eat Itself and Jesus Jones to explore sampling and hip-hop beats. The Age of Chance album *One Thousand Years of Trouble* established a template for noisy, sample-heavy dance-rock in 1987, but Pop Will Eat Itself and Jesus Jones were able to combine it with catchy songs that secured them commercial success and brought ideas from electronic dance music into the indie arena – although American hip-hop and house productions continued to evolve much more rapidly than most of their British emulators could follow.

As the eighties came to an end, the use of electronics and sampling had blurred the boundaries between indie rock and dance music, as the use of Burroughs-meets-Bomb-Squad samples, raging electronics, dub basslines and post-Tackhead industrial hip-hop beats was perfected by bands like Meat Beat Manifesto and Renegade Soundwave, cultish innovators who existed on dance music's weirder fringes. Former industrial bands also started to make house and techno: Cabaret Voltaire recorded parts of their *Groovy, Laidback and Nasty* album in Chicago with housemaster Marshall Jefferson, while experimental noise-music duo Greater Than One became rave anthem-makers GTO.

Some indie bands had been commissioning 12-inch remixes of their singles for years, but now it became common practice for them to engage club DJs to remodel their work. London acid house scene luminaries like Paul Oakenfold, Andrew Weatherall and Terry Farley, aided by studio engineers who knew the right buttons to press, began completely remaking records for bands like Happy Mondays and Primal Scream, deconstructing their songs and introducing more rhythmically-focused structures that offered new directions for alternative rock.

Weatherall's remix of Primal Scream's bluesy ballad 'I'm Losing More Than I'll Ever Have' was a key moment; it took the original apart, dosed it with 125mg of MDMA and remade it as a completely new work with a new name, 'Loaded', simultaneously giving the band a critically-acclaimed hit, a new musical perspective and a complete career revitalisation. It was little wonder that DJs came to be seen by record companies as sonic alchemists, capable of transforming leaden-footed indie rock into dancefloor gold.

Primal Scream's *Screamadelica* album, co-produced by non-musician Weatherall with input from The Orb, proved to be the peak moment of the indie-dance phenomenon; an ecstatic odyssey that soared to a transcendental plateau with the narcotised breakbeat dub of 'Higher Than the Sun'. 'Because he wasn't aware of the rules, he broke them,' Primal Scream's Bobby Gillespie said of Weatherall after the influential DJ's death in 2020. 'No one else would have thought of constructing tracks like he did.'[31]

Bleep Techno and Breakbeat Hardcore
'What we're making is modern electronic funk music.'
DJ Parrot, Sweet Exorcist[32]

Like Gerald Simpson across the Pennines in Manchester, Winston Hazel was a dancer. The son of Caribbean immigrants from the Windrush generation, Hazel had been part of a Sheffield b-boy crew called Smac 19, a group of first-generation UK breakdancers. He also used to organise coaches to transport clubbers from Sheffield to jazz-funk all-dayers in cities around the north and the Midlands, and soon started running his own club nights too.

This was partly out of necessity; in Sheffield, as elsewhere in Britain in the 1980s, racist door policies meant that young Black men were often turned away from city-centre clubs. 'The only way to make sure you could definitely have a night out was to put the night on yourself,' Hazel says.

He teamed up with DJ Parrot, who had been running the Jive Turkey soul, funk and electro night in Sheffield since 1985, attracting a mixture of hardcore dancers from the all-dayer circuit, city hipsters and local electronic musicians like Stephen Mallinder and Richard Kirk of Cabaret Voltaire. 'In my head, there were obvious parallels between the rhythmic electronic music of Sheffield and so many of the records being played in the Black clubs of the time,' says Parrot.

Jive Turkey was a club 'for all the misfits in the city', says Hazel. When house music arrived, they had their very own sound. 'Sonically, the rawness of it was incredible and you could hear it was Black music with the elements of soul and funk in there,' he enthuses. 'It was a continuation of what had come before it, but it sounded new and that galvanised people.'

Sheffield already had some infrastructure to support forward-thinking electronic musicians – Cabaret Voltaire's Western Works and FON Studios, whose name was an acronym for 'Fuck Off Nazis'. Built by post-industrial funk band Chakk, FON employed a talented young audio engineer and drum-machine programming adept called Robert Gordon. There was also FON Records, a shop run by Steve Beckett and Rob Mitchell, where Hazel also worked and from where the Warp record label would be launched.

Warp's debut release in 1989, 'Track With No Name', heralded a new British electronic sound that drew on sound system culture for its bass weight and dub space, as well as Chicago house and Detroit techno for its drum patterns and cosmic synthetics. Credited to Forgemasters in tribute to the Sheffield steel company of the same name, with a 909 beat and a hint of the industrial legacy of Cabaret Voltaire, it was made quickly and cheaply by Gordon, Hazel and Sean Maher at Gordon's house. Gordon had just bought a sampler, a synth and an Atari computer, and they made the track to test it all out.

'I brought a record to sample, 'Abele Dance' by Manu Dibango, and we sampled that and 'Track With No Name' was constructed within four hours, finished,' says Hazel. 'Basically it's an electronic funk track. Robert brought the reggae influence. I brought the futuristic and soulful influence.' Its chattering machine rhythm evoked the sounds of the city itself. 'When we were kids, you could hear the drop hammers going off in the forges all day and all night, heavy industrial rhythms bouncing across the city from the steelworks, and those were the kind of sounds that came through into our music.'

'Track With No Name' was one of a series of remarkable records made over a couple of years around the turn of the 1990s in Yorkshire cities like Sheffield, Leeds and Bradford; minimalistic tracks whose exhilarating depth-charge basslines and Kraftwerk-style bleeping tone signals led them to become known as 'bleep techno' or 'bleep and bass'. The style – adored by ravers who liked their music tough and bottom-heavy – was first laid out by Unique 3, a group of hip-hop and electro heads from Bradford who had been members of the Solar City Rockers breakdance crew. Their self-released debut, 'The Theme', sounded like it came from another dimension: a mesmeric electrical storm of bleeps circling like flying saucers above ominous sub-bass drones crafted from low-end feedback.

Hazel remembers how the young bleep techno producers would come down to the club nights he and Parrot were running in Sheffield, bringing tapes of their tunes. 'Obviously they'd also heard this new music that was coming out of Chicago and Detroit at the same time as us and they were trying out similar styles and then bringing them down to our nights on cassette, and we'd play them. It was crews from Leeds and Bradford – Nightmares on Wax, the Unique 3 lot and then, a bit later, LFO and Ital Rockers. We were the people that had come from the all-dayer circuit and the jazz-funk scene and moved forward into this new form of music and started remaking it.'

In his book about bleep and bass, *Join the Future*, Matt Anniss argues that the music grew out of a nexus between electro, dub reggae, house and hip-hop, jazz-funk all-dayers, blues dances, multiracial inner-city clubs and illegal after-hours parties. It could only have been created in the UK, believes Hazel. 'It was completely British music, made in Britain by British kids.'

Vital to the development of the sound was Warp Records co-founder Gordon, who had picked up on the affinity between the reggae steppers groove and the four-to-the-floor rhythms of house music, a connection that would also be explored by Smith & Mighty in Bristol. Gordon came from a reggae background; as a teenager, he would buy hobbyist magazines like *Practical Electronics* and build kit that he could then sell. 'The reggae sound systems were buying custom equipment so I taught myself how to make it. I made what I considered the best dub sirens and the best preamps. I think I was earning more money than my mum,' he recalls.

The second Warp bleep-and-bass 12-inch came out of Leeds: 'Dextrous' by Nightmares on Wax, whose members were also former breakdancers. 'Dextrous' grew from an attempt to copy the SH-101 bass clang of 'Voodoo Ray' but ended up sounding very different indeed.

Even more entrancing in its alien beauty was 'Testone' by Sweet Exorcist – Parrot and Cabaret Voltaire's Richard H. Kirk – which was also released on Warp in 1989. Thrillingly stark and throbbing with funk, 'Testone' was recorded on an Atari computer that the duo hardly knew how to work, using a test oscillator for its signature bleeps that echoed the Yellow Magic Orchestra's 'Computer Game'. 'Being as it was me and Kirky, both officially non-musicians, I suppose it was always likely to turn out sounding a bit different,' says Parrot. 'Testone' had a feeling of post-punk weirdness about it that set it aside from a lot of the dancefloor tunes being made at the time, a style that the duo further developed with the bonkers wonkiness of their 'Clonk' series.

Kirk said that he and Parrot initially made 'Testone' to 'give people a blast at the Jive Turkey night'.[33] Warp's next release was also made for a club: The Warehouse in Leeds. It was created by LFO – Mark Bell and Gez Varley, who had also been breakdancers in the electro era and felt a real kinship with the other Yorkshire bleep-techno musicians. 'A lot of the lads, they're all the same background – breakdancing, buying electro records and then getting their first drum machines, and then house music came along so everybody got into house,'[34] said Varley.

Bell and Verley recorded their debut, also called 'LFO', with Warehouse DJ Martin Williams in his attic studio using a budget-price Kawai K1 synth to create the icy deep-space chords that opened the record and a Texas Instruments speak-and-spell machine for the vocal. Again, dub-influenced bass was the throbbing heart of it all, a seismic force that literally made dancefloors shudder. Varley explained that the track's monstrous sub-bass groan was added to thrill dancers at the illegal blues parties they used to go to in Leeds' Chapeltown area: 'Right, let's put in some heavy bass, they're going to go *mental!*'[35] With its insistent rave-bleep riff, 'LFO' was cheaply made but sounded colossal. Dropping like a vacuum bomb at the height of the rave era, it was a peak moment for British techno.

The emergence of bleep techno as a sound, with producers competing to deliver ever more resonant bass and mind-altering FX to entrance their hometown dancers across the north of England, showed how new strains of electronic music could mutate rapidly in the hothouse environment of the club scene. If one producer's sound tore up the dancefloor, it would be immediately imitated by others, sometimes in such a radical way that the intended copy became something completely different. If that happened, the imitation would then be imitated itself, potentially triggering yet further imitations and mutations.

In dance music culture, innovations were often made through this collective process of sonic hybridisation; a process enabled by a supportive audience of ravers who were eager for ever weirder, wilder noises and heavier, more propulsive beats. The impact made by Unique 3, LFO and Sweet Exorcist inspired producers all over the country to make their own bleep tracks, from Nexus 21 in Stafford to Rhythmatic in Nottingham, Tricky Disco in London, Original Clique in Bedford and Fantasy UFO and Hypersonic in Essex.

After working with LFO, Martin Williams moved on to set up his own Bassic label and further develop the dub-house synergy with tracks by Ital Rockers and Ability II. But Warp Records moved in another direction, convincing LFO they should record an album rather than focusing on 12-inch releases. Co-founder Steve Beckett, an admirer of independent labels like Mute and Factory, believed that Warp's artists should be 'making electronic albums people could appreciate from start to finish, rather than just being one-off dance records'.[36]

LFO's *Frequencies* paid tribute to Bell and Varley's electro roots and worked as home listening without compromising its techno intensity; it was a creative and critical success that paved the way for Warp to transform itself into the definitive UK electronic albums label of the nineties, issuing records that twisted and abstracted dance music tropes and established idiosyncratic producers like Aphex Twin as auteur figures.

'That was the second phase of the label, where we signed Aphex Twin, Autechre, Black Dog and B12, and we went onto a different level, because these artists became really respected in their own right making real cutting-edge music that was pushing the boundaries of electronic music,'[37] Beckett said.

This was a restless, fast-moving period in British electronic dance culture. While producers in Yorkshire were developing bleep and bass, London-based trio The Black Dog had begun to make tracks like 'Virtual' and 'The Weight', which heralded the Detroit-inflected, introspective and emotive style that would become known by the contentious name of 'intelligent dance music' or IDM. Elsewhere in London, young producers on the rave scene were creating their own UK-specific variant of house and techno – breakbeat hardcore.

Like bleep techno, breakbeat hardcore was largely pioneered by Black British descendants of the Windrush generation and built on the legacy of sound system culture and the hip-hop scene. It also revelled in its love of bass, although it was only when jungle emerged in the nineties that the low-end achievements of Unique 3 and LFO were rivalled. However, instead of exploring the application of dub techniques to house, the London variant prioritised the breakbeat, the sonic spine of hip-hop, and picked up on ideas from radical rappers like Public Enemy and the venturous sampling methods of their production team, The Bomb Squad.

As teenagers, Philip 'PJ' Johnson and Carlton 'Smiley' Hyman had run their own sound system, Heatwave, playing illegal blues dances; future drum and bass star DJ Hype (Kevin Ford) would cut up hip-hop beats as PJ and Smiley rapped. The duo's first records under the name Shut Up and Dance established their rough-and-ready style: speeded-up breakbeats, insouciantly pirated samples and gruffly barked vocals full of acerbic social commentary. 'We'd take old Def Jam tracks, push them from 100 to 130bpm, and let rip on the mike,'[38] Smiley later recalled.

With their first release '5678', they initially thought they were making an edgier British version of hip-hop, but found that ravers adored their boisterous energy and carefree naughtiness; it helped that many of the hardcore dancers on London's initially multiracial rave scene in the late eighties also loved hip-hop. 'We didn't really see ourselves as rave, but it fitted obviously to the whole rave thing,' said PJ. 'We were making a lot rawer sound than that, a lot rawer – keeping it with the sound system vibe.'[39]

This was the style that would become known as hardcore – British breakbeat house with hip-hop and reggae elements, speeded-up rhythms and barmy vocal samples. Shut Up and Dance merrily pilfered snippets of music from mainstream stars like Prince, Eurythmics and Suzanne Vega for their tracks. 'We've always loved pop stuff. It was what we grew up on,' explained Smiley. 'Use samples that are good. Just 'cause it's obscure, so what? Doesn't mean it's good. Use something that's good. Like when was the last time you heard Kate Bush in a sample? Kate Bush is a genius. You should use things like that.'[40]

This light-fingered attitude would eventually get them into trouble after they sampled Marc Cohn's 'Walking in Memphis' for their hit 'Raving I'm Raving' without securing legal clearance. The Mechanical-Copyright Protection Society, which collects royalties for songwriters, then dug into their back catalogue and found various other uncleared borrowings. Legal action ensued.

PJ and Smiley's Shut Up and Dance label issued records by other Black British talents who created new hybrid styles of electronic dance music and found themselves adopted by ravers hungry for hard-hitting beats. The Ragga Twins, Deman Rocker and Flinty Badman (brothers David and Trevor Destouche) had been reggae MCs on the Unity sound system and brought serious dancehall style to breakbeat hardcore. Like bleep techno, their music was one of the precursors to jungle and drum and bass: tracks like 'Spliffhead' and 'Hooligan 69' mixed ragamuffin incantations with raggedy grooves and deranged electronic bleeps and squawks. Flinty Badman said that Shut Up and Dance were looking to create a new ragga-rave style and told them to 'chat like you chat on the sound system, don't go in the studio and water it down like a nice record, we want it ruff.'[41]

Another wholly uncommon performer whose records were produced by Shut Up and Dance was Nicolette, a British-Nigerian jazz singer who had also fallen in love with rave culture, which she saw as a 'heart-opening' social movement that traversed social and ethnic divides with music that was 'ritualistic… almost shamanic'.[42] Nicolette's bewitchingly intimate, guileless vocals, combined with PJ and Smiley's spaced-out arrangements, created sultry breakbeat nocturnes that seemed to exist in another world from a lot of the electronic dance music of the time.

Shut Up and Dance and the Ragga Twins were not the only British reggae and hip-hop musicians adopted by the rave scene. There was also Britcore rapper Silver Bullet, whose spiky, urgent singles 'Bring Forth the Guillotine' and '20 Seconds to Comply' featured declamatory vocals and ominous samples from films like *Halloween* and *Robocop*. Both became pirate-radio favourites and prefigured the breakbeat-heavy techno-punk style that would be developed in the early nineties by The Prodigy.

Shut Up and Dance's former sound system colleague DJ Hype also helped develop the hardcore sound with the trippy productions he made with The Scientist (Phivos Iatropoullos). 'The Exorcist' and 'The Bee', with its insistent buzzing synth, were both weird, noisy records, but ravers loved them. 'They had that turntablism mentality that came from Hype and I also had a bit of that punk attitude. I was into post-punk industrial electronic music, so for me it was about twisting up the sound,' says Iatropoullos, who cites Depeche Mode, The Human League and BBC Radiophonic Workshop composers Delia Derbyshire and John Baker among his formative influences.

'The Exorcist' also highlighted how the emerging hardcore sound was accelerating away from its house and techno roots as DJs sought to raise the frantic energy of the ravers ever higher. 'On pirate radio and in the clubs, all the DJs would be speeding up the records to plus-eight [on Technics turntables], so I was making these tracks at the BPM I was hearing the DJs play, which meant everything naturally turned out faster,' Iatropoullos explains.

The use of ominous samples became another characteristic of the hardcore sound, exemplified by 'Mr. Kirk's Nightmare' by 4Hero, a 1990 rave anthem that began with a policeman telling a man his son has died of an overdose, before thrashing forwards into a storm of looped Isley Brothers breaks running backwards as well as forwards, queasy bleeps and ragga bass.

It was one of the first tracks put out by Reinforced Records, which would become one of the most important drum and bass labels and release Goldie's astonishingly inventive Rufige Crew records. 'Mr. Kirk's Nightmare' anticipated the darkcore rave sound that emerged as harsher sonic moods descended upon the euphoric sound of early rave. 4Hero's Mark Mac said it was intentionally sinister: 'We were saying, "If someone hears this and they're tripping, it's gonna freak them out, they ain't gonna want to trip again".'[43]

Independent productions like 'Mr. Kirk's Nightmare' were made using rudimentary equipment pushed to its limits in the now-established DIY traditions of electronic music in the UK. What was different in the rave era was that a killer track recorded at home and issued by an independent label not only had the potential to become a mass-selling hit but could also lead to a lifelong career in electronic music.

The huge outlaw parties of 1989, sometimes known as 'orbital' raves because many were staged near M25 London Orbital Motorway, served as entry points to electronic dance music for countless thousands of youths who were beguiled by the thrills of illegal nocturnal festivities, mind-altering drugs and hypnotic rhythms. As well as transforming many young initiates' perceptions of what music could sound like, the illegal raves provided a name for a duo formed by two brothers from a village in Kent that lay close to the M25.

Orbital's Paul and Phil Hartnoll had been teenage fans of bands like Kraftwerk, Cabaret Voltaire and Australian industrialists Severed Heads, and had grown up with the BBC Radiophonic Workshop's soundtracks to the TV programmes they watched. 'As a kid, they would always give me this feeling of weirdness – it was kind of unsettling, it sounded sort of wrong and cold and broken and a bit lonely, but I was drawn to it as well,' says Paul Hartnoll. 'I was always interested in those kinds of sounds, like the music for [SF marionette series] *Captain Scarlet* [by Barry Gray] when the Ondes Martenot would come in with those spooky kind of Theremin-type noises.'

The Hartnoll brothers started out making music by 'trying to sound like New York electro or New Order' in a spare bedroom at home, using cheap drum machines and synths that they picked up secondhand. 'We were finding things like old [Roland] SH-09s and SH-101s, which were like £40, nobody wanted them because all the big names wanted big, modern digital synths and samplers, and so people like us were able to go around buying all these old analog synths,' Paul Hartnoll recalls. In Chicago and Detroit, impecunious musicians used whatever technology they could acquire to create house and techno; Orbital were doing something similar in the UK, he believes. 'The music wasn't made on the equipment you wanted, necessarily – it was made on the equipment you could afford.'

As well as the trippy frequencies of acid and the Afrofuturist harmonics of Detroit techno, Orbital loved the directness of punk rock, which led them to base a lot of their tracks on powerfully compelling riffs. 'British dance music was very riff-based – big chord samples played like a lead line, these glorious kind of riffs that were instantly enjoyable: "Yeah, this feels good!" I think that accounts for the success of people like The Prodigy as well, and I think it was influenced by punk,' says Hartnoll. 'A lot of us were too young to have been punks in the very first flush of it, but we had that second wave of people like the Dead Kennedys and Crass and Flux of Pink Indians. A lot of the sampling I did from those kinds of records, because that's what I had in my record collection. I didn't have a selection of rare grooves and funk so I was sampling what I had.'

The making of Orbital's riff-based debut 'Chime' was emblematic of how DIY electronic music was made in the rave era. It was initially produced at home using an Akai sampler, a 909 rhythm box, a 303 acid machine and a budget-priced Yamaha DX100 synth; Hartnoll says it was made in a couple of hours as an experiment to test out some equipment. 'That means the track was made totally unselfconsciously and just came out as the glorious rave anthem that it ended up being.'

The Hartnoll brothers took the track to pirate-radio DJ Jazzy M, who set up his own independent label in order to release it in an edition of 1,000. But first Hartnoll had to deal with one of the biggest expenses of the entire process. 'Jazzy M sent me away and said, "Go and put it on a metal cassette so that it's the best quality that we can have." And it was like £3.50. And I was like, "Bloody hell, this is really expensive!" and I was really unsure about having to invest in it.'

'Chime' was still one of the centrepieces of Orbital's live set almost four decades later when they invited surviving veterans of the Radiophonic Workshop to make a guest appearance with them at the Bluedot festival at the Jodrell Bank space observatory. 'They taught us everything we know!' yelled Phil Hartnoll as the venerable gentlemen in their casual shirts, slacks and matching Orbital-style head-torch glasses took to the stage for a wild rave rendition of the *Doctor Who* theme – illuminating a British electronic music lineage that led from musique concrète and early sixties SF TV all the way through to house and techno.

One of them was Dick Mills: 'It's easy to say that you're humbled, but I really am,' says Mills, who joined the Workshop back in 1958, when he was still in his early twenties. 'We're proud as anything to have played a part in electronic music history, this wonderful tapestry of sounds.'

By the end of the 1980s, although avant-garde electro-acoustic music remained relatively obscure, electronic dance music had developed into a kind of contemporary folk culture, expressing the consciousness and concerns of its community in an ever-evolving sonic narrative. But while British electronic musicians often saw themselves as visionary futurists, the music they were making was part of a continuum that stretched back to World War II and carried echoes of much that had gone before it – radiophonic effects, musique concrète loops, psychedelic abstraction, dub disorientation, sound system bass weight, Enoesque ambience, industrial weirdness, electro-pop fizzle and electro-funk sizzle, hip-hop bricolage and the compulsive rhythms of house and techno.

Over the decades since World War II, technological developments had brought the production of electronic music from the avant-garde margins into the popular mainstream of British culture. Electronic instruments had become more expressive, more sonically versatile, easier to use and more portable. They had also become more affordable, making them more accessible to wider communities and increasing numbers of non-musicians, including marginalised outsiders – a trend that would continue into the 1990s and beyond.

Back in 1945, a young composer like Tristram Cary could only dream of buying a reel-to-reel tape machine that would allow him to laboriously chop up and reassemble pieces of magnetic tape to make music. Even then, few people wanted to listen to such unusual sounds. By 1990, teenagers could cut tracks on their home computers using purpose-made software and command a mass audience if their music was exciting enough. The DIY spirit of British electronic music-making – rooted in the post-war independent sonic research of composers like Cary and Daphne Oram and the tape-recorder experiments of amateurs and hobbyists, as well as the make-do-and-mend inventiveness of the Radiophonic Workshop – had become the inspiration for a global popular culture.

All this happened as electronic technology became increasingly integrated into everyday existence in the decades after World War II, permeating every sphere of life. Technological optimism underpinned a culture of electronic music-making that was enraptured by the idea of the future, constantly reaching towards the new, propelled by the machines that could make dreams come true.

By the end of the 1980s, as technology continued to develop at exhilarating speed, electronic music-making had become increasingly democratised. Jungle, drum and bass, UK garage, psytrance, dubstep: all these styles and more lay ahead in a culture that was surging forward with what felt like unstoppable dynamism.

Here and now, or so it seemed at the time, anything might be possible.

ACKNOWLEDGEMENTS

This one goes out to Mirka and Alex, and to all my friends in the wonderful world of electronic music, wherever you are.

For research materials, help with contacts and photographs, advice and support, I would like to thank Siamak Amidi, Dave Anderson, Matt Anniss, Nigel Ayres, Vanya Balogh, Janet Beat, Richard Bernas, Slobodan Brkić, Basil Brooks, Caro C, John Cavanagh, Simon Crab, Jon Dasilva, John Earls, Nia Gvatua, Malu Halasa, Ian Helliwell, Steve Hillage, Brian Hodgson, Jovanka Lekić, Ian Levine, Chris Long, Adrian Loving, Steve Malins, Stephen Mallinder, Vie Marshall, Graham Massey, Mark Moore, Mariam Murusidze, Colin Potter, Mike Power, Hillegonda Rietveld, Gabriella Smart, Colin Steven, Wolfgang Tillmans, Jill Westwood and Greg Wilson.

I want to express particular gratitude to James Gardner for his generosity in sharing insights and suggesting essential reading, and to Dave Rimmer and Kirk Degiorgio for reading the manuscript and offering much-needed advice.

Special thanks are due to my agent, Matthew Hamilton, and to David Barraclough, Claire Browne and everyone at Omnibus Press. I would also like to thank the Society of Authors and the Authors' Foundation for providing a grant to help with the research.

For creative inspiration (and for broadcasting my show), thanks to Tata Janashia, Nina Bochorishvili and all the crew at Mutant Radio.

All quotes in the book are from my own interviews unless indicated otherwise. Much gratitude to everyone who gave up their time to be interviewed: Neil Arthur, Mark Ayres, Nigel Ayres, Harvey Bainbridge, Dave Ball, Richard Barbieri, Richard Barratt, Lawrence Batchelor, Janet Beat, Russ Bell-Brown, Richard Bernas, Matt Black, Tim Blake, Dennis Bovell, Basil Brooks, Arthur Brown, Richard James Burgess, Caro C, Chris Carter, Jayne Casey, Simon Crab, Thomas Crimble, Jon Dasilva, DJ Paulette, Dave Dorrell, Mikey Dread, Julia Dunn, Barry Evangeli, Catherine Ford, John Foxx, Neil Fraser, Ron Geesin, Miquette Giraudy, Manda Glanfield, Robert Gordon, Pete Q. Harris, Paul Hartnoll, Winston Hazel, Ian Helliwell, William 'Lez' Henry, Steve Hillage, Anderson Hines, Brian Hodgson, Phivos Iatropoullos, Mark

Iration, Donald Johnson, Milo Johnson, Errol Kennedy, Paddy Kingsland, Keith LeBlanc, Thomas Leer, Mark Leslie, Don Letts, Kermit Leveridge, Ian Levine, Mick MacNeil, Stephen Mallinder, Vie Marshall, Graham Massey, MC Duke, Barry Miles, Daniel Miller, Dick Mills, Mark Moore, Stephen Morris, Adi Newton, Gary Numan, Graeme Park, Elizabeth Parker, Alex Paterson, Mike Pickering, Colin Potter, Andrew Powell, Princess Julia, Steve Proctor, Nick Raphael, Eddie Richards, Hillegonda Rietveld, Kev Roberts, John Rocca, Adrian Sherwood, Tim Simenon, Gerald Simpson, Stephen Singleton, Jill Smith, Steven Stapleton, Ian Anthony Stephens, Ann Swinton, Christopher Thomson, Tony Thorpe, Stephen Thrower, Cosey Fanni Tutti, Dave VJ, David Vorhaus, Rick Wakeman, Martyn Ware, Pete Waterman, Jill Westwood, John Whybrew, Greg Wilson, Trevor Wishart and Ed Wynne.

Some of the people who were interviewed for the book passed on before it was finished: RIP Francis Monkman, Mark Stewart and Peter Zinovieff.

For archive materials, thanks to the Daphne Oram archive at Goldsmiths, University of London, the Tristram Cary archive at the University of Adelaide's Barr Smith Library, the Delia Derbyshire archive at the University of Manchester, the WikiDelia online archive, Ray White's *The White Files* website, Michael Kane's *Record Mirror* online archive, *The Wire*, *Electronic Sound*, *The Quietus*, the *IT* online archive, the *Oz* archive at the University of Wollongong, the *Mu:zines* online archive, the Manchester Digital Music Archive, the *More Dark Than Shark* Brian Eno online archive, the Black Music History Library website, Greg Wilson's *Electrofunkroots* website, Simon Dell's *Encyclopaedia Electronica* website, Simon Crab's *120 Years Of Electronic Music* website and Rock's Back Pages. I also want to express my gratitude to all the authors and journalists who wrote books and articles that I've quoted from – unfortunately way too many to list here, but if you're one of them, thank you.

Finally, love as always to my brothers Richard and Will, and to all the members of the extended Collin clan.

NOTES

Introduction
1. Brian Eno, 'The Studio as Compositional Tool – Part 1', *Down Beat*, July 1983
2. Richard James Burgess, *The History of Music Production*, Oxford University Press, New York, 2014
3. Daphne Oram, *An Individual Note*, Galliard Paperbacks, London, 1972
4. Tara Rodgers, *Pink Noises*, Duke University Press, Durham, 2010
5. John Lennon, *Skywriting by Word of Mouth*, It Books, New York, 2010

Journey Into Space – Musique Concrète and Radiophonic Sound
1. Letter to Daphne Oram from Yehudi Menuhin, 29 December 1960, Daphne Oram Archive, Goldsmiths, University of London
2. Interview conducted by Gabriella Joy Smart for her thesis *Tristram Cary: Scenes from a Composer's Life*, University of Adelaide, 2010
3. *Lumen, The University of Adelaide Magazine*, Winter 2005
4. International Churchill Society website
5. *The Music Show*, ABC Radio National, 11 February 2006
6. Tristram Cary, 'Electronic Music: A Call for Action', *The Musical Times*, April 1966
7. *The Music Show*
8. Ibid.
9. *The Composer, Journal of the Composers' Guild of Great Britain*, No. 9, Spring 1962
10. Handwritten transcript of interview with Daphne Oram, unknown date, Daphne Oram Archive, Goldsmiths, University of London
11. Tristram Cary, *Illustrated Compendium of Musical Technology*, London, Faber & Faber, 1992
12. *What the Future Sounded Like*, directed by Matthew Bate, Porthmeor Productions, 2007
13. Ibid.
14. Report to BBC managers, November 1956, Daphne Oram Trust website
15. 'Transcript of an interview', Tower Folly, Kent, 1 June 1991, from the Hugh Davies Archive, quoted in Nicola Anne Candlish, *The Development of Resources for Electronic Music in the UK, with Particular Reference to the Bids to Establish a National Studio*, Durham University, 2012
16. Ibid.
17. *Contemporary Music Review*, Volume 11, 1994
18. David Kynaston, *Austerity Britain 1945-51*, Bloomsbury, London, 2010
19. Daphne Oram, letter to Richard Francis, Managing Director of BBC Radio, 17 January 1983, Daphne Oram Archive, Goldsmiths, University of London
20. Report to Brian George, BBC Head of Programme Operations, November 1956, Daphne Oram Archive, Goldsmiths, University of London

21. Louis Niebur, *Special Sound: The Creation and Legacy of the BBC Radiophonic Workshop*, Oxford University Press, New York, 2014
22. Charlotte Higgins, *This New Noise: The Extraordinary Birth and Troubled Life of the BBC*, Guardian Faber Publishing, London, 2015
23. Desmond Briscoe and Roy Curtis-Bramwell, *The BBC Radiophonic Workshop: The First 25 Years*, BBC, London, 1983
24. Ibid.
25. Ibid.
26. *The Daily Telegraph and Morning Post*, 7 October 1957
27. Jo Hutton, *Radiophonic Ladies*, Sonic Arts Network, 2000
28. Briscoe and Curtis-Bramwell, *The BBC Radiophonic Workshop: The First 25 Years*.
29. *The Observer* and *The Times*, 1957, specific dates unspecified, quoted in ibid.
30. Newspaper cutting, unknown source, unknown date, Daphne Oram Archive, Goldsmiths, University of London
31. *The Times*, 24 May 1958
32. *BBC Sound Broadcasting News*, 27 May 1958, Daphne Oram Archive, Goldsmiths, University of London
33. *The Guardian*, 24 January 2003
34. *Sisters with Transistors*, directed by Lisa Rovner, Willow Glen Films/Anna Lena Films 2020
35. Francis Bacon, *New Atlantis*, originally published in 1627, republished by the *Project Gutenberg* website, 1 December 2000
36. *The Alchemists of Sound*, directed by Roger Pomphrey, BBC Four, 2003
37. Mark Ayres, sleeve notes for reissued *BBC Radiophonic Music* album sleeve, BBC Records 2002
38. Sleeve notes for *Doctor Who at the BBC Radiophonic Workshop Volume 1: The Early Years 1963-1969*, Mute Records, 2005
39. *Radio Times*, December 1960, exact date unknown
40. F.C.Brooker, *Radiophonics in the BBC*, BBC Engineering Division Monograph Number 51, November 1963
41. *The Times*, 8 October 1957
42. Newspaper cutting, unknown source, unknown date, Daphne Oram Archive, Goldsmiths, University of London
43. Ibid.
44. *Daily Mirror*, 6 February 1962
45. Letters to the *Radio Times*, November 24/November 10 respectively, 1960, quoted in Briscoe and Curtis-Bramwell, *The BBC Radiophonic Workshop: The First 25 Years*
46. Ibid.
47. Niebur, *Special Sound*
48. Daphne Oram, letter to Richard Francis
49. *Sight & Sound*, April 2014
50. *Manchester Evening News*, 11 July 1960
51. *British Movietone News*, 19 February 1962
52. *Tape Recording*, May 1960
53. *Daily Telegraph*, 16 January 1968
54. Ian Helliwell, *Tape Leaders: A Compendium of Early British Electronic Music Composers*, Velocity Press, West Wickham, 2021
55. F. C. Judd, *Electronic Music and Musique Concrète*, Forruli Classics, Potters Bar, 2013

56. Helliwell, *Tape Leaders: A Compendium of Early British Electronic Music Composers*
57. *Amateur Tape Recording*, November 1963
58. *Amateur Tape Recording*, August 1959
59. *Amateur Tape Recording*, March 1960
60. Helliwell, *Tape Leaders: A Compendium of Early British Electronic Music Composers*
61. Ibid.
62. *The Guardian*, 14 July 1961
63. BBC website, 8 April 2011
64. Judd, *Electronic Music and Musique Concrète*
65. *The Quietus*, 29 May 2013
66. Robert O'Byrne, *Desmond Leslie: The Biography of an Irish Gentleman*, Lilliput Press, Dublin 2010
67. Ibid.
68. Ibid.
69. Ibid.
70. John Cavanagh, 'Delia Derbyshire: On Our Wavelength', *Boazine* 7, unknown date, republished by delia-derbyshire.org, 2017
71. *The Delian Mode*, directed by Kara Blake, Philtre Films 2009
72. Hutton, *Radiophonic Ladies*
73. Ibid.
74. Interview with John Cavanagh, *Original Masters*, BBC Radio Scotland, 1997, exact date unknown
75. The Guardian, 7 July 2001
76. Ibid.
77. Briscoe and Curtis-Bramwell, *The BBC Radiophonic Workshop: The First 25 Years*
78. *Tomorrow's World*, BBC, 9 December 1965

An Electric Storm – Space-Age Pop and Psychedelia
1. Briscoe and Curtis-Bramwell, *The BBC Radiophonic Workshop: The First 25 Years*
2. *Daily Mirror*, 7 December, 1963
3. Ibid.
4. Peter Howell, *Radiophonic Times*, Obverse Books, Edinburgh, 2021
5. Ibid.
6. Briscoe and Curtis-Bramwell, *The BBC Radiophonic Workshop: The First 25 Years*
7. *The Guardian*, 6 July 2001
8. *Tristram Cary: Scenes from a Composer's Life*, thesis by Gabriella Joy Smart, University of Adelaide, 2010
9. John Repsch, *The Legendary Joe Meek: The Telstar Man*, Cherry Red Books, London, 2001
10. Barry Cleveland, *Joe Meek's Bold Techniques*, ElevenEleven Publishing, Agoura Hills, 2015
11. Repsch, *The Legendary Joe Meek*
12. Ibid.
13. *Melody Maker*, 8 February 1964
14. *Melody Maker*, 6 January 1962
15. Repsch, *The Legendary Joe Meek*
16. *International Times*, 16 January 1967
17. *Record Collector*, 21 September 2007

18. George Martin with William Pearson, *With a Little Help from My Friends*, Little, Brown, Boston, 1995
19. Interview with Alan Freeman for *Rave* magazine, quoted in Steve Turner, *Beatles '66*, HarperCollins, New York, 2016
20. Kenneth Womack, *Sound Pictures*, Chicago Review Press, Chicago, 2018
21. Michael Hill, 'The Oratory of Harold Wilson', in Andrew S. Crines, Richard Hayton (editors), *Labour Orators from Bevan to Miliband*, Manchester University Press, Manchester, 2014
22. Jeff Nuttall, *Bomb Culture*, MacGibbon & Kee, London, 1968
23. Michael Hicks, *Sixties Rock*, University of Illinois Press, Champaign, 1999
24. Turner, *Beatles '66*
25. Jonathon Green, *Days in the Life*, Pimlico, London, 1998
26. Ibid.
27. Barry Miles, *Paul McCartney: Many Years from Now*, Secker & Warburg, London, 1997
28. Ibid.
29. *International Times*, 16 January 1967
30. Timothy Leary, Ralph Metzer and Richard Alpert, *The Psychedelic Experience*, Penguin, London, 2008
31. *Ultimate Classic Rock*, 6 April 2016
32. Kenneth Tynan, *Tynan Letters*, Vintage, London, 2012
33. George Emerick, *Here, There and Everywhere*, Gotham Books, London, 2006
34. Ibid.
35. Ibid.
36. Ian MacDonald, *Revolution in the Head*, Chicago Review Press, Chicago, 2007
37. Emerick, *Here, There and Everywhere*
38. *Marc Myers' Jazzwax*, Jazz FM website, 12 September 2012
39. Womack, *Sound Pictures*
40. *International Times*, 16 January 1967
41. Womack, *Sound Pictures*
42. *New Musical Express*, 26 November 1967
43. *Far Out* magazine, 26 June 2022
44. Mark Prendergast, *The Ambient Century: From Mahler to Moby – The Evolution of Sound in the Electronic Age*, Bloomsbury, London, 2003
45. *Melody Maker*, 9 November 1968
46. *New Musical Express*, 9 November 1968
47. *The Beatles Anthology*, Chronicle Books, London, 2002
48. *Mojo*, October 2000
49. *The Guardian*, 22 March 2003
50. BBC website, 16 November 2008
51. *Surface* magazine
52. BBC website, 16 November 2008
53. Green, *Days in the Life*
54. *International Times*, 31 October 1966
55. Jon Savage, *1966: The Year the Decade Exploded*, Faber & Faber, London, 1966
56. Mark Blake, *Pigs Might Fly*, Aurum Press, London, 2007
57. Ibid.
58. Green, *Days in The Life*

59. Julian Palacios, *Syd Barrett & Pink Floyd: Dark Globe*, Plexus Publishing, London, 2010
60. *News of the World*, 12 February 1967
61. *Hansard*, 28 July 1967
62. Interview with Chris Salewicz, Pink Floyd Fan Club website, 1987
63. Robert Adlington (editor), 'Introduction: Avant-Garde Music and the Sixties', *Sound Commitments*, Oxford University Press, New York, 2009
64. Interview by James Gardner for *These Hopeful Machines*, Radio New Zealand website, 15 July 2013
65. Palacios, *Syd Barrett & Pink Floyd: Dark Globe*
66. Briscoe and Curtis-Bramwell, *The BBC Radiophonic Workshop: The First 25 Years*
67. Interview with John Cavanagh, *Original Masters*, BBC Radio Scotland, 1997, exact date unknown
68. *Surface* magazine
69. Ibid.
70. 'Brief Lives – JB Obituary', *The John Baker Tapes*, Trunk Records, 2008
71. *The Times*, 15 February 1997
72. *Caught by the River* website, 29 July 2008
73. Ibid.
74. Ibid.
75. *Tomorrow's World*, BBC One, 6 March 1968
76. Post by 'Gyro', *EEVblog Electronics Community Forum*, 23 April 2016
76. Trevor Pinch and Frank Trocco, *Analog Days: The Invention and Impact of the Moog Synthesizer*, Harvard University Press, Cambridge, 2002
78. Interview conducted by Gabriella Joy Smart
79. *The Guardian*, 20 October 2015
80. *The Music Show*, ABC Radio National, 11 February 2006
81. Pinch and Trocco, *Analog Days: The Invention and Impact of the Moog Synthesizer*
82. John Cage, *Silence: Lectures and Writings*, Wesleyan University Press, Middletown, 2013
83. *International Times*, 13 March 1970
84. Dominic Sandbrook, *White Heat: A History of Britain in the Swinging Sixties*, Abacus, London, 2009
85. *The Quietus*, 6 April 2021
86. Helliwell, *Tape Leaders: A Compendium of Early British Electronic Music Composers*
87. Rodgers, *Pink Noises*
88. Music Now, Sounds of Discovery press release, quoted in Benjamin Piekut, 'Indeterminacy, Free Improvisation, and the Mixed Avant-Garde', *Journal of the American Musicological Society*, December 2014
89. *International Times*, 23 August 1968
90. Letter from Berk to a friend, quoted in *The Wire*, October 2015
91. *The Guardian*, 16 February 2017
92. New York University website, 2009
93. Nick Mason, *Inside Out: A Personal History of Pink Floyd*, Phoenix, London, 2011
94. Ibid.
95. *Sound and Vision*, Spring 2017

Other Side Of The Sky – Space Rock, Prog And Ambient
1. *International Times*, 8 October 1970

2. Ray Foulk with Caroline Foulk, *The Last Great Event: When the World Came to the Isle of Wight 1970 – Volume 2*, Medina Publishing, Cowes, 2020
3. *Sounds*, 17 October 1970
4. Carol Clerk, *The Saga of Hawkwind*, Omnibus Press, London, 2006
5. Foulk, *The Last Great Event: When the World Came to the Isle of Wight 1970 – Volume 2*
6. *International Times*, 28 January 1970
7. *International Times*, 14 January 1970
8. *Prog*, 6 May 2016
9. *Hawkwind* album cover, Liberty Records 1970
10. *Vice*, 1 March 2015
11. *What the Future Sounded Like*
12. Joe Banks, *Hawkwind: Days of the Underground*, Strange Attractor Press, London, 2020
13. Ian Abrahams, *Hawkwind: Sonic Assassins*, Lumoni Press, 2016
14. Banks, *Hawkwind: Days of the Underground*
15. *Uncut*, September 2007
16. Nik Turner and Dave Thompson, *The Spirit of Hawkwind 1969-1976*, Cleopatra Books, Los Angeles, 2016
17. *Record Collector*, May 2002
18. Tim Gadd, 'Robert Calvert – Ramblings at Dawn', 1982 interview, posted on YouTube, 15 December 2012
19. *International Times*, 8 October 1970
20. Clerk, *The Saga of Hawkwind*
21. Ibid.
22. *Melody Maker*, 12 August 1972
23. *Prog*, 25 October 2019
24. *Slate*, 14 August 2012
25. *Mole Express*, Issue 19, November 1971
26. 'Malcolm Cecil on Creating TONTO', National Music Centre video, YouTube, 5 June 2020
27. David Weigel, *The Show That Never Ends: The Rise and Fall of Prog Rock*, W.W. Norton, New York, 2017
28. *Prog Rock Britannia*, directed by Chris Rodley, BBC4, 2009
29. Ibid.
30. Interview by Mark Powell, Cherry Red Records YouTube channel, 15 September 2008
31. Ibid.
32. Musicians' Union, 'Don't Fall for It', *Musicians Union Journal*, 1967, quoted in Sarah Angliss, 'Mimics, Menaces, or New Musical Horizons', in Frode Weium, Tim Boon (editors), *Material Culture and Electronic Sound*, Smithsonian Institution Scholarly Press, Washington DC, 2013
33. Pete Townshend, *Who I Am*, HarperCollins, London, 2012
34. Ibid.
35. AOL, 5 October 2006, republished on PeteTownshend.net
36. PeteTownshend.net
37. Mason, *Inside Out: A Personal History of Pink Floyd*
38. *Sound on Sound*, October 2009
39. Ibid.

40. Anil Prasad, 'Terry Riley: Lighting Up Nodes', *Innerviews*, 2014
41. Udi Koomran interviews Daevid Allen, 2005, Planet Gong website
42. Ibid.
43. Daevid Allen, *Gong Dreaming 2: The Histories & Mysteries of Gong from 1969-1979*, SAF Publishing, London, 2009
44. Ibid.
45. Ibid.
46. Ibid.
47. Turner and Thompson, *The Spirit of Hawkwind 1969-1976*
48. *It's Not Only Rock'N'Roll* website, 24 March 2013
49. *Rolling Stone*, 22 July 1971
50. George McKay, *Senseless Acts of Beauty: Cultures of Resistance Since the Sixties*, Verso, London, 1996
51. Andy Beckett, *When the Lights Went Out: Britain In The Seventies*, Faber & Faber, London, 2010
52. *International Times*, 6 September 1973
53. Penny Rimbaud, *Shibboleth: My Revolting Life*, AK Press, London, 1999
54. Penny Rimbaud, *The Last of the Hippies: An Hysterical Romance*, PM Press, Oakland, 2015
55. Clerk, *The Saga of Hawkwind*
56. *The Guardian*, 14 June 1997
57. *Keyboard*, July 1981
58. David Sheppard, *On Some Faraway Beach: The Life and Times of Brian Eno*, Orion, London, 2015
59. Bracewell, *Roxy: The Band That Invented an Era*
60. Michael Nyman, *Experimental Music: Cage and Beyond*, Cambridge University Press, Cambridge, 1999
61. Prendergast, *The Ambient Century: From Mahler to Moby – The Evolution of Sound in the Electronic Age*
62. Sheppard, *On Some Faraway Beach: The Life and Times of Brian Eno*
63. *The Telegraph*, 15 October 2011
64. Simon Frith and Howard Horne, *Art into Pop*, Methuen, London, 1988
65. *The Guardian*, 14 June 1997
66. *Roxy Music* album sleeve notes by Simon Puxley, Island Records 1972
67. *Oz*, September 1972
68. *The Guardian*, 14 June 1997
69. Dave Ball, Electronic Boy: *My Life In and Out of Soft Cell*, Omnibus Press, London, 2020
70. Martin Aston, *Breaking Down the Walls of Heartache: How Music Came Out*, Constable, London, 2016
71. *The Guardian*, 12 November 2006
72. *Mojo*, April 1997
73. Ibid.
74. *Q*, November 1990
75. *Discreet Music* sleeve notes, Obscure Records 1975
76. Erik Satie, quoted in Cage, *Silence: Lectures and Writings*
77. Harry Sword, *Monolithic Undertow: In Search of Sonic Oblivion*, White Rabbit, London, 2022

78. *Ambient 1: Music for Airports*, sleeve notes, Polydor 1978
79. *Keyboard Wizards*, Winter 1985
80. *New York Times*, 12 August 1979
81. *Musician*, November 1979
82. Brian Eno, *A Year with Swollen Appendices*, Faber & Faber, London, 1996
83. *Los Angeles Times*, 16 April 1987
84. Hugo Wilcken, *David Bowie's Low (33⅓)*, Bloomsbury Continuum, London, 2014
85. *Playboy*, September 1976
86. *Mojo*, February 2007
87. *Uncut*, exact date unknown, republished by davidbowie.com
88. Sheppard, *On Some Faraway Beach: The Life and Times of Brian Eno*
89. *Rolling Stone*, 17 May 2012
90. Tony Visconti with Richard Havers, *Tony Visconti: The Autobiography – Bowie, Bolan and the Brooklyn Boy*, HarperCollins, London, 2007
91. Ibid.
92. *Sound Opinions*, Show 529, 14 January 2016
93. *Ultimate Classic Rock*, 18 May 2014
94. Interview with John Cavanagh, *Original Masters*, BBC Radio Scotland, 1997, exact date unknown
95. Niebur, *Special Sound*
96. *Surface* magazine
97. Red Bull Music Academy website, 19 September 2013
98. Delia Derbyshire website, 2017
99. Sonic Boom, letter in *The Wire*, September 2001
100. *The Times*, 18 July 2008
101. *The Mail on Sunday*, 20 March 2005
102. Frances Morgan, 'Delian Modes: Listening for Delia Derbyshire in Histories of Electronic Dance Music' in *Dancecult: Journal of Electronic Dance Music Culture 9*, 2017

This is Entertainment – Industrial Music and Post-Punk Futurism
1. *The Quietus*, 25 January 2023
2. *The Wire*, September 2004
3. Jon Savage, *This Searing Light, The Sun and Everything Else: Joy Division – The Oral History*, Faber & Faber, London, 2019
4. Banks, *Hawkwind: Days of the Underground*
5. *The Quietus*, 25 January 2023
6. *Pitchfork*, 30 June 2014
7. *Gunrubber*, February 1977, reprinted in *Cabaret Voltaire: A Collection of Interviews 1977-1994*, Fabio Méndez, 2021
8. *Y*, issue three, 1981
9. *NME*, September 1981, exact date unspecified, reprinted in *Cabaret Voltaire: A Collection of Interviews 1977-1994*
10. *The Wire*, October 1996
11. Cosey Fanni Tutti, *Art Sex Music*, Faber & Faber, London, 2017
12. Richard King, *How Soon is Now?: The Madmen and Mavericks Who Made Independent Music 1975-2005*, Faber & Faber, London, 2012
13. *Spin*, 21 June 2012

14. *Industrial Soundtrack for the Urban Decay*, directed by Travis Collins and Amélie Ravalec, Les Films du Garage 2015
15. Genesis P-Orridge with Tim Moir, *Nonbinary: A Memoir*, Abrams Press, New York, 2021
16. *The Wire*, October 2011
17. V. Vale and Andrea Juno (editors), *RE/Search 6/7: Industrial Culture Handbook*, RE/Search 1983
18. P-Orridge, *Nonbinary: A Memoir*
19. Bob Osborn, *Futurism and the Futurists*, quoted in Thom Holmes, *Electronic and Experimental Music: Technology, Music, And Culture*, Routledge, Abingdon, 2008
20. *120 Years of Electronic Music* website
21. Drew Daniel, *Throbbing Gristle's 20 Jazz Funk Greats (33⅓)*, Bloomsbury Continuum, London, 2008
22. P-Orridge, *Nonbinary: A Memoir*
23. *The Wire*, October 1996
24. Tutti, *Art Sex Music*
25. *Daily Mail*, 19 October 1976
26. Daniel, *Throbbing Gristle's 20 Jazz Funk Greats (33⅓)*
27. Jon Savage, 'The Tape Decays', sleeve notes for Throbbing Gristle's *Five Albums* box set, Fetish Records, 1982
28. *The Wire*, July 2007
29. The Desperate Bicycles, 'The Medium Was Tedium' single sleeve, Refill Records, 1978
30. *Sounds*, 26 November 1977
31. *Ireallylovemusic* website, 2005, exact date unspecified
32. Richard Evans, *Listening to the Music the Machines Make: Inventing Electronic Pop 1978-1983*, Omnibus Press, London, 2022
33. Obituary published by Mute Records, November 2002, quoted in Simon Dell, *From the Port to the Bridge: The Story of Robert Rental and Thomas Leer*, encyclopaediaelectronica.com, 2018
34. *The Guardian*, 7 January 2013
35. Martin Lilleker, *Beats Working for a Living: Sheffield Popular Music 1973-1984*, Juma, Sheffield, 2005
36. *Sounds*, August 1985, exact date unspecified, reprinted in *Cabaret Voltaire: A Collection of Interviews 1977-1994*
37. Sean Turner, 'Complete Guide to the Human League 1977-1980', blindyouth.co.uk
38. *GQ*, 23 October 2020
39. Martin James, *Fatboy Slim: Funk Soul Brother*, London, Sanctuary, 2002
40. Red Bull Music Academy website, 24 May 2016
41. *The Word*, October 2011
42. *Record Mirror*, 21 August 1982
43. Thomas Dolby, *The Speed of Sound: Breaking the Barriers Between Music and Technology – A Memoir*, Icon Books, London, 2018
44. *The Word*, October 2011
45. *Classic Rock & Culture*, 3 January 2017
46. *PopMatters*, 4 October 2011
47. *Washington Independent Review of Books*, 14 March 2017
48. *MusicTech* website, 14 December 2017

49. *Tomorrow's World*, BBC, 22 November 1979
50. *Shapers of the 80s* website, 13 February 2015
51. Steve Strange, *Blitzed!: The Autobiography of Steve Strange*, Orion, London, 2002
52. *Observer Music Monthly*, 4 October 2009
53. Gary Kemp, *I Know This Much: From Soho to Spandau*, Fourth Estate, London, 2009
54. *Daily Mirror*, 3 March 1980, quoted in Dominic Sandbrook, *Who Dares Wins: Britain, 1979-1982*, Penguin, London, 2019
55. *Melody Maker*, 1980, exact date unspecified, quoted in Sandbrook, *Who Dares Wins: Britain, 1979-1982*
56. Kemp, *I Know This Much: From Soho to Spandau*
57. Wesley Doyle, *Conform to Deform: The Weird and Wonderful World of Some Bizzare*, Jawbone Press, London, 2023
58. Ibid.
59. *Riverside*, BBC2, 1983, exact date unknown, Karen Howarth YouTube channel, 27 September 2020

Just Can't Get Enough – Synth-Pop and Art-Rock
1. Marc Almond, *Tainted Life: The Autobiography*, Pan Books, London, 2000
2. Ibid.
3. *Record Mirror*, 16 February 1980
4. Joanna Demers, *Listening Through the Noise: The Aesthetics of Experimental Electronic Music*, Oxford University Press, New York, 2010
5. *The Face*, October 2001
6. Dave Rimmer, *New Romantics: The Look*, Omnibus Press, London, 2003
7. Almond, *Tainted Life: The Autobiography*
8. Ibid.
9. Ibid.
10. *The Quietus*, 26 November 2021
11. Matthew Collin, with contributions by John Godfrey, *Altered State: The Story of Ecstasy Culture and Acid House*, Serpent's Tail, London, 1997
12. Ibid.
13. *Finn Johannsen* website, 16 August 2010
14. *Nottingham Post*, 28 November 2008
15. *NME*, 29 July 1978
16. *The Guardian*, 4 April 2003
17. *Record Mirror*, 19 December 1981
18. *The Guardian*, 13 December 2021
19. *Record Mirror*, 14 March 1981
20. *Record Mirror*, 8 August 1981
21. *Sound on Sound*, February 2007
22. *Melody Maker*, 22 September 1984
23. *NME*, 5 September 1981
24. Jonathan Miller, *Stripped: Depeche Mode*, Omnibus Press, London, 2009
25. *Uncut*, 19 February 2015
26. *Electronic Sound*, June 2018
27. *NME*, 17 April 1982
28. *Synth Britannia*, BBC Four, 16 October 2009
29. *Electronic Sound*, September 2023

30. *Record Mirror*, 10 March 1984
31. *NME*, 20 December 1984
32. *Recoil* website, date unspecified
33. Steve Malins, *Depeche Mode: The Biography*, André Deutsch, London, 2009
34. Ian Gittins, *Depeche Mode: Faith and Devotion*, Palazzo, London, 2018
35. Miller, *Stripped: Depeche Mode*
36. *The Face*, January 1989
37. *MLive*, 22 August 2013
38. *The Face*, January 1989
39. Savage: *This Searing Light, The Sun and Everything Else: Joy Division – The Oral History*
40. Bernard Sumner, *Chapter and Verse (New Order, Joy Division and Me)*, Thomas Dunne Books, New York, 2014
41. Ibid.
41. King, *How Soon is Now?: The Madmen and Mavericks Who Made Independent Music 1975-2005*
43. Sumner, *Chapter and Verse (New Order, Joy Division and Me)*
44. *The Guardian*, 11 February 2013
45. Peter Hook, *The Haçienda: How Not to Run a Club*, Simon & Schuster, London, 2009
46. *The Guardian*, 23 March 2010
47. Stephen Morris, *Fast Forward: Confessions of a Post-Punk Percussionist Volume II*, Constable, London, 2020
48. *Liverpool Echo*, 8 May 2013
49. *The Word*, May 2010
50. Ibid.
51. Trevor Horn, *Adventures in Modern Recording: From ABC to ZTT*, Nine Eight Books, London, 2022
52. *Sound International*, September 1980
53. *Musician, Player and Listener*, November 1980
54. Samantha Bennett, *Modern Records, Maverick Methods: Technology and Process in Popular Music Record Production 1978-2000*, Bloomsbury Academic, New York, 2019
55. Horn: *Adventures in Modern Recording: From ABC To ZTT*
56. *The Independent*, 24 January 2014
57. Paul Harkins, 'Following the Instruments, Designers, and Users: The Case of the Fairlight CMI', *Journal on the Art of Record Production*, July 2015
58. *Q*, January 1989
59. *Beat This: A Hip-Hop History*, directed by Dick Fontaine, BBC, 1984, quoted in Paul Gorman, *The Life & Times of Malcolm McLaren: The Biography*, Constable, London, 2020
60. *The Face*, December 1982
61. *Record Mirror*, 19 March 1983
62. *Rolling Stone* website, 22 July 2022
63. *Music Technology*, December 1989
64. *Number 1*, 23 February 1985
65. Holly Johnson, *A Bone in My Flute*, Arrow Books, London, 1995
66. Ibid.
67. *Number One*, 21 April 1984

68. *Sounds*, 14 January 1984
69. *Number One*, 21 April 1984
70. Paul Flynn, *Good as You: From Prejudice to Pride – Thirty Years of Gay Britain*, Ebury Press, London, 2017
71. *The Times*, 14 February 1985
72. Johnson, *A Bone in My Flute*
73. Timothy Warner, *Pop Music – Technology and Creativity: Trevor Horn and the Digital Revolution*, Ashgate Publishing, Aldershot, 2003
74. *The Queer Bible* website, October 2018
75. *Number One*, 24 March 1984
76. *The Washington Post*, 4 November 1984
77. *The Queer Bible* website, October 2018
78. Aston: *Breaking Down the Walls of Heartache: How Music Came Out*
79. Ibid.
80. Norman Fowler, *AIDS: Don't Die of Prejudice*, Biteback Publishing, London, 2014
81. *Record Mirror*, 16 June 1984
82. *The Guardian*, 4 April 2003
83. Bryony Sutherland and Lucy Ellis, *Annie Lennox: The Biography*, Omnibus Press, London, 2001
84. *Classic Pop*, 21 September 2017
85. Marcus Barnes, 'The Revolution Was Televised: Imagination's Influence on 80's Black Britain' in Adrian Loving, *Fade to Grey: Androgyny, Style & Art in 80s Dance Music*, Design-Diversity.org, Washington D.C., 2020
86. Ibid.
87. *NME*, 25 April 1981
88. Interview by Martyn Ware, *Electronically Yours* podcast, 15 July 2021
89. *Huffington Post*, 8 October 2013
90. *Attitude*, August 1994
91. Chris Heath, *Pet Shop Boys, Literally*, Penguin, London, 1991
92. BBC Radio 2, *This Cultural Life*, 16 April 2022
93. *Pet Shop Boys, Literally*, ibid.
94. Sleeve notes to Pet Shop Boys, *Please*, CD reissue, 2001
95. Ibid.
96. Heath, *Pet Shop Boys, Literally*
97. Ibid.
98. Pet Shop Boys, *Please*, CD reissue
99. Sleeve notes to Pet Shop Boys, *Actually*, CD reissue, 2001
100. Sleeve notes to Pet Shop Boys, *Behaviour*, CD reissue, 2001
101. *Meet Paul McCartney*, ITV, 7 August 1980
102. *Electronics & Music Maker*, March 1986
103. *Sound on Sound*, March 1987
104. *Q*, April 2018
105. *The Scotsman*, 12 February 2012
106. Graeme Thomson, *Themes for Great Cities: A New History of Simple Minds*, Constable, London, 2022
107. *Sound on Sound*, January 1987
108. *The Boston Globe*, 3 July 1980
109. *Sound on Sound*, January 1987

110. *Salon*, 20 March 2001
111. *Electronics & Music Maker*, October 1982
112. Ibid.
113. *Record Mirror*, 10 January 1981
114. *The Guardian*, 21 August 2014
115. Robert Fink, 'ORCH5, or the Classical Ghost in the Hip-Hop Machine', in Eric Weisbard (editor), *Listen Again: A Momentary History of Pop Music*, Duke University Press, Durham, 2007
116. Howell, *Radiophonic Times*
117. Brian Hodgson, 'My Years in the Mildewed Wedding Cake', *The White Files* website, 2021
118. *Electronics & Music Maker*, October 1985
119. Howell, *Radiophonic Times*, ibid.

Coughing Up Fire – Dub Reggae and Sound Systems
1. *Duke Vin and the Birth of Ska*, directed by Gus Berger, Gusto Films & Hackney Film Collective, 2008
2. Ibid.
2. Julian Henriques, *Sonic Bodies: Reggae Sound Systems, Performance Techniques, and Ways of Knowing*, Continuum, London, 2011
4. Mike and Trevor Phillips, *Windrush: 75 Years of Modern Britain*, HarperCollins, London, 1999
5. Lloyd Bradley, *Bass Culture: When Reggae Was King*, Penguin, London, 2001
6. *The Independent*, 21 November 2012
7. 'British Reggae', *Aquarius*, directed by Jeremy Marre, London Weekend Television, 18 September 1976
8. *Duke Vin and the Birth of Ska*
9. Bradley, *Bass Culture: When Reggae Was King*
10. *The Sunday Times*, 4 February 1973
11. *NME*, 21 February 1981
12. *Sound Business*, directed by Molly Dineen, 1981
13. Linton Kwesi Johnson, 'Jamaican Rebel Music', *Race & Class*, Volume 17 Issue 4, April 1, 1976
14. *World in Action*, ITV, 30 January 1978
15. Interview by Steve Vibronics, *Life in Dub Podcast #3*, *Mixcloud*, date unspecified
16. William 'Lez' Henry, *What the Deejay Said: A Critique from the Street!*, Learning by Choice Publications, London, 2006
17. Anna Arnone, *Sound Reasoning*, Arandora Press, 2017
18. Interview by Steve Mosco, 1984, exact date unspecified, republished by *Dub Club Y2K* website
19. Louis Chude-Sokei, 'Dr. Satan's Echo Chamber', *Chimurenga* website, 9 March 2013
20. *The Wire*, January 2001
21. *Sounds*, 26 November 1977
22. *Red Bull Music Academy* website, 2014
23. Ibid.
24. *Digital Media* channel, YouTube, 12 April 2023
25. Interview by Steve Mosco

26. *NME*, 21 February 1981
27. *The World* website, 13 February 2014
28. *Race Today*, May 1975
29. Licklemor Productions channel, YouTube, 2022, exact date unspecified
30. Interview by Uli Nefzer, *Way Above the Level* website, 23 September 2009
31. Sleeve notes for *An England Story: The Culture of the MC in the UK 1984-2008*, Soul Jazz Records, 2008
32. Tricky with Andrew Perry, *Hell Is Round the Corner*, Blink Publishing, London, 2020
33. *Sounds*, 15 January 1983, quoted in Stephen Hebditch, *London's Pirate Pioneers: The Illegal Broadcasters Who Changed British Radio*, TX Publications, London, 2015
34. John Hind and Stephen Mosco, *Rebel Radio: The Full Story of British Pirate Radio*, Pluto Press, London, 1985
35. Hebditch, *London's Pirate Pioneers: The Illegal Broadcasters Who Changed British Radio*
36. *Analogue Foundation* website, 29 January 2019
37. Caribbean Celebrities Radio, 18 September 2021
38. *Entertainment Report* podcast, YouTube, 17 October 2022
39. Interview by Gregory Mario Whitfield, *Uncarved.org* website, 2003
40. *The Wire*, July 2008
41. Paul Sullivan, *Remixology: Tracing the Dub Diaspora*, Reaktion Books, London, 2014
42. *The Wire*, July 1997
43. *Venue*, 12 April 1991
44. *Bugbear Music*, Soundcloud, 17 March 2014
45. *The Wire*, October 2018
46. Interview by DJ Stryda, Falasha Recordings website, date unspecified
47. Interview by Steve Vibronics, *Life in Dub Podcast* #11, date unspecified
48. Interview by Greg Whitfield, *3:AM Magazine*, 2003

Tearin' Down the Avenue – Electro and Hip-Hop
1. *The Face*, May 1984
2. Muggs and Stevens, *Bass, Mids, Tops: An Oral History of Sound System Culture*
3. *The Guardian*, 6 October 2006
4. Tricky with Perry, *Hell Is Round the Corner*
5. Muggs and Stevens, *Bass, Mids, Tops: An Oral History of Sound System Culture*
6. *VNA Magazine*, May 2014
7. *The Face*, May 1984
8. *The Guardian*, February 2022
9. *The Arts Fuse*, 26 July 2018
10. Comment by Anthony Anderson, posted on the *80sgroovevinyl* channel, YouTube, date unspecified
11. Interview by Bill Brewster for *DJHistory.com*, Red Bull Music Academy website, 9 March 2018
12. *Electrofunkroots* website, 2004
13. *The Electricity Club* website, 18 August 2012
14. *The Wire*, January 2002
15. *Electronics & Music Maker*, November 1984
16. *Overground* magazine, 1984, quoted in *Cabaret Voltaire: A Collection of Interviews 1977-1994*

17. *Electronic Sound* website, 14 June 2018
18. *Electro Rock*, directed by Richard Gayer, PolyGram Music Video, 1985
19. 'The Early Stages of Hip-Hop in London', YouTube, 19 June 2012
20. *Jocks & Nerds*, Summer 2015
21. BBC Radio 1Xtra, 2 October 2018
22. Ibid.
23. *The Guardian*, 16 November 2021
24. *Bad Meaning Good*, directed by Tim Westwood, BBC Two, 5 August 1987
25. *Jocks & Nerds*, Summer 2015
26. *Old to the New* website, 9 June 2011
27. *Red Bull Music Academy* website, date unspecified
28. Lloyd Bradley, *Sounds Like London: 100 Years of Black Music in the Capital*, Serpent's Tail, London, 2013
29. Phillips, *Windrush: 75 Years of Modern Britain*
30. Ibid.
31. Bradley, *Sounds Like London: 100 Years of Black Music in the Capital*
32. *Soul Underground*, September 1989
33. !K7 Music website, August 2004
34. Don Letts with David Nobakht, *Culture Clash: Dread Meets Punk Rockers*, SAF Publishing, London, 2007
35. *The Guardian*, 14 October 2013
36. Muggs and Stevens, *Bass, Mids, Tops: An Oral History of Sound System Culture*
37. *i-D*, June 1990
38. *The Wire*, September 1994
39. Phil Johnson, *Straight outa Bristol: Massive Attack, Portishead, Tricky and the Roots of Trip-Hop*, Hodder & Stoughton, London, 1996
40. Greg Tate, 'Trick Baby', quoted in Alexander G. Weheliye, *Phonographies: Grooves in Sonic Afro-Modernity*, Duke University Press, Durham, 2005
41. Tricky with Perry, *Hell is Round the Corner*
42. *Straight No Chaser*, Winter 1995
43. Muggs and Stevens, *Bass, Mids, Tops: An Oral History of Sound System Culture*
44. 'Bristol Headz Special Edition', *Headz Zine*, Autumn 2021
45. *Ban Ban Ton Ton* website, 18 December 2018

Unnatural History – Experimentalists, Industrialists and Noise-Musicians
1. David Keenan, *England's Hidden Reverse: A Secret History of the Esoteric Underground*, Strange Attractor Press, London, 2014
2. Coil manifesto, 1983
3. *The Guardian*, 11 December 2004
4. *England's Hidden Reverse*, ibid.
5. Coil press release, 9 April 1985
6. Keenan, *England's Hidden Reverse: A Secret History of the Esoteric Underground*
7. *Keyboard Magazine*, July 1987
8. *The Wire*, July 2006
9. *The Wire*, May 2001
10. *Fact Magazine*, 3 November 2010
11. Ibid.
12. Ibid.

13. *The Wire*, August 2007
14. Ibid.
15. FAQ v3.01, Susan Lawly Records website, 28 August 2011
16. *The Wire*, August 2007
17. *Little White Earbuds* website, 19 September 2012
18. *The Quietus*, 11 July 2012
19. Jennifer Wallis (editor), *Fight Your Own War: Power Electronics and Noise Culture*, Headpress, London, 2016
20. *Sounds*, unknown date, republished in 'A Brief Nurse with Wound History', *Ultima Thule* website
21. *Unsound*, Volume Two Number Three/Four, date unspecified
22. Doyle, *Conform to Deform: The Weird and Wonderful World of Some Bizzare*
23. Samuel Galloway and Joseph Sannicandro, 'Queer Noise', in Sarah Raine and Catherine Strong (editors), *Towards Gender Equality in the Music Industry: Education, Practice and Strategies for Change*, Bloomsbury Academic, New York, 2019
24. Interview by David Keenan, Red Bull Music Academy website, 27 March 2015
25. *The Quietus*, 27 July 2015
26. *Sounds*, 7 May 1983
27. *The Wire*, November 2017
28. *The Wire*, April 2010
29. *The Edge*, January 1998, republished by muslimgauze.org
30. Sleevenotes for Muslimgauze, *Maroon*, 1995
31. *Glissando*, Issue 21, 2013
32. *Bidoun*, summer 2007
33. Nigel Ayers, *Electronic Resistance*, Amaya Productions, San Francisco, 2021
34. Leaflet for concert at the Whiskey a Go Go, London, 23 May 1982, reproduced in ibid.
35. *Sounds*, 11 June 1983
36. *The Quietus*, 14 April 2010

Pump Up the Volume – Samplemania, Hi-NRG and Dance-Pop
1. *Cut*, December 1987
2. *Music Technology*, January 1989
3. *Q*, December 1987
4. King, *How Soon Is Now?: The Madmen and Mavericks Who Made Independent Music 1975-2005*
5. *Modern Records, Maverick Methods: Technology and Process in Popular Music Record Production 1978-2000*
6. *Music Technology*, November 1987
7. *The Guardian*, 19 July 2021
8. *The Guardian*, 4 July 2017
9. *Cut*, December 1987.
10. *Electronics & Music Maker*, July 1986
11. *Record Mirror*, 27 February 1988
12. *The Face*, September 1990
13. Evans, *Listening to the Music the Machines Make: Inventing Electronic Pop 1978-1983*
14. Jimmy Cauty and Bill Drummond, *The Manual (How to Have a Number One the Easy Way)*, KLF Productions, London, 1988

15. *The Wall Street Journal*, unknown date, cited in *Music Technology*, March 1991
16. *Rolling Stone*, 24 April 2018
17. *Q*, December 1987
18. Mark Katz, *Capturing Sound: How Technology Has Changed Music*, University of California Press, Berkeley, 2010
19. Press release for reissue of Brian Eno and David Byrne, *My Life in the Bush of Ghosts*, Virgin/EMI, 2006
20. *Rolling Stone*, 2 April 1981
21. *Sounds*, 7 March 1981
22. *The Guardian*, 11 August 2022
23. Ian Levine, *Leap Years*, privately published manuscript (courtesy of Ian Levine), 2018
24. Jeremy Norman, *No Make-Up: Straight Tales from a Queer Life*, Elliott & Thompson, London, 2013
25. Alkarim Jivani, *It's Not Unusual: A History of Lesbian and Gay Britain in the 20th Century*, Michael O'Mara Books, London, 1997
26. *Evening Standard*, 28 September 2023
27. Louis Niebur, *Menergy: San Francisco's Gay Disco Sound*, Oxford University Press, New York, 2022
28. *Record Mirror*, 30 July 1983
29. Levine, *Leap Years*
30. Ibid.
31. BBC News website, 16 October 2005
32. Norman, *No Make-Up: Straight Tales from a Queer Life*
33. Levine, *Leap Years*
34. *Stuff and Nonsense* interview, YouTube, 29 March 2021
35. Ibid.
36. Biography by Jimmy Somerville, *Official Jimmy Somerville Fan Page* website, date unspecified
37. *Electronic Beats*, 11 March 2015
38. Phil Harding, *PWL: From the Factory Floor*, Cherry Red Books, London, 2015
39. Ibid.
40. *A Journey Through Stock Aitken Waterman* podcast, Episode 8, 2022
41. *NME*, 18 July 1987

Emotions Electric – House, Techno, Acid
1. *The News*, 13 August 2016
2. *New Musical Express*, 12 December 1987
3. T-Coy biography, LTM Recordings website, date unspecified
4. Luke Bainbridge, *Acid House: The True Story*, Omnibus Press, London, 2014
5. Oona King, *House Music: The Oona King Diaries*, Bloomsbury, London, 2008
6. Dave Swindells, *Acid House As It Happened*, Idea, London, 2022
7. Matt Anniss, *Join the Future: Bleep Techno and the Birth of British Bass Music*, Velocity Press, West Wickham, 2019
8. Muggs and Stevens, *Bass, Mids, Tops: An Oral History of Sound System Culture*
9. Hebditch, *London's Pirate Pioneers: The Illegal Broadcasters Who Changed British Radio*
10. Ibid.
11. *Magic Feet* fanzine, 1997, exact date unspecified

12. Ibid.
13. *Convulsion* fanzine, 1992, exact date unspecified
14. *The Guardian*, 12 November 1988
15. *Pioneer DJ* website, date unspecified
16. Collin (with Godfrey), *Altered State: The Story of Ecstasy Culture and Acid House*
17. *New Musical Express*, 22 October 1988
18. Hillegonda C. Rietveld, 'Voodoo Rage: Blacktronica from the North', in Jon Stratton, Nabeel Zuberi (editors), *Black Popular Music in Britain Since 1945*, Ashgate Publishing, Farnham, 2014
19. Bainbridge, *Acid House: The True Story*
20. Simon Trask, 'Rhythm Nation', in Chris Kempster (editor), *History of House*, Sanctuary Publishing, London, 1996
21. Graham Massey, Facebook post, 2 April 2021
22. Collin (with Godfrey), *Altered State: The Story of Ecstasy Culture and Acid House*
23. Hook, *The Haçienda: How Not to Run a Club*
24. *Mixmag*, 20 May 2019
25. *i-D*, March 1990
26. *Join the Future* website, 10 September 2010
27. 'Ambient House – The Facts?', KLF Communications press release, 1990
28. Sheppard, *On Some Faraway Beach: The Life and Times of Brian Eno*
29. *The Wire*, April 1999
30. Collin (with Godfrey), *Altered State: The Story of Ecstasy Culture and Acid House*
31. *The Guardian*, 23 February 2020
32. *i-D*, December 1990
33. *Dazed Digital*, 8 November 2011
34. *Rough and Ready Muso Interviews*, Soundcloud, date unspecified
35. Ibid.
36. Red Bull Music Academy website, 2007, exact date unspecified
37. Ibid.
38. *Melody Maker*, 6 June 1992
39. *Blog to the Old School* website, 6 May 2009
40. *DJHistory.com*, 2005, republished by Red Bull Music Academy website, 23 January 2019
41. *Data Transmission* website, August 9, 2019
42. Muggs and Stevens, *Bass, Mids, Tops: An Oral History of Sound System Culture*
43. *We Love Jungle* website, date unspecified

INDEX

3D (Robert Del Naja) 236, 256, 257, 258
4AD 130, 175, 294, 295
4Hero 353
4th Street Orchestra, The 213
10cc 87
23 Skidoo 118, 265, 269, 277, 290, 345
52nd Street 173
400 Blows 288, 290, 306, 333, 345
801 (group) 84
808 State 336, 337–8, 343

A Certain Ratio 135, 173, 239, 325
A Guy Called Gerald (Gerald Simpson) xiii, 334–7
Aba Shanti-I 204, 230–1
ABBA 306
ABC 135–6, 173
Ability II 350
Abrams, Colonel 324
acid house and rave culture 327–34, 341–6
Acidica Lights 97
Adam and the Ants 249
Adamski (Adam Tinley) 340
Adamski, George 28
Addis, Tony 326
Adlington, Robert 55
Adonis 323
Adrenalin M.O.D. 333
African Head Charge 225
Afrika Bambaataa 142, 168, 172, 178, 201, 237, 241, 248–9, 296
Age of Chance 345

Akai samplers 227, 297, 303, 354
Allen & Blewitt 249
Allen, Daevid 88–90, 91, 92
Allen, Mike 246
Allen, Stu 332, 336
Almond, Marc 149, 150, 153–4, 156–60, 162, 268
Alpha and Omega 230
Altered Images 172
amateur tape recording 21–5, 27
Amateur Tape Recording 23
ambient house 343–4
ambient music 104–6
AMM 45, 51, 54, 94, 275
Amnesia (club) 328, 339
Amon Düül/Amon Düül II 75, 275
Anderson, Dave 73
Anderson, Paul 'Trouble' 254, 331
Anderton, James 316
Andrews, John 97, 342
Andrews, Tony 97
Anger, Kenneth 65
Angus, Colin 345
Anniss, Matt 348
Aphex Twin 155, 301, 342, 350
A. R. Kane 294
ARP synthesizer 80, 82, 84, 86, 138
Art of Noise 57, 176, 179–80
Arthur, Neil 150, 156
Ash Ra Tempel 90
Asher, Jane 44
Atari computer 232, 303–4, 349
Atkins, Juan 142, 172

Atmosfear 242
Attrition 281
Autechre 350
Avraamov, Arseny 16
Ayler, Albert 44
Ayres, Mark 11, 12, 57
Ayres, Nigel 79, 280, 281, 282, 286–8

B Movie 150
B12 350
Babbitt, Milton 5
Baby Ford 332
Babylon (film) 214–15
Bacon, Alice 54
Bailey, Derek 69
Bainbridge, Harvey 80
Baker, Arthur 172–3, 190, 242–3
Baker, John 30, 55, 57–9, 109, 201, 202, 353
Baker, Richard Anthony 58, 59
Balance, John (Geff Rushton) 265, 266–9, 280
Balch, Antony 89
Balfe, Dave 175
Ball, Dave 70, 103, 153–4, 156–60, 344
Ballard, J. G. 57, 77, 130, 133, 137, 140, 160, 176
Bam Bam 345
Band Aid 183
Bandez, Annie Anxiety 223
Bang the Party 326–7, 337
Bangs, Lester 104
Banks, Joe 77
Barbieri, Richard 190, 192–3
Barker, Andrew 335–6

377

Barnes, Marcus 186
Barrett, Aston 228
Batchelor, Lawrence 'Kid' 304, 326–7, 331, 339–40
BBC 4-5, 8-10, 15, 78, 181, 318, 334
BBC Radiophonic Workshop: *BBC Radiophonic Music* album 56, 57; Brian Hodgson 11–12, 13, 14, 30, 31, 201; concert with Orbital 355; critics and admirers 13–14; David Cain 57; Delia Derbyshire 30–1, 32, 35–7, 56, 109; *Doctor Who* series 34, 35–7; early commissions 11, 13; establishment 7–8, 9, 10–12; influence xi, 37–8, 354; John Baker 55, 57–8; last days 201–2; rock musicians' visits 55–6, 64–5, 85; School Radio projects 37–8, 57; techniques and innovations 12–13, 30, 109, 201
Beat, Janet 18–20
Beatles, The 42–3, 44, 46–51, 67, 71, 87, 91, 108, 137, 153, 176, 212, 257, 305
Beatmasters, The 301–2, 307, 325
Beckett, Steve 347, 350
Bee Gees 85, 243
Beer, Andrew 290, 333
Bell, Mark 349
Bell-Brown, Russ 229–30
Bellotte, Pete 80, 87–8
Beloved, The 337–8
Bennett, Samantha 177, 295–6
Bennett, William 271–2
Berio, Luciano 5, 31, 44, 45
Berk, Ernest 17–18, 68–9, 94

Bermange, Barry 56
Bernas, Richard 93, 94
Bernelle, Agnes 28, 150
Berry, Ron 282
Best, Philip 272
Big Audio Dynamite 221, 245–6
Big in Japan 175
Billy's (club) 145–6, 148
Birtwistle, Harrison 62
Black, Matt 254, 303, 305, 307–8, 309
Black Dog, The 342, 350–1
Black Sabbath 80
Blackwell, Chris 66, 223
Blah Blah Blah 149, 150
Blair, David 249
Blake, Stacia 72, 77, 78, 79
Blake, Tim 90, 91, 92
Blancmange 150, 156, 172
bleep techno 347–50
Blitz (club) 146–8
Blood Shanti 231
Blue Beat 223
Boddy, Ian 282
Bogart, Neil 88
Bomb Squad, The 309, 345
Bomb the Bass 240, 296–8, 301
Bourbonese Qualk 283, 285–6
Bovell, Dennis 'Blackbeard' 208, 211, 212–14, 222, 228
Bowie, David 82, 92, 103, 106–8, 114, 115, 128, 133, 140, 148, 149, 154, 160, 165, 169, 186, 192, 193, 194, 198, 338
Boy George 103, 339
Boyle, Mark 54
Bradley, Lloyd 207, 253
breakbeat hardcore 351
Briottet, Danny 295
Briscoe, Desmond 9, 10–12, 13, 14, 35, 57, 70
Britain, post-war: activism and protests 78, 103, 181–2, 185, 284–5; art

school musicians 100–1, 136–7, 157; Black communities and racist policing 207, 210, 213, 215, 217; computing & gaming 155; consumer boom 15; counterculture 44, 51–3, 73, 75, 78–9, 120; homophobic stigmatisation 40–1, 58–9; popular culture influences 25–6, 43–4; societal changes 2, 43, 58; Thatcher government and social discord 119, 163, 182, 185, 188; Windrush generation and racism 206, 210, 221, 253
British Electric Foundation (B.E.F.) 162, 164
British Nationality Act 1948 206
British Recording Club 23
Brock, Dave 74, 75–6, 80, 95–6
Broken Glass 236, 238, 240, 247
Bronski, Steve 184
Bronski Beat 184–5, 268, 317
Brooks, Basil 96–7
Broome, Ralph O. 24
Broughton, Edgar 75
Brown, Arthur 84–5, 92
Brown, James 107, 220, 250, 252, 289, 294, 296, 298, 305, 306, 307
Brown, Miquel 311, 313
Bruford, Bill 80
Bryars, Gavin 94
Buchanan, Shaun 316
Buchla, Don 64
Buckmaster, Paul 106
Budd, Harold 106
Budgie 175
Buggles, The 154, 176
Burden, Ian 161

Burgess, Richard James xi, 144–5, 147, 172, 198–9, 324
Burns, Pete 180, 186
Burroughs, William S. 44, 45, 89, 115–16, 122, 127, 265, 345
Burston, Paul 312
Bush, Kate 197, 198–200, 351
Buzzcocks 116, 117
Byrd, Gary 249
Byrne, David 308–9

Cabaret Voltaire 112–19, 127, 132, 150, 224, 244–5, 265, 277, 290, 346
Cage, John 4, 16, 18, 53, 55, 64, 67, 93, 94, 136, 273
Cagneys (club) 149–50
Cain, David 57
Calder, Clive 240–1
Calix, Mira 342
Callis, Jo 161
Calvert, Robert 77, 78, 188, 191
Camden Palace (club) 290, 324, 326
Camel 82
Can 75, 76, 127, 130, 165, 193
Cardew, Cornelius 67, 101
Carlos, Wendy 63, 82, 134
Caro C 111
Caroline K 286–8
Carter, Chris 117, 121–3, 127, 262–5, 279
Cary, Tristram: academic career 59; BBC commissions 9, 37; commercial works 59; 64; concerts, 1968 17–18, 32, 59–60; electronic experimentation 2–3, 6; Electronic Music Studios (EMS) 62, 63, tape recorders' potential 1–2, 5, 345

Casey, Jayne 175–6, 180
Casio synthesizers 131, 155, 286, 303
Cassidy, Larry 173
Castle Records 22
Catherall, Joanne 161
Cauty, Jimmy 290, 305–7, 341, 343
Cecil, Malcolm 80–1, 342
Chakk 345, 347
Cherry, Neneh 256, 298
Chicory Tip 80, 194
Chinnery, Derek 181
Chris and Cosey 262–5, 279, 282, 290
Christopherson, Peter 122, 123, 265–9
Chude-Sokei, Louis 211
Churchill, Winston 2
Clarke, Johnny 215, 229
Clail, Gary 227–8
Clarke, Malcolm 24
Clarke, Vince 164, 165–6
Clash, The 117, 131, 179, 213, 245–6, 248, 249, 255, 256, 270
Clavioline 39
Clayton, Jace 284
CLEM magazine 281
Cleveland, Barry 39
Clock DVA 127, 132–3
Cluster 85, 104
Cockerell, David 61, 62, 63, 303
Cocteau Twins 175
Coil 150, 266–9, 279
Coldcut 254, 303–4, 305, 307–8
Coleman, Ornette 44, 132
Coles, Richard 317
Collier, Nicola 337
Collins, Phil 198
Colourbox 221, 290, 294
Columbia-Princeton Electronic Music Centre 5
Come 271
Communards, The 317
Confusion (club) 339
Connell, Andy 239–40
Cook, Norman 304, 339

Cookie Crew 247, 251, 302
COUM Transmissions 119–21, 122, 124–5
Council Collective, The 188
Count Suckle (Wilbert Campbell) 207
Cowley, Patrick 312–13, 314
Coxsone, Lloyd 207, 208, 211–12
Crab, Simon 284, 285–6
Crass 94, 284–5, 287, 354
Creation Rebel 213, 223
Crimble, Thomas 74, 75
Cunningham, Merce 67
Current 93 269–70
Currie, Billy 138, 147, 191
Curtis, Ian 169, 170
Curved Air 83–4
Cybotron 142, 237
Czukay, Holger 193, 246

Dada movement 113, 115
Daddy Colonel 217
Daddy G 255–6, 257, 258, 304
D.A.F. 165, 174, 288
Dale, Colin 254, 331
Dance Theatre Commune 68–9, 94
Dasilva, Jon 329–30
Dave VJ 253, 254
Davies, Hugh 11, 17, 70–1, 93, 277
Davies, Michael (DikMik) 74, 76, 90
Davies, Peter Maxwell 31
Davis, Dennis 107
Davis, Rik 142
Davis, Rob 333
Dead Kennedys 354
Dead or Alive 319
Deadly Headley 223
Dean, Hazell 313, 316–17
Delirium (club) 328
Demers, Joanna 154–5
Demon Boyz 250
Depeche Mode 150, 164–8, 172, 193, 289, 353

Derbyshire, Delia:
  1970s art project
    collaborations 110;
  BBC Radiophonic
    Workshop 30–1, 32,
    56, 109, 201; 'Carnival
    of Light' 50, 51;
    concerts, 1968 17–18,
    32, 60; David Vorhaus
    collaborations 65–6;
    death and posthumous
    media coverage 110;
  Doctor Who series 35–7;
    early influences 29–30;
    musical collaborations
    31–2, 56–7, 85; Paul
    McCartney 50; Pink
    Floyd's visit 55–6;
    status as innovator xii,
    111; Unit Delta Plus
    61–2
Derek B 250
Desperate Bicycles, The
  127
Dettmar, Del 78
Disciples, The 229–30, 231
Divine 318
Dizzy Heights 248, 249
DJ Alfredo 328
DJ Hype 351, 352
DJ Kool Herc 178
DJ Laurent 265
DJ Parrot 118, 330, 346,
  347, 349
DJ Paulette 148–9
D-Mob 334
Dobrowolski, Andrzej 5
Doctor Who xi, 34–7, 83, 91,
  108, 110, 201, 306,
  313, 316, 355
Doctors of Madness 115
Dolby, Thomas 143–4, 241
Dorrell, Dave 292, 293,
  294, 296, 328
Double Dee and Steinski
  294, 298, 304
Dougans, Brian 333
Doyle, Roger 277
Dread, Mikey 209, 214
Dread and Fred 229
Dread Broadcasting
  Corporation 218

drug culture and music
  44–6, 53, 54, 74–8,
  90, 98, 158–9, 170,
  268–9, 328–30
drum machines: Bentley
  Rhythm Ace 84, 85;
  Boss 165, 170, 279;
  Farfisa 114; Linn 155,
  161, 198, 200, 315,
  319; Oberheim DMX
  155, 171, 227; Roland
  138, 158, 172, 173,
  228, 265, 303, 325,
  333, 347, 354
Drummond, Bill 175,
  305–7, 341, 343
Dub Judah 230
dub reggae and sound
  systems 205–32
Dubuffet, Jean 274
Duddell, William x
Dudley, Anne 176, 178,
  179–80
Dug Out, The (club) 256
Duke Vin (Vincent Forbes)
  205–6, 207, 208
Dunbar, Sly 221, 228
Dunkley, Simon 77
Dunn, Julia 68–9
Dwyer, Bill 'Ubi' 95
Dwyer, Terence 27

Eat Static 342
Ecstasy, Cindy 158, 159
Edwards, Rupie 211
Egan, Rusty 145–7, 149,
  172, 291
Einstürzende Neubauten
  150, 167
El-Dabh, Halim 5
Electribe 101 337
electro 235–46
Electro Rock (documentary)
  247
Electronde x
elektronische musik 5–6
Elizabeth Archer and the
  Equators 225
Ellitt, Jack 16
ELO 87, 191
Emerick, Geoff 46
Emerson, Keith 81, 82

Emerson, Lake and Palmer
  (ELP) 81, 82, 131
E-Mix 300, 339
EMS (Electronic Music
  Studios): establishment
  62–4; Synthi 100 84,
  97; Synthi AKS 87,
  96, 108, 114; VCS3
  synthesizer 78, 79, 81,
  82, 83–4, 85, 86,
  100
Emulator synthesizers 155,
  171, 172, 239, 243,
  244, 245
Enemy Within, The 188
Eno, Brian: 801 member
  84; ambient music
  104–6, 343; Basil
  Kirchin 69; Bowie
  'Berlin Trilogy'
  collaboration 106–7,
  108; influence on
  electronic artists 114,
  129, 131–2; musical
  influences 98–9;
  post-punk production
  projects 137; Roxy
  Music 99–100, 101–2;
  sampling 308–9; solo
  recordings 103–4;
  tape recorder uses xi,
  100, 103, 105; VCS3
  synthesizer 81, 100,
  101
Eric B. & Rakim 294,
  307–8
Eskimo Fox 225
Eurythmics 164, 166, 186,
  351
Evangeli, Barry 318, 319
Evasions, The 249
Evelyn, George 235–6,
  237,
Eventide Harmonizer
  107–8, 162
Everett, Kenny 249
EXPO 58, Philips Pavilion
  15–16
E-Zee Possee 339

Fabian, Jenny 54
Fabio 331

Face, The 148, 238
Factory Records 130, 132, 169, 173, 223, 239, 325, 350
Fad Gadget 165
Fagandini, Maddalena 12, 13, 30, 41–2
Fairbairn, Nicholas 125
Fairlight xi, 155, 177–8, 196, 198–9, 200, 201, 267, 315, 320
Family Quest 248, 249
Farley, Terry 346
Farley 'Jackmaster' Funk 243, 324
Farren, Mick 44, 95
Fast Product 130, 134
Fast Set, The 150
Fats Comet 227
Faust 127, 129, 274, 275, 285
Faver, Colin 254, 290, 324, 326, 331
Fearon, Phil 241
Fernandez, Akin 333
Ferry, Bryan 100, 101–2, 136, 149
Fingers Inc 323
Fink, Robert 201
Finley, Karen 299
Fisher, Mark 225, 281
Fistfuck 276
Fletcher, Andy 165, 167, 168
Flux of Pink Indians 354
Fluxus 49, 52, 100, 120, 122, 275
Flynn, Paul 184
FON Studios 347
Forgemasters 322, 323, 347
Formula, Dave 194
Fothergill, John 273–4
Foulk, Ray 74
Fowler, Norman 185
Fox, Samantha 305
Foxx, John 136–8, 147, 149, 154
Frankie Goes to Hollywood 175, 180–3, 186, 339
Franklin, Keith 326
Fraser, Neil (Mad Professor) ix, 211, 219–21, 259, 288, 290, 344
free festivals, 1970s 95–7
Freeez 201, 242–3
Fresh 4 236, 259
Fripp, Robert 82, 103, 108, 129
Frith, Simon 100
Froggy 238, 305
Front 242 289, 290
Fry, Martin 135–6, 173, 339
Fung, Trevor 328
Funkapolitan 248
Future, The (group) 133

Gabriel, Pascal 296–7, 298, 299
Gabriel, Peter 191, 194, 196–8, 303
Gagarin, Yuri 25–6, 134
Gahan, Dave 164, 165, 167
Garage, The (club) 325
Gardner, James 37–8, 62–3
Garratt, Sheryl 329
Geesin, Ron 67, 69–70, 130, 157
Genesis 82, 122, 170, 196
Gentle Fire 93, 94, 277
Gentle Giant 82
Gerhard, Roberto 20, 31–2
Gibb, Robin 85
Gibbs, Joe 224
Gibson, William 293
Gilbert, Gillian 170, 171
Gillespie, Bobby 346
Gilmour, David 53
Gilroy, Paul 255
Gina X Performance 146
Ginsberg, Allen 44
Giraudy, Miquette 92, 342
Glanfield, Manda 302, 307
Glass, Philip 87, 300, 301
Glastonbury Fair (festival) 92–3, 94
Goldie 247, 353
Goldman, Vivien 215–16
Gong 88, 89–93, 97, 194, 342
Goon Show, The 8, 11, 13
Gordon, Robert 347, 348
Gore, Martin 164, 167, 168
Grainer, Ron 35
Grandmaster Flash 162, 179, 236, 239, 248–9, 294, 303, 304
Gray, Barry 27, 109, 354
Green, Nigel 241
Greenfield, Dave 195
Greengate sampler 288, 291
Greensleeves label 223
Gregory, Glenn 162–3
Grogono, Peter 62
Groove 325
Grooverider 331
Groupe de Recherches Musicales 5
GTO 346
Guru Josh 340
Gysin, Brion 89, 225, 245, 265

Haçienda, The (club) 174, 240, 323, 325–6
Hague, Stephen 189, 308
Haig, Paul 195
Haigh, Robert 277
Halasa, Malu 255
Halpern, Stephen 106
Hamilton, James 238
Hammond Novachord x, 64
Hancock, Herbie 80, 179, 334
Hannett, Martin 169, 173
Hardcastle, Paul 243–4
Harding, Phil 320–1
Hardrock Soul Movement 253
Hardy, Ron 168
Harmonia 104
Harris, Bon 289–90
Harris, Pete Q. 240–1
Harris, Simon 250
Harrison, George 44, 45, 50
Harrison, Jonty 278
Harrow, David 223
Hartnoll, Paul & Phil 354–5
Hassell, Jon 193

381

Hawkwind 73–80, 93, 95, 96, 116, 120, 188, 194, 282, 336, 338
Haza, Ofra 307–8
Hazel, Winston 236, 323, 346–8
Heaven (club) 184, 189, 310–12, 316, 341
Heaven 17 132, 162–4
Hebditch, Stephen 218, 331
Heddle, John 334
Hedges, Mike 172
Helliwell, Ian 22, 24, 25
Henderson, Dave 279
Hendrix, Jimi 74, 75, 91, 120
Henriques, Julien 206
Henry, Pierre 5–6, 19, 32, 65
Henry, William 'Lez' 205, 209, 210, 216, 218
Henze, Hans Werner 62
Herndon, Holly 27
Hicks, Michael 44
Higgins, Charlotte 8
Higgins, Terence 316
Hijack 250
Hillage, Steve 90–2, 194, 342
Hines, Anderson & Carson 252–3
hi-NRG 310–15, 317–19
Hinton, Joie 342
hip-hop 246–60, 334–7
Hit Squad MCR 336
Hodgson, Brian: BBC Radiophonic Workshop 11–12, 13, 14, 30, 31, 201; Brian Jones visit 64–5; 'Carnival of Light' 50; David Vorhaus collaborations 65–6; *Doctor Who* series 34–5, 36–7; musical collaborations 85, 109; space, fascination with 25; Unit Delta Plus 61–2
Hollis, Mark 191
Holmes, Trevor F. 24

Hook, Peter 172, 339
Hooper, Nellee 255, 256, 258, 304
Hooykaas, Madelon 110
Hope, Wally 95
Hopkins, John 'Hoppy' 53
Horn, Trevor 176–8, 179–80, 181, 182–3, 303
Horne, Howard 100
Horrocks, James 296
Hoskyns, Barney 187
Hotline 325
Howell, Peter 36, 201, 202
Human League, The 108, 130, 131–2, 133–5, 160–2, 164, 243, 353
Humphreys, Paul 132
Hurley, Steve 'Silk' 324
Hyman, Carlton 'Smiley' 351
Hyslop, Kenny 195

Ian B 25, 304
Iatropoullos, Phivos 352–3
i-D 148
Imagination 186–7
industrial music 113–27, 132–3, 264–77
Industrial Records 123, 124, 127
Intermodulation 93, 94
International Carnival of Experimental Sound (ICES 72) 94
International Times (*IT*) 44, 53, 65, 68, 73, 75, 78, 95
Iration Steppas 230, 231–2
Irdial Discs, 333
Irie, Tippa 217, 251
Island Records 66, 221, 223
Isle of Wight Festival, 1970 73–4
Ital Rockers 348, 350

Jackson, Martin 239–40
Jackson, Steve 254, 331
Jagger, Mick 54, 65
Jah Tubbys 217, 230
James, Greg 238
Japan 191–3

Jay, Joey 254
Jay, Norman 253, 254
Jazzie B 254, 255, 258, 304
Jazzy M 331, 355
Jeczalik, J.J. 178, 179
Jefferson, Marshall 323, 324, 332, 344, 346
Jenkins, Roy 95
Jerome, Steve 189
Jesus Jones 345
Jesus Loves You 339
Jivani, Alkarim 311–12
Jive Bunny 310
Jive Records 240–1
Jive Turkey (club) 347, 349
John, Elton 80, 158
John, Leee 186, 187
Johnson, David 146
Johnson, Donald 173
Johnson, Holly 175, 180–1, 183
Johnson, Linton Kwesi 207, 209, 213
Johnson, Matt 129
Johnson, Milo 256, 257–8
Johnson, Philip 'PJ' 351
Jolley, Steve 187
Jolly Roger, 333
Jones, Brian 64–5
Jones, Bryn 282–4
Jones, Gareth 167
Jones, Grace 183, 186, 343
Jones, Mick 245, 246
Jones, Stuart Wynn 27
Journey into Space (radio programme) 8, 25
Joy Division 79, 168–71
Judd, Fred C. 21, 22–3, 26–7, 29, 116, 220
Judge Jules 254
Jumpin Jack Frost 330
Justified Ancients of MuMu, The (The JAMs) 305–6

Kamins, Mark 174
Karn, Mick 192, 193
Katz, Mark 308
Keenan, David 266
Kelday, Paul 282
Kember, Pete (Sonic Boom) 110

Kemp, Gary 147, 148
Kennedy, Errol 186–7
Kerr, Jim 193, 194
Kevorkian, François 168, 242, 301
Khan, Chaka 287
Khan, Morgan 239–40, 248, 287
Khider, Ibrahim 284
Killing Joke 116, 213
Kilminster, Lemmy 76, 77–8
King, Oona 329
King, Peter 217
King Crimson 64, 80, 81–2, 212
King Tubby 38, 104, 211, 232
Kingdom Come 84–5, 92
Kingsland, Paddy 31, 58–9, 85, 109, 201–2
Kirchin, Basil 69
Kirk, Richard H. 113–14, 115–16, 118, 119, 244–5, 349
Kiss FM 254, 331
KLF, The 175, 290, 306, 341, 343
Kneale, Nigel 14
Knuckles, Frankie 190, 314, 323, 324
Korg synthesizers 20, 130, 131, 132, 134, 155, 158, 159, 189, 194, 325
Korgis, The 155
kosmische music 75, 85, 90, 104, 106, 125, 275, 282, 341
Koziman, Elisabeth 110
Kraftwerk 55, 85, 96, 106, 107, 128, 130, 132, 135, 136, 137, 138, 142, 144, 146, 153, 169, 193, 194, 237, 241, 342, 348, 354
Krause, Bernie 65
Krause, Dagmar 83
Kristina, Sonja 83, 84
Krush 325
Kynaston, David 6

Lacey, Bruce 121
Lacey, John 121, 122
Laidley, Herbie 239, 240
Lake, Greg 81
Lambert, Douglas 310, 316
Lambert, Verity 35
Land of Oz (club) 341–2
Landscape 144–5
Langan, Gary 178
Language Lab, The (club) 248
Last Few Days 265
Lawrence, Leslie 326
Leary, Timothy 46
LeBlanc, Keith 188, 223, 225–7
Ledrut, Jean 41
Lee, Dave 333
Leer, Thomas 127–30
Legend (club) 171, 237, 238, 335
Legendary Pink Dots 281
Lennon, John xiii, 45, 46, 47, 49–50, 71
Lennox, Annie 186
LePage, Denis & Denyse 313
Lepke (Leroy Anderson) 218
Leslie, Desmond 28–9, 69, 150
Leslie, Mark 28, 29
Letts, Don 244, 245, 246, 255
Levan, Larry 168, 174, 187, 238, 242, 246, 301
Levene, Keith 138, 223
Leveridge, Kermit 238, 240, 252
Levine, Ian 189, 238, 310, 313–15, 316, 324
Lewis, John 109, 154, 316
Leyton, John 40, 185
LFO 348, 349, 350, 351
LGBTQ+ issues: HIV-AIDS musicians' responses 185, 190, 267–8, 315–7; homophobic stigmatisation 40–1, 58–9, 185; political activism 103, 181, 15; positive images 103, 154
Li Yuan-Chia 110
Lift, The (club) 326
Lim, Roger 202
Liquid Len and the Lensmen 76
Lloyd-Langton, Huw 74–5
Lockwood, Annea xii, 67
London Posse 247, 251
Loose Ends 241
Lowe, Chris 189–90
Luening, Otto 5
Luminophone x–xi
Lusardi, Mark Angelo 242
Lustmord 270, 285
Lynn, Vera x
Lynott, Phil 191

M (group) 154
M/A/R/R/S 292, 294–6, 306
Mac, Mark 353
MacDonald, Ian 47
Macka B 210
Mackay, Andy 99–100, 102
Mackintosh, CJ 294
MacNeil, Mick 193–4, 195
Maderna, Bruno 5
Madonna 172, 300
Magazine 147, 194, 239
Maher, Sean 347
Mallinder, Stephen 113–14, 116, 118–19, 244–5
Manasseh 228–9, 254
Mantronix 201, 248
Manzanera, Phil 84
Margouleff, Robert 80–1
Marie, Kelly 316
Marinetti, Filippo 126, 180
Mark, Louisa 212
Marsh, Iain Craig 133–4, 161, 162–4
Marshall, Vie 250–1
Martin, Billie Ray 300, 337
Martin, George 41–3, 46, 47–8, 178, 212

Mason, Nick 70, 87, 94
Massey, Graham 335, 336, 338, 339
Massive Attack 221, 226, 236, 255, 256, 257, 258, 259
Mastermind 239, 253
Matthewman, Gordon 331
Matthews, Carl 282
Matthews, Harry Grindell x–xi
Matumbi 212, 213
Maximum Joy 255
MC Buzz B 252
MC Duke 247–8, 251
MC Mell'O' 248, 252
MC Tunes 252, 335
McCarthy, Carlton 258
McCartney, Paul 41, 43, 44–5, 46–7, 48, 49, 50–1, 54, 64, 71, 115, 178, 191
McCluskey, Andy 131, 132
McCutcheon, Les 314
McDonald, Skip 225–6, 227
McGee, Billy 268
McGee, Brian 195
McGlashan, Colin 208
McKay, George 95
McLaren, Malcolm 150, 178–9, 235–6, 300–1
McLaren, Norman 16
McPhee, Tony 84
McWhinnie, Donald 7, 9
Meat Beat Manifesto 345
Mechanical-Copyright Protection Society 352
Meek, Eric 39
Meek, Joe 38–41, 42, 91, 121, 185
Mel and Kim 320
Mellotron 47, 48, 64, 82, 84
Melody Maker 40, 49, 79, 148
Menges, Chris 214
Metabolist 129, 149
MFSB 300
MIDI technology 227, 244
Mighty, Ray 259

Miles, Barry 44–5, 50–1, 65, 68
Miller, Daniel 70, 130–1, 157, 165–6, 167, 271, 277
Millington, Mark (Mark Iration) 231–2
Mills, Dick 8, 10, 11, 14, 15, 31, 36, 37, 57, 355
Ministry 226, 270, 288
Minogue, Kylie 319, 333
Mitchell, Rob 347
Mixmaster Morris 105, 341–2
Monie Love 247, 251
Monkman, Francis 83–4
Moody Boys, The 290
Moog synthesizers 22, 50, 63, 64–5, 80, 82, 87, 187, 189, 212
Moorcock, Michael 53, 77
Moore, Mark 146, 296, 298–301, 328
More, Jonathan 254, 303, 305
Morgan, Frances 111
Morley, Paul 179–80, 180
Moroder, Giorgio 80, 87–8, 125, 170, 171, 183, 192, 195, 312
Morris, Stephen 79, 108, 168–70, 172–3, 174
Moyet, Alison 166, 243
Mr C 324, 331, 345
Mr Monday 340
Muggs, Joe 236
Munkacsi, Kurt 300
Murray, Pauline 195
Music Now 67
Music of Life label 250
Musicians' Union 85
musique concrète 1–2, 5–6, 9, 10, 12, 15, 22, 28–9, 76, 86–7, 274, 277, 281, 355
Muslimgauze 282–284
Mute Records 130, 165–6, 223, 296, 321, 350

Nagle, Paul 282
Naked Lunch 150

Naked Software 67, 93, 94
Nancy Noise 328
Nash, Brian 181
Nayman, Rex 148
Nelson, Bill 191
Nelson, Trevor 254
Nesbitt, Alex 7
Neu! 79, 106, 136, 193, 275
Neu Electrikk 150
Neutron Records 135
Neville, Richard 51
New Age Steppers 223
New Musical Express (*NME*) 48, 49, 164, 187, 321, 325
New Order 79, 170–3, 174, 239, 242, 339, 345
Newley, Anthony 56
Newton, Adi 132–3
Newtrament 234, 239, 249
Nexus 21 350
Nicolette 352
Niebur, Louis 15, 109, 314
Nightmares on Wax 236, 348, 349
Nine Inch Nails 226, 270, 271, 288
Nitzer Ebb 289–90
No Smoke 327
Noah, Bonjo Iyabinghi 225
Nocturnal Emissions 79, 280, 281, 286–8, 290
Norman, Jeremy 311, 316
Norris, Richard 344
Numan, Gary 108, 135, 138, 139–42, 149, 154, 165, 193, 237
Nurse with Wound 273–5, 279
Nuttall, Jeff 43
Nylon, Judy 104
Nzinga Soundz 221

O Yuki Conjugate 281
Oakenfold, Paul 328, 333, 341, 346
Oakey, Phil 133–4, 160–1, 162, 183, 186
Oblique Records 128
O'Dell, Alaura 276
Oliveros, Pauline 5, 103
Ollis, Terry 78

Ondes Martenot 27, 354
Ono, Yoko 49, 53, 56
On-U Sound 223, 224–5
Oppenheimer Analysis 282
Oram, Daphne: BBC, early career 4–5, 6–7, 10, 16; BBC Radiophonic Workshop 10–12, 15–16; childhood musical interests 4; commercial works 17; electronic experimentation xiv, 6, 16–17; home studio 16–17, mentorship role 17, 60, 71; concerts 13–14, 17–18, 24; Oramics machine 16, 18; status as innovator xii, 14, 16, 17, 111
Orb, The 105, 341, 342–4, 346
Orbit, William 300–1
Orbital 340, 354–5
ORCH5 200–1
Orchestral Manoeuvres in the Dark (OMD) 131, 132, 143, 200
Orlando, Bobby 172, 189, 313
Orton, Richard 71, 277
Oz (magazine) 51, 78, 102
Ozric Tentacles 97–8, 342

Pablo, Augustus 212, 290
Palmer, Carl 82
Papa Levi 217
Paradise Garage (club) 171, 174, 187, 238, 242,
Pareles, Jon 309
Paris is Burning (film) 300
Park, Graeme 304, 325
Parker, Elizabeth 202, 343
Parker, Evan 69
Partington, Darren 335–6, 338
Paterson, Alex 105, 341, 343–4
Pathak, Heman 273–4, 276
Paul, Les 76
Pearce, Stevo 149–150, 156, 245

Peech Boys 299
Peel, John 135, 213, 303
Pellay, Lana/Alan 223
Penderecki, Krzysztof 5
Pepler, Merv 342
Perry, Lee 'Scratch' 38, 104, 138, 211, 221, 224, 228, 319
Pet Shop Boys 188–90, 201
Pettibone, Shep 190
Pickering, Mike 173–4, 304, 325–6, 328
Pink Floyd 51, 52, 53–6, 70, 75, 76, 77, 86–7, 91, 92, 120
Pink Industry 175–6
Piper, Deirdre 67
Pips (club) 148–9
pirate radio stations 218–19, 254, 331–2
Pitt, Arthur 75
Plank, Conny 136, 138, 276
Plantone label 223
Pointon, Malcolm 117
Pop, Iggy 107, 149
Pop Group, The 213, 226, 255
Pop Will Eat Itself 345
P-Orridge, Genesis 119–21, 122–3, 124, 125, 126–7, 265–6, 269, 344
Portion Control 288–9, 290
Potter, Colin 274, 277, 279–80
Powell, Andrew 94
Powell, Enoch 210
Practical Electronics 116–17, 121, 220
Prendergast, Martin 325–6
Price, Martin 336, 338
Primal Scream 344, 346
Prince 142, 201
Princess Julia 145, 148
Proctor, Steve 149–50
Prodigy, The 240, 288, 340, 352, 354
progressive rock 81–98
psychedelia 51–5, 64–5, 67

Psychic TV 150, 265–6, 269, 344
Public Enemy 252, 294, 309, 345, 351
Public Image Ltd (PiL) 116, 138, 195, 213

Quaker City 210, 217
Quando Quango 173–4, 325
Quantick, David 321
Queen 108, 183

Radiodiffusion Télévision Française 5
Ragga Twins, The 352
Raidl, Tim 330
Rampling, Danny 254, 328, 331
Rampling, Jenni 331
Random, Eric 118
Ranking Ann 221, 222
Ranking Miss P 218
Raphael, Nick 228–9
Read, Mike 181
Record Mirror 154, 161, 238, 305, 313
Record Shack 313–14
Reeder, Mark 171
Regular Records 128
Reid, Benji 236
Reinforced Records 353
remixing ix, 159, 162, 172, 187, 208, 220, 224, 244, 246, 295, 300, 307–8, 344, 346
Renegade Soundwave 295, 345
Rental, Robert 127, 128–30, 131
Revell, Graeme 271
Rexy 148
Reynolds, Ambrose 175
Reznor, Trent 226, 271
Rhythm King 296, 297, 301–2
Rhythmatic 350
Richards, Eddie 290, 291, 304, 324, 331, 333–4
Richards, Keith 54
Rietveld, Hillegonda 173–4, 337

385

Riley, Terry 44, 67, 83, 86, 89, 94, 103, 129, 136
Rimbaud, Penny 94, 95
Rimmer, Dave 156
RIP (club) 330–1, 345
Roberts, Kev 314
Robertson, Sandy 309
Robie, John 172, 243, 244, 288
Robinson, Valerie 'Lady V' 221–2
Rocca, John 241, 242–3
Rock Against Racism 213,
Rock City (club) 323
Roddenberry, Gene xiii
Rodney P 250, 251
Roeg, Nicolas 9, 65, 106
Rogerson, Diana 276, 277
Roland: Microcomposer 144–5, 162; TB-303 bass synthesizer 164, 173, 265, 288, 303, 325, 327, 333, 354; TR-808 drum machine 158, 159, 172, 173, 228, 237, 243, 244, 258, 265, 286, 303, 325, 336; synthesizers 134
Rolling Stones, The 44, 54, 64–5, 75, 301
Rose Royce 299
Ross, Diana 195
Rosso, Franco 214
Roxy Music 81, 84, 100, 101–2, 103, 114, 136, 137, 186, 192, 193
Royal College of Music Electronic Studio 59
Rubin, Rick 345
Rushent, Martin 161–2, 172, 196
Russolo, Luigi 126, 179, 273
Rutherford, Paul 180–1, 184, 339
Ruthless Rap Assassins 252, 253
Ruts/Ruts DC 213, 221
Ryrie, Kim 201

Saint, The (club) 314–15

Sakamoto, Ryuichi 193, 213
sampling and copyright debate 294–8, 307–8
San Francisco Tape Music Centre 5
Sandbrook, Dominic 66–7
Satie, Erik 104, 106, 259, 277
Saunderson, Kevin 168, 172
Savage, Jon 53, 126, 128
Sax, Trevor 217
Saxon Sound International 217–18, 251, 258
Scargill, Arthur 188
Scarr, Howard 96, 97
Schaeffer, Pierre 5–6, 9, 16, 42, 82, 114, 136
Schulze, Klaus 85, 282
Scientist, The 352
Scratch Beatmasters 335–6
Seal 340
Section 25 173, 345
Sema 277
Sender, Ramon 5
S'Express 296, 298, 300, 301
Shaka, Jah xi, 211, 215–17, 228–9, 230, 231, 326
Shakespeare, Robbie 212, 221, 228
Shamen, The 345

Shelley, Pete 116, 195–6
Sheppard, David 99
Sherman, Bim 223
Sherwood, Adrian 168, 188, 213, 222–5, 226–7, 245
Shocklee, Hank 309
Shoom (club) 300, 328, 329, 338, 344
Shreeve, Mark 282
Shut Up and Dance 351–3
Sigue Sigue Sputnik 195
Silicon Teens 165
Silver Apples 66, 76, 121
Silver Bullet 352
Simenon, Tim 296–8

Simple Minds 108, 193–5
Sinclair, Jill 180
Sinfield, Peter 81–2
Singing Arc x
Singleton, Stephen 135–6
Siouxsie and the Banshees 149, 172
Sista Culcha 221
Sister Audrey 221
Slits, The 213, 223
Sly and the Family Stone 85
Smash Hits 156, 189
Smiley Culture 217, 251
Smith, Jill 121
Smith, Richard 266
Smith, Rob 256, 259, 260
Smith, Wayne 228
Smith & Mighty 258, 259–60, 348
Smykle, Paul 'Groucho' 221
Smyth, Gilli 89, 92
Soft Cell 70, 103, 149, 150, 152–4, 156–60, 162, 172, 185, 268, 279, 344
Soft Machine 54, 85, 89
Solid Space 282
Some Bizzare 150, 156, 245
Somerville, Jimmy 184–5, 317
Sommerville, Ian 45
Sonique 300
Soul II Soul 226, 253, 254–5, 258, 259, 320, 326
Sound Iration 228, 230
Sounds 74–5, 128, 150, 274, 279, 309
Souster, Tim 86, 94
Space (band) 146, 172
space rock 75, 77
space travel, composition influence 25–7
Spandau Ballet 147, 172, 192
Sparks 156
Spectrum (club) 327, 333, 341
Spinmasters, The 335–6, 338

SPK 127, 271, 285, 288
Spooky Tooth 65
Stansfield, Elsa 110
Stapleton, Steven 270, 273–6
Starr, Ringo 63
Stephens, Ian Anthony 313, 314, 315
Stewart, Diane 92
Stewart, Mark 225–7, 256, 258–9, 268, 286
Stock Aitken Waterman 294–5, 318, 319–21
Stockhausen, Karlheinz 5, 6, 9, 10, 11, 20, 29, 42, 43, 45, 49, 64, 71, 82, 86, 92, 93, 94, 104, 192, 275
Stonehenge Free Festival 95, 96–7
Stooges, The 132, 169
Storm Bugs 149, 281–2
Strange, Steve 145–7, 148, 291
Stranglers, The 195
Stravinsky, Igor 200–1
Street Sounds label and compilations 239–40, 248, 287, 290, 335
Studio di Fonologia Musicale di Radio Milano 5
Studio Eksperymentalne Polskiego Radia 5
Studio für Elektronische Musik des Westdeutschen Rundfunks 5
Stylophone 85, 128, 157
Subotnick, Morton 5
Sugar Hill Records 173, 223, 225, 297
Sugarhill Gang 237, 242, 245, 249
Suicide 117, 131, 156, 174
Sulley, Susan Ann 161
Summer, Donna 87–8, 107, 125, 134, 170, 171, 176, 185, 193, 195
Sumner, Bernard 117, 169–71, 173

Susie Q 251
Sutcliffe, Alan 17
Swain, Tony 187
Sweet Exorcist 118, 349, 350
Swindells, Dave 331
Sylvian, David 192, 193
Synclavier synthesizers 155, 158–9, 166–7, 177, 303
synth-pop 153–90
System 7 342

Tackhead 223, 227, 287, 305, 345
Talk Talk 191
Tandy, Richard 87
Tangerine Dream 55, 96, 122, 282
Tape Recording 17, 23
Taubman, Martin x
T-Coy 325, 326, 327
T-Cut-F 325
Tebbit, Norman 255
Techno Twins 196
Telex 146
Tennant, Neil 188–90, 312
Test Dept 150, 188
Thatcher, Margaret 119, 148, 156, 163, 185, 188, 189, 190, 210, 221, 248, 284, 285, 286, 321, 334
Theremin x, 27, 84, 354
Theremin, Leon x
Third Mind Records 279
Thomas, Evelyn 315
Thompson, Dave 94
Thompson, Kirk (DJ Krust) 236
Thompson Twins 164
Thomson, Christopher 68
Thorne, Mike 157, 158–9, 185
Thorpe, Tony 288, 290, 306, 333
Throbbing Gristle 66, 117, 120, 122–5, 127, 128, 130, 157, 165, 263, 264, 265, 266, 269, 270, 271, 273, 275, 280, 281, 284

Thrower, Stephen 266–9, 281
Tibet, David 265, 269–70, 275, 277
Timelords, The 306
Tong, Pete 320
TONTO 80–1
Tonto's Expanding Head Band 81, 342
Toop, David 106, 235
Topley-Bird, Martina 259
Topping, Simon 325, 326
Tornados, The 38, 40
Townshend, Pete 86, 94
Tricky 218, 236, 258–9
Tricky Disco 350
'Trip, The (club) 331
Trojan label 223
Trunk, Jonny 69
Trunk Records 20, 59, 69
Tubeway Army 139, 140–1
Turing, Alan 61
Turner, Nik 75, 77, 78, 93
Turner, Tina 164
Tutti, Cosey Fanni 111, 119–21, 122–3, 124–6, 262–5, 276
TW Funk Masters 242
Tynan, Kenneth 46

UFO (club) 54, 76, 84, 85, 86, 89, 100
UK-made house music 324–7
Ultravox 136, 137–8, 142, 146, 147, 149, 183
Unique 3 348, 350, 351
Unit Delta Plus 61–2
United Dairies label 274, 275, 277
United States of America, The (band) 66
Up, Ari 223
Ure, Midge 147, 183, 191
Ussachevsky, Vladimir 5

Vangelis 155, 304, 344
Varèse, Edgard 15
Varley, Gez 349
Vaucher, Gee 94
Vego, Jah 207, 208

387

Velvet Underground, The 53, 75, 116, 124, 132
Vice Versa 135–6, 173
Vincent, Robbie 238
Visage 147, 168
Visconti, Tony 107–8
Vorhaus, David 36, 65–6, 200, 201

Wakeman, Rick 81, 82–3, 212
Walklett, Davy 273
Walters, John L. 145, 198
Ware, Martyn 131–2, 133–4, 161, 162–4
Warehouse, The (club, Leeds) 149, 157, 349
Warehouse, The (club, Chicago) 324
Warp Records 277, 347–9, 350
Warrener, Patrice 90
Warrior, Jah 230
Warriors Dance label 327
Wasp synthesizer 129, 131, 271
Waterman, Pete 295, 317, 318–19, 320–1, 333
Waters, Roger 55, 56, 70
Watson, Chris 113–14, 115, 116, 117, 119, 244
Watson, Maurice 239, 328
Watson, Noel 239, 328
Watts-Russell, Ivo 294, 295

Way, Darryl 84
Weatherall, Andrew 176, 344, 346
Welch, Elizabeth 127
Weller, Paul 188, 339
Westwood, Jill 276
Westwood, Tim 248
Wham! 183, 249
White, Mark 135
White Noise 66, 109, 200
Whitehouse 271, 272
Whiteley, Joseph Forrest x
Who, The 86
Whodini 241
Whybrew, John 288–9
Wild Bunch, The 255, 256–8, 259
Wild Style (film) 236
Wilde, Kim 155
Wilder, Alan 167
Willesden Dodgers, The 240–1
Williams, Brian 270–1, 278
Williams, Edward 96
Williams, Martin 349, 350
Williams, Tony 242
Willie Wee 256
Wilson, Delroy 212
Wilson, Greg 172, 237, 238, 239–40, 330
Wilson, Harold 43
Wimbish, Doug 225–6, 227
Windsor Free Festival 95, 97

Wire 116, 158–9
Wishart, Trevor 277–8
Witter, Simon 325
Wobble, Jah 138, 214
Wonder, Stevie 80, 81
Wright, Adrian 134, 160–1, 162
Wynne, Ed 97–8

X, Malcolm 215, 225

Yamaha synthesizers 155, 319–20, 354
Yazoo 166, 168, 299
Yes 80, 82, 122, 180, 212
York University Electronic Music Studio 277–8
Young, David 31
Young, Martyn 294, 296
Young, Steve 294
Youth (Martin Glover) 116, 191, 290, 321

Zephaniah, Benjamin 210–11
Zimmer, Hans 176, 315, 324
Zinovieff, Peter 17–18, 50, 59–62, 63–4, 78, 97, 84
Zorch 96–7
ZTT label 180, 183, 338
Zulu Nation 178, 179, 238, 249